# Impact of Mass Media

## CURRENT ISSUES

Third Edition

Edited by
## Ray Eldon Hiebert
*University of Maryland*

with a foreword by
## Carol Reuss
*University of North Carolina at Chapel Hill*

Longman *Publishers USA*

W024064

16. 6. 95

**Impact of Mass Media: Current Issues,
Third Edition**

Longman, 10 Bank Street, White Plains, N.Y. 10606

Associated companies:
Longman Group Ltd., London
Longman Cheshire Pty., Melbourne
Longman Paul Pty., Auckland
Copp Clark Longman Ltd., Toronto

Acquisitions editor: Kathleen M. Schurawich
Production editor: Victoria Mifsud
Text design: Joseph DePinho
Text design adaptation: Betty L. Sokol
Cover design: LCI Design
Production supervisor: Richard C. Bretan

**Library of Congress Cataloging-in-Publication Data**

Impact of mass media : current issues / edited by Ray Eldon Hiebert;
    with a foreword by Carol Reuss.—3rd ed.
      p.   cm.
    Includes index.
    ISBN 0-8013-0838-0
    1. Mass media—United States.   2. Mass media—Influence.   3. Mass
media—Social aspects.   I. Hiebert, Ray Eldon.
  P92.U5I46   1994
  302.23'0973—dc 20

                                                                93-42401
                                                                  CIP

1 2 3 4 5 6 7 8 9 10-MA-9897969594

## Credits

# Contents

# Foreword

Nothing could be more important to a liberal education than an understanding of mass media, the way they affect our lives, the way they have changed, and the way they have changed America and the world. This book amply demonstrates the enormous impact that television, radio, newspapers, and magazines have had on our culture, our society, our politics, and our government. It also sheds light on mass media's effects on key current issues such as crime, violence, war, minorities, and gender. But this book does not present simple solutions; it attempts to show many sides of the issues concerning the impact of mass media—the legal, moral, ethical, and economic dilemmas, including some that are highly controversial.

Ray Hiebert and I were both involved in the inception of this book and served as co-editors of its first two editions. But much has happened since the first edition of this book was published in 1985, and my duties as associate provost of a major public university have not allowed me the time to keep up with the rapid developments that have characterized mass media in the past few years. Professor Hiebert, fortunately, has been able to continue this project, editing the third edition himself. He brings to the task his experience as a journalist for both newspapers and broadcasting, many years as a teacher of journalism and mass communication, and an author and editor of many articles and books on the field. Added to that now is his global view of mass communication since he has traveled and lectured in many countries of the world, served as academic advisor to the Voice of America since 1981, and since 1991 has been director of the American Journalism Center in Budapest.

Since our field of mass communication has been changing so rapidly, this book has also changed. This is not just a third edition with a few new essays. This is, in fact, an entirely new book. Professor Hiebert has endeavored to keep up with the changes in mass media by selecting an entirely new set of current essays, while at the same time retaining the basic structure of the original book.

Please read this book carefully. It will not only help to make you a better communicator and a better journalist; it can also help to make you a better consumer of mass media, and a better citizen.

Carol Reuss, Associate Provost
University of North Carolina at Chapel Hill

# Acknowledgments

The following reviewers offered helpful comments and suggestions.

Kwadwo Anokwa, Butler University
Tom Draper, University of Nebraska—Kearney
James Featherston, Louisiana State University
Diane Furno-Lamude, University of New Mexico
Mary Beth Holmes, University of Scranton
George Johnson, James Madison University
Bill Loges, University of Denver
Jan Whitt, University of Colorado

# Impact of
# Mass Media

# Introduction

In the 1990s, the last decade of our century, there can be little doubt about the power and impact of mass media. Consider just a few examples: The communist world collapses, and mass media play a key role. In the Persian Gulf war, the American government seems to be as much concerned with influencing the media as with fighting the enemy. Our politicians are judged not on their ideas or their leadership but on their ability to project a winning image in the media. Athletes no longer seem as engaged in athletic competition as they are in competing for huge salaries as mass entertainers on mass media.

Most of us have had some direct experience with the impact of media on our lives, and we have witnessed their power in molding institutions and shaping events. What still is arguable is whether that power is being used for good or for ill. In this debate, there are many sides—and that is what this book is all about.

We should begin by defining our terms. Basically, we divide mass media into two categories: print—newspapers, magazines, and books—and electronic—radio, television, and motion pictures. These instruments of communication must be able to carry messages quickly to audiences so large they could not be gathered together in any one place at any one time. Mass media audiences are thus apt to be diverse, heterogeneous, and multicultural. The mass communicators themselves are not people with whom these audiences have personal contact; they are remote and anonymous. The messages of communication are usually transient, impermanent; for radio and television, the messages are here one moment, gone the next; the messages of newspapers last only a day, magazines only a week or a month; book and film messages last a bit longer, but in an age of mass media, even they are displaced quickly.[1]

In spite of their impermanence, mass media messages have power. Many scientific studies have confirmed that we no longer turn as often to our families, friends, neighbors, religious organizations, or social institutions for the news and information we need about ourselves, our communities, and our world. We now depend mostly on mass media. The same is true for much of our entertainment. Studies show that Americans spend more than half their leisure time—activities other than eating, sleeping, or working—on mass media, and the majority of that time is spent watching television.

Television, in fact, has in many ways become the most powerful of all the mass media, which is why it gets more emphasis in this book. Simply put, we spend more time on television and are more concerned about its impact than all the other media together.

In any discussion of mass media, we must also include advertising, which isn't a medium itself but is so inextricably woven into the fabric of most mass media that it must not be ignored. By advertising we mean the purchase of time or space in the print and electronic media to present a specific message. The advertiser is not usually employed by the medium, but by providing its principal financial support, it plays a key role in the mass communication process.

Increasingly, public relations (PR) has also become an essential part of mass media. Like advertising agency personnel, PR counselors are not employees of any medium. They are outsiders who seek to influence the content of mass media by packaging the news that is presented there, by shaping personalities, and by staging events, all to achieve a particular mass message and, the PR counselors hope, a particular mass response. It is no longer possible to separate mass media and public relations; we cannot understand one without the other.

Government plays a unique role in mass media in the United States. Unlike most other countries, in America the government does not own or operate any mass media that are readily available for public consumption within the country. (An exception is the Voice of America, the federal government's radio station, which is broadcast only on shortwave and aimed at other countries.) Also unlike many other countries, the American government rarely provides financial subsidies or support for the mass media. (One exception here is government support for public broadcasting.) The American philosophy about the government's relationship to mass media comes from the First Amendment to the Constitution: "Congress shall make no laws abridging freedom of speech or freedom of the press." (The primary exception are the laws that govern broadcasting, but these laws have little to say about broadcasting content.)

Thus, government plays a minor role in controlling the media. There are few laws and few institutional supports. Rather, mass media in the United States are market driven. They are basically businesses, set up to make a profit, and to do so they must provide a commodity people want. To sell advertising time or space, the medium must have an audience that the advertiser wants to reach. If the medium does not get a large enough audience to bring in enough money in subscriptions or advertising sales to cover its costs, it will go out of business.

This brief sociological description of mass media in the United States explains much of why they do what they do. We may like or dislike mass media, but unless we understand the reasons for their formats and contents, we will be less able to criticize them constructively and to work for improvements.

These instruments of mass communication have been twentieth-century phenomena. Some, like electronic media, were inventions of the twentieth century, whereas print media, although invented earlier, were essentially reinvented in this century to reach the masses. Advertising developed much earlier, but in the twentieth century it has become a massive and to some extent a scientific industry. Public relations is the quintessential twentieth-century phenomenon, perhaps the very symbol of our age.

So the impact of mass media is a fitting subject as we approach the end of the century. For much of the 1900s, scholars have argued about the real power of mass media. Now most of them seem willing to concede that the media have power and impact, even though questions remain about the precise nature of that impact or the actual cause-and-effect relationship.

Do the media make things happen, or do they merely report on what has happened? Do the media make us act and influence our opinions, or do they merely reflect our actions and feelings? Scientists and scholars still haven't given us conclusive answers to these kinds of questions, no doubt because there are so many variables. Every answer must be qualified by many conditions. So we still must quote two social scientists from the middle of the century, Bernard Berelson and Morris Janowitz:

> The effects of communication are many and diverse. They may be short-range or long-run. They may be manifest or latent. They may be strong or weak. They may derive from any number of aspects of the communication content. They may be considered as psychological or political or economic or sociological. They may operate upon opinions, values, information levels, skills, taste, or overt behavior.[2]

This doesn't mean that it is useless to be concerned about the impact of the mass media. It does mean that we must be exceedingly careful in making generalizations and in assigning blame. The effects of mass media must be measured and predicted on a case-by-case basis, taking into consideration all the variables in each situation.

This book is not a scientific examination of the specifics of the impact of mass media. Instead, it presents current arguments about that impact by some leading thinkers, experienced observers, and thoughtful critics.

Questions about the impact of mass media usually engender heated debate. The arguments raised here may be among the most important of our age because in one way or another we are all affected by mass media. And we have all debated these questions ourselves, ever since we emerged from behind the dark glasses of childhood to realize that the TV tube and the silver screen and the printed word may not, after all, represent reality.

When we realize that the illusions we have received from mass media are exactly that—illusions, not real or accurate or perfectly matched to our perceptions—we become disillusioned. The first time we read a newspaper story that describes an event about which we had personal knowledge, we are likely to say, "Hey, that's not the way it was; I saw it myself and it didn't happen that way at all." The first time we visit a television studio and see the painted sets for the local news show, we say, "Gee, I thought that was the real city skyline behind the anchorperson." The first time we go to Washington, D.C., and see the White House, we remark, "It's so small! It seemed so much bigger on television!"

This book is about the illusions we get from mass media and our disillusionment when we find out that everything isn't the way we thought it was. Dispelling these illusions may be one of the most important responsibilities of education. In America today young people spend more time in front of the television set than they do in class. By the time the average American graduates from high school, he or she will have spent about 12,000 hours in class and about 19,000 hours watching the tube. The illusions and disillusionments of young people in our society are greater than they have ever been in any society before.

What can we believe? What is true and what is not? Education must provide a way to answer these questions. We have to be educated about mass media if we want to steer a clear course between illusions, on the one hand, and disillusionment, on the other.

This book takes up some of the current issues concerning mass media and examines them from several different perspectives. Some of the authors presented here are vigorously in favor of mass media and defend them. Others are opposed and critical. And some try to take a balanced approach.

In the third edition of this book, the current issues are quite different than in the first or second edition. Every article in this book is new. The issues are changing. Mass media themselves are changing, and that in itself has become a major media issue. Also, the world is changing; it is a much different place already than it was only a few years ago, in 1988, when the second edition of this book was published. Since then the whole Soviet empire has collapsed, the Iron Curtain has come down, the Berlin Wall has been demolished, and communism (which prevailed in much of the world in 1988) has been discredited as a viable political and economic system. (Some say that the free mass media of the West played a key role in this world revolution.) America, too, has changed, and so have Europe and the Third World. Thus change itself has become a key issue.

Other issues have also changed. We're not so concerned about media access as we once were (although we probably should be), nor are we as concerned about business and the media or religion and the media. But other issues—responsibility, ethics, violence, sex, politics, government, war, minorities, gender, age, culture, and technology—are still as important in the 1990s as they were in 1988.

One thing is sure: The age of mass communication has made it possible for us to gain access to far more information than any society ever had before. Information is indispensable to a complex and advanced civilization. We are an information-hungry society; we need an ever-increasing number of facts to maintain and increase our standard of living. Information today is a commodity we are willing to pay for. We also have more leisure time. We depend on the mass media to provide much of our information and entertainment.

We have often been told that information is power. The question is, what do we have to do to ensure that the information we receive from mass media will serve our needs, not the purposes of someone else?

This book is designed to help readers formulate their own conclusions about the role of mass media in their lives. Conflicting arguments are often presented here deliberately. These arguments should be discussed, and new facts and perspectives should be considered so that each person can reach his or her own conclusions. Only in this manner will truth emerge from this vast marketplace of facts and ideas—truth for each individual.

Today, mass media are too important for us not to know where we stand on the issues affected by communication. Mass media are too essential to be ignored. And the issues raised by mass media will no doubt continue to grow in importance in the foreseeable future.

## NOTES

1. For a good sociological definition of mass media, see Charles R. Wright, *Mass Communication: A Sociological Perspective*, 3d ed. (New York: Random House, 1986).
2. Bernard Berelson and Morris Janowitz, *Reader in Public Opinion and Communication* (New York: Free Press, 1966), p. 379.

# 1

# Changing Mass Media

Mass media are technology-based industries. They depend on machines to make them work—printing presses, broadcasting transmitters, cameras, projectors, radio and television receivers, and much more. Increasingly, they depend on high-tech equipment, especially computers. The technical developments that took place during World War II made mass television possible and greatly expanded the entire world of electronics. And since that time technological changes have been taking place in our society at an ever-increasing rate. Mass media technologies have changed many times, which have caused changes in mass media themselves, which have caused changes in content, which have caused changes in audiences, which have caused changes in mass media effects.

For print and electronic media, these changes have produced several important results: They have made the communication process faster, cheaper, and easier. This has led to a great proliferation of media, both mass and specialized. This has also reduced the role of the gatekeeper between the communicator and the audience. And perhaps most important, it has allowed the communicator to be far more accurate in directing information to a specific audience.

In printing, earlier technologies had produced giant presses that made possible large daily newspapers, but these production plants were so expensive that relatively few newspapers could afford to stay in business. Beginning in the 1960s, the introduction of photo-offset lithography reduced the cost of printing. In the 1970s and 1980s, the introduction of computers reduced the cost of printing and editorial production, and gave the writer/reporter more control over his or her work. In the late 1980s, the introduction of desktop publishing technologies, using personal computers, made the production of the printed word so inexpensive that the average person can now afford to be a publisher.

Similar changes have taken place in the electronic media. Before 1950, movies had to be made in large studios, using bright lights and large and expensive sound and camera equipment. Radio and television transmitters were large and ungainly. A television camera was the size of a desk, and lights in a TV studio had to be so bright that their heat was almost unbearable. The technological changes that began after World War II and have continued to the present have miniaturized and improved the equipment and made it available at a fraction of its earlier cost. Today, we can hold a TV camera in the palm of our hand; a radio transmitter can fit in a suitcase; high-speed film allows movies to be made with small cameras and lightweight sound equipment on location anywhere. As with print media, it is now possible for the average person to be in the electronic communication business.

Other technological developments have aided in the expansion of electronic media. FM broadcasting, which was developed in the 1950s and 1960s, more than doubled the frequencies available to radio. Cable TV, which was developed in the 1970s and 1980s, multiplied the TV possibilities by a factor of ten or more. Video cameras and tape recording—lightweight, inexpensive, and easy to operate—make it possible for anyone to be a movie producer.

Perhaps the most important technological development has been the computer, now an essential part of all mass communication. In the mid-1960s, computers were unheard of in the communication business. One computer was the size of a large classroom, used hundreds of vacuum tubes that had short lifetimes, and cost millions of dollars. Today, a small desk- or laptop computer that is faster and more reliable, with more memory and more functions, can be purchased for not much more than a thousand dollars. This technology is being put to use in almost every aspect of mass communication.

Finally, the computer has allowed one other development that is changing mass communication as much as anything else—market research. Putting together our increased knowledge of human psychology, our use of statistical tools, and the computer to analyze data, we can now predict a number of communication outcomes with considerable reliability and solve a number of communication problems with considerable success. We can discern what audiences want, what they will pay attention to, and what they will pay for. We can find particular segments in a mass society who want a certain communication product or whom we want to reach with a particular message. And we can measure audience response to communicated messages.

All this has made the mass communication process more reliable. More messages can be communicated. Audiences are more likely to find particular messages that suit their interests and points of view. Communicators are more likely to be able to reach the audiences they seek.

And all of this is changing the landscape of mass media. This first section gives some examples of the global spread of communication as a result of the new technologies and their impact on mass media.

# 1

# Global Mass Media Empires

## *by* Carl Bernstein

*Editor's Note:* American mass media, especially the entertainment media, have become global industries, changing both those who consume their products and those who create them. American mass media, for example, now get 85 percent of the world's revenue from pay-TV, 75 percent from television, 55 percent from home videos, 55 percent from movies, 50 percent from sound recordings, and 35 percent from book sales.

In European theaters, 70 percent of box-office receipts are for American films. In India, half of all film imports come from the United States. In Peru, 90 percent of all films shown are American. In Japan, American movies produce long lines of customers at the movie theaters.

In television, U.S.-made movie videos bring in $1.9 billion from abroad. In Europe, two-thirds of all programming is American. European syndication of U.S. shows such as "Dallas" earned $1 billion in 1990.

The United States also dominates the sound-recording markets of the world even though American recording firms lose more than $30 million annually to pirates. Michael Jackson's recording of "Bad" sold 135,000 copies in India alone.

Carl Bernstein, formerly an editor at *Time*, was a reporter at the *Washington Post* when he and Robert Woodward made journalistic history by uncovering the Watergate scandal during the Nixon administration. Before joining *Time*, he was a broadcast executive at ABC. This article appeared in *Time*, December 24, 1990.

Just outside Tokyo 300,000 people troop through Japan's Disneyland each week, while 20 miles outside Paris a new city is rising on 8 sq. mi. of formerly vacant land. Once Euro Disney Resort opens for business in 1992, forget the Eiffel Tower, the Swiss Alps and the Sistine Chapel: it is expected to be the biggest tourist attraction in all of Europe. In Brazil as many as 70% of the songs played on the radio each night are in English. In Bombay's thriving theater district, Neil Simon's plays are among the most popular. Last spring a half-dozen American authors were on the Italian best-seller list. So far this year, American films (mostly action-adventure epics like *Die Hard 2* and *The Terminator*) have captured some 70% of the European gate.

America is saturating the world with its myths, its fantasies, its tunes and dreams. At a moment of deep self-doubt at home, American entertainment products—movies, records, books, theme parks, sports, cartoons, television shows—are projecting an imperial self-confidence across the globe. Entertainment is America's second biggest net export (behind aerospace), bringing in a trade surplus of more than $5 billion a year. American entertainment rang up some $300 billion in sales last year, of which an estimated 20% came from abroad. By the year 2000, half of the revenues from American movies and records will be earned in foreign countries.

But the implications of the American entertainment conquest extend well beyond economics. As the age of the military superpowers ends, the U.S., with no planning or premeditation by its government, is emerging as the driving cultural force around the world, and will probably remain so through the next century. The Evil Empire has fallen. The Leisure Empire strikes back.

"What we are observing," says Federal Reserve Board Chairman Alan Greenspan, "is the increasing leisure hours of people moving increasingly toward entertainment. What they are doing with their time is consuming entertainment—American entertainment—all over the industrialized world."

For most of the postwar era, hard, tangible American products were the measure of U.S. economic success in the world. Today culture may be the country's most important product, the real source of both its economic power and its political influence in the world. "It's not about a number, though the number is unexpectedly huge," says Merrill Lynch's Harold Vogel, author of the 1990 book *Entertainment Industry Economics*. "It is about an economic state of mind that today is dominated by entertainment."

What is the universal appeal of American entertainment? Scale, spectacle, technical excellence, for sure: *Godfather Part III. Batman.* The unexpected, a highly developed style of the outrageous, a gift for vulgarity that borders on the visionary: a Mötley Crüe concert, for example, with the drummer stripped down to his leather jockstrap, flailing away from a calliope riding across the rafters of the Meadowlands Arena in New Jersey. Driving plots, story lines and narrative: a Tom Clancy hero or one of Elmore Leonard's misfits. Indiana Jones' strength of character, self-reliance, a certain coarseness, a restless energy as American as Emerson and Whitman.

"People love fairy tales," observes Czech-born director Milos Forman, "and there is no country that does them better than the United States—whatever kind of fairy tales, not only princesses and happy endings. Every child dreams to be a prince: every adult has a secret closet dream to be Rambo and kill your enemy, regardless if it's your boss or communists or whoever."

Donald Richie, the dean of arts critics in Japan, sees a broader appeal. "The image of America radiates unlimited freedom, democracy, a home of the people," says Richie. "This certainly appeals to the Japanese, who live in a very controlled, authoritarian society." Jack Valenti, president of the Motion Picture Association of America, concurs, arguing that American entertainment—particularly movies, television and rock—was a primary catalyst in the collapse of communism in Europe and the Soviet Union.

On a recent visit to China, David Black, the supervising producer for *Law & Order*, watched young Chinese sell bootleg copies of Chuck Berry and Jerry Lee Lewis tapes in Shanghai. "In Hollywood," says Black, "we are selling them the ultimate luxury: the fact that people don't have to live the life they're born into. They can be a cowboy, a detective, Fred Astaire—and that's what America is selling now. The hell with cars. Cars are just wheels and gears. People want to be able to play at being other people more than they want transportation."

The process exacts a spiritual cost. At work sometimes in the iconography of American popular culture is a complex nostalgia for the lost American soul. Madonna is not Monroe, Stallone is not Billy Wilder. But they are cultural forces with an authority and resonance uniquely American. Such gilded presences radiate signals of material success and excess on a scale heretofore unknown in popular entertainment. Perhaps more important, their influence—as models for imitation, objects of media attention—far outweighs that of the traditional heroes and heroines in what may have been an earlier and more accomplished age. The very adulation that the global stars receive simultaneously diminishes and trivializes them, as if they were mere image and electricity.

Money, lavish production, the big-budget blockbusters that only the American movie studios are willing to finance—these are part of the appeal. And of course the newness of it all, whether in music or film or TV. Only in the U.S. does popular culture undergo almost seasonal rituals of renewal.

Giovanni Agnelli, the Italian automobile industrialist, adds another factor: quality. "What is unique about American movies and popular music and television?" asks Agnelli. "They are better made; we cannot match their excellence."

Nor, it seems, can anyone else on the world stage right now. Matsushita's purchase of MCA, like Sony's ownership of CBS Records and Columbia Pictures, signals a recognition of the value of integrating the yin and the yang of leisure economics, the hardware of VCRs and DAT and the software of music and programming. "Our entertainment is the one thing the Japanese can't make better or cheaper than us," says David Geffen, the largest single shareholder in the recent MCA-Matsushita deal. "That's why they are buying in. But they will have zero influence in the product. Companies don't decide what gets made; the content of American entertainment is inspirationally motivated."

Michael Eisner, chairman of Walt Disney Co., and other industry executives argue that the unique character of American entertainment is the result of the polyglot nature of the society itself—and the clash of cultures and races and traditions within it. The U.S. is the only country in the world with such a heterogeneous mix, uniquely able to invent rap music, Disney World, Las Vegas, rock 'n' roll, Hulk Hogan, Hollywood and Stephen King.

A whole school of traditional economists is worried, however, that infatuation with the entertainment business and its glitzy success is symptomatic of a self-indulgent, spendthrift society deep into self-deceit. "The pre-eminence of entertainment is illusory success," warns Allen Lenz, economist for the Chemical Manufacturers Association. "It's no substitute for manufacturing. We need balance in our economy, not just the goods of instant gratification. The future of America is not in Michael Jackson records, $130 Reeboks and *Die Hard 2*. The fact is, you can't make it on Mickey Mouse."

Or can you? Disney's Eisner is part of a powerful cadre of modern-day Hollywood moguls who have acquired what their predecessors only hoped to have: real global power—economic, social, political.

They exercise it through their stewardship of global entertainment conglomerates in the midst of a communications revolution that has changed the nature of the world. Eisner, Fox's Rupert Murdoch, Paramount's Martin Davis, Steve Ross of Time Warner (which owns the parent company of TIME), Ted Turner of Turner Communications, record executive Geffen, superagent Michael Ovitz and others have an astonishing influence on what the world sees, hears, reads and thinks about.

"The most important megatrend of the century is the availability of free time," maintains Italian Foreign Minister Gianni De Michelis, who is working on a book about the new dynamics of global economy. "This is the reason the U.S. will remain the most important economy in the world—because its GNP is increasingly geared to entertainment, communications, education and health care, all of which are about individuals 'feeling well,' as opposed to the 19th century concept of services intended to protect the workplace and production."

De Michelis' notion illustrates another aspect of today's entertainment business: the lines between entertainment, communications, education and information are increasingly blurred, and the modern U.S. entertainment company is uniquely positioned to provide software in all four areas.

Just as the auto industry determines the basic health and output of a host of other industries (steel, plastics, rubber), the American entertainment business has become a driving force behind other key segments of the country's economy. As a result of this so-called multiplier effect, the products and profits of dozens of U.S. industries are umbilically tied to American entertainment: fast food, communications technology, sportswear, toys and games, sporting goods, advertising, travel, consumer electronics and so on. And the underlying strength of the American economy, many economists believe, has a lot to do with the tie-in of such businesses to the continued growth and world dominance of the American entertainment business and the popular culture that it exports.

"The role of entertainment as a multiplier is probably as great as, or greater than, any other industry's," observes Charles Waite, chief of the U.S. Census Bureau of Economic Programs. "Unfortunately, there's no exact way to measure its effect." But if the American entertainment industry's boundaries were drawn broadly enough to include all or most of its related businesses, some economists believe, it could be credited with generating more than $500 billion a year in sales.

Though the business is increasingly global, the domestic entertainment industry is still the backbone, and it is still thriving. The enormous profits of the '80s are being reduced by the recession. But the amount of time and money the average postadolescent American spends in the thrall of entertainment remains astounding: 40 hours and $30 a week, if industry statistics are to be believed. By the time U.S. culture goes overseas, it has been tried, tested and usually proved successful at home.

Americans this year will spend some $35 billion on records, audio- and videotapes and CDs, almost as much as they will spend on Japanese hardware manufactured to play them. In the air-conditioned Nevada desert, the opening of two gargantuan amusement centers dedicated to gambling and show business—the Mirage and Excalibur hotels—is leading Las Vegas toward its biggest year ever. In Nashville the country-music business is keeping the local economy afloat amid a tide of regional recession. Felix Rohatyn, the fiscal doctor, says the only hope for New York City, laid low by the collapse of the boom-boom Wall Street economy of the '80s, is to turn it into a tourist attraction keyed to entertainment. But the industry is also undergoing profound change in its essential financial and cultural dynamic: moving toward the European and Asian customer as a major source of revenue while moving away from American network television as the creative and economic magnet. *Rambo III* earned $55 million at home but $105 million abroad.

Another effect of globalization: rather than waiting months or years before being released outside the country, American movies and television programs are beginning to enter the foreign marketplace in their infancy and even at birth—and boosting profits. Universal opened *Back to the Future II* in the U.S., Europe and Japan simultaneously. The film made more than $300 million, and the receipts were available months earlier than usual, accruing millions of dollars in interest.

The pervasive American presence is producing a spate of protectionist measures around the world, despite vigorous protests by American trade negotiators. The 12 members of the European Community recently adopted regulations requiring that a majority of all television programs broadcast in Europe be made there "whenever practicable."

Leading the resistance to the American invasion has been France and its Culture Minister, Jack Lang, a longtime Yankee basher who has proclaimed, "Our destiny is not to become the vassals of an immense empire of profit." Spurred by Lang, who has gone so far as to appoint a rock-'n'-roll minister to encourage French rockers, non-French programming is limited to 40% of available air time on the state-run radio stations. But even Alain Finkelkraut, the highbrow French essayist and critic who is no friend of pop culture, concedes, "As painful as it may be for the French to bear, their rock stars just don't have the same appeal as the British or the Americans. Claude François can't compete with the Rolling Stones."

In Africa, American films are watched in American-style drive-in theaters to the accompaniment of hamburgers and fries, washed down with Coca-Cola. One of the biggest cultural events in Kenya in recent weeks has been the national disco-dancing championships. But in Nairobi last month, two dozen representatives of cultural organizations held a seminar on "Cultural Industry for East and Central Africa" and concluded that something must be done to roll back Western (primarily American) dominance of cinema, television, music and dance. "Our governments must adopt conscious policies to stop the dazzle of Western culture from creeping up on us," Tafataona Mahoso, director of the National Arts Council of Zimbabwe, told the gathering.

In Japan too, where the influence of American entertainment is pervasive, the misgivings are growing. "Younger people are forgetting their native culture in favor of adopting American culture," says Hisao Kanaseki, professor of American literature at Tokyo's Komazawa University. "They're not going to see No theater or Kabuki theater. They're only interested in American civilization. Young people here have stopped reading their own literature."

Though movie admissions cost about $12 in Japan, customers seem willing to pay that to stand in the aisles for American films. "To the Japanese, American movies are hip and trendy, and Japanese audiences would rather die than be unfashionable," says William Ireton, managing director of Warner Bros. Japan.

Aside from the Islamic world, where laws based on fundamentalist strictures often forbid access to *any* entertainment, there seem to be very few places where that is not the case. Even in secular Iraq, teenagers jam the half a dozen or so little shops in downtown Baghdad that sell pirated copies of American rock-'n'-roll tapes and where the walls are covered with posters of Madonna and Metallica.

The exponential growth of the American entertainment industry since the late 1970s has taken place in an era of extraordinary affection and goodwill toward the U.S. in the industrialized world. In Europe, Asia and even Latin America, anti-Americanism is lower than at any time since the Vietnam War. The phenomenon is in part self-fulfilling: to a large extent that goodwill can be traced to the projection of America as seen through its popular culture rather than to the nation's actual political or social character. If anything, there is an increasing dissonance between what America really is and what it projects itself to be through its movies and music.

"Even in Nicaragua, when we were beating their asses in the most horrible way, they had this residual love for us," observes author William Styron, who visited the country during the *contra* war. "They love us for our culture, our books, our heroes, our baseball players, our sports figures, our comic strips, our movies, everything. They had this consummate hatred of Reagan, but underneath was enormous love and affection for us as a kind of Arcadia."

The American entertainment business captures much that is appealing, exuberant—and excessive—about the American character. The fantasies and limitless imaginations of Americans are a big part of who they are. It is also, ironically, the source of America's moral authority. For it is in the country's popular culture—movies, music, thrillers, cartoons, Cosby—that the popular arts perpetuate the mythology of an America that to a large extent no longer exists: idealistic, rebellious, efficient, egalitarian. In the boom time of their popular culture, Americans have found new ways to merchandise their mythologies. This is what America manufactures in the twilight of the Reagan era.

Christopher Lasch, the social historian who wrote *The Culture of Narcissism*, sees the development of an entertainment-oriented economy as the final triumph of style over substance in the U.S. Lasch believes the most singular American psychological characteristic—the desire for drama, escape and fantasy—has come to dominate not only American culture and politics but even its commerce. "It's all of a piece. Its effect is the enormous trivialization of cultural goods. Everything becomes entertainment: news, political commentary, cultural analysis," he says. "The most significant thing about the process is that it abolishes all cultural distinctions, good and bad, high and low. It all becomes the same, and therefore all equally evanescent and ultimately meaningless."

Is the imperialism of American popcult smothering other cultures, destroying artistic variety and authenticity around the world to make way for the gaudy American mass synthetic? "It's a horrible experience to go to the most beautiful place in the world only to turn on *Crossfire*," says Leon Wieselthier, the literary editor of the *New Republic*.

"I've always felt that the export of our vulgarity is the hallmark of our greatness," says Styron, who lived for many years in Paris and whose books always sell well in France. "I don't necessarily mean to be derogatory. The Europeans have always been fascinated by wanting to know what's going on with this big, ogreish subcontinent across the Atlantic, this potentially dangerous, constantly mysterious country called the U.S. of A." American popular culture fills a vacuum, vulgar or not. "French television is a wasteland: ours is a madhouse. But at least it's vital," says Styron. "*Dallas* and *Knots Landing* and the American game shows are filling a need in France."

Susan Sontag, whose 1964 essay *Notes on "Camp"* broke new ground in interpreting American popular culture, expresses doubt that the vitality of European culture will be extinguished by America's onslaught. "The cultural infrastructure is still there," she says, noting that great bookstores continue to proliferate in Europe. Rather than regarding Americans as cultural imperialists, she observes wryly, "many Europeans have an almost colonialist attitude toward us. We provide them with wonderful distractions, the feeling of diversion. Perhaps Europeans will eventually view us as a wonderfully advanced Third World country with a lot of rhythm—a kind of pleasure country, so cheap with the dollar down and all that singing and dancing and TV."

How long will the American cultural hegemony last? "I think we are living in a quasi-Hellenistic period," says Chilean philosopher Claudio Veliz, a visiting professor of cultural history at Boston University, who is writing a book on the subject.

"In 413 B.C., Athens ceased to be a world power, and yet for the next 300 years, Greek culture, the culture of Athens, became the culture of the world." Much as the Greek language was the lingua franca of the world, Veliz sees the American version of English in the same role. "The reason Greek culture was so popular is very simple: the people liked it. People liked to dress like the Greeks, to build their buildings like the Greeks. They liked to practice sports like the Greeks; they liked to live like the Greeks. Yet there were no Greek armies forcing them to do it. They simply wanted to be like the Greeks."

If America's epoch is to last, the underlying character of American culture must remain true to itself as it is pulled toward a common global denominator by its entertainment engine. But danger signals are already present: too few movies characterized by nuance, or even good old American nuttiness; more and more disco-dance epics, sickly sweet romances and shoot-'em-up, cut-'em-up, blow-'em-up Schwarzenegger characters: rock 'n' roll that never gets beyond heavy breathing and head banging; blockbuster books that read like T shirts. The combination of the foreign marketplace and a young domestic audience nourished on TV sitcoms, soaps and MTV may be deadly.

The strength of American pop culture has always been in its originality and genuineness: Jimmy Stewart and Bruce Springsteen, *West Side Story* and *The Graduate*; Raymond Chandler and Ray Charles, the Beach Boys and Howdy Doody, James Dean and Janis Joplin. It would be a terrible irony if what America does best—celebrate its own imagination—becomes debased and homogenized by consumers merely hungry for anything labeled MADE IN THE U.S.A.

Another American century seems assured, though far different from the one now rusting out in the heartland. The question is, Will it be the real thing?

# 2

# The Last Gasp
# of Mass Media?

## *by* Joshua Levine

*Editor's Note:* While America's mass media have become global entertainers, the media are changing at home. To survive in the fast-changing
American world, mass media are becoming less massive. Falling ratings,
alternative media, and narrow-interest programming are eroding television's mass audience.

This article illustrates how broadcasting is becoming narrowcasting,
how mass media are becoming specialized and even individualized. The
future promises even more change in that direction. By the year 2000,
experts predict that 40 percent of American homes will have interactive
television, where individual viewers actually become part of the communication process, for example, by shifting camera angles at sporting
events or by selecting various levels of skill and difficulty for aerobic
exercises.

A major step toward individualizing media will be taken when the nation is wired with fiber optic cable sometime in the early twenty-first
century. This, says James Ogilvy, president of the research firm Holen
North America, "will completely destroy the very idea of mass media"
because it will open so many possibilities for sending and receiving individualized messages.

Joshua Levine is the marketing editor of *Forbes* magazine, where this
article appeared on September 17, 1990.

Mark Stahlman, 42, a securities analyst with Alex. Brown & Sons, is a prize
catch for marketers. Along with his wife and two children, he lives in affluent
Montclair, N.J., just outside New York City. With his high income, prestige address and growing family, he's in the market for lots of upscale goods and services. But Stahlman's not biting on the usual lures.

Instead of network television, Stahlman each night zips through 42 cable
channels while thumbing through some of the 30 special interest magazines
he subscribes to. Everything from the *Wine Spectator* to *Road & Track*. More
often than not, Stahlman confesses, most end up half-read in a 4-foot pile.

Because there's simply not enough time. Certainly not enough to allow much network televiewing.

Yet, while the most attractive part of its audience is drifting away, TV networks have been steadily raising their prices. In 1980 the average price for 30 seconds of prime time on the networks was $63,800. Thirty seconds of network prime time [in 1990] goes for an average of $112,600. That's a 76% jump in prices.

Faced with the decline in network televiewing and with rising prices for TV time and advertising space, people with goods and services to sell are looking for more efficient ways to reach potential customers. Thus the TV networks and mass circulation magazines are finding they can no longer prosper merely by delivering tons of undifferentiated audiences to advertisers.

"The way mass media work now, advertisers simply 'buy eyeballs,'" as one ad agency media director puts it—hoping that Stahlman's will be among them. But in the future, advertisers will demand that the media pinpoint not only the age and income of their prospects but also their psychology and buying patterns. Often this won't be done program by program and page by page but in combinations of magazines, TV programs, books and videotapes. Knowing who it is he wants his message to reach, the marketer will demand a media package that promises to deliver his target audience—not just an audience. If Mark Stahlman is in a marketer's target group, he will look for advertising media that can deliver Mark Stahlman and not just any pair of eyes.

"That is clearly what is coming," says Rupert Murdoch, whose News Corp. is buying and building exactly these sorts of bundled media options on a global scale. Looking ahead to when homes will get 100 or more cable or satellite channels, Murdoch says there will be "a lot more fragmentation in the audience and a lot more targeted broadcasting."

Within ten years, maybe sooner, those mass media that can't subdivide their audiences like this to include the Stahlmans of this world will be crippled—or worse.

Back in 1978 ABC, NBC and CBS had a lock on viewers, with 90% of the television audience during prime time. By [1989] that had dropped to 64%, with independents (including Murdoch's new Fox network) up to 24% and cable channels at 22%. Worse for the networks, the viewers they have lost are often people like Mark Stahlman.

By [1989] roughly half of U.S. households could choose from among more than 30 TV channels. With so many choices, the audience becomes, as Rupert Murdoch says, "fragmented." Each fragment offers different viewer profiles and correspondingly different marketing opportunities. Only [a few] years ago less than a third had so many options. Viewing choices will only multiply in the decade ahead, according to a report issued by New York-based ad agency Ogilvy & Mather. That will further undermine network viewing.

The networks argue they've hit bottom. Not everyone agrees. "There's really no mass media left," says Eugene DeWitt, who runs his own media buying company. "The Emperor's got no clothes."

Mass-circulation magazines face the same dilemma the TV networks face. They offer a somewhat undifferentiated audience, and that isn't what marketing people generally want.

Faced with an avalanche of new competition from specialized interest publications—nearly 3,000 new titles hit the newsstands in the last ten years—the general interest, mass-circulation magazine industry is currently suffering through a gruesome downturn. All this has disturbing echoes of the demise in the 1950s and 1960s of such powerhouse national magazines as *Collier's*, *Look* and the *Saturday Evening Post*.

*Reader's Digest*, the most widely read general interest magazine, is down to 16.3 million readers from a high of 18.4 million in 1977. Over the same period, *TV Guide*'s circulation has dropped by more than 4 million—which is more than the combined circulations of *Travel & Leisure, Working Woman* and *House Beautiful.* "You probably won't see *Time* magazine grow," concedes Reginald Brack, president of the Time Inc. Magazine Co., a division of Time Warner. He's being optimistic. Actually, *Time* is shrinking. *Time*, the largest-circulation newsweekly, is down to 4 million readers from its peak of 4.8 million in 1986. Twice in the last two years it reduced the circulation it guarantees to advertisers, because it was becoming increasingly costly to maintain the old levels and because advertisers were less and less interested in sheer numbers.

Most disturbing to advertisers, the defectors from the mass media tend to be richer, better-educated people who can afford specialized material that fits their needs more snugly. Which leaves mass television and magazine audiences increasingly made up of a "media underclass" that will only become more impoverished over time.

Take women aged 25 to 54, a basic audience sector in TV advertising. On average, the poorest 40% of the audience sees 77% of the prime-time commercials, while the richest 40% sees only 8%. Instead of watching a network show, the more affluent women are probably spending their time reading *Architectural Digest*, the *National Review, Town & Country* or the *New Republic.* Or, if televiewing, they may be watching Bravo or the Arts & Entertainment Network.

"The networks are straining to maintain the institution, but the institution is dying like a tree—from the inside out," says David Braun, who runs the media services department for the merged Kraft General Foods. "Suddenly you notice there's no wood in the middle."

Some advertisers have already noticed, and are acting on it. Starting on Labor Day, for example, Buick began sponsoring a series of six syndicated television shows devoted to winners of the Medal of Honor. The programming is designed in response to the profile of Buick buyers, who are conservative, mature, decidedly not flashy and earn at least $35,000 a year.

The problem is, these people don't watch much television. So Buick and *U.S. News & World Report* devised a series of six special sections on these medal winners to run in the magazine the weeks the broadcasts air. Afterwards, the inserts will be bound in book form and sold in bookstores and newsstands. Buick, aware that its target audience does not watch much television, hopes the inserts are getting readers to watch the TV series. This is the kind of thing Rupert Murdoch is talking about when he says the future lies in bundled media: Here Buick is using a bundle comprising magazines, special-interest TV and books. "We're going to have to bend the mass media to our needs," says Phil Guarascio, who can do quite a bit of bending with the $1 billion ad budget he throws around as head of advertising at GM.

Kraft General Foods' David Braun agrees. Ten years ago Braun's job was relatively easy: To snare women aged 25 to 54, the basic target market for a product like Grape Nuts cereal, Braun used to call the three television networks, the seven big women's service magazines and *Reader's Digest*. Mission accomplished.

Today Braun considers about 100 magazines for Grape Nuts, and ends up placing ads in as many as 30, including *Backpacker, Prevention* and *Shape*. Braun still buys network television but supplements that with numerous cable channels and syndicated shows to reach his target audience.

Gordon Link, media director at McCann-Erickson Worldwide, the New York-based ad agency, says when the networks' share of viewers dips to 40%, their days as a mass medium will be over. When will that be? David Braun thinks it could happen within five years.

Not surprisingly, the networks say that will never happen. They've banded together to form the Network Television Association to mount the first-ever trade campaign to convince advertisers they're alive and well.

Mass magazines may have more flexibility than network television moving into an age of more specialized audiences. *Time* magazine is considered the leader among big publishers in slicing and dicing its circulation. Using a process called selective binding, Time recently began inserting specially targeted ads into 900,000 copies of *Time, Sports Illustrated* and *People* that go only to subscribers who have just moved. The ads, from makers of appliances, carpeting and other home improvement items, zero in on the likeliest prospects for these products.

Time says it's too early to say how this is working. But it's certainly not clear that a focus on demographics alone is going to placate advertisers. For many years now, *Time* has offered advertisers over 200 demographically and geographically targeted editions, ranging from business executives to college students. But more than 70% of *Time*'s advertising still runs in the full edition, roughly the same percentage as ten years ago. Meanwhile, the cost of fragmenting press runs balloons the cost of producing the magazine—higher costs that get passed on to the advertisers.

In future, selective binding and a companion process, inkjet printing, will let mass magazines treat their circulations much like direct-mail lists—at a fraction of the cost. This way an advertiser can, in theory at least, reach only those *Time* readers it considers worth reaching, not the full subscription list. Says

Time Warner's Reginald Brack: "Dozens of advertisers are already running their own databases against our subscription list."

Chevrolet is matching a list of owners of competing makes with *Time*'s circulation. With inkjet printing, Chevy can address those readers by name in the ad, possibly steering them to their nearest Chevy dealer for a test drive. *Time* readers who don't own the make of car Chevy is targeting will never see the ad, which is supposed to run later this year.

Not surprisingly, that kind of customized service doesn't come cheap. A full bells-and-whistles *Time* magazine ad using both selective binding and inkjet printing costs about $45 per thousand readers, compared to *Time*'s $30 average. By contrast, a comparable direct-mail campaign averages about $400 per thousand.

The next step: *Time* and other magazines will turn selective binding loose on their editorial copy, tailoring the mix of articles to the taste of individual readers—the ultimate response to specialized reader needs. Will it work? Skeptics say that people with specialized interests—which means all of us—are more likely to turn to a specialty magazine than to look at *Time* for what they want to know. Cat lovers will prefer cat magazines to articles about pets in *Time*; for fans of popular music, *Rolling Stone* will probably be more popular than an issue of *Time* with a few extra articles about pop music.

But TV broadcasters can't subdivide the airwaves the way magazines can cut and paste their pages. Publicly, at least, they say they don't have to. With deep-pocket budgets to spend on splashy programming, networks say a majority of viewers will always choose to watch them. But that may be wishful thinking. CBS figured it could pull in male viewers by shelling out $3.6 billion over four to seven years for the rights to a broad range of big-time sporting events like baseball's All-Star Game and auto racing's Daytona 500. So far, it's not working that way. Ratings for the Daytona 500 [in] February [1990], for instance, dropped to 7.3, from 8.1 in 1989, and CBS is whispering to Wall Street that it's facing big losses this year.

The networks' programming advantage will keep shrinking as cable operators and syndicators boost their spending on original programming, most notably sports. ESPN now carries about 160 major league baseball games each season and 8 National Football League games. Ted Turner's TNT cable network has a big chunk of NBA basketball, with 75 regular-season games. News junkies—an educated and affluent lot, by and large—will probably turn first to CNN rather than wait for the evening network television news.

Rupert Murdoch's Fox network has also proved there are alternatives to mass programming. Fox has corralled huge numbers of viewers aged 12 to 34 with brash, irreverent shows like *In Living Color* and *The Simpsons* that speak directly to youth in their own voice. Targeted TV.

That approach has obviously appealed to advertisers. Fox raked in $550 million in advance advertising commitments for the new season, up from $300 million [in 1989]. CBS took in only $900 million, and it airs seven nights a week to Fox' five. Says McCann-Erickson's Link: "The networks argue that they couldn't have done what Fox did. I say bull!"

At least one of the networks is hedging its bets. [In] February [1990], NBC joined forces with Murdoch's News Corp., Cablevision Systems and Hughes Communications to form Sky Cable, the first U.S. direct broadcast satellite (DBS) venture. Sky Cable will enter orbit and start beaming programming to the home via napkin-size satellite dishes in late 1993. It will also give niche TV programming a significant boost. Sky Cable will carry as many as 108 channels, many of which will resemble special interest magazines. "Programming of the future will have to be niche-oriented to succeed," says Marc Lustgarten, vice chairman of Cablevision Systems Corp. A channel carrying only westerns, or science fiction shows? Why not, says Lustgarten. But advertisers won't be buying piddling audiences of wrangler-lovers or sci-fi freaks. They'll buy demographic packages of viewers on a number of these niche channels.

Christopher Whittle, whose Whittle Communications is 50% owned by Time Warner, is gearing up to launch Special Reports TV this fall. This outfit will put video disc players in the waiting rooms of 20,000 pediatricians, obstetricians and family doctors. Whittle's pitch is simple: Here's a way to reach potential customers that your regular advertising somehow missed. Says Whittle: "Since there's less time to consume media today, we try to figure out places where people still have the time."

Future Whittle screens may appear in airports and even the workplace. More fragmentation of the mass markets, less money and time for the mass media.

# 3

# Beyond Broadcast Journalism

## *by* Jon Katz

*Editor's Note:* Broadcasting may be one of the best examples of the end of mass media—not the only example, just one of the best, perhaps because it can make best use of the array of new electronics available today.

Changes in broadcasting are among the most important in our culture. As the author of this article points out, "The challenges strike at the heart of how issues are examined, at what viewers see, at what a news medium is and does."

Just as CNN has changed world news gathering and TV news viewing, so other new forms of broadcasting are changing politics and government and the way we view these institutions on television. C-Span and local cable news are good examples. In the same way, MTV is changing our definitions of news, pay-TV is changing traditional ways of paying for television, remote equipment is changing the way we watch television, and the telephone hooked up to the television and our computers will ultimately change nearly everything else.

Jon Katz is a former executive producer of CBS "Morning News" and a contributing editor of the *Columbia Journalism Review* and *Rolling Stone*. This article originally appeared in the *Columbia Journalism Review*, March/April 1992.

It isn't fashionable to like TV, but there seems to be no stopping it. If kids aren't playing interactive video games on the screen, parents are shopping on it, ordering movies, watching Congress vote, or tuning in continual weather forecasts and up-to-the-second sports. We can see Nelson Mandela walk out of jail, watch Cruise missiles roar over Baghdad, sit in on public discussions of public officials' sexual behavior, join jurors in once-forbidden courtrooms.

Yet television's very success has knocked one of its crown jewels—broadcast journalism—off its pins. It no longer seems feasible for news to compete in its current form with all the other things that can now be done with/on/via a television set. In fact, commercial broadcast news, network and local, is struggling to survive in its native habitat.

For broadcasters in general, and broadcast journalists in particular, the worst is by no means over. In the coming months, new technological Godzillas will be stirring. The '90s will see additional evolutionary leaps for the box that dominates our living rooms. Some changes will be instantly apparent, on display in stories like the presidential campaign. Others will evolve less noticeably. But news media already battered by recession, defecting youth, cable and VCR competition, and tabloid telecasts have little relief in sight.

The challenges described below are not simply economic—they strike at the heart of how issues are identified and examined, at what viewers see, at what a news medium is and does. Broadcast journalism may have to redefine its mission, its fundamental sense of purpose and reason for being.

## Local Cable News

Later [in 1992], when Time Warner plugs in its twenty-four hour cable news operation—New York One News—in New York City, a new age of truly local television news will dawn. A few states and major cities (including Washington) already have local cable news channels, but New York's will be the largest and most visible. Individual TV stations have always called their news programs local, but few are. Most are regional outlets whose newscasts air a mere dozen daily stories, plus sports and weather. Grass-roots news—fires, city council elections, zoning board flaps, high school football—has been the almost-exclusive province of daily and weekly newspapers.

Local cable news operations will change that. Programming around the clock, they'll have more news time to fill in one day than a network news division or local commercial station gets in weeks. They have the air time already, and satellite trucks and ENG (electronic news gathering) vans—which send microwave signals back to station receivers—have given cable operations the cost-effective technology with which to originate live from anywhere: a Christmas Eve concert by your local church choir, the high school's commencement ceremonies. Soccer league championships will come to television in the same manner that the Olympics now do—live and at considerable length. Imagine the viewership when your township council debates whether or not to double your property taxes, or the board of education decides whether or not to offer free condoms to high school students, and the local cable channel invites you to register your opinion via touch-tone phone.

If all politics is local, news is even more so. The existing mainstream media, broadcast and print, will have to contend with live news not just from Moscow but from Main Street. Television will be able to tell you where all those sirens are headed, and show you the fire as well.

Local cable will pose serious new challenges for advertising and marketing departments, since retailers—furniture stores, home appliance chains, discount houses—will find broadcast advertising opportunities more affordable and appealing.

Time Warner has also recently begun signing up subscribers to the country's first 150-cable channel operation in Queens, New York. Called Quantum, and described by company officials as a "video highway" into the home, the new channel brings an additional technological dimension and potential to television. It offers about half again as many additional channels as the largest systems now in operation, providing cable companies the means to offer specialized experimental, informational, educational, and other services. The system includes fifty-seven channels for pay-per-view movies and special events, with sixteen different movies available at all times—there's even a NASA channel. Quantum will eventually offer new high-definition television, interactive voice technology, and links with computers, fax machines, and a new generation of PCNs—personal communication networks.

## The Video Culture Will Expand

More than 40 million home entertainment systems—Nintendo, Sega, Genesis—are now installed in American homes. New services like the Miami-based Video Jukebox Network allow subscribers to dial up their own music videos. The network now has 13 million subscribers. Sports channels are experimenting with interactive controls that would permit viewers to choose from a variety of camera angles, in effect making each viewer his or her own director. Specialized programming will join with Baby Bell computer systems and home entertainment programs to ensnare anyone with a TV set.

In January [1992], the Federal Communications Commission designated a special radio frequency for interactive over-the-air television services. The frequency would allow television users to order take-out food from local restaurants, pay credit card and utility bills, and call up sports scores by operating remote control devices.

MTV, the cable music channel, has its own daily and weekend news broadcast and a staff of reporters and broadcasters. While MTV news concentrates on rock music, it has also aired stories on politicians like David Duke and non-music issues like AIDS and human rights. The video culture has spawned its own print publications as well. *Entertainment Weekly*, one of the fastest-growing magazines in America, often skillfully and professionally crosses the line between traditional issues and popular culture, especially in areas where the two fuse. The magazine recently devoted a cover story to sexual harassment in the entertainment industry, and another to the controversy surrounding the movie *JFK*.

## Pay-per-View

The Olympics have always been considered a quasi-news event, a marriage between geopolitics, nationalism, and sports. The 1972 terrorist attack on the Israeli Olympic team in Munich and the barring and readmission of South Africa from competition made clear that world sports and world politics can merge.

But [in 1992], NBC [made] broadcasting history by presenting 1,080 hours of Barcelona Olympics on pay-per-view cable channels, along with the

network's free coverage. The costs vary, depending on how many events viewers subscribe to watch, but network officials estimate the average cost will be
$125. Regardless of whether sports addicts or regular Olympics fans will pay
extra to watch more complete coverage of specific events, pay-per-view presents a significant challenge to the already pressed commercial networks. Many
mainstream journalists have viewed the approach of pay-per-view television
with horror, concerned that the free dissemination of information that characterized broadcast journalism will be impeded. Possibly, but another option is
that busy, distracted Americans will be able to choose the type of news and spe-
cial-event programming they want, when they want it.

## C-SPAN

Cable's public service channel will become one of the most important sources
of government and political news in America, probably during this presidential
election year. C-SPAN already is on all day in many news bureaus, lobbyists' and
bureaucrats' offices, and public interest group headquarters, broadcasting congressional debates, key policy speeches, and discussions. During the presidential campaign—when the networks all say they will send fewer people, devote
less airtime, and spend less money—C-SPAN will be offering round-the-clock
mainstream press conferences, call-ins, debates, and conferences with no journalists to get in the way. When it isn't airing congressional debates, it might air
the Russian Evening News, as it does every day at 6 P.M., go live to Portsmouth,
New Hampshire, for President Bush's address to the local Rotary Club, invite
*Washington Post* reporter Bob Woodward to take calls about the series he recently co-authored with David Broder on Vice-President Dan Quayle, broadcast *JFK* producer Oliver Stone's luncheon address to the National Press Club,
or air Joint Congressional Economic Committee Hearings on a proposed "Marshall Plan for America." "The networks used to be the video record of the campaign," said Tim Russert, senior vice-president of NBC News, in an interview
with *The New York Times* in December. "Now C-SPAN has taken that role."

## Trawlers

One of the most-feared new phenomena in broadcasting is the growing tendency of switcher-armed viewers to "trawl" through the channels on cable and
commercial networks, skimming past one broadcast after another, pausing only
briefly. Networks refuse to release surveys they've commissioned that disclose
precise numbers on the enormous audience shifts, and for good reason: one of
the annoyances viewers no longer need endure, even for a second, is commercials. Subscribers pay for cable, guaranteeing cable operators some revenue
aside from commercial time, but networks have no such fallback.

Trawling presents serious public policy implications, as well as electronic
ones. One network executive conceded that during the gulf war, "our

overnights [ratings] told us that millions of people would shift to CNN the second a commercial came on. Often they wouldn't come back. It's amazing, but on a given night when there's a big story, you have literally millions of people—huge chunks of the country—jumping back and forth to avoid commercials or boring guests." It also raises the question of whether Americans will have the patience to focus on serious issues—health care, homelessness, violence—when it's so easy to hop to movies around the clock.

## The Baby Bells

Newspapers and broadcasters had been dreading—and lobbying against—the unleashing of these potential communications monsters for years. They've lost. The federal courts have freed these companies—calling them babies is like calling the Terminator "Toodles"—to enter the information market with computers that access financial and other information, and with message systems that will expand Americans' ability to chat electronically with like-minded people nationwide. This technology has existed for some years, but the Baby Bells, which already own and operate many of the telephone lines and transmission systems the technology requires, have the marketing and economic muscle to make them attractive to consumers.

Sometime in the next year the Baby Bells are expected to offer information ranging from sports scores to stock market quotations, from electronic storage of medical and dental records to home banking and shopping and video services that allow students to view school lectures from home. The technology will enable users to control appliances remotely and to display electronic Yellow Pages, which newspaper publishers dread will displace classified advertising. Telecommunications analysts believe Congress will eventually allow the Baby Bells to compete directly with cable companies by offering television programs.

## Live Real-time Coverage of *Everything*

You Were There and you will be there more and more frequently. The gulf war, the aborted coup in the former Soviet Union, the Clarence Thomas-Anita Hill confrontation, and the William Kennedy Smith trial highlighted an emerging pattern in big-story coverage, one that is born of TV technology but functions almost independently of traditional journalistic notions.

All these stories were covered live, in "real time." All connected the viewer in unprecedentedly direct ways. The role of the correspondent seemed much diminished. Reporters and anchors were hosts, telling us where we were and, most of the time, where we were going, but seeming to know little more than the rest of us about what was really happening, or what it meant.

In the William Kennedy Smith trial, cable continued to shoulder aside the technological, legal, and cultural barriers that have blocked TV from many of the country's courtrooms, demonstrating again how specialized cable news coverage can provide airtime not available to commercial broadcast news, and in the case of specialized channels like the Court Channel, specialized expertise about the subjects like the law as well.

Even when the biggest stories erupt—the gulf war, Clarence Thomas—the commercial networks can't afford to air them as extensively as cable. It costs too much now for the networks to junk hours of prime-time entertainment, but covering live news is precisely what cable is set up to do.

The challenge for broadcast news has never seemed more fundamental: at a time when television technology can take us almost everywhere to cover almost anything, what precisely is the new role of the broadcast journalist? To introduce live coverage? Or to explain, shape, and comment on it?

## Retrenchment for Most Fixed-time Newscasts

The great fixed-time newscasts of network and local news—America's common bulletin boards through the '60s, '70s, and mid-'80s—are fragmented and in disarray. With cable news on the air around the clock, why should we wait for half an hour of evening news? And even if we wanted to sit down and watch, everybody's too busy.

Breaking hard news will become the virtually exclusive province of cable news channels, which have no expensive entertainment broadcasts to preempt when war or scandal breaks out. In vivid contrast to the expensive, cumbersome anchor-bureau model of the networks—which kept correspondents and producers sitting around in distant bureaus with nothing to do much of the time while paying anchors millions of dollars a year for appearing on the air about eight minutes a day—cable news organizations like CNN are models of efficiency. There are no multimillion-dollar anchors; many more reporters and producers make a lot less money; and because the network is on twenty-four hours a day, its bureaus can be used more regularly and efficiently.

These days the networks all seem headed in different directions. GE—NBC's new owner—has drawn enormous fire within NBC and in other news media for its sometimes heavy-handed and brutal cost reductions, so much so that it is reportedly considering selling the network to one of the giant entertainment conglomerates like Paramount or Disney. That is especially ironic, because GE seemed to understand from the beginning that information technology would alter journalistic function. NBC recently acquired the Financial News Network and began its own video wire service, the News Channel. In the long run, from an economic standpoint, NBC seems the best equipped to survive in the fragmented, cable-driven world of TV news.

ABC, on the other hand, appears to be the best positioned for the short run. Its news division seems the likeliest to stay in the evening news business. Of the Big Three, its owner—Capital Cities—seems to best understand the broadcast culture, managing to quietly make its news division more efficient while acquiring and leaving intact its most visible symbols—including the strongest lineup in broadcast journalism.

CBS News, which has settled down somewhat since the relentless and highly public bloodletting of Laurence Tisch's early regime, seems quieter but still adrift. It has yet to publicly articulate a new sense of direction to replace the institution Tisch decimated. It has not moved in new directions, as NBC has, or beefed up its anchor stable, as has ABC. Aside from *48 Hours*, broadcasting's flagship news division still seems stunned by years of layoffs and budget cuts, a raccoon lying in the road as the car speeds away.

## Newsmagazines Will Grow

Network news has no choice but to back away from hard news. News divisions, pressed to find revenues for their tightfisted new owners and showcases for their news personalities, will continue to retreat to the new generation of prime-time newsmagazines. These broadcasts make sense both economically—they cost a fourth of a prime-time entertainment broadcast—and journalistically; they are less hidebound than evening news broadcasts, freer to use dramatic video and range away from reporter-clogged institutions like the White House and the State Department.

CBS has finally stopped bouncing the gritty, dramatic *48 Hours* from one time slot to another, and the broadcast has boosted its ratings as viewers have finally been able to figure out where to find it. ABC News has also stuck with its new newsmagazine, *PrimeTime Live*, giving it time to recover from its disastrous and over-hyped start nearly three years ago. There are reports that Sam Donaldson, co-anchor of *PrimeTime Live*, will leave the broadcast to anchor his own new newsmagazine program, and that NBC News will bring out its own newsmagazine this spring.

The newsmagazines' great but closely guarded secret is that they are much closer to the highly successful tabloid telecasts like *Hard Copy* and *Inside Edition* than they are to traditional news division newscasts or documentaries. With their emphasis on crime, sensationalism, and celebrity, they are mining territory the evening news always considered unworthy. For the newsmagazines to continue to compete with the booming tabloids, they will have to get even racier. They will. For better or worse, commercial broadcast news will make its last stand here.

The news media persist—at their peril—in covering this revolution as an amalgam of toys, or as more bad habits for kids. It is, in fact, a new culture of information, profoundly reshaping the leisure time and information habits of tens of millions of Americans.

At least some of these changes will be evident during the presidential campaign. When the Bush campaign wanted to expose its embattled vice-presidential nominee to a skeptical nation in 1988, aides simply walked Dan

Quayle over to the anchor booths at the Republican convention for chats with Bernard Shaw, Dan Rather, Peter Jennings, and Tom Brokaw. In 1992, with the possible exception of CNN, there won't be anchors at the Republican convention or on the scene at key presidential primaries.

The three commercial networks have announced that their anchors will cover only the Democratic convention in New York, a cheap limo ride across town from their headquarters. They will also scale back the number of reporters, producers, and camera persons assigned to the primaries, the campaign, and the election, all of which will get less airtime. The networks can't afford to cut deeply into prime-time entertainment revenues and can't compete directly with the ubiquitous, lower-paid, more mobile legions of CNN.

It is unclear how politicians will get their messages across in a system as fragmented as broadcast journalism. Challengers without the power of a president to command media attention will have a more difficult time than ever getting through to a public mesmerized by a staggering array of video choices. It is also unclear how journalists will transmit *their* messages. Just as newspapers were—many still are—reluctant to concede television's permanence and relevance, so broadcast news executives and producers have been slow to react to the manner in which technology has made news instantaneously available.

Whether broadcast news does or doesn't respond, this technology will continue to supplant, thus alter, one of the most basic functions of the reporter: to take us where we can't go ourselves.

Like much of the mainstream print media it has challenged and in some ways supplanted, broadcast journalism tends to equate the status quo with responsible, ethical journalism and to view the new video culture as a cross between prostitution and Armageddon. Because it has been so slow to respond to the evolution of its own medium, to permit real diversity of opinion and creatively distinct news programming, broadcast journalism has allowed itself to be perceived as dying, in a constant state of retrenchment and cutback. Yet television news is hardly becoming extinct; it is spreading all over the place.

In one sense, commercial broadcast journalism is freer to experiment and innovate than at any time since its inception. News divisions may have lost much of the virtual monopoly on the daily presentation of news they came to hold through their evening newscasts, and they may no longer be able to compete effectively on breaking stories. But that leaves a lot of room—for real commentary, more reports, and reporting away from the media clusters in Washington and New York, a revival of investigative units looking at crime, waste, and corruption, and closer looks at largely untapped subjects like science, technology, popular culture, and religion.

As for the tube itself, we may like it or not, but we can probably all agree that, whatever its shortcomings, there is one thing it will continue to do brilliantly: grow.

# 4

# Identity Crisis of Newspapers

## by Doug Underwood

*Editor's Note:* Newspapers are in a state of transition. Although they are still the largest mass medium in terms of the number of people they employ and total annual revenues, they have been sorely tried by the competition from television and new alternative media. Evening papers have been particularly vulnerable. Today people seem to come home after work and watch TV news rather than read the evening newspaper. Many evening dailies have gone out of existence in the past decade.

The newspaper industry is now trying to reinvent itself in the age of electronics. Editors and publishers are brainstorming to discern how to keep their old readers and win new ones, especially the young. Part of this effort is inspired by new technologies, which newspaper people feel they must bring to their business. Another part is simply inspired by the success of television. In fact, some newspapers are trying to reinvent themselves as television.

Perhaps the first and most famous such effort was the development of *USA Today*, founded in 1982. It uses satellite transmissions to beam electronic images of its pages to twenty-six printing plants around the United States, allowing it to be printed and distributed simultaneously nationwide, the first truly national newspaper, competing directly with national network television. The paper also makes heavy use of vivid color, striking graphics, and punchy writing of short news items, in the mode of TV news. Moreover, it sells its copies on the streets in newspaper boxes that have been deliberately designed to look like TV sets.

Many newspapers have copied *USA Today*, but in the 1990s newspapers have to do much more to reinvent themselves as viable mass media. This article summarizes such efforts. Doug Underwood is a former daily journalist who is now on the communications faculty at the University of Washington in Seattle. This article appeared in *Columbia Journalism Review*, March/April 1992.

Recently, readers of *The Kansas City Star* were treated to an intriguing new audio-electronic feature. In a box above a six-paragraph feature story about a rock band headed by Chicago White Sox pitcher Jack McDowell, readers were invited to dial a number to hear some of the band's music. Thirteen hundred people dialed into the newspaper's audio "StarTouch" system to hear brief samples of McDowell's songwriting, singing, and guitar playing.

These days boxed invitations abound as reporters at the *Star* strive to turn the newspaper into a "navigational tool" for readers using their telephones to gain access to the *Star*'s new audio system. "We're turning this technology over to the newsroom," says Scott Whiteside, until recently the *Star*'s vice-president for new product development. "We've told them, 'You have the privilege of re-defining journalism. Nobody has done this before.'"

After decades of wringing their hands about the coming of the Information Age but doing little about it, newspaper executives are embarking on the "reinvention" of the daily newspaper—the newest buzzword in industry circles. They have been frightened into doing so by the persistence of their circulation problems, by setbacks in their fight to keep the Bell companies out of the information delivery business, and by the depth of the recession, which has sped the collapse of the industry's retail advertising base.

Gannett's "News 2000" program is a case in point. Editors of local Gannett newspapers are quite literally remolding their beat structures and newsroom organization to respond to perceived reader interests. The just-implemented program is part of Gannett's effort to encourage its local newspapers to pay greater attention to community issues. At the Gannett-owned daily in Olympia, Washington, for example, editors have replaced traditional beats with "hot topic" teams, slapped limits on story length and jumps, added extensive reader service lists, and replaced some reporters with news assistants who gather "news-you-can-use" data from local agencies.

Gannett has taken its cue from the trend-setting *Orange County Register*, which shook up newspaper traditionalists two years ago with its switch to reader-friendly beats like "malls" and "car culture," and from Knight-Ridder's experimental newspaper in Boca Raton, Florida, with its test-marketed formula of news nuggets, pastel hues, multiple graphics, and reader-grabbing features.

Newspapers are also experimenting once again with electronic videotext systems. Many journalists thought videotext was dead when Knight-Ridder shut down its pioneering Viewtron program in the mid-1980s because it couldn't sign up enough subscribers (see "What Zapped the Electronic Newspaper?" CJR, May/June 1987). These days newspapers in Albuquerque and Fort Worth are making a go of modest, low-investment videotext systems that give readers access to electronically archived material that can't be fitted into the daily newshole. At the same time, newspapers in Denver and Omaha shut down more elaborate and expensive videotext experiments, saying there was not yet a market for videotext in their cities. Meanwhile, newspaper executives are watching (nervously, in many cases) as new computer developments point toward the time when today's newspaper, television, computers, and the telephone will be blended into a single multimedia instrument.

Futurists say that all this is just the Information Age finally catching up with newspapers. Paul Saffo, a research fellow at the Institute for the Future in

Menlo Park, California, argues that paper is becoming outmoded as computers become society's principal way of storing data. "We'll become paperless like we became horseless," he says. "There are still horses. But little girls ride them."

Amid all the flailing about as newspapers prepare for an uncertain tomorrow, three general strategies can be discerned: efforts to save the newspaper as it is, efforts to augment the newspaper electronically, and efforts to look beyond the newspaper-on-print.

## The Future of the Newspaper-as-It-Is

In recent years, front pages with more "points-of-entry" and "scannable" news, marketing programs developed in tandem with the news department, and "news-you-can-use" and reader-written features have proliferated. And yet there is no evidence that the focus on readers—and the fixation on marketing and packaging and redesigns associated with it—has done anything to improve newspapers' prospects. Indeed, even the industry's own consultants now caution against expecting circulation growth from redesigns or the adoption of reader-driven marketing formulas.

James Batten, the chairman of Knight-Ridder, a chain known for the high quality of its journalism, launched what he called a "customer-obsession" campaign, an important part of which was the redesigned *Boca Raton News*. It showed initial circulation jumps. However, last summer the *News* dismissed two circulation managers after their departments allegedly overstated the newspaper's paid circulation—a sign of the pressure the newspaper is feeling to show results for Knight-Ridder.

Today's editors, says Susan Miller, Scripps Howard's vice-president/editorial, have come to believe that reader-driven newspapering can be a "higher calling." The vast majority of staffers are becoming accustomed to the idea that "newspapers are to be of service to readers and are not staffed by a Brahmin class that was chosen to lecture the population," Miller says, adding, "People who refuse to be service-oriented will leave in disgust and say we're pandering and will call us bad names—but they will leave."

Bill Walker, a former *Sacramento Bee* reporter, is one who left. In a piece titled "Why I Quit" in *The San Francisco Bay Guardian*, he wrote: "Nowadays, editors spend their days taking meetings in glass offices, emerging only to issue reporters instructions like this: 'Get me a 12-inch A1 box on the city's reaction to the tragedy. Talk to teachers, kids, the mayor, the bishop. Focus on the shock, the sadness, the brave determination to move on. And don't forget the homeless. We've got color art from the shelter.' Meanwhile, the promotions director is already producing a cheery drive-time radio spot to plug the story. . . . We used to have a saying: no matter how bad journalism was, it beat selling insurance for a living. But no more."

Miller, for her part, predicts that the economics of the industry will lead to a thinning of the ranks of mid-level management. At many organizations those ranks were swollen as newspapers put more emphasis on the planning and packaging of the news product. Miller thinks that the leaner newsroom of the future will mean that more power will be placed in the hands of front-line troops. Bill Baker, Knight-Ridder's vice-president/news, says that the emphasis newspaper companies will be putting on innovation will make entrepreneurial thinking in the newsroom more valued. He adds that several new information products being developed by "The Edge of Knight-Ridder," an internal product-development program, were created by veteran reporters who have "the appetite to follow through on them."

Still, newspaper managers may find it difficult to abandon the traditional hierarchy or change their ways of thinking. Publishers oriented to the bottom-line and newspaper managers who made their way up in a safe, monopolistic environment tend to be wary of creative risk-taking. The temptation to hire another consultant, order up another readership survey, or let an industry organization do their thinking for them will, in most cases, win out over coming up with their own ideas and then investing in them.

## Beefing It Up Electronically

Newspapers are making a marginal profit at best in their efforts to find an audience that wants access to an electronic menu of items like restaurant and movie reviews, expanded news stories, sports scores, advance classified ads, business news, and public records. The most popular form of access has been telephone info-lines, and newspapers like *The Kansas City Star* are integrating them into the full operation of the newspaper. Videotext systems are still considered risky, but even editors at newspapers that have abandoned videotext agree that the market for electronic newspapering is growing.

That's certainly the way Gerry Barker, marketing director for *The Fort Worth Star-Telegram*'s "Startext" electronic information service, sees it. "The generation coming out of school who are very computer-oriented—these are the readers of tomorrow," Barker says. "People have misjudged it. It's a social revolution that's happening out there. You can't throw dollars and technology at this and expect it to hatch. It's evolutionary. Just because we built a few Edsels doesn't mean the car is wrong."

Many analysts attribute the failure of early videotext efforts to the attempt by newspapers to transfer the newspaper-on-print too literally onto the computer. "The newspaper's approach to news has to change in order to be successful in transmitting information electronically," says Richard Baker, director of corporate communication for CompuServe, a twenty-two-year-old computer communications company with more than 900,000 customers. "Newspapers and magazines have to embrace the concept of sharing the creation of the news. There needs to be a willingness and openness to let the readers have a much greater hand in determining what's the news." Baker adds that the key to CompuServe's success is the development of customized information and interactive "bulletin boards."

The pressure on newspapers to become all-service information companies has grown recently as the newspaper industry has lost court efforts to keep the telephone companies out of the electronic information business. The experience of the French Minitel system, which gives telephone users in France access to telephone directories and a variety of interactive and communications services via mini-computers, is seen as the model for how U.S. telephone companies may use their monopoly powers to move in on newspapers' most lucrative business. Yet everything ultimately argues for a partnership between newspapers and the telephone companies—and that may already be happening. For example, *The Seattle Times* (whose publisher, Frank Blethen, has been one of the vocal critics of the Baby Bells) recently announced that the *Times* was negotiating to team up with US West to be a data provider on the telephone company's information network.

## The Paperless Newspaper

With the coming developments in electronic data delivery, many newspaper futurists believe the newspaper-on-print faces a perilous future. They say videotext operations and the new computer pagination systems—by means of which newspaper pages are fully designed and laid out on the computer screen—are simply crude, first steps toward the multimedia systems that will come to dominate the information industry. In software systems that are already on the market, computer users can pull from the computer's memory a variety of audio-visual material—including printed text, mobile graphics, video images, music, special effects—which let users create their own multimedia productions.

These developments—combined with the advances in computer-transmitted television—present enormous implications for both newspapers and broadcasters. Digital broadcasting—by means of which images are transmitted in a code used by computers—promises to provide a truly multimedia system that will allow text, graphics, and video images to be transmitted to the computer screen. It doesn't take a rocket scientist to see how this development will increase the pressures to blend the now-separate media forms, and companies in the U.S. and Japan have been hurrying digital technology to the marketplace much faster than many predicted.

Many communications conglomerates, now integrated across newspaper and broadcast divisions, are well structured to take advantage of those developments. Knight-Ridder officials are planning for the day (which they see happening within this decade) when these multimedia newspapers will be available on portable, touch-sensitive, flat-panel displays.

Roger Fidler, the director of new media development for Knight-Ridder, predicts a "bright future" for the "essence" of the newspaper. "I don't see print disappearing," he says. "But I see it taking a different form. The question is not whether there will be newspapers in the next century, but who will publish them. I'm not convinced the majority of the newspaper companies today will be in business in the next century."

So what will it be like to be a journalist in the brave new information world? The minimalistic journalism brought about by reader-friendly newspapering has done much to turn news into just another commodity in the marketplace. And as newspapers join the electronic competition, newspaper journalists are likely to find themselves ever more subject to the forces of technological change, the demands of perpetually updating the news for electronic services, and the pressure to think of their work in marketing terms.

As with many other professions in the go-go 1980s, marketing and the bottom-line have become the by-words of newspapering, and new information technologies offer much to encourage that trend. In the years ahead, newspaper companies—and newspaper professionals—can probably expect to bump up and down on a rocky ride of diminished profit margins, failed efforts at experimentation, and intrusions into their markets.

That's the potential dark side. But there are also reasons to be optimistic. The endless newshole promised by computers does offer an answer to the ever-shrinking news columns—and could hold hope for journalists frustrated by the design gimmicks that have increasingly circumscribed the work life of those who produce the text. Newspapers have always been at the base of the information pyramid, providing much of the in-depth information that is then compressed and marketed by the electronic information purveyors. As the explosion of information continues, there will be even more need for highly skilled journalists to root through it, filter out what's important, and help put it into perspective. The demand for more specialty reporting skills, the opportunities for more creative and analytical writing, and the chance to use data bases to do more sophisticated investigative reporting are all potential upsides of electronic newspapering.

Newspaper journalists should also take heart from the fact that virtually none of those who gaze into the future are predicting the near-term demise of the newspaper-on-print. Technology, so far, has been unable to match the efficient way the eye can scan the newspaper page or the way a newspaper can be folded up and carried around—or the way it can be read while breakfasting over coffee and bagels on a Sunday morning.

Newspapers understand their local, or their specialty, markets. And they can offer an intelligent voice in a world where the cacophony of other media seems to be drowning the public in noise it doesn't want to hear. "There are things about a newspaper that are attuned to the human spirit," says Bill Baker of Knight-Ridder, "and it'll be there forever."

# II

# Mass Media and
# a Changing World

Much has been made of the role mass media have played in the political changes that have taken place worldwide in the past few years. George P. Shultz, former secretary of state, told a Stanford student audience in 1990 that the recent dramatic upheaval in the Eastern bloc was a byproduct of the emergence of the information revolution. The world is changing rapidly and we are living in a new age, Shultz said: "I think it's been apparent for quite some time that the more open and more free [political] system works better [than a closed totalitarian system such as Soviet communism]. It works better from a moral standpoint, and it works better from an economic standpoint. But there has emerged over a period of time, and I think with increasing force in the 1980s, the information revolution, a change in the nature of how things work."

Shultz noted how the all-news cable television network, CNN, was readily available throughout much of the world and brought world events to a global audience. . . . "Information goes around so readily that by now . . . whenever anything important happens anywhere, it is known about everywhere. When I traveled as Secretary of State . . . I would go to the Soviet Union and watch CNN. Go to China, and watch CNN. Go to our operations center for the State Department, which is a 24-hour, seven-day-a-week operation, and of course it's getting this huge flow, thousands and thousands of cables every day. But we also have on CNN."

Mass media recently played a key role in changing not only the totalitarian regime of the former Soviet empire but also many oppressive regimes in Africa, Asia, and Latin America and the apartheid policies of South Africa. But eastern Europe has been the most striking example. Dana Braunova, a Czechoslovakian journalist, recalled the events as she watched them unfold:

It all began [in Czechoslovakia] on November 20, 1989, when the non-party news-papers dared to denounce the brutal police attack on a student demonstration. Thus the "media revolt" got underway and Czechoslovakia's journalists began to report on events openly and honestly. It was not an easy job, especially for those working for hard-line directors in the state press, radio and TV agencies. Their de-termination proved to be decisive in communicating with the provincial popula-tion, since police had taken steps to prevent the delivery of non-state newspapers outside Prague.

With the previously distorted TV and radio coverage, people outside the capi-tal had no real knowledge of the situation in Prague, nor for the reasons for the students' strike and the subsequent rallies. This lack of information could well have isolated cities and towns and made it easy for the security forces to crush the movement for democracy and human rights.

In addition to the mass media, wall posters played a unique role in keeping in-formation flowing. Distributed by students and opposition groups, the posters de-nounced police brutality and campaigned for human rights.[1]

Two days after the attack on students, nearly 400 journalists met in Prague, denounced police brutality, called for an investigation, rejected the monopoly of the Communist party, and called for a general strike. They then formed a syndicate of Czech journalists, the first nonpolitical journalistic organization in Czechoslovakia since the Communists had come to power.

What happened in Czechoslovakia was also taking place in Hungary, Poland, East Germany, Romania, Bulgaria, and the Soviet Union itself, all dramatically symbolized by the demolishment of the Berlin Wall. The forty-year Cold War had come to an end.

In 1989, Ted Koppel of ABC-TV produced a documentary called "Revolu-tion in a Box." It showed how video cameras were being used to produce un-derground video news shows, which were then surreptitiously distributed to people eager to learn what was really going on in the closed society of com-munism. Koppel believed that the camcorder was democratizing the world be-cause it was a tool of mass communication in the hands of ordinary people. It is no longer possible, in this new age of communication technology, said Koppel, for totalitarian regimes to exercise complete and absolute control over the lives of the people they rule. For if people can communicate, if they can get access to information, they can acquire control of their own lives.

Perhaps it is too early to tell whether Koppel's theory will continue to pre-vail. But the decade of the 1990s certainly started off in a way that would make us think he was right.

**Note**

1. From *The Democratic Journalist*, as quoted in *Action*, January–February 1990, pp. 1–2.

# 5

# TV That Changed Our Lives

## *by* David Halberstam

*Editor's Note:* In 1989, the television celebrated its fiftieth birthday. Although the technology had been demonstrated as early as the 1920s, regular programming did not start until 1939. At that time a few limited programs were received only by a handful of rich people. Until the late 1940s a TV receiver was far too expensive for the average person.

During World War II, much was done to perfect and produce electronic gear of all sorts for the war effort, from radar and sonar to walkie-talkies and field transmitters. When the war was over, the factories producing these war products fell idle until someone realized they could mass-produce TV sets. Of course there had to be a mass audience of consumers who wanted to buy affordable sets. And to get such consumers, television had to produce programs that mass audiences wanted to watch.

By 1950, a TV industry capable of gaining a mass audience was in place, and in that year TV sets priced under $100 came on the market for the first time. That had been considered the breakthrough point for mass consumers, and when those sets became available at $99, mass consumers bought and mass audiences began to watch.

Looking back at the early years of television as a mass medium, it is quite easy to see landmarks that made an impact on our lives, our politics, and our culture. That is what David Halberstam does in this article. A former *New York Times* reporter, he is the author of a number of books dealing with modern history and the role of mass media. This article was originally published in *TV Guide*, May 6, 1989.

That television has altered our lives dramatically is now a given. Perhaps the first evidence came in the late 1940s and early '50s during the rise of the Milton Berle show, when a remarkable amount of social activity stopped on Tuesday night. Restaurants and nightclubs, suddenly empty because of the competition with Berle, changed their schedules and closed for the evening. Throughout the East Coast, where most of the television sets were located, toilets flushed as if on signal during the commercials and at the show's conclusion. If that was the first sign, there have been countless others as television has transformed our society politically, culturally, demographically. Trying to make a short list of moments on television that changed our lives is not easy. But here, for better or worse, are six such important events.

### December 1955–December 1956: Martin Luther King and the Montgomery Bus Boycott

When the Montgomery (Ala.) bus boycott began, network news was still relatively new and primitive. But ordinary Americans already were forming a way of gaining information, sitting down every night in front of their screens, watching the news on television, creating in the process what Daniel Schorr later called "a national evening séance."

Montgomery and its aftermath saw the rise of an immensely skilled leader who blended the nonviolence of Gandhi's teaching with the visceral new power of modern communications. King became in those years nothing less than a teledramatist. He chose his enemies carefully, the cruder the segregationist the better, and in so doing he learned how to bring the evil of segregation to the surface; in the process he gave television news its first great running story, one with action, drama and moral dimension.

King was a keen student of modern communications; he learned daily how to deal with the rising power of the media, scheduling his protests in time to make the evening news shows. The response of the average white American to these events was startling: within nine years a series of court decisions and new federal laws granted complete political and legal freedom to blacks. In the process King's protest movement stimulated television's desire for film and thus for action and, eventually, pseudo-action. Not surprisingly, in the '60s, protesting groups went into the streets because that was where the cameras were.

### September 1956: Elvis Presley Goes on The Ed Sullivan Show

Sullivan, a good traditionalist who ran a CBS Sunday night variety show, prided himself on the quality of his taste and was always aware that he was entering people's homes. As such, he had publicly vowed that Elvis, whom he considered a vulgarian, would never go on his show. Then, in early 1956, Elvis's manager, Col. Tom Parker, booked Presley on Milton Berle's show for two appearances. Up went Berle's ratings. Then Steve Allen, who had a variety show that went directly against Sullivan with marginal success, signed Elvis for an appearance. Now, despite a very tame visit by the rocker, Allen beat Sullivan.

Sullivan immediately surrendered. No matter that it was the most sanitized appearance imaginable. The old had capitulated to the new. It was the start of something profound: the youth culture.

### December 1958: The New York Giants-Baltimore Colts Sudden-Death NFL Title Game

It was a remarkable game: two great teams at the height of their powers playing the new, faster, more exciting pro game at an almost-perfect level. Because it coincided, as did some of these other events, with the spread of television, an entire nation watched, though in some parts of the country where television was still relatively new, many people watched in bars. The game marked many things: the ascent of pro football to a level enjoyed in the past only by baseball; the explosion of sports as a crucial ingredient in an America that was becoming a new television-driven, entertainment-oriented society; and, perhaps most importantly, it marked the ability of television to find an event that it favored (that is, something it could cover well) and virtually reinvent it, taking it from something ordinary to something that was part of the national fabric.

### September 1960: The First Kennedy-Nixon Debate

Not only was it the watershed event in the 1960 campaign, but it greatly legitimized the medium itself. Until that moment it was still fashionable among much of the nation's intelligentsia to boast that they did not watch television and, indeed, did not even own a television set. Now, owning a television set was mandatory for an engaged citizen.

In addition, it was the moment that changed politics in America. Politicians had always gone where people gathered, and now they were gathering in their homes. It signaled the mediazation of American politics and the parallel decline of the party system. Only four years later, in 1964, both Presidential campaigns were devoted to getting the candidates on television.

### August 1965: The Coverage by CBS's Morley Safer of the Burning of Vietnamese Hutches by the American Marines in the Village of Cam Ne

It was a vital moment, not just in the war, but in the way many Americans came to look at their own country. Safer was with a Marine unit when it came into a Vietnamese village outside of Da Nang; three marines had been wounded earlier in the day (quite possibly by friendly fire), and the troops were in a rage by the time they reached Cam Ne. They literally tore it apart, and Safer and his cameraman, Ha Thuc Can, had dramatic footage of the marines setting fire to the peasants' huts. (Only heroic intervention by Can prevented the marines from using flamethrowers in a deep hole where a bunch of women and children were cowering.)

In countless Westerns, it was John Wayne and the cavalry who rode up to save women and children from the Indians. But this time it was as if the image were reversed, as if our boys were the villains. The night the report aired, the phones rang off the hook at CBS from people protesting that what they had just seen could not have happened.

It was a landmark piece of reporting, a great reporter present at precisely the right place and time, and it accelerated a process in which Americans saw the true complexity of a very different war.

### November 1979–January 1981: The Iran Hostage Drama

Nothing reflected so completely the power of television over the political process as the taking of the hostages in the American embassy by Iranian students. It was the ultimate volatile media event, and in no small degree it was responsible for the unseating of a President, Jimmy Carter. Carter, doing poorly in the polls at the moment the hostages were taken, later canceled campaign appearances in Iowa and deliberately magnified the crisis because it made him more *Presidential* in contrast to his Democratic challenger, Sen. Edward Kennedy. It put Carter on the front page and on the evening news, just as it squeezed Kennedy off.

Alas for Carter: live by the tube, die by the tube. For it also escalated the crisis in the public mind, and it made the Ayatollah Khomeini Carter's equal. The Ayatollah quickly understood the uses of television, and in the ensuing crisis he kept the Carter Presidency hostage. The crisis was one that the networks loved: unlike many other serious issues, it provided constant photo opportunities. Normally in the process of American communications, print defines and television amplifies, but in this case, television defined and, because the story went so deep into the bloodstream, print dutifully responded. As such there was something ominous in that change as well.

# 6

# Did TV Undo an Empire?

## *by* John Simpson

---

*Editor's Note:* In Romania, East Germany, and Czechoslovakia, television neither kept the masses quiet nor led the revolution, writes John Simpson. What it did was serve as a community bulletin board for historic revolts.

This article was originally published in *World Monitor* in March 1990. Simpson, foreign editor of BBC television, traveled to Berlin, Prague, Budapest, and Bucharest, among other cities, to cover the revolutions of 1989.

---

The great dictator stood on the balcony of his party headquarters. The square below was filled with expectant faces and obedient banners. He knew the people loved him: All his courtiers told him so. He began to tell them how the Russians were trying to undermine Romania's independence by stirring up trouble in the distant city of Timişoara; only he didn't mention the Russians by name. He grew heated. The demonstrators in Timişoara were just hooligans and class enemies. He paused, then started thanking the organizers of that day's meeting. It was then that the booing began.

As Romanian television broadcast this comic and terrible moment live, several things started happening at once. Nicolae Ceauşescu's face showed his utter, horrified amazement at the reaction of the ordinary people in the square. His chief of security lost his head: Coming up behind Ceauşescu, he said loudly enough for the microphone to pick up, "They're starting to break in." The official cameraman's hand started trembling so much the picture shook alarmingly. Back at the television station there was a total failure of nerve. Someone in panic ordered the picture to be cut. The screen went to a lurid red blank.

To everyone who was watching, television had effectively announced the impending fall of the regime. Thousands immediately came out onto the streets. Less than 24 hours later, Ceauşescu and his wife were fugitives. After two more days they were executed. To all those who believe that television was responsible for the revolutions in Eastern Europe in 1989, and they are many, Romania seems the crowning proof.

As the Eastern European dominoes fell, one by one, beginning with Poland and Hungary, continuing with East Germany and Czechoslovakia, and ending in Romania, most of the key events took place in front of the television cameras. It's tempting to assume that the one has made the other happen. There's an easy logic to the idea; it stands to reason. The past few months provide us with virtual laboratory conditions in which to test the theory out.

Somehow, though, it doesn't quite work. What people mean when they say television made the revolutions happen, is that it created the atmosphere in which the population as a whole lost faith in its rulers and slowly turned against them. But in the early days of each of the relevant revolutions—in East Germany, in Czechoslovakia, and in Romania—control of the television station remained with the old regime's loyalists until the critical moment had passed. Television followed the revolution; it did not precede it.

Romanian television, for instance, was scarcely a hotbed of anti-Ceauşescu sentiment. It was slavishly obedient to him. As a result of the chronic power shortages in Romania, television was permitted to broadcast for only three hours a night. There was a news bulletin about the doings of the Ceauşescu family at the start of transmission, and a news bulletin about the doings of the Ceauşescu family at the end of transmission. In between there were programs about the doings of the Ceauşescu family.

Like the stars of some dreadful soap opera, Nicolae and Elena and Nicu and Ilie and the rest of them posed for the cameras, took possession of bunches of flowers, made speeches without number, and were awarded honorary degrees in subjects they couldn't even spell. The viewers loathed it. In self-defense they ran the considerable risk of smuggling in videos from the outside world. Failing that, they watched Bulgarian television, which can be received in Bucharest and much of southern Romania. It was almost as bad, but at least it didn't feature the Ceauşescus.

Romanian television played not the slightest part in building up the opposition to Ceauşescu; nor did it tell the country's viewers about the revolutions that were taking place elsewhere in Eastern Europe. Hungarian, Yugoslav, Bulgarian, and Soviet television, which could all be received in parts of Romania, passed on the news in varying degrees, but the best source of information was the Western radio stations. The BBC and Radio Free Europe broadcast detailed accounts in Romanian of what was going on. Time and again in the streets of Bucharest people told me how much they appreciated the foreign radio broadcasts. I don't remember hearing anyone mention foreign television.

So in the Romanian example, television may have shown viewers the key moment of Ceauşescu's weakness, but it didn't start the revolution. Nor did it start the previous revolution, in Czechoslovakia in late November.

Czechoslovakia is a more developed country than Romania, and the regime, though unpleasant, never tried to cut people off from the outside world to the same extent. Sizable parts of Czechoslovakia could receive West German and Austrian television, and people everywhere could hear BBC and Radio Free Europe programs in Czech and Slovak. Almost everyone in the country knew that the East German regime was crumbling, that the Russians were doing nothing to shore it up, and that the Berlin Wall had been breached.

Even so, most people thought the Communist government in Czechoslovakia would survive for at least another year. It was the government itself that ensured its own downfall. Two weeks after the Berlin Wall was opened, demonstrations started in earnest in Prague. Naturally, no picture of the demonstrations appeared on Czechoslovak Television (CST). On Nov. 17 the government decided to act. It ordered the riot police to attack the crowds with batons and tear gas. Immediately the story went round that someone had been killed. As it happened, the story was untrue; the government in some desperation even paraded the student who was supposed to be dead on television, and showed that he was very much alive. But the damage had been done. The stolid, usually unheroic Czechs poured out onto the streets in greater and greater numbers. The government did not dare to use force again. Eventually, it surrendered and resigned.

For part of this time a protracted battle had gone on inside Czechoslovak Television about whether to show coverage of the daily protests. Eventually the opposition at CST won, and the demonstrations were shown. They grew even bigger as a result. But by that stage the outcome of the process was no longer in doubt. Television gave the process of revolution an extra push and helped to consolidate what had happened. But it played no part in creating the revolutionary atmosphere. That was done, as in Romania, by the government itself. Its use of violence and brutal repression over the years meant that people were desperate for change. Directly the possibility arose, the crowds came out onto the streets.

In the old, romantic pronunciamentos of South America, you had to take over the radio and television stations and start broadcasting inflammatory messages to the nation. In the revolutions in Eastern Europe the television stations went over to the side of the crowd only when it was clear who was going to win. What defeated the Communist governments in East Germany, Czechoslovakia, and Romania was the tactic of getting the crowds out in the streets, giving them the feeling that they could win, and increasing the pressure until the critical mass was obtained.

Ceauşescu and the other leaders of Communist Eastern Europe thought of television rather in terms of George Orwell's "1984": For them, it was an instrument of mass hypnosis, which operated in every dwelling to keep the inhabitants loyal. As the Romanian example shows, Big Brother completely failed in his appointed task.

But television didn't have the power to create the revolutions of "1989" either. It isn't a force in itself. It's simply the most effective notice-board for the community. And the notice which state-run television, usually despite itself, presented to the Eastern European viewer was that the Marxist-Leninist system was not, after all, invulnerable.

Because the state controlled everyone's lives and had its representatives in every factory and every block of flats, the system had always been regarded as permanent. It could, perhaps, be reformed; but revolution was assumed to be out of the question. The realization that this was no longer so swept right through Eastern Europe far faster than anyone expected. Television was part of the process by which political change ceased to be unthinkable.

# 7

# The Revolution Has Been Televised

## *by* Tara Sonenshine

*Editor's Note:* Although Eastern European communism has collapsed, the Communist party still controls China. The reason, according to Tara Sonenshine, is television. East Germans were able to see the pro-democracy demonstrations in Tiananmen Square on their TV sets in June 1989. But Chinese citizens were able to see very little of what occurred in their own country, and they were not able to see much of what subsequently occurred in East Germany when the Berlin Wall came down in November 1989.

Tara Sonenshine argues that the powerful video images of Tiananmen Square fueled East Germany's peaceful revolution. She is editorial producer for Koppel Communications, Ted Koppel's independent production company. This article originally appeared in the *Washington Post*, October 2, 1990.

It's not too much of an exaggeration to say that the German revolution began in Tiananmen Square. When troops moved against Chinese pro-democracy demonstrators on June 4, 1989, the events filled television screens around the world, but perhaps nowhere with so much effect as in East Germany. There, millions of people watched anxiously as Chinese students and citizens waged a war of nerves against the government—and then lost in a brutal military crackdown.

Pastor Tureck remembers the impact of those images from Beijing on his parishioners in Leipzig. "We saw Tiananmen Square here in Leipzig on West German television . . . and it influenced our world," he recalls. "Although people were afraid, they were also filled with hope." Many East Germans gathered in the wooden pews of Pastor Tureck's quaint little church after seeing reports from China to discuss what the events in China might mean for their own burgeoning protest movement.

Erich Honecker also watched the reports from Tiananmen. They had, according to Princeton University Prof. James McAdams, one of the leading American experts on the GDR, "a paradoxical effect. The East German government knew people were watching things play out in China, and they felt pressured into taking a stand. Honecker had to take a hard-line position to make it clear to the people that such behavior would not be tolerated."

Honecker had tried to keep East German television from covering the Beijing uprising, but the strategy backfired: West German TV was broadcasting the images and enabling citizens and the leadership of East Germany to see what was happening. The East German government's response of open support for what the Chinese leadership did in Tiananmen created anger and frustration among the East German citizenry.

Of course, Tiananmen Square was only one of the powerful video images of revolution that reached East Germany in the banner year of 1989, albeit perhaps the most galvanizing. There were also images from Poland—Gen. Jaruzelski standing with Lech Walesa, whose hand was clenched in a Solidarity victory salute. There were images from Hungary—soldiers cutting the barbed wire fence along the Austro-Hungarian border. There were images from Czechoslovakia—freedom trains carrying jubilant East Germans to the West.

Television was, for the people of East Germany, a window through which they could witness the revolutionary changes taking place around them. It allowed them to take part in the broad movement to unseat communism around the world. It filled them with the courage to confront a police state known for its brutal repression of dissent. It gave them information and knowledge—with which they could challenge the old ways of looking at the world.

When Mikhail Gorbachev burst upon this television scene in 1985, with his new ideas of perestroika and glasnost, the old guard of the East German leadership resisted as best it could. Honecker was a traditionalist, a product of the old school, and so he used traditional means to fight back. He censored Gorbachev's speeches in East Germany. He banned Soviet articles. Bern Beyer, an East German economist, recalls being angered by the strategy. "We could see Gorbachev on television, but only the privileged were allowed to read the complete text of what he had to say."

Again, the strategy backfired. Honecker failed to realize, until it was too late, the power of television as a motivator of public opinion. Honecker could keep Gorbachev out of the libraries, but he could not keep him out of the living room. On West German television came pictures of the new Soviet leader in action—kissing babies in Britain, shaking hands with Margaret Thatcher and Helmut Kohl, drawing crowds on the streets of Washington, escorting Ronald Reagan around Moscow.

Daniela Dahn, an East German writer and former television producer, recalls how the contrast frustrated people. "There was a lot of pent-up anger in the country, and the East German TV media did nothing to even hint that the system was prepared to change. Meanwhile people could get television from the West, from West Germany. And we watched as glasnost developed in the Soviet Union. We could see it."

Not everything people saw from the Soviet Union was positive. In 1987 television carried the first pictures of the Chernobyl nuclear accident. Prof.

McAdams was living in East Germany at the time. "It was the first convincing sign of the universal crisis of socialism. Here was a cloud over everyone's head. East German television tried to say it was no big deal. West German television showed picture of Bavarian supermarkets dumping their vegetables. The public trust was further eroded."

This erosion of public trust reached its pinnacle with the tearing down of the barbed wire fence along the border between Austria and Hungary. While West German television was showing pictures of ecstatic East Germans driving across the border, East German television carried an official statement on its state-run ADN network criticizing Hungary for the "organized smuggling of human beings." Within days of that report, thousands of East Germans who feared climbing the Berlin Wall flooded Hungary in hopes of taking the long road to West Germany. "Television gave us information, sometimes information on how to leave the country," says Daniela Dahn.

Such mass departures were a traditional fear of the East German leadership, and it used traditional means to try to prevent them. Beginning with the construction of the Berlin Wall in 1961, the state had tried to limit travel to the West and contacts between citizens of East and West. At first the policy included curtailing the spread of information by television and other means. In the early 1960s youth brigades harassed those who tried to watch Western TV. Television antennas were torn down or turned around in an effort to scramble the incoming signal from West Germany. When the West Germans changed to a new PAL system of broadcasting, East German television refused to convert the signal for viewing.

But technology moved faster than the political leadership. People were able to turn the antennas back around or to buy converters on the black market. Honecker finally reached a decision in the mid-1970s to abandon efforts to cut the East off from Western television. He chose instead to counter it with propaganda from within. As McAdams explains, "the policy changed from one of isolation from the West to one of insulation from the West."

Television might actually show people the excesses of capitalism— homelessness, drugs, unemployment. East German television would be used to propagate the positive values of socialism. Honecker instituted "Black Channel," a government propaganda program that put its own spin on news from the West and provided pro-East German programs. Bern Beyer recalls how "Black Channel" would use video of Gorbachev with negative commentary running over it. "You would see a positive image but hear an East German negative opinion being expressed. Most viewers understood the difference."

As a television producer for East German television, Dahn learned firsthand what it was like to play by Honecker's rules. "One of the shows I produced was canceled by the government because it was too controversial. It exposed the unfair wages being paid young people in the GDR. Another program about pollution in the GDR was cut because it used real data. We were not supposed to use real data because people were not supposed to know how bad the water was that they were drinking."

Since then, people have been introduced to programs like "Klartext," which provide investigative reports on everything from the old Stasi or state security to new political developments. A program called "1199," named for the postal zip code in East Berlin, is targeted to youth, with up-to-date music videos and cultural stories from the West.

Dahn says that the television revolution has had positive and negative effects. "The percentage of people who watch the GDR nightly news has risen from about 4 percent to 45 percent. . . . There are communities around Hanover that have demanded that their city administrators install satellite dishes so they can watch East German news."

The downside is that literature has at least temporarily lost its attraction. "Theaters are empty, and books just aren't being bought anymore. Fiction, in particular, is not attracting people's attention."

The geographic and cultural closeness of the two Germanys made the impact of West German television on the GDR even more magnified. People in East Berlin who watched the news from West Germany heard reports in their own language and saw pictures of a country just next door. The irony is that television has been both a means and an end.

Ron Asmus, an expert on East Germany for the Rand Corp., has been looking at the root causes of the revolution. "The two things that drove the revolution were the desire for freedom and affluence—and the sense of a single German nation. On the first, the media appealed to the East German pent-up consumerism. People want a BMW, they want to go to the Bahamas. . . . And this revolution was, in part, about the desire for a VCR."

By late September of 1989 the revolution had spread to all corners of the GDR. Massive protests finally persuaded Honecker to cut off Western media coverage. Journalists were blocked from entering East Berlin and other cities. No foreign media were present in Leipzig when a massacre was averted by last-minute compromises between the church and the local Communist Party. Television cameras were not there to record the events.

But Honecker's last-ditch effort to curtail Western coverage of the protest movement failed. By Oct. 16 the crowds in Leipzig had swelled to 100,000. Two days later, Honecker resigned, citing ill health. On Oct. 30, "Black Channel," the government propaganda program, aired its last program.

Those who had their television sets tuned in to the evening news on Nov. 9 heard a hastily read, ill-prepared statement by Gunther Shabowski, an East German Politburo member. "Today, the decision was made that makes it possible for all citizens to leave the country through East German crossing points." Seemingly unsure himself of what that meant, Shabowski tried to suggest that it was not the fall of the Berlin Wall. "This does not mean that we mean to tear it down."

But millions of viewers heard those words and raced to Checkpoint Charlie, one of the most famous of the Wall's crossings. In a country where only 30 percent of the population has a telephone but 90 percent has television, the quickest way to verify information is on the streets. Border guards at the Wall crossings had not even been issued new instructions. They learned that something dramatic had happened the same way everyone else did—through television.

In the days and weeks after the fall of the Berlin Wall, East German television aggressively covered the news and began in-depth investigations into the corruption of the Honecker regime. In fact, it was East German television that carried the first pictures of the fancy dachas and lavish hunting lodges that had housed the top officials of the Communist Party. Stories of pollution in East Germany were also run—completely changed, says Bern Beyer of the East Berlin Institute of Politics and Economics. "It is, at times, even more aggressive than West German television."

There is a final irony: in China, where some of the impetus for revolutions in Eastern Europe originated, citizens have not been able to see the results. The Chinese leadership, unlike Erich Honecker, understands fully the impact of television. The dramatic images of the crumbling of the Berlin Wall were barely seen in the homes of ordinary Chinese citizens.

# 8

# Ten Days That Shook the White House

## by Daniel Schorr

*Editor's Note:* The revolution in the former Soviet bloc is certainly not the only example of the power of television. That power not only has changed communist countries but also is constantly changing America as well, and it will continue to change the world as long as free mass media prevail.

This article shows how television changed the policies of the Bush administration on the Kurdish issue. But it wasn't television alone that made the message effective; it was television in concert with the printed word.

Daniel Schorr, now senior news analyst for National Public Radio, was for many years a correspondent for network radio and television. This article was originally published in the *Columbia Journalism Review*, July/August 1991.

Score one for the power of the media, especially television, as a policy-making force. Coverage of the massacre and exodus of the Kurds generated public pressures that were instrumental in slowing the hasty American military withdrawal from Iraq and forcing a return to help guard and care for the victims of Saddam Hussein's vengeance.

The Kurdish tragedy was only one in a season of worldwide disasters—the typhoon in Bangladesh, earthquakes in Soviet Georgia and Costa Rica, famine in Africa. Scenes of suffering flitted past American television audiences, a succession of miseries almost too rapid and stark to be absorbed.

But the suffering of the Kurds stood out from the others. This was not a natural catastrophe, but a man-made disaster, and one that had a special claim on the American conscience. It was America, after all, that had invaded Iraq and shaken loose the underpinnings of authority. It was America's president, George Bush, who, on February 15, called on the "Iraqi military and the Iraqi people" to rise up and "force Saddam Hussein . . . to step aside." It was President Bush who, on February 27, had ordered an abrupt cessation of hostilities, leaving the Iraqi dictator with enough armor and aircraft to put down Shiite and Kurdish uprisings. And, finally, it was the Bush administration that, after first warning the Iraqi regime not to use helicopter gunships against its own people, then stood by while they were used to strafe Kurds fleeing to the mountains in the north.

Americans became dimly aware, in the month after the war stopped and the rebellions had started, that their government, having burst the floodgates in Iraq, was trying to run away from the flood. There was even a whisper of tacit collusion with the dictator whom Bush had called "worse than Hitler." *The New York Times* reported on March 27 that the administration had "decided to let President Saddam Hussein put down rebellions in his country without American intervention." This in the name of avoiding being dragged into what the president called "a Vietnam-style quagmire," and in response to Saudi Arabian and Turkish concerns about the possible disintegration of Iraq.

The administration had every reason, at first, to believe that the public supported a policy of getting the troops home quickly and avoiding involvement in ethnic strife. There was some criticism, but it was mainly confined to the editorial pages of newspapers. The Bush administration, like the Reagan administration, seems to work on the premise that print does not move people; only television, with its visceral impact, does.

The Kurds had been let down by America before. As disclosed in the report of the House Intelligence Committee in 1976 (of which I obtained a draft before the House voted to suppress it), President Nixon had the CIA sponsor a Kurdish uprising against Saddam Hussein, starting in 1972, as a favor to the Shah of Iran. When the Shah and Saddam settled their differences, support for the insurrection was withdrawn and the Kurds were abandoned to an Iraqi attack. ("Our movement and people are being destroyed in an unbelievable way, with silence from everyone," Mustafa Barzani, father of the current Kurdish leader, wrote to Secretary of State Henry Kissinger on March 10, 1975. "We feel, Your Excellency, that the United States has a moral and political responsibility towards our people, who have committed themselves to your country's policy.") Thousands were killed and 200,000 fled to Iran, of whom 40,000 were forcibly returned to Iraq.

I reported this on CBS in 1976, but it was a "tell story" without the pictures needed to let the audience experience the dimensions of American betrayal. And it made little impression. So now, in March 1991, the Bush administration was not overly concerned with "tell stories" and commentaries about how America was turning its back on the Kurds.

Jim Hoagland wrote in *The Washington Post* of "an American bug-out from the Persian Gulf," and William Safire wrote in *The New York Times* that the president had experienced "a failure of nerve." But "a senior presidential aide" told *Time* magazine, "The only pressure for the U.S. to intervene is coming from columnists and commentators." And a "top White House aide" (probably Chief of Staff John Sununu in both cases) told *Newsweek*, "A hundred Safire columns will not change the public's mind. There is no political downside to our policy."

Famous last words, politically speaking. What the White House did not seem to realize was that, by the end of March, the issue, as perceived by the public, was changing from military intervention in support of a revolution to compassionate intercession for the victims of Saddam Hussein's genocidal methods. By then, while hundreds of thousands of Kurds and Shiites were being driven into Iran, where they could not be easily seen by the world, hundreds of thousands more Kurds were being driven into the rugged mountains bordering Turkey, where they could be vividly witnessed by television.

The vast panorama of suffering, and perhaps even more the individual portraits of agony, seemed overwhelming. Not easily forgotten were scenes like that of the little girl, her bare feet sinking into the freezing mud, or of the little boy, his face burned, possibly by napalm. The anguished face of a child peered up from the cover of *Newsweek*, with the caption, addressed to Mr. Bush, "Why won't he help us?" In a BBC report on *The MacNeil/Lehrer NewsHour*, a woman asked, "Why did George Bush do nothing?"

The quagmire-shunning Bush administration was slow to react, concentrating on a formal cease-fire to speed the return of American troops and continuing to emphasize its refusal to be involved in "an internal conflict."

**April 2:** On a golf course in Florida, in strange juxtaposition with evening news scenes of shivering and starving refugees, the president brushed off questions about the continued Iraqi use of helicopter gunships against the Kurds, saying, "I feel no reason to answer to anybody. We're relaxing here."

A senior official told *The Washington Post* that the reticence was deliberate: "Engaging on the issue gains us nothing. All you do is risk raising public concerns that are not there now. . . . "

**April 3:** By now the administration was becoming aware of American and European "concerns," and had begun scrambling for a policy of compassion without intervention. On the Florida golf course, Mr. Bush said, "I feel frustrated any time innocent civilians are being slaughtered. But the United States and these other countries with us in this coalition did not go there to settle all the internal affairs of Iraq."

Later that day came a written statement in the president's name, departing from the administration's passive role: "I call upon Iraq's leaders to halt these attacks immediately and to allow international organizations to work inside Iraq to alleviate the suffering. . . . The United States is prepared to extend economic help to Turkey through multilateral channels."

**April 4:** Appearing with Japanese Prime Minister Toshiki Kaifu in Newport Beach, California, Mr. Bush said, "We will do what we can to help the Kurdish refugees." But he also stuck with the position that no American parent "wants to see United States forces pushed into this situation, brutal, tough, and deplorable as it is."

By this time, the Kurdish insurrection all but crushed, television was showing a mass exodus into the mountains. A widely distributed Associated Press photo showed a ten-year-old girl in a hospital in northern Iraq being comforted by her mother. The child had lost a hand and an eye in an Iraqi helicopter attack.

**April 5:** In Newport Beach, a dogged President Bush declared, "We will do what we can to help there without being bogged down into a ground-force action in Iraq." Again, the press office, hours later, came up with a written new policy—the Air Force would start dropping food, blankets, and clothing to Kurdish refugees in northern Iraq.

As a public-relations answer, the air drops did not go over very well. The supplies landed in random places; television showed where some Kurds had been killed by falling bales.

**April 8:** Europe was looking at television, too, seeing reporting—particularly in Britain—that was often more vivid and comprehensive than American television was showing. At a European Community meeting in Luxembourg, British Prime Minister John Major proposed the creation of a protected "enclave" for the Kurds in northern Iraq. Secretary of State James Baker, visiting Luxembourg, saw on television what Europeans were seeing. Then, at the bidding of President Bush, worried about an impression of American insensitivity to the refugees' plight, Baker proceeded to the Turkish border. The seven-minute visit turned into a photo opportunity of a special sort. It focused on scenes of desperate Kurds, one saying, in English, "Please, Mr. Baker I want to talk to you. You've go to do something to help us."

**April 11:** A Reuters dispatch from Washington noted, "Searing pictures of suffering Iraqi refugees have clouded America's gulf war triumph and given President Bush a devilish political problem." Part of his problem was that his vacillation on the Kurdish issue had helped to bring down his approval rating from 92 to 80 percent in a *Newsweek* poll (78 percent in a Gallup poll).

**April 12:** The administration announced that American troops would be going back into Iraq as part of a relief operation called "Provide Comfort." Military encampments would be set up, guarded by coalition forces, eventually to be turned over to the United Nations. The announcement came so suddenly as to catch off base Defense Secretary Richard Cheney who, an hour before, had told a news conference that there had been no decision to "actually put forces on the ground in Iraq."

Within a two-week period, the president had been forced, under the impact of what Americans and Europeans were seeing on television, to reconsider his hasty withdrawal of troops from Iraq. As though to acknowledge this, Mr. Bush told a news conference on April 16, "No one can see the pictures or hear the accounts of this human suffering—men, women, and, most painfully of all, innocent children—and not be deeply moved."

Military victory over Iraq was threatening to turn into political and moral defeat. The polls that had shown Americans overwhelmingly wanting troops home in a hurry were now showing that Americans did not want to abandon the Kurds, even if that meant using American forces to protect them.

It is rare in American history that television, which is most often manipulated to support a policy, creates an unofficial plebiscite that forces a change in policy.

In a column on May 5, *New York Times* television critic Walter Goodman underscored what the medium had wrought when "it compelled the White House to act despite its initial reluctance." But he also raised the question, "Should American policy be driven by scenes that happen to be accessible to cameras and that make the most impact on the screen?"

The question is a reasonable one. But, in the case of the Kurds, it was not the pictures alone that forced the change. These were not random pictures of random suffering, but pictures that dramatized the suffering of a people for whom Americans felt some responsibility. It was that combination that overwhelmed governmental passivity.

# III

# Mass Media and a Changing America

As we saw in the last section, mass media have played a powerful role in bringing about what appears to be a better world: freer and more open, more democratic and less totalitarian, and with more individual choices and options and less likelihood that despots can succeed. But have mass media really made the world better for everyone?

Many critics, looking at the United States, say that mass media are making America worse, not better. The particular villain is television, but motion pictures, advertising, slick magazines, cheap novels, and even daily newspapers are given a share of the blame as well.

Of course, we can ask the age-old question, who is really to blame? Is it the media themselves? Is it the owners, producers, directors, and editors—the so-called gatekeepers—of mass media? Is it the creative writers and artists and reporters? Is it the advertisers and PR firms who try to get their messages into mass media and to influence media for their own purposes? Is it lawmakers, who should be passing laws to bring about stricter control of mass media, or the government, which should be administering those laws? Or is it—some might say, God forbid!—the consumer, the mass majority, the great American audience that influences media content by its choices in the marketplace?

Many would say the ultimate responsibility rests with customers—readers, listeners, and viewers. They make their selections from a great variety of options; they can turn off the television or switch channels; they can choose from any number of newspapers, magazines, movies, radio programs, and books. They can also choose to avoid mass media; they can converse with family and friends, work in the garden, play games, or do aerobic exercises.

As we have pointed out, Americans spend more than half their leisure time on mass media, most of it mediocre fare. It is their choice. They are not required to do so, and there are plenty of other options.

When we examine what people choose when they have a free choice, the results are not particularly helpful. For example, the *National Enquirer*, a tabloid sold in supermarkets that deals mainly in sex, sleaze, gossip, half-truths and total lies, sells about 20 million copies a week. The *New York Times* doesn't sell that many copies in a week of daily issues. In the Washington, D.C., area, for example, recent Audit Bureau of Circulations figures show the number of people who subscribe to each of the following publications:

| | |
|---|---|
| *National Enquirer* | 54,731 |
| *New Yorker* | 26,898 |
| *Soap Opera Digest* | 22,302 |
| *Scientific American* | 17,820 |
| *Weight Watchers* | 17,784 |
| *Guns & Ammo* | 9,688 |
| *Harper's* | 7,799 |

Perhaps children and the poor have fewer options, and studies show that these two population groups are most likely to spend the most time watching television—with disastrous results, according to some critics, especially for children, who are most vulnerable to the impressions they get from television.

Should the government exercise some degree of authority over children's television, in an otherwise free society, to protect the young? Many people think so. Others see such a move as an opening for government encroachment in all other areas of personal and civil liberties. For these people, the solution might better be family control, in which parents dictate what and how their children watch television and join with their children to help them interpret the fantasies and fictions of television from a normal point of view.

A problem here is that fewer and fewer households have parents at home during the early years of a child's life; more and more children are spending those most impressionable preschool years in day-care centers, where television is often used as an easy baby-sitter and pacifier.

A corollary problem is that adults themselves don't seem to have better taste than children. For example, studies show that adults are turning away from newspapers. Is this because they don't want factual reporting and intelligent analysis? Or are newspapers themselves trying too much to be glitzy products to keep up with television? One thing is sure: The power of the news media at the beginning of the 1990s seems to have declined considerably from the days when journalists exposed the scandal of Watergate and brought about the resignation of an American president.

# 9

# So Many Media, So Little Time

## by Richard Harwood

*Editor's Note:* Americans spend more time on mass media than do people in most other societies of the world. The average American spends 21 percent of his or her time working, 31 percent sleeping, and 48 percent in other activities. Of these other activities, 78 percent is spent on mass media, or eight hours and fifty-two minutes per day. More than half of that media time, actually 58 percent, is spent on television, not even including home videos.

Unfortunately, by far the largest percentage of our mass media time is devoted to entertainment, not information. News time and news audiences seem to be shrinking in America. Where will it all lead?

Richard Harwood is a long-time Washington journalist, columnist, and former ombudsman for the *Washington Post*, a job that required him to be the newspaper's conscience. This column was published in the *Washington Post* on September 2, 1992.

There are 8,760 hours in a 365-day year. Adolescents, according to the folklore, spend most of that time thinking or dreaming about sex. Adults have other, although not necessarily more interesting, demands on their time.

Adjusting for vacations, weekends, holidays and illness, the average full-time worker in the course of a year puts in about 1,824 hours at the job. Sleep, at 7½ hours a night, accounts for 2,737 hours.

The largest share of our time, however, is claimed by the "media"—3,256 hours a year, or about nine hours a day. This estimate comes from Veronis, Suhler & Associates, a reputable investment banking house in New York, specializing in the communications industry.

Where does this "media" time go? These are the daily average calculations, based on the Veronis, Suhler data:

*Television including cable:* Four hours and nine minutes.
*Radio including drive time:* Three hours.
*Recorded music:* 36 minutes.
*Daily newspapers:* 28 minutes.
*Consumer books:* 16 minutes.
*Consumer magazines:* 14 minutes.

*Home video:* Seven minutes.
*Movies in theaters:* Two minutes.

This is a big business, the nation's ninth largest, ranking just below aerospace and just above electronic equipment and its components. The adult consumers of all this amusement and information spent last year $108.8 billion on the "media"—about $353 per person. Advertisers spent another $80 billion to bring it to us.

Our lives and our economy are affected in many ways. The "media" are a great engine in our consumer society. They provide the jobs for hundreds of thousands of technicians, writers, artists, performers, intellectuals, pseudo-intellectuals and the orally accomplished. They shape our attitudes and beliefs and put pictures of the world into our heads.

We can't quantify those influences or rank them in any order of importance. Does rap music or the editorial page of the New York Times have greater impact on the minds of our youth? Which history of the assassination of John Kennedy is a greater popular "truth"—the Warren Commission report or the film "JFK"? Are "family values" more affected by speeches from George Bush and Dan Quayle or by TV sitcoms, soap operas, hillbilly music, Ann Landers and Oprah?

James Carey, dean of the College of Communication at the University of Illinois, ruminates on these questions in an essay published in the Kettering Review:

"We have inherited . . . a journalism of the expert and the conduit, a journalism of information, fact, objectivity and publicity. It is a scientific conception of journalism: it assumes an audience to be informed, educated by the journalist and the expert. . . . [But] today the most important parts of our culture are in the arts, in poetry, in political utopianism, in the humanities. . . . The [scientific] metaphor that has governed our understanding of journalism in this century has run into trouble. Neither journalism nor public life will move forward until we actually rethink, redescribe, and reinterpret what journalism is; not the science or information of our culture but its poetry and conversation."

I'm not sure I understand what he is saying. Not all of us can or necessarily ought to be minstrels, poets, troubadours or conversationalists. But it is obvious from the Veronis, Suhler data that he is right in one sense—newspapers, books and magazines are now marginal claimants on our time and attention, occasional voices in the noise of the crowd. The marketplace is saying that other "media" occupy the large spaces in our lives.

It is also obvious that the politicians [in 1992]—Bill Clinton and Al Gore, in particular—understand that there may be more effective ways than an hour on "Meet the Press" to get into our heads and hearts. Clinton does a saxophone recital on the "Arsenio Hall Show." Gore evokes Elvis Presley in his acceptance speech. Murphy Brown is the year's new political icon. Major Dad is summoned to certify the legitimacy of the president of the United States. The Walter Lippmanns and James Restons of journalism once commanded audiences with the great men of public affairs, men (and women) who now pander to Katie Couric and CNN.

The Public Broadcasting Service, the most "scientific" and information-driven medium in the television wasteland, struggles against MTV and "Entertainment Tonight" to maintain a 2 percent share of the prime-time minutes. Its blood cousin, National Public Radio, attracts only 10,000 of the 2.5 million teenagers tuned in at any time to the radio spectrum. The audience erodes for the evening news as portrayed by the major networks. General Electric, owner of NBC, contemplates the sale of its money-losing news division to an independent syndicator. Newspapers remain profitable, but their audience share has declined steadily for three decades. The news magazines are reinventing themselves in fits and starts in an uncertain quest for greater relevance.

Our understanding of these changes is limited. The new media world was never planned; it came upon us largely through technological mutations and unforeseen opportunity. We don't know where it is headed, whether "journalism and public life will move forward" under its influence or will undergo greater trivialization.

The historical data from Veronis, Suhler contain a very faint suggestion that we are entering a withdrawal phase in our addiction to the media. We gave them 59 fewer hours of our time on Earth [in 1991] than in 1986. This may reflect more discriminating standards of consumption. On the other hand, it could be the cumulative result of these many years of sleep deprivation.

# 10

# Is TV Ruining Our Children?

## *by* Richard Zoglin

*Editor's Note:* Although a number of groups are pressing for laws to bring some control to children's television, over the past forty years the way children grow up has already been profoundly changed. Children are introduced to the real world—and taught their ABCs—earlier than ever. But they may be affected by an overdose of TV violence. Even sitcoms change childhood notions by showing that adults don't always know what they're doing.

Richard Zoglin covers media issues for *Time*. He was aided in this article, which appeared in *Time* on October 15, 1990, by the reporting of William Tynan.

Behold every parent's worst nightmare: the six-year-old TV addict. He watches in the morning before he goes off to school, plops himself in front of the set as soon as he gets home in the afternoon and gets another dose to calm down before he goes to bed at night. He wears Bart Simpson T shirts, nags Mom to buy him Teenage Mutant Ninja Turtles toys and spends hours glued to his Nintendo. His teachers says he is restless and combative in class. What's more, he's having trouble reading.

Does this creature really exist, or is he just a paranoid video-age vision? The question is gaining urgency as the medium barges ever more aggressively into children's lives. Except for school and the family, no institution plays a bigger role in shaping American children. And no institution takes more heat. TV has been blamed for just about everything from a decrease in attention span to an increase in street crime. Cartoons are attacked for their violence and sitcoms for their foul language. Critics ranging from religious conservatives to consumer groups like Action for Children's Television have kept up a steady drumbeat of calls for reform.

[In 1990] Congress took a small step toward obliging. Legislators sent to President Bush a bill that would set limits on commercial time in children's programming (a still generous 10 $\frac{1}{2}$ minutes per hour on weekends and 12 minutes on weekdays). The bill would also require stations to air at least some educational kids' fare as a condition for getting their licenses renewed. Bush has argued that the bill infringes on broadcasters' First Amendment rights, but

**65**

...in, who vetoed a similar measure [1988]) he is expected
...

...s at reform, as well as critics' persistent gripes about
...en's TV, skirt the central issue. Even if the commer-
...were reined in, even if local stations were persuaded to air
...y children's fare, even if kids could be shielded from the most ob-
...able material, the fact remains that children watch a ton of TV. Almost
...aily, parents must grapple with a fundamental, overriding question: What is
all that TV viewing doing to kids, and what can be done about it?

Television has, of course, been an inseparable companion for most American youngsters since the early 1950s. But the baby boomers, who grew up with Howdy Doody and Huckleberry Hound, experienced nothing like the barrage of video images that pepper kids today. Cable has vastly expanded the supply of programming. The VCR has turned favorite shows and movies into an endlessly repeatable pastime. Video games have added to the home box's allure.

The average child will have watched 5,000 hours of TV by the time he enters first grade and 19,000 hours by the end of high school—more time than he will spend in class. This dismayingly passive experience crowds out other, more active endeavors: playing outdoors, being with friends, reading. Marie Winn, author of the 1977 book *The Plug-In Drug*, gave a memorable, if rather alarmist, description of the trancelike state TV induces: "The child's facial expression is transformed. The jaw is relaxed and hangs open slightly; the tongue rests on the front teeth (if there are any). The eyes have a glazed, vacuous look. . . ."

Guided by TV, today's kids are exposed to more information about the world around them than any other generation in history. But are they smarter for it? Many teachers and psychologists argue that TV is largely to blame for the decline in reading skills and school performance. In his studies of children at Yale, psychologist Jerome Singer found that kids who are heavy TV watchers tend to be less well informed, more restless and poorer students. The frenetic pace of TV, moreover, has seeped into the classroom. "A teacher who is going into a lengthy explanation of an arithmetic problem will begin to lose the audience after a while," says Singer. "Children are expecting some kind of show." Even the much beloved *Sesame Street* has been criticized for reinforcing the TV-inspired notion that education must be fast paced and entertaining. Says Neil Postman, communications professor at New York University and author of *Amusing Ourselves to Death:* "*Sesame Street* makes kids like school only if school is like *Sesame Street*."

Televised violence may also be having an effect on youngsters. Singer's research has shown that prolonged viewing by children of violent programs is associated with more aggressive behavior, such as getting into fights and disrupting the play of others. (A link between TV and violent crime, however, has not been clearly established.) Other studies suggest that TV viewing can dampen kids' imagination. Patricia Marks Greenfield, a professor of psychology at UCLA, conducted experiments in which several groups of children were asked to tell a story about the Smurfs. Those who were shown a Smurfs TV cartoon beforehand were less "creative" in their storytelling than kids who first played an unrelated connect-the-dots game.

But the evidence is flimsy for many popular complaints about TV. In a 1988 report co-authored for the U.S. Department of Education, Daniel Anderson, professor of psychology at the University of Massachusetts in Amherst, found no convincing evidence that TV has a "mesmerizing effect" on children, overstimulates them or reduces their attention span. In fact, the report asserted, TV may actually increase attention-focusing capabilities.

Nor, contrary to many parents' fears, have the new video technologies made matters worse. Small children who repeatedly watch their favorite cassettes are, psychologists point out, behaving no differently from toddlers who want their favorite story read to them over and over. (The VCR may actually give parents *more* control over their kids' viewing.) Video games may distress adults with their addictive potential, but researchers have found no exceptional harm in them—and even some possible benefits, like improving hand-eye coordination.

Yet TV may be effecting a more profound, if less widely recognized, change in the whole concept of growing up. Before the advent of television, when print was the predominant form of mass communication, parents and teachers were able to control just what and when children learned about the world outside. With TV, kids are plunged into that world almost instantly.

In his 1985 book, *No Sense of Place,* Joshua Meyrowitz, professor of communication at the University of New Hampshire, points out that TV reveals to children the "backstage" activity of adults. Even a seemingly innocuous program like *Father Knows Best* showed that parents aren't all-knowing authority figures: they agonize over problems in private and sometimes even conspire to fool children. "Television exposes kids to behavior that adults spent centuries trying to hide from children," says Meyrowitz. "The average child watching television sees adults hitting each other, killing each other, breaking down and crying. It teaches kids that adults don't always know what they're doing." N.Y.U.'s Postman believes TV, by revealing the "secrets" of adulthood, has virtually destroyed the notion of childhood as a discrete period of innocence. "What I see happening is a blurring of childhood and adulthood," he says. "We have more adultlike children and more childlike adults."

What all this implies is that TV's impact is pervasive and to a large extent inevitable. That impact cannot be wished away; all that can be done is to try to understand and control it. Reforms of the sort Congress has enacted are a salutary step. Networks and stations too—though they are in the business of entertainment, not education—must be vigilant about the contents and commercialization of kids' shows.

The ultimate responsibility still rests with parents. The goal should not be—cannot be—to screen out every bad word or karate chop from kids' viewing, but rather to make sure TV doesn't crowd out all the other activities that are part of growing up. These counterbalancing influences—family, friends, school, books—can put TV, if not out of the picture, at least in the proper focus.

# 11

# Crack and the Box

## *by* Pete Hamill

*Editor's Note:* Americans have the money to buy drugs, says the author of this article, and the supply is plentiful. But almost nobody in power asks why people spend good money on them.

Pete Hamill here suggests that the drug plague coincides with the un-spoken assumption of most TV shows: that life should be easy. Such a view encourages people to pop a pill, smoke some dope, inhale some powder, or inject some liquid for an easy way out of the problems of life. He suggests that watching television itself can be addictive and, thus, en-courages addictive behavior of all sorts.

Hamill is a columnist for *New York Newsday*. The original version of this article first appeared in *Esquire* magazine in May 1990.

One sad rainy morning [in 1990], I talked to a woman who was addicted to crack cocaine. She was 22, stiletto-thin, with eyes as old as tombs. She was living in two rooms in a welfare hotel with her children who were two, three and five years of age. Her story was the usual tangle of human woe: early pregnancy, dropping out of school, vanished men, smack and then crack, tricks with johns in parked cars to pay for the dope. I asked her why she did drugs. She shrugged in an empty way and couldn't really answer beyond "makes me feel good." While we talked and she told her tale of squalor, the children ignored us. They were watching TV.

Walking back to my office in the rain, I brooded about the woman, her zombielike children, and my own callous indifference. I'd heard so many ver-sions of the same story that I almost never wrote them anymore: The sons of similar women, glimpsed a dozen years ago, are now in Dannemora or Soledad or Joliet; in a hundred cities, their daughters are moving into the same loveless rooms. As I walked, a series of homeless men approached me for change, most of them junkies. Others sat in doorways, staring at nothing. They were addi-tional casualties of our time of plague, demoralized reminders that although this country holds only two percent of the world's population, it consumes 65 percent of the world's supply of hard drugs.

*Why*, for God's sake? Why do so many millions of Americans of all ages, races and classes choose to spend all or part of their lives stupefied? I've talked to hundreds of addicts over the years; some were my friends. But none could give sensible answers. They stutter about the pain of the world, about despair or boredom, the urgent need for magic or pleasure in a society empty of both. But then they just shrug. Americans have the money to buy drugs; the supply is plentiful. But almost nobody in power asks, *Why?* Least of all, George Bush and his drug warriors.

William Bennett talks vaguely about the heritage of '60s permissiveness, the collapse of Traditional Values and all that. But he and Bush offer the traditional American excuse: It Is Somebody Else's Fault. This posture set the stage for the self-righteous invasion of Panama, the bloodiest drug arrest in world history. Bush even accused Manuel Noriega of "poisoning our children." But he never asked why so many Americans demand the poison.

And then, on that rainy morning in New York, I saw another one of those ragged men staring out at the rain from a doorway. I suddenly remembered the inert postures of the children in that welfare hotel, and I thought: *television.*

Ah, no, I muttered to myself: too simple. Something as complicated as drug addiction can't be blamed on television. Come on. . . . But I remembered all those desperate places I'd visited as a reporter, where there were no books and a TV set was always playing and the older kids had gone off somewhere to shoot smack, except for the kid who was at the mortuary in a coffin. I also remembered when I was a boy in the '40s and early '50s, and drugs were a minor sideshow, a kind of dark little rumor. And there was one major difference between that time and this: *television.*

We had unemployment then; illiteracy, poor living conditions, racism, governmental stupidity, a gap between rich and poor. We didn't have the all-consuming presence of television in our lives. Now two generations of Americans have grown up with television from their earliest moments of consciousness. Those same American generations are afflicted by the pox of drug addiction.

Only 35 years ago, drug addiction was not a major problem in this country. We had some drug addicts at the end of the 19th Century, hooked on the cocaine in patent medicines. During the placid '50s, Commissioner Harry Anslinger pumped up the budget of the old Bureau of Narcotics with fantasies of reefer madness. Heroin was sold and used in most major American cities, while the bebop generation of jazz musicians got jammed up with horse.

## TV Generation

Until the early '60s, narcotics were still marginal to American life; they weren't the $120 billion market they make up today. If anything, those years have an eerie innocence. In 1955 there were 31.7 million TV sets in use in the country (the number is now past 184 million). But the majority of the audience had grown up without the dazzling new medium. They embraced it, were diverted by it, perhaps even loved it, but they weren't *formed* by it. That year, the New York police made a mere 1,234 felony drug arrests; in 1988 it was 43,901. They confiscated 97 *ounces* of cocaine for the entire year; [in 1990] it was hundreds of pounds. During each year of the '50s in New York, there were only about a hundred narcotics-related deaths. But by the end of the '60s, when the first generation of children *formed* by television had come to maturity (and thus to the marketplace), the number of such deaths had risen to 1,200. The same phenomenon was true in every major American city.

In the last Nielsen survey of American viewers, the average family was watching the television seven hours a day. This has never happened before in history. No people has ever been entertained for seven hours a *day.* The Elizabethans didn't go to the theater seven hours a day. The pre-TV generation did not go to the movies seven hours a day. Common sense tells us that this all-pervasive diet of instant imagery, sustained now for 40 years, must have changed us in profound ways.

Television, like drugs, dominates the lives of its addicts. And though some lonely Americans leave their sets on without watching them, using them as electronic companions, television usually absorbs its viewers the way drugs absorb their users. Viewers can't work or play while watching television; they can't read; they can't be out on the streets, falling in love with the wrong people, learning how to quarrel and compromise with other human beings. In short, they are asocial. So are drug addicts.

One Michigan State University study in the early '80s offered a group of four- and five-year-olds the choice of giving up television or giving up their fathers. Fully one-third said they would give up Daddy. Given a similar choice (between cocaine or heroin and father, mother, brother, sister, wife, husband, children, job), almost every stone junkie would do the same.

There are other disturbing similarities. Television itself is a consciousness-altering instrument. With the touch of a button, it takes you out of the "real" world in which you reside and can place you at a basketball game, the back alleys of Miami, the streets of Bucharest, or the cartoony living rooms of Sitcom Land. Each move from channel to channel alters mood, usually with music or a laugh track. On any given evening, you can laugh, be frightened, feel tension, thump with excitement. You can even tune in *MacNeil/Lehrer* and feel sober.

But none of these abrupt shifts in mood is *earned.* They are attained as easily as popping a pill. Getting news from television, for example, is simply not the same experience as reading it in a newspaper. Reading is *active.* The reader must decode little symbols called words, then create images or ideas and make them connect; at its most basic level, reading is an act of the imagination. But the television viewer is *passive* and doesn't go through that process. The words are spoken to him by Dan Rather or Tom Brokaw or Peter Jennings. There isn't much decoding to do when watching television, no time to think or ponder before the next set of images and spoken words appears to displace the present one. The reader, being active, works at his or her own pace; the viewer, being passive, proceeds at the pace determined by the show. Except at the highest levels, television never demands that its audience take part in an act of imagination. Reading always does.

In short, television works on the same imaginative and intellectual level as psychoactive drugs. If prolonged television viewing makes the young passive (dozens of studies indicate that it does), then moving to drugs has a certain coherence. Drugs provide an unearned high (in contrast to the earned rush that comes from a feat accomplished, a human breakthrough earned by sweat or thought or love).

And because the television addict and the drug addict are alienated from the hard and scary world, they also feel they make no difference in its complicated events.

The drug plague also coincides with the unspoken assumption of most television shows: Life should be *easy.* The most complicated events are summarized on TV news in a minute or less. Cops confront murder, chase the criminals and bring them to justice (usually violently) within an hour. In commercials, you drink the right beer and you get the girl. *Easy!* So why should real life be a grind? Why should any American have to spend years mastering a skill or craft, or work eight hours a day at an unpleasant job, or endure the compromises and crises of a marriage? Nobody *works* on TV (except cops, doctors and lawyers).

Love stories on television are about falling in love or breaking up; the long, steady growth of a marriage—its essential dailiness—is seldom explored, except as comedy. Life on television is almost always simple: good guys and bad, nice girls and whores, smart guys and dumb. And if life in the real world isn't that simple, well, hey, man, have some dope, man, be happy, feel good.

Most Americans under the age of 50 have now spent their lives absorbing television; that is, they've had the structures of drama pounded into them. Drama is always about conflict. So news shows, politics and advertising are now all shaped by those structures. Nobody will pay attention to anything as complicated as the part played by Third World debt in the expanding production of cocaine; it's easier to focus on Manuel Noriega, a character right out of *Miami Vice,* and believe that even in real life there's a Mister Big.

What is to be done? Television is certainly not going away, but its addictive qualities can be controlled. It's a lot easier to "just say no" to television than to heroin or crack. As a beginning, parents must take immediate control of the sets, teaching children to watch specific television *programs,* not "television," to get out of the house and play with other kids. Elementary and high schools must begin teaching television/media literacy as a subject, the way literature is taught, showing children how shows are made, how to distinguish between the true and the false, how to recognize cheap emotional manipulation. All Americans should spend more time reading. And thinking.

For years, the defenders of television have argued that the networks are only giving the people what they want. That might be true. But so is the Medellin cartel.

# 12

# Are There New Rules of History?

## *by* Jeffrey A. Frank

*Editor's Note:* The trial of four police officers for beating a black man, Rodney King, following a car chase in Los Angeles raises important issues not only about justice but also about our sense of history. The thirty seconds of tape that contained the beating was shown over and over again, during the trial and on world television, leaving the searing impression of certain guilt. But the jury, putting that thirty seconds into the larger context, decided that the police officers were not guilty.

Most of the world has seen only the reality of the thirty seconds on tape, so most of us would have voted for a guilty verdict. But what is reality, and more important in a sense, what is justice? Is guilt or innocence determined only by thirty seconds of videotape? Is it determined by the public based on TV viewing?

Even if the court still determines guilt or innocence, television today seems to determine history, says the author of this article. And that has forever changed reality, if not justice.

Jeffrey A. Frank is an editor of the "Outlook" section of the *Washington Post,* where this article appeared on May 3, 1992.

Ten years from now, when the case of Rodney King is remembered—and it will be—it is not the official verdict that will be recalled. Few will be able to say whether it was three, or five or more policemen who beat a Los Angeles man senseless, and fewer still will be able to remember their names.

What won't go away—what will make its way into textbooks and documentaries and, finally, into the scrapbook of the late 20th century—is the image. More specifically, it is the blurred, videotaped image of a man who was kicked, clubbed, shocked with a stun gun and otherwise roughed up by a group of uniformed members of the Los Angeles Police Department.

In that way, a kind of meta-verdict—a transcendent judgment—will have been reached by much of America and, very likely, by history. It is the sort of verdict that's been reached before: after the shootings by National Guardsmen on the Kent State campus; after the handgun execution of a Viet Cong suspect by police chief Nguyen Ngoc Loan; and in our political life, notably after what was judged to be a "police riot" at Chicago's 1968 Democratic convention. Such a verdict, in time, affects the way a nation regards its past—and, ultimately, how a nation regards itself.

In the case of Rodney King and the LAPD, the enduring images are interlocking. Beyond the ghostly video footage of King being clubbed and kicked are pictures of Darryl Gates, the LAPD chief who, to the relief of many, is about to step down; the accused policemen themselves, in civilian clothing, looking very much like the folks who just moved into the house four doors down in a mostly white neighborhood; and, as the week ended, the urban warfare on the streets of Los Angeles, highlighted (provoked? exaggerated?) by still more video cameras.

Much, perhaps all, of this is intimately related to the presence of television in American life. And though it is almost too obvious to note in an age when the tube is so intrusive, in fact television has by now changed not only the rules of history but the nature of historical fact.

"There are events," former NBC News chief Reuven Frank has observed, "which exist in the American mind and recollection primarily" because of television. And Bill McKibben, in his new book, "The Age of Missing Information," points out that history itself "is weirdly foreshortened—for instance, all anniversaries from the TV period are marked with great care and attention, at least if whatever happened was captured on film." Thus, the shootings at Kent State were commemorated in rich detail as the 20th anniversary of the event drew near.

But this is also an era that is fond of the arguments of deconstructionism—breaking texts and images into their component pieces looking for meanings. It is a process that may eventually persuade those who listen too attentively to confuse cause and effect: What you see is not necessarily what happened, you are told; and when what you see is broken down into enough pieces, you may come to think that you are suddenly seeing something else.

For someone like George Orwell, this would be no less than an assault on objective reality. And those who'd watched the video of the King beating and then heard the verdict no doubt felt they'd witnessed just such an assault.

On videotape, and subsequently on millions of TV screens, a fellow human was treated like a punching bag. The human may not have been altogether admirable, but he writhed on the ground and his bones were broken. In the outer world, though, 12 Ventura County jurors watched the video numerous times, in slow motion and freeze-frame, and eventually decided not that someone had been badly beaten but that there was not enough evidence to convict four policemen of using excessive force.

In the late 20th century, such a verdict is often not the one that lasts. Sgt. Koon, along with officers Powell, Briseno and Wind may go back to their pre-King lives (though it is difficult to imagine that their lives can be the same), but beyond their circle, the meta-verdict of guilt has been registered. That verdict, along with images of what actually happened to Rodney King in March 1991, has already mutated into *fictional* video, in a recent episode of "L.A. Law" that involved police brutality.

Much the same thing has happened with other meta-verdicts in the 45 years or so since television has been upon us. Often, the blue images put forth by cathode-ray tubes leave a surprising after-image. Often, this happens in cases altogether unlike the case of Rodney King.

When Police Commissioner Theophilus Eugene "Bull" Connor deployed fire hoses against civil rights protesters, the citizens of Birmingham, Ala., were never asked to render a formal judgment. They may have been embarrassed by Connor's tactics (as members of the LAPD were clearly embarrassed by the behavior of the four men on trial), but Connor kept his job and his place in the community (although he was defeated in a mayoral contest). It was loops of film, played repeatedly on America's TV sets, that gave Connor his unenviable place in history. It was Martin Luther King's eloquent 6,500-word "Letter From Birmingham Jail" that summed up the meta-verdict.

After the Anita Hill-Clarence Thomas confrontation, polling data indicated that America was inclined to believe that Thomas was telling the truth when he denied having sexually harassed Hill. But the passage of time suggests that a more transcendent judgment has been recorded. Signs of that have been measured by what voters did in statewide primaries in Pennsylvania (where an Anita Hill defender won) and Illinois (where a Thomas defender was unseated) and in heightened sensitivity to the harassment issue. Contradictory verdicts, official and public, seemed to follow the rape trial of William Kennedy Smith; even many of those who would have voted to acquit will forever see him pursued by the woman behind the blue dot.

Reuven Frank has observed that the "highest power of television journalism is not in the transmission of information but in the transmission of experience." In the case of Rodney King, it was an unnervingly silent videotape that conveyed (and continues to convey) the experience.

Again and again, the objective reality: batons in the air, the blurred figure on the ground, the 4-1 ratio of police to civilian. The beating of Rodney King, repeated thousands of times, came to exist in the American mind just as certainly as the explosion of the Challenger. And it was the dissolution of the link between image and reality—the incomprehensible distance between reality's image and a jury's judgment—that brought forth so much pure rage.

"Today, the globe has shrunk in the wash with speeded-up information movement from all directions," Marshall McLuhan has said, and in the speed-up, an increasing number of verdicts on events have been rendered, even as the details vanish: An American senator will forever have been weeping in the New Hampshire snow in 1972. A kneeling young woman, hysterical, will forever be weeping over the dead at Kent State. The Saigon police chief will forever be blowing out a man's brains. And now there is this L.A. beating, something never seen before in quite this way, in such—literally—blow-by-blow detail.

For the latter part of [that] week, America was besieged by still more images: Somber newscasters who kept repeating the phrase, "the acquittal of four white policemen." The relieved smile on the face of Officer Laurence M. Powell, who had been singled out for committing the worst violence against King. The fire and smoke and rage seen on the streets of America's second largest city. Political leaders, black and white, condemning the verdict and condemning the violence. And all this carried with it another reminder (of which no more are needed) that the distance between the world of Rodney King and mainstream American society is great, and seemingly unbreachable.

But on a more enduring level, something else happened: the larger verdict simultaneously became part of the American mind and the American past. In the television age, the brutalizing of Rodney King became American history, revved up into the present: fast-forward and reverse and freeze-frame—the image that attaches itself to society, gets under its skin, and changes it forever. What we see, in history's new blur, is what we were.

# IV

# Freedom and Responsibility

In the United States, mass media probably have more freedom than in any other country in the world. Even countries similar to the United States in legal systems and political philosophies—such as Canada, the United Kingdom, New Zealand, and Australia—have all adopted, since World War II, public policies that are more restrictive of press and mass media than anything in America.

Britain and Australia, for example, have an Official Secrets Act, which allows the government to withhold information it deems threatening to its security, and the government can prosecute the press if the press publishes or broadcasts such information. In the United States, we have a Freedom of Information Act, which carefully limits what the government can withhold and forces the government to divulge any other information that citizens and the press might want. But the main difference is this: If mass media publish or broadcast information that the U.S. government has legally withheld, they cannot be prosecuted for doing so. In general, in the United States, the burden of responsibility to protect government secrets rests with the government, not with the press.

In our most kindred countries—Britain, Canada, Australia, and New Zealand—broadcasting is much more restricted than it is in the United States. These countries all have large national broadcast systems that are quasi-governmental institutions, funded largely by taxpayers. Even though they might pride themselves on their independence, these institutions—the BBC in Britain, CBC in Canada, ABC in Australia—often bend to the direct orders of their governments.

The U.S. government owns no public broadcasting except the Voice of America (VOA), our external broadcast service allowing America to inform the world about our policies and our version of the news. Since there is little chance of making a profit from this kind of venture, it must be supported by the government or it wouldn't exist. Congress, which provides the subsidy for the VOA, also insists that it broadcast only on shortwave aimed abroad, not at American audiences, because we don't want government interference in the information process.

The government does provide some financial support for public broadcasting, again largely because there hasn't been enough profit in educational programming in the past. PBS and NPR, the television and radio services of public broadcasting, are trying to raise their own funds from sponsors, viewers, and listeners in order to reduce their dependence on the government.

All other broadcasting in America is strictly private business. Radio and television have to operate within guidelines set by the Federal Communications Commission, but the print media have virtually total freedom from government interference. Nonetheless, U.S. broadcasters with a license to broadcast can do almost anything they want to do to make a profit.

Many people, perhaps a growing number, feel that American mass media are too free, that some limits ought to be imposed on some of their actions. Even a majority of journalism students, in a poll recently taken at the University of Maryland, indicated that the press had too much freedom, which many antimedia groups seek to limit. Many others want to force mass media, through legal means, to be more responsible.

At the same time, from another direction, there are those who would set limits on the freedom of speech if what is said belittles a particular group, especially if that groups is a minority in society and has been traditionally denigrated. We have come to be concerned about the "political correctness" of our speech.

Does the near absolute legal freedom of speech and of the press in the United States give individuals or the press the freedom to be irresponsible? And what is irresponsibility? Most of us would agree that it is irresponsible to falsely yell "Fire!" in a crowded theater. Is it irresponsible to use derogatory language when referring to minority groups, women, or anyone? Where should the line be drawn on freedom?

Clearly, if mass media operate in an irresponsible manner in the opinion of the majority, that majority can insist on laws that would place limits on their actions. Even the Constitution, and its First Amendment guaranteeing freedom of speech and of the press, can be changed by a two-thirds majority of all the states. It has already been amended twenty-six times.

For the journalist, the demand for press responsibility has often been perceived as a way of controlling the press. Who determines what is responsible and what is irresponsible? The journalist would like to have that determination made by readers, listeners, and viewers, through their choices of media in an open marketplace, rather than by the government. Yes, the journalist would say, without controls there may be some irresponsibility in the media, but an irresponsible press is much less to be feared than an irresponsible government. Only an absolutely free press, even if it is occasionally irresponsible, can guarantee freedom from an irresponsible or corrupt or despotic government.

# 13

# Reflections on the First Amendment

## *by* George E. Reedy

*Editor's Note:* "If the press didn't tell us, who would? A simple question; and its answer is as old as the nation: No one." This statement, by Robert H. Wills, president in 1990 of the Society of Professional Journalists, Sigma Delta Chi, reflects the sentiments of most American journalists.

Protection for such sentiments comes from the First Amendment to the Constitution, which says, in part, "Congress shall make no law abridging freedom of speech or freedom of the press." Yet the absolute freedom that the First Amendment guarantees has come under increasing attack.

In this article, George E. Reedy defends the First Amendment. He was President Lyndon Johnson's press secretary in 1964–1965, but he started his professional career as a journalist, and he is now the Nieman professor emeritus at Marquette University. This article was first published in *The Quill* in March 1990.

What is badly needed in the United States today is a simple statement chiseled in stone over the entrance to every public building and every educational institution and inscribed on indestructible billboards along every major highway. It should read:

> Freedom of speech is freedom of the press and freedom of the press is freedom of speech; if either is cut, both will bleed and personal freedom will die.

It is more than passing strange that Americans need such a reminder. We have lived as free men and women with that principle for nearly two centuries while personal freedom in every nation that has controlled the press has gone down the drain.

Perhaps freedom has in some sense been too successful in the United States, because most of us have come to take it for granted.

There are even those today who believe that a free press is a luxury that we can discard temporarily when it appears to conflict with our needs in time of crisis. This philosophy cropped up nearly 16 years ago in the chief minority opinion on the Pentagon Papers case and, while it did not control the final decision of the Supreme Court, only three justices rejected it in its entirety.

Those Founding Fathers, led by James Madison, who forced adoption of the First Amendment, had no illusions regarding "temporary" press restraints. They knew that even a short-term suspension of press freedom would always become permanent, and it would not be confined to the press alone. Freedom is a package in which the various elements gather strength from each other, and none of them can be surgically excised, like an inflamed appendix, without all collapsing.

The First Amendment, which everyone talks about but which few read, says: "Congress shall make no law respecting an establishment of religion, or prohibiting the free exercise thereof; or abridging the freedom of speech, or of the press; or the right of the people peaceably to assemble, and to petition the Government for a redress of grievances."

This is remarkably lucid language. It says in unmistakable terms that we Americans can believe what we want to believe, say what we want to say, publish our thoughts in an effort to convince others, and assemble those who agree with us to try to persuade our government to do what we think it should do.

Obviously, freedom to speak and publish also means freedom to inquire. Control the chain at any point and we become helpless subjects of arbitrary rule.

What is equally important in modern times is that the First Amendment does not confer a special privilege on the press. The privilege is *freedom to publish,* on paper or by electronic means, and it is a privilege that belongs to every American—whether he or she writes books, newsletters or ordinary letters.

The press is an institution that publishes daily and therefore resorts to the First Amendment more often than do other institutions and individuals. But the freedom to publish is still a privilege that belongs to all of us, without which freedom of speech would be meaningless.

In a mass society, it does little good for me to whisper my political views to close friends. If I hope to accomplish anything, I must find a way of publishing my opinions so they can be read or heard by others.

I have never been able to decide in my own mind whether a free society produces a free press or a free press produces a free society. I suspect that the two go together, along with protections against arbitrary administration of the laws.

History, however, is very revealing on the relationship. Every dictatorship that has come to power in our memory has begun by seizing the press as the first step toward abolishing personal liberty. Men and women who cannot publish cannot fight back. Furthermore, without a press free to dig out facts without governmental supervision, we have no means of calling governmental officials to account. We cannot change—nor can we protest against—that which we do not know.

The right to learn, to investigate, to express opinions, to demand account-ability—these rights were vital at the time the First Amendment was written. They are even more crucial now in an era of big government in which unsavory or merely incompetent deeds can be concealed in the labyrinthian corridors of buildings that house tens of thousands of federal workers, and in which telling facts and plans and statistics can be tucked away in impenetrable footnotes to trillion-dollar budgets.

Without a full-time corps of journalists intensively analyzing the workings of the governmental machine, we are helpless against a bureaucracy that, however well intentioned it may be, is certainly not going to inform us of its shortcomings.

People in power do not like to be disturbed, and freedom of speech and press is always disturbing.

In modern times, the most popular rationale for restraining the press in-volves "national security." I am placing the phrase in quotes deliberately be-cause it is usually voiced in the same tones of reverence as those employed when reciting the Lord's Prayer. National security is a phrase intended to put an end to thought rather than to stimulate discussion.

Most of us are somewhat uncertain as to the exact meaning of the phrase, national security, but we all know that it somehow involves our survival as a peo-ple. In a world of atomic bombs, space stations, and potential laser-beam weapons, we are very quick to buy any proposals to guarantee our future. It seems to make a lot of sense for us to take steps that withhold from possible en-emies information as to how we can fight back if attacked.

No one can seriously argue that there is no information whose publication should be withheld temporarily at certain times. But that is not really a prob-lem. In this century, our nation has fought four major wars with no compulsory press censorship. When those wars are reviewed, it is apparent that in no in-stance did we suffer any setback because national security secrets were re-vealed by the press.

American journalists are as patriotic as anyone else and do not want to see their country defeated. In the name of national security, they have in the past entered into voluntary agreement to defer publication, and the voluntary agree-ments have worked.

Nevertheless, journalists who value their craft and trust the American peo-ple do not knowingly lie to protect someone's conception of the national inter-est. There have been charges that news correspondents painted an overly gloomy picture of what happened in Vietnam and thus sapped our morale. But that smacks of an alibi invented for covering up the pursuit of a disastrous na-tional policy. If we are to censor the press for being "downbeat," we might as well give up freedom altogether.

There is another side to the national security issue, however. It is that even in instances where deferring information can be justified, we pay a heavy price for it. First, if something should go wrong, the American people will not be prepared for it and can easily panic. At the first publicly known setback in a previously secret national policy, the morale of the people will suffer and confidence in the government will begin to shrink.

Second, if some things are censored that should be censored, the people then would have no means of knowing whether other things that should *not* have been censored have been censored.

Third and most important, is that secrecy limits the number of minds that can be brought to bear on a subject. It prevents genuine, adversarial discussion, which is the only process that gives us conclusions in which we can have confidence.

There is ample, historical precedent to establish the importance of all three of these points. One of the great strengths of the Allies in World War II was the absolute insistence of the British Broadcasting Corporation that it be the first to announce every defeat. As a result, the British were able to take setbacks calmly. And when the BBC announced victories, those reports were believed all over the world—and the inhabitants of the Axis countries were disheartened no matter what their own governments said.

When we finally entered Japan at the end of the war, we discovered that the Japanese had realized that their government was feeding them censored news and consequently the rumor mills were working overtime. The people knew they were on the losing end when their government told them they were winning.

To my mind, the most direct argument against censorship, official or self-imposed, can be derived from the tragic series of events of 1961 labeled "the Bay of Pigs." The plan to invade Cuba was absolutely harebrained and any genuine adversarial discussion would have blown it out of the water. But it was kept secret within a small circle, and it is amazing what follies can be contrived by the minds of even the most brilliant men and women when they are thinking in isolation. The failure of the invasion held us up to scorn and ridicule, and to this day our standing in Latin America suffers.

One important American newspaper got hold of the story in advance but soft-pedaled it at the request of the State Department. Had the account been placed on page one, the invasion would have been called off and today we would be a stronger nation.

Secrecy in any form damages a nation. I have travelled extensively in Latin America and Asia. Everywhere, on both continents, I have encountered a disturbing attitude. It is that every American—journalist, businessman or even tourist—is thought to be a probable CIA agent who is to be trusted only after thorough investigation.

I cannot but wonder whether the CIA can ever have accomplished anything in those areas that makes up for what we have lost in standing. I was in Chile before the election that made Salvador Allende president, and it was apparent from ordinary conversations in Santiago that his only real strength with the people was the widespread belief that United States agents were trying to keep him from the presidency.

There is, unfortunately, an all too widespread belief that our security rests upon our ability to spring unexpected surprises upon other nations that may become hostile. This is a belief that can be held only by ignoring the real world in which we live. It fails to account for a key development of the modern age: that science and technology have abolished secrecy or any possibility of attaining it.

In modern times, it is possible to withhold information from ordinary citizens who do not have the necessary background to understand what they are looking at. But we are wasting our time if we think we can withhold such information from governments.

The modern reality encompasses teams of scientists in the Soviet Union, in Great Britain, in France, in mainland China, in the United States—men and women who have all read the same books and, in many instances, studied under the same professors. These scientists and technicians and analysts read the same publications and talk to each other at international congresses. They have access to satellites that constantly report to them construction projects of any size in other countries.

Furthermore, when we speak of the weapons of today, we are talking about objects of massive size that are being manufactured in enormous plants employing tens of thousands of people. There is nowhere a basement where a scientist with long hair is peering through a cracked microscope to come up with a death ray. The marvels of the last quarter of the 20th Century are the results of team effort—team efforts on such a massive scale that the process and the results cannot be hidden.

Our real security lies in intelligent and open use of our resources, including the men and women who adapt and direct the new technologies, and who are willing to work because they feel themselves to be a vital part of our society.

There is only one way such people can function effectively, and that is through the fullest and freest discussion. In the modern world, that means the public must be fully informed as to what its government is doing. Dictatorships can stay in power as long as they are successful. But they crumple at the first setback. Free people have the resiliency that enables them to recover from defeat.

It would be idle not to recognize the current reality. There are many people who say they have lost their confidence in a free press. Some think that the press spends too much time "taking out after people" and treating them with arrogance if not with insolence. Others believe that the press is too gloomy and is printing too much "bad news"—with the implication that "good things" would happen if "good news" were printed.

It is not difficult to sympathize with those points of view. The only trouble is that bad news is created by bad or misguided people. It is not printed because the press wants to "get" somebody but because we cannot make a better world unless we know what is wrong.

While the press is a "watchdog," in that it alerts the rest of us to what is happening in the world, when it comes to doing something about a matter, I am my own watchdog, as is every other American. It is not the press that takes after political leaders, but the people themselves when they find that the leaders have done something wrong. No newspaper or news magazine or network has ever brought down a president or caused a governor to be tossed out of office.

There is little doubt that we live in a world where most of the news is bad. We face crushing debts; irresponsible dictators who somehow must be kept in check; famine conditions in many parts of the world; and the ever present shadow of nuclear war. It is little wonder that a free press is required to bring us bad news under such circumstances.

If the press does *not* bring us bad news, the bad events will not go away. All that will happen is that we, the American people, will lose our ability to act and react intelligently. Much as we would like to do so, we cannot dig a hole and hide.

The First Amendment to the Constitution speaks with elegant simplicity. It belongs to me, to you, to every American. It does not establish a kind of subsidy for an industry nor is it a device for an evasion of responsibility.

There are some people, of course, who will use the First Amendment responsibly and others who will use it irresponsibly. But if we start giving pieces of it away, it will all perish—what we like and what we don't like.

Freedom of the press means freedom to obtain and to publish the knowledge without which we cannot manage our own affairs. We have done very well as a free people. Let's keep it up.

# 14

# Siege of the First Amendment

## *by* Nicols Fox

---

*Editor's Note:* There are many attacks on the freedom of mass media these days. The executive branch of government itself makes 6.8 million documents secret annually, and the number is rising each year. Some members of Congress have suggested amending the Bill of Rights to limit freedom of speech and of the press. At the same time, according to the author of this article, "anti-smut activists, liberal academics, and aggressive libel plaintiffs" all want to curb speech and mass media.

Nicols Fox, an associate editor of the *Washington Journalism Review*, frequently writes about government and the arts. This article was published originally in the *Washington Journalism Review* (now the *American Journalism Review*), December 1990.

Which is worse: to burn the flag or tell a racist joke? It would depend, it seems, on your political perspective. But in a rare confluence of thinking, those who want to prevent either one from taking place aren't worrying very much about First Amendment rights. The stakes are too high, they say. Racism tears at the fabric of society; flag burning tarnishes our most visible national symbol. Some things are more important than free speech.

Both liberals and conservatives, with what they feel are the best of intentions, are increasingly attempting to control various forms of expression. Sometimes the challenges are direct; sometimes they are subtle and insidious, but some basic principles and important institutions are under attack. Newspapers and networks, entertainers and artists, college students and outspoken citizens—someone has been trying to tell them all what they can and can't say.

Speech has always had its limitations, and traditionally they have been set by the courts. Essentially, the limits pertain to national security or the defamation of another's character. On an ongoing basis the Supreme Court fine-tunes the First Amendment. Changes occur incrementally and at a glacial pace. Trends are not always easy to spot.

But, increasingly, the most obvious assaults on free speech and expression are coming not so much from the Supreme Court as from lower courts, local officials, corporations, government agencies and citizen groups. If the government and corporations want to limit speech for self-serving reasons—to stay in power or to control their employees—other groups, with a growing intolerance for the offensive, are being tempted to try and ban what they don't like.

Art has traditionally been a bellwether of cultural change. Like some law of social physics, every challenge to conventional morality from the art world has almost invariably prompted an "equal and opposite reaction" from some element of the community. As art became more provocative, a collision was perhaps inevitable. High-visibility arrests on obscenity charges of the rock group 2 Live Crew for explicit lyrics, and of Dennis Barrie, the director of Cincinnati's Contemporary Art Center, for displaying the sexually explicit and homoerotic photographs of Robert Mapplethorpe have revealed an American mind set, a remnant of our Puritanical beginnings. As if the country's flirtation with permissiveness during the 60s and 70s got out of hand, the folks who argued for "Whatever turns you on" are being asked to turn it off.

Both 2 Live Crew and Dennis Barrie were found not guilty in jury trials, and for a moment the worst fears of those concerned about the First Amendment seemed overwrought and unwarranted. But the shopkeeper who sold the records of 2 Live Crew was found guilty of selling pornography, and attempts to censor culture in the past several years have increased. One editor of a national art publication said the incidents reminded her of the birds in Alfred Hitchcock's avian chiller, quietly but persistently accumulating.

In Arlington, Virginia, "about an inch" was trimmed from the exposed penis of a sculpture in a public park; in Richmond a gallery had to cover a window display containing male nudes with brown paper when protests were lodged; in Maryland an exhibition of contemporary art was termed "satanic" and challenged. Stores selling copies of *Life* magazine featuring the history of the bra were boycotted in one New England town; in the Northwest parents tried to remove the issue from a school library.

But the definition of "offensive" extends beyond the sexual and the irreligious to the political. In Chicago protesters gathered when a piece of art invited people to step on the flag; later a work of art depicting the late Mayor Harold Washington in lingerie was forcibly removed from a gallery by two irate aldermen; in Washington, D.C., a cartoon of George Bush was removed from an exhibition of prints at the International Monetary Fund, and an outdoor work of art by a black artist depicting Jesse Jackson in whiteface saying "How ya like me now?" was torn down by angry black men who failed to appreciate its irony.

Isolate the outright attempts to censor and they look like random blips on a radar screen, the anomalies of a kind of post-modern cultural confusion. But Judith F. Krug, executive director of the Office for Intellectual Freedom of the American Library Association, says, "These public incidents set the arena in which it is more acceptable to challenge the specific kinds of materials that may be available." A 1988 report said that challenges to library books and school materials increased by 168 percent in the previous five years. Krug suspects that many more go unnoticed.

A recent survey by the new Thomas Jefferson Center for the Protection of Free Expression in Charlottesville, Virginia, indicated a general confusion over the First Amendment and what it covers. Almost half of those polled said that government has the right to prevent newspapers from publishing nude photographs, and nearly 30 percent said that freedom of expression did not extend to newspapers. Forty percent said that they didn't believe the First Amendment protected the arts and entertainment or that protecting such expression wasn't as important as protecting the spoken word.

People for the American Way, which each year publishes a survey of "Attacks on the Freedom to Learn," reported that attempts to censor school libraries or educational material occurred in 42 states and doubled in the Northeast between 1988 and 1989. Works that parents challenged ranged from "Lysistrata," the comedy by Aristophanes, to Maya Angelou's *I Know Why The Caged Bird Sings.* But parents regularly attempt to remove books that variously: teach reproduction or evolution, feature the occult or fail to support a strong military by promoting the concept of pacifism.

Fear of the offensive has bred some unlikely coalitions. Liberal feminist groups have joined the Reverend Donald Wildmon and his conservative American Family Association in attacking pornography. And ironies abound. Artist groups that would argue against any restrictions for grants given out by the National Endowment for the Arts have nevertheless protested art seen as promoting racial stereotypes. The work of a Japanese commercial artist which depicted a blackface minstrel in top hat and bow tie happily sipping away at his advertised soda was vandalized when it hung at the Parsons School of Design in New York City. Later, students held a protest in the gallery chanting, "Hey, hey, ho, ho, racist art has got to go."

And Actors Equity, in a highly publicized case, recently refused to allow the Caucasian Jonathan Pryce, who had played the part of a Eurasian in the London production of "Miss Saigon," to play the part here, saying that the character should be played by an Asian. A howl of protest and ridicule from nearly everyone eventually convinced the union to back down.

What does the dyslexic, agnostic, insomniac do at night?

He sits up wondering if there is a dog.

What's wrong with this joke? Technically, at least, it violates the speech codes of several universities. Some of the strongest challenges to the First Amendment are coming from these, the very bastions of free thought. They were inspired by the high dropout rates for minority students, considered to have been brought on by a hostile learning environment. But already speech codes have been made campus law by a dozen institutions. Nat Hentoff, a syndicated columnist for the *Village Voice* who frequently writes about First Amendment issues, finds this trend "the most dismaying dimension of First Amendment activity since the McCarthy era."

At the University of Michigan, he wrote, a student read aloud a limerick that made fun of the alleged homosexual acts of a nationally known sports figure. Under the university's Policy on Discrimination and Discriminatory Harassment by Students in the University Environment, this recitation was cited as "intimidating behavior" by another student. Although the offending student apologized at once, his thoughts on homosexuality were considered to need correction. His written apology was printed in *The Michigan Daily,* and he was "sentenced" to attend a gay rap session for educational purposes.

"The speech police are now on campus," says Hentoff. Between September 1988 and April 1989 under a university policy that prohibits "any behavior, verbal or physical, that stigmatizes or victimizes an individual on the basis of race, ethnicity, religion, national origin, sex, sexual orientation, creed, ancestry, age, marital status, handicap or Vietnam-era veteran status," more than 146 complaints were processed by officials.

One person's free speech is another's insult, and the argument over which is which has split the seemingly unsplittable. The California affiliate of the American Civil Liberties Union disagreed with the Michigan affiliate on whether speech codes at universities are needed to counter an apparent increase in racial unrest on American campuses. Not long ago, in a suit brought by the Michigan ACLU, Michigan's policy was declared unconstitutional by U.S. District Judge Avern Cohn. But the California affiliate supports Stanford's policy, which places sanctions on speech similar to those under the Michigan code.

The code is so broad that Hentoff says "wise students will take a vow of silence."

The trend worries Mark Goodman, director of the Student Press Law Center in Washington, who has found that some anti-harassment codes "pose a direct threat to student publications." Ironically, Goodman notes, the codes are well-intentioned. "The problem of racism is very serious," he says, "but the response is so wrongheaded I have trouble understanding how educators can defend them."

But, says the Thomas Jefferson Center's Director Robert O'Neil, a former president of the University of Virginia, universities implement speech codes "out of a sense of desperation and as a last resort when other approaches prove inadequate."

Goodman points out that the codes can have an effect opposite to the one intended. Minority publications, he notes, now have some very harsh words to say about other campus groups. "I have seen comments from black student publications strongly critical of white America. Under these regulations, those could be censored as easily as [comments] about blacks." He points out that various groups could end up being "the victims of the policies they created." O'Neil echoes this sentiment: "Restrictive codes may create at least as many problems as they solve and may not serve the goal of increased tolerance, understanding and civility in the academic community."

Hentoff addressed the same possibilities in reacting to the suspension of CBS's Andy Rooney for alleged anti-gay remarks. "What . . . celebrators of

Rooney's humiliation do not realize is that this kind of corporate yielding to silencers cuts both ways. [Former CBS News President] David Burke has greatly encouraged all kinds of pressure groups—including those who are not fond of blacks or gays—to believe that they too can remove someone they find offensive if they put on enough heat."

Prior to the framing of the American Constitution, both George Mason and John Adams championed the concept of a free press. And yet that document held no such guarantees. They were thought to be unnecessary. It was James Madison, a convert to the idea that minority views deserved to be expressed, and a proponent of the need for a bill of rights, who wrote to Thomas Jefferson pointing out that individual rights guaranteed only by the opinion of the majority could be eliminated whenever that opinion changed.

"When it comes to the rights and liberties of *individual* dissenters, a democratic majority can be as repressive as a king," says Hentoff in his book *The First Freedom.*

But nothing is harder to hold onto than freedom. In 1798, only seven years after the ratification of the Bill of Rights, Congress passed the Alien and Sedition Acts, a blatant attempt by the Federalist Party, then in control, to still opposition from Jefferson's party, the Democratic-Republicans. One Federalist target was the Republican press.

The first victim, Congressman Matthew Lyon of Vermont, was charged for writing to the *Vermont Journal* claiming that the administration of John Adams had, "in an unbounded thirst for ridiculous pomp, foolish adulation and selfish avarice," forgotten the public welfare. Lyon was jailed and fined. But freedom of the press has always looked better in theory than in practice, especially to the person being written about. No less a defender of freedom than Jefferson, who in 1798 came to Lyon's defense, would, less than six years later, complain to Governor Thomas McKean of Pennsylvania about the irresponsible Tory (Federalist) press which was then attacking him.

Leonard Levy, in his book, *Jefferson and Civil Liberties: The Darker Side,* noted that Jefferson, in an "entirely confidential letter," reminded McKean that while the federal government was prevented from moving against the press, the individual states were not. Said Jefferson, "a few prosecutions of the most prominent offenders would have a wholesome effect in restoring the integrity of the presses."

In fact, throughout modern history there have been forceful attempts to suppress civil liberties in America when it was thought warranted by conditions. During the First World War and shortly thereafter, pressure against those considered radical or subversive was intense. The Wobblies, an organization of workers espousing a socialist philosophy, were repeatedly silenced when they attempted to speak out in public. Teddy Roosevelt issued wartime warnings to church groups with pacifist leanings, advising them, with little thought of the doctrine of separation of church from state, to fly the flag from their steeples to demonstrate their loyalty.

After the war, fear of Bolsheviks, radicals, aliens and labor agitators remained, and attacks on the First Amendment continued. "The Red Menace" era was to follow. During the infamous Palmer Raids in 1920, 4,000 suspected radicals were rounded up during the night of a 33-city dragnet. Hentoff notes, "Among many newspapers supporting the roundups, *The Washington Post,* answering minority complaints that the Bill of Rights had been violated, lectured: 'There is no time to waste on hairsplitting over infringement of liberty.'"

As recently as 1942 the Supreme Court ruled that libelous statements, obscenity and "fighting words" fell outside the protection of the First Amendment. Since then a series of Supreme Court decisions has fine-tuned libel law, establishing the right of the plaintiff to explore the state of mind of the perpetrator to determine if malice were a factor—and now, to have access to notes and records to reveal more clearly that state of mind.

Gene Roberts, former executive editor of *The Philadelphia Inquirer* and now on the faculty of the University of Maryland, is one of those concerned about the censorious effect of libel laws. Corporations and local governments, he recently noted in a series of speeches, have begun suing individuals for libel when they speak out at town meetings and before city councils. Even circulating a petition, "written by voters, signed by voters and presented by voters to a court" has been found by a court to have defamed the politician it was designed to recall.

More and more critics, he says, are losing jury trials, and the awards have been substantial. In an overwhelming majority, he concedes, the verdicts have been reversed by higher courts, but the critics have been put to heavy expense and trouble, "to the point that it becomes easy to rationalize staying quiet instead of speaking out."

Increasingly, newspapers are being subjected to intimidating libel suits, increasing caution among editors—expecially those at small, independent papers without the resources to fight. Several editors admitted to Roberts that there were letters to the editor they had not published, editorials they had not written and investigative reporting they had not done—all out of fear of libel action.

The Supreme Court's recent *Milkovich* decision, which said that opinion is not necessarily a defense against libel, may increase that caution. Clearly the possibility exists that an editor with two op-ed pieces to choose from will select the one less likely to result in a lawsuit. Although Bruce Sanford, a Washington lawyer who works with the Society of Professional Journalists, doubts that the ruling will have much effect on what is being written, in the next breath he says, "There will certainly be censorship or self-censorship," which he points out will be "antithetical to First Amendment interests."

For some that is a discouraging thought. Paul McMasters, Deputy Editorial Director of *USA Today* and national freedom of information chairman of the SPJ, fears, too, that editors will self-censor. If they do so, it will be in an atmosphere where editorial pages are already "homogenized," he says.

Geneva Overholser, editor of the *Des Moines Register* and chairman of the First Amendment Committee of the American Society of Newspaper Editors, agrees: "Editorial pages are not as vigorous as they used to be."

Says Jane Kirtley, executive director of the Reporters Committee For Freedom Of The Press: "Sure, there is self-censorship. Everyone denies it but everyone engages in it. After the recent Supreme Court ruling on libel, we are going to see news organizations more chary about which op-ed pieces they run, about what letters they run. It's not that they think they would lose if it came to a suit, it's just they will think it's not worth it to have to defend it."

In 1985, years before the latest ruling, Gene Roberts wrote, "We are in the midst of a genuine First Amendment crisis. The libel problem is real. It is frightening. It is menacing to a nation that has thrived and flourished on vigorous dissent and unfettered criticism of government and its officials."

"It's a kind of timid era, a fearful era," notes Geneva Overholser.

And that, says Hentoff, is when the First Amendment is usually most endangered—"when the nation is most fearful: a time of war, for instance, or during a period when there is much anxiety about an outside menace."

The irony today is that the anxiety seems to be self-induced by internal confusion over values and priorities at a time when the traditional external adversary, communism, is no longer as threatening.

The past decade has seen a building up of defenses by the federal government even as the external adversary began to weaken. In 1982 an executive order from the Reagan White House extended the McCarran Internal Security Act. Federal employees with access to sensitive information were required to sign agreements to submit any writings to pre-publication review for the rest of their lives—a condition that applied not only to those dealing with classified information but also with classifiable information, thus extending the control of information further than ever before. They were also required to submit to lie detector tests during any investigation of information leaks. Says Donna Demac, author of *Liberty Denied,* "By late 1989, secrecy contracts had been signed by approximately three and a half million people, according to the head of the Information Security Oversight Office, which oversees executive branch security programs."

And the secrecy extends along with government grants into the scholarly arena. Demac says that Jonathan Knight of the American Association of University Professors "has described the controls that prevail today on American campuses as 'subtle, institutionalized censorship with the greatest potential to corrode scientific freedom.' "

In the same period the United States Information Agency restricted the entry of dozens of films into the United States by refusing to approve them as fit for educational or other use. One film labeled "political propaganda" was produced by the National Film Board of Canada on the perils of nuclear war; another was on acid rain. In all, according to the General Accounting Office,

41 percent of all foreign films were classified by the Department of Justice as propaganda.

Colombian journalist Patricia Lara was jailed and deported when her name was found on an Immigration and Naturalization Service list of some 40,000 people suspected of "subversive Communist or terrorist activities." In 1989, not long after that incident, Congress passed a two-year ban on the ideological exclusion of temporary visitors but retained it for those seeking permanent residence.

Obtaining documents under the Freedom of Information Act has also become increasingly difficult, according to Demac and many others. Those who have attempted it report confronting obstacle after obstacle. On June 11 *The New Yorker*'s "Talk of the Town" column noted the recent release of Oliver North's notebooks, which "constitute nothing less than a contemporaneous handwritten history of the most secret workings of the United States national-security apparatus during the Reagan Administration." They were, the writer notes, withheld from the American people until May 1990.

"For more than three years, North, his lawyers and the Reagan and Bush White Houses had successfully stymied even congressional efforts to obtain the notebooks, unexpurgated," *The New Yorker* said.

The recent release was an achievement for the information-advocacy groups that succeeded where others had failed, but it only highlights the problem and the growing concern. "There is something fundamental that is violated in a democracy when the White House can classify documents as 'Codeword/Top Secret' in order to suppress politically damaging information," Senator John Kerry was quoted as saying by *The New Yorker*.

Says Richard O. Curry in his 1988 book *Freedom at Risk: Secrecy, Censorship and Repression in the 1980s*, the policies of the Reagan Administration reflect *"radical departures* from the past. This is revealed not only by the comprehensive scope of the administration policies, but its ability to *institutionalize* secrecy, censorship, and repression in ways that will be difficult if not impossible, to eradicate."

Recently the historian Warren I. Cohen resigned as chairman of the State Department's Advisory Committee on Historical Diplomatic Documentation because committee members, all of whom had security clearances, had been denied what traditionally had been their right to review material the department was excluding from its publications. Says Cohen in an essay in *World Monitor*, "At a time when the Soviet Union and its former satellites are revealing their most terrible secrets . . . the U.S. government is publishing blatantly fraudulent accounts of its activities in Guatemala, Iran and Southeast Asia in the 1950s. Indeed, much of the historical record published recently by the Department of State in its renowned 'Foreign Relations of the United States' series may distort and misrepresent American activities abroad."

Some of the censorship we see in America—and, indeed, many decisions to speak or print—are directly related to economics. *The Detroit Free Press,* when seeking approval of a joint operating agreement from the Justice Department that would have a direct economic impact on the newspaper, killed a political cartoon lampooning then Attorney General Ed Meese.

But the news is not all bad. Most convictions on obscenity charges or harsh libel judgments take place in lower courts where judicial "inexperience . . . is sometimes a factor," says Jane Kirtley. The convictions are generally reversed.

Put the freedoms Americans enjoy against a global backdrop and the contrast is striking. Protected by a written Bill of Rights and an independent judiciary habituated to defending those rights, Americans are proud to be living in the longest existing constitutional democracy; they tend to feel secure, even complacent. But couple pride with complacency and the effect can be blinding. It is difficult to see what we are predisposed to ignore: that as secure as our rights seem to be, they can be undermined by abuse, ignorance and carelessness. It is also too easy to consider, without thinking, that justice or a collective "right" might require the suppression of an individual's or a corporation's rights.

Few would maintain, for instance, that smoking is of any benefit to society, but the rights of tobacco companies to free speech through advertising have clearly been disregarded in light of the perceived social benefit in denying these rights. Says *USA Today*'s McMasters, "Anti-tobacco groups are good people, but when they call for special laws that forbid that sort of advertising that restricts speech, they are taking a very short view."

Robert O'Neil declares the First Amendment to be "in perilous condition across the nation." The Thomas Jefferson Center's survey shows, he says, "an alarming gap in support for pure speech—utterance of the spoken word—[as opposed to] other forms of expression, including freedom of the press." Those who thought entertainment could legally be restricted, for instance, were highly protective of their own right to speak out. He notes that improving public understanding of the meaning of these guarantees will be a major task of the new center.

McMasters says, "My feeling is that the First Amendment defenders and advocates have to do a lot better job of defending and explaining the First Amendment. We've got to be a little less self-righteous and a little more forthcoming about speech responsibility."

Supreme Court Justice David Souter, during his recent confirmation hearings, remarked that it is a mistake "to assume that the only guardians of the Constitution are the judges." He was referring to members of Congress and the president, who have sworn to uphold the Constitution. But he might have been speaking to the American people at large.

There is a nervousness in America. The very vastness and diversity of the country makes it seem almost unmanageable. The speed of modern communications has meant that information and ideas are exchanged without the time that once existed to reflect and adjust to change. Our government seems ineffectual, our institutions fragile. The systems we devised in gentler times hardly seem up to the task of governing, let alone shaping the culture. Creating consensus becomes daunting. The result is a collective frustration, and frustration breeds unease. Inevitably there is the temptation to turn to simple and direct solutions, to control or ban or limit expression seen as undesirable by whatever means and at every level—school libraries, town meetings, city councils—whenever and wherever values are perceived to be threatened.

Ironically, it is not a foreign power that is threatening the First Amendment, but Americans themselves. American individuals who often are aiming only for a common good, Americans frightened by the unruly, unpredictable nature of freedom.

Some recent decisions in the courts have been reassuring. But it is time to start paying attention. James Madison warned, "There are more instances of the abridgment of the freedom of the people by the gradual and silent encroachments of those in power than by the violent and sudden usurpations."

Today Paul McMasters says: "It is a sort of a double irony that at the time the U.S. seems to be having second thoughts about the First Amendment, we see Tiananmen Square and Eastern Europe looking to us as the model of what free speech can mean. It's a cliché because it's true. We have hundreds of congressmen wanting to amend the Bill of Rights to prevent one form of free speech. We have an administration that is stamping 6.8 million documents secret each year. And then we have the Rev. Donald Wildmon [who campaigned against Robert Mapplethorpe's photographs].

"It's my feeling that we really don't need a First Amendment if the only speech [we protect] is speech we like."

Tolerance should be the catch phrase for the 90s, says Jane Kirtley. "Whenever we have thought police marching through the streets, no matter how noble the intentions, we have to stop and think, 'Is this really what we want?' "

# A Trash Course in Free Speech

### *by* Howard Kurtz

*Editor's Note:* One of the most crucial concerns of freedom and responsibility in the last decade of the twentieth century has been the raising of questions about political correctness (PC). What is PC? It's easier to say how it came about than to try to provide a comprehensive definition.

One characteristic of the last third of the 1900s has been increased concern about individual and group rights. It started, no doubt, with civil rights and the concern by African-Americans that they had not been treated equitably in America. Other groups then began to make similar claims—for women's rights, for gay and lesbian rights, for Hispanic rights, and more.

However, the right to freedom of speech and press as guaranteed by the First Amendment can run into direct conflict with individuals' or groups' rights to protect themselves from those who would say or print things they don't like. And if the mass media communicates messages that offend, to what extent can individuals or groups strike back? These are questions and issues raised by a host of actions on college and university campuses in the past few years.

Howard Kurtz is a media reporter for the *Washington Post,* where this article was published on July 29, 1993.

A new form of protest is all the rage on college campuses across the country: stealing, dumping or burning student newspapers.

While national attention has focused on the University of Pennsylvania, where black students seized thousands of copies of the student paper in April [1993], at least 18 similar campus incidents in recent months have received little publicity.

The grievances of those grabbing the papers range from allegations of racism or sexism to embarrassment over negative articles. But these assaults on the First Amendment have sparked little outrage, and college administrators have generally taken a hands-off approach.

"We've never had this many thefts in a short period of time," said Mark Goodman, executive director of the Student Press Law Center, a nonprofit group in Washington that monitors such incidents.

"The thing that is most frustrating is the attitude of school administrators. If they've expressed any concern at all—and most haven't—it's been very mild. Nobody has outright condemned it and said it won't be tolerated on this campus."

In one case, a college administrator turned out to be part of the problem. At Middle Tennessee State University, Associate Dean Judy Smith apologized for taking two dozen copies of the student paper, Sidelines. These were among hundreds of copies that had disappeared during a freshman orientation session.

Sam Gannon, editor of Sidelines, said Smith acknowledged that she was troubled by a front-page story about a student leader who had just been arrested in a local bank robbery.

"She told me it was an embarrassment to herself and the university and that wasn't the kind of light she wanted new students to see the university in," Gannon said. "I asked if she was aware that this was censorship."

Smith later maintained that she thought she was disposing of an outdated issue. "It was just an unfortunate mistake," spokesman John Lynch said. A student also admitted stealing papers and has written a letter of apology.

College papers are particularly vulnerable to theft because they are distributed in bulk at central locations. Since the publications are generally free, the thefts rarely lead to arrests and are often treated as harmless pranks.

Some critics see the colleges' failure to punish the culprits as a symptom of political correctness. A Wall Street Journal editorial lambasted the University of Pennsylvania for "political craveness" by "accommodating political zealots."

In that incident, 14,000 copies of the Daily Pennsylvanian were thrown in the trash by black students protesting a columnist who criticized affirmative action, Malcolm X and the Rev. Martin Luther King Jr. The university president, Sheldon Hackney, who has been nominated to head the National Endowment for the Humanities, has been faulted for not responding more aggressively.

Hackney said at the time that "two important university values, diversity and open expression, seem to be in conflict."

University spokeswoman Barbara Beck said Hackney "really did say right from the beginning that this was wrong." She said the eight students accused in the theft will be brought before a student judicial panel this fall.

Asked about possible punishment, Beck said the students might "become involved in a program in which they work with other students, or do a project that leads to some kind of understanding of what they did and how to work with others."

The Daily Pennsylvanian theft may have sparked a rash of copycat incidents. Days later at Pennsylvania State University, thieves took 6,000 copies of the Lionhearted, which has often attacked gay people and women's studies. Two hundred were burned on the lawn of a trustee of the paper.

The offending issue featured a full-page sketch of a woman in a bikini with a sign, "Feminist at Work." Criminal charges were filed this month against two female ex-students, one of whom headed a group called Womyn's Concerns.

Several of the incidents have a racial element. At Dartmouth College, black students repeatedly removed copies of the Dartmouth Review from dormitory halls after the paper reported that a member of the Black Freshman Forum had been charged with assaulting two female students. The Review is an independent conservative paper published off campus.

M. Lee Pelton, Dartmouth's dean of students, did not denounce the thefts. He said in a letter that those who seized the papers "have neither broken any laws nor violated the College's Code of Conduct. . . . One group feels that the other has printed materials which are deliberately provocative and hurtful, while the other feels that its right to make known its views has been impaired."

Dartmouth spokesman Alex Huppe said that "it's probably wrong for an administration to come in and heavy-handedly work out student-to-student problems. It's not up to the administration to force them to get along with each other." He said piles of newspapers in dormitory halls are "in the category of litter."

Joe Burbach, editor of the Badger-Herald at the University of Wisconsin at Madison, said 100 black students held a rally to denounce the newspaper and burn a stack of copies. He said they objected to a cartoon that likened the Cleveland Indians mascot to Little Black Sambo. Eight hundred papers were later stolen from drop-off points, Burbach said.

The dean of students focused her comments on the paper's right to publish. Spokesman Terry Devitt said the university took no action because it could not find the thieves. "This is something we take very seriously," he said.

But Burbach said college officials "didn't say people shouldn't be taking the Badger-Herald's papers. It was a very marginal and weak response by the university."

One theft that led to prosecution took place in March [1993] at Southeastern Louisiana University. Mark Morice, the only student member of the state's regional college board, was freed on $25,000 bond after charges that he arranged for fraternity pledges to steal 2,000 copies of the Lion's Roar. The issue carried an article critical of the school's Student Government Association.

Other incidents seem to revolve around personal embarrassment. At California Polytechnic State University, 6,000 copies of the Mustang Daily were dumped after the paper refused to kill a story about a student arrested on peeping Tom charges. Managing Editor Todd Hogan said the student had pleaded with editors not to run the story, but that there is no evidence tying him to the theft.

"From a reporter's standpoint, we're really upset," Hogan said. "We work real hard to put out a quality newspaper. You're just depriving students of news."

In one case, the motive seems to have been old-fashioned capitalism. After the University of North Carolina won the NCAA basketball championship in April, a local store scooped up hundreds of copies of the Daily Tar Heel and sold them for $3.95 apiece.

# 16

# Stop Making Sense

## *by* Christopher Lasch

*Editor's Note:* Some critics say mass media are failing to meet their responsibilities by being too bland and too objective. In this article, a widely published historian and media critic laments the current state of American journalism and calls for a return to the fiery partisan prose that characterized newspapers in the past.

Some of the blame, according to this author, lies with advertising and public relations. "Responsibility came to be equated with the avoidance of controversy," partly because of advertising and public relations. "The decline of the partisan press and the rise of a journalism professing rigorous standards of objectivity do not assure a steady supply of usable information," which is what is really necessary to make democracy and freedom possible.

The original version of this article first appeared in the Spring 1990 issue of the *Gannett Center Journal.* This version was published in *NewsInc.,* December 1990.

Let us begin with a simple proposition: What democracy requires is public debate, not information. Of course it needs information too, but the kind of information it needs can be generated only by vigorous popular debate. We do not know what we need to know until we ask the right questions, and we can identify the right questions only by subjecting our own ideas about the world to the test of public controversy. Information, usually seen as the precondition of debate, is better understood as its by-product. When we get into arguments that focus and fully engage our attention, we become avid seekers of relevant information. Otherwise, we take in information passively—if we take it in at all.

From these considerations it follows that the job of the press is to encourage debate, not to supply the public with information. But as things now stand the press generates information in abundance, and nobody pays any attention. It is no secret that the public knows less about public affairs than it used to know. Millions of Americans cannot begin to tell you what is in the Bill of Rights, what Congress does, what the Constitution says about the powers of the presidency, how the party system emerged or how it operates. Ignorance of public affairs is commonly attributed to the failure of the public schools, and only secondarily to the failure of the press to inform. But since the public no longer participates in debates on national issues, it has no reason to be better informed. When debate becomes a lost art, information makes no impression.

Let us ask why debate has become a lost art. The answer may surprise: Debate began to decline around the turn of the century, when the press became more "responsible," more professional, more conscious of its civic obligations. In the early nineteenth century the press was fiercely partisan. Until the middle of the century papers were often financed by political parties. Even when they became more independent of parties they did not embrace the ideal of objectivity or neutrality. In 1841 Horace Greeley launched his *New York Tribune* with the announcement that it would be "a journal removed alike from servile partisanship on the one hand and from gagged, mincing neutrality on the other." Strong-minded editors like Greeley, James Gordon Bennett, E. L. Godkin, and Samuel Bowles did not attempt to conceal their own views or to impose a strict separation of news and editorial content. Their papers were journals of opinion in which the reader expected to find a definite point of view, together with unrelenting criticism of opposing points of view.

It is no accident that journalism of this kind flourished during the period from 1830 to 1900, when popular participation in politics was at its height. Eighty percent of the eligible voters typically went to the polls in presidential elections. After 1900 the percentage began to decline sharply. Torchlight parades, mass rallies, and gladiatorial contests or oratory made nineteenth-century politics an object of consuming popular interest.

In the midst of such politics, nineteenth-century journalism served as an extension of the town meeting. It created a public forum in which the issues of the day were hotly debated. Newspapers not only reported political controversies but participated in them, drawing in their readers as well. And print culture rested on the remnants of an oral tradition: Printed language was still shaped by the rhythms and requirements of the spoken word, in particular by the conventions of verbal argumentation. Print served to create a larger forum for the spoken word, not yet to displace or reshape it.

The "best men," as they liked to think of themselves, were never altogether happy with this state of affairs, and by the 1870s and 1880s their low opinion of politics had come to be widely shared by the educated classes. The scandals of the Gilded Age gave party politics a bad name. Genteel reformers—"mugwumps," to their enemies—demanded a professionalization of politics, designed to free the civil service from party control and to replace political appointees with trained experts.

The drive to clean up politics gained momentum in the Progressive Era. Under the leadership of Theodore Roosevelt, Woodrow Wilson, Robert La Follette, and William Jennings Bryan, the Progressives preached "efficiency," "good government," "bipartisanship," and the "scientific management" of public affairs, and declared war on "bossism." These reformers had little use for public debate. Most political questions were too complex, in their view, to be submitted to popular judgment. They liked to contrast the scientific expert with the orator—the latter a useless windbag whose ranting only confused the public mind.

Professionalism in politics meant professionalism in journalism. The connection between the two was spelled out by Walter Lippmann in the Twenties, in a series of books that provided a founding charter for modern journalism—an elaborate rationale for a journalism guided by the new idea of professional objectivity. Lippmann held up standards by which the press is still judged.

In Lippmann's view, democracy did not require that people literally govern themselves. Questions of substance should be decided by knowledgeable administrators whose access to reliable information immunized them against emotional "symbols" and "stereotypes" that dominated public debate. The public, according to Lippmann, was incompetent to govern itself and did not even care to do so. A complex industrial society required a government carried on by officials who would necessarily be guided—since any form of direct democracy was now impossible—by either public opinion or expert knowledge. Public opinion was unreliable because it could be united only by an appeal to slogans and "symbolic pictures." Truth, as Lippmann conceived it, grew out of disinterested scientific inquiry; everything else was ideology. Public debate was at best a disagreeable necessity. Ideally, it would not take place at all; decisions would be based on scientific "standards of measurement" alone.

The role of the press, as Lippmann saw it, was to circulate information, not to encourage argument. The relationship between information and argument was antagonistic, not complementary. He did not take the position that argumentation was a necessary outcome of reliable information; on the contrary, his point was that information precluded argument, made argument unnecessary. Arguments were what took place in the absence of reliable information.

Lippmann had forgotten what he learned (or should have learned) from William James and John Dewey: that our search for reliable information is itself guided by the questions that arise during arguments about a given course of action. It is only by subjecting our preferences and projects to the test of debate that we come to understand what we know and what we still need to learn. Until we have to defend our opinions in public, they remain opinions in Lippmann's pejorative sense—half-formed convictions based on random impressions and unexamined assumptions. It is the act of articulating and defending our views that lifts them out of the category of "opinions," gives them shape and definition, and makes it possible for others to recognize them as a description of their own experience as well. In short, we come to know our own minds only by explaining ourselves to others.

The attempt to bring others around to our own point of view carries the risk, of course, that we may adopt their point of view instead. We have to enter imaginatively into our opponents' arguments, if only for the purpose of refuting them, and we may end up being persuaded by those we sought to persuade.

Argument is risky and unpredictable—and therefore educational. Most of us tend to think of it (as Lippmann thought of it) as a clash of rival dogmas, a shouting match in which neither side gives any ground. But arguments are not won by shouting down opponents. They are won by changing opponents' minds.

If we insist on argument as the essence of education, we will defend democracy not as the most efficient but as the most educational form of government—one that extends the circle of debate as widely as possible and thus forces all citizens to articulate their views, to put their views at risk, and to cultivate the virtues of eloquence, clarity of thought and expression, and sound judgment. From this point of view, the press has the potential to serve as the equivalent of the town meeting.

The rise of the advertising and public-relations industries, side by side, helps to explain why the press abdicated its most important function—enlarging the public forum—at the same time that it became more "responsible." A responsible press, as opposed to a partisan or opinionated one, attracted the kind of readers advertisers were eager to reach: well-heeled readers, most of whom probably thought of themselves as independent voters. These readers wanted to be assured that they were reading all the news that was fit to print, not an editor's idiosyncratic and no doubt biased view of things. Responsibility came to be equated with the avoidance of controversy because advertisers were willing to pay for it. Some advertisers were also willing to pay for sensationalism, though on the whole they preferred a respectable readership to sheer numbers. What they clearly did not prefer was "opinion"—not because they were impressed with Lippmann's philosophical arguments but because opinionated reporting did not guarantee the right audience. No doubt they also hoped that an aura of objectivity, the hallmark of responsible journalism, would rub off on the advertisements that surrounded columns of print.

In a curious historical twist, advertising, publicity, and other forms of commercial persuasion themselves came to be disguised as information and, eventually, to substitute for open debate. "Hidden persuaders" (as Vance Packard called them) replaced the old-time editors, essayists, and orators who made no secret of their partisanship. And information and publicity became increasingly indistinguishable. Today, most of the "news" in our newspapers consists of items churned out by press agencies and public-relations offices and then regurgitated intact by the "objective" organs of journalism.

The decline of the partisan press and the rise of a journalism professing rigorous standards of objectivity do not assure a steady supply of usable information. Unless information is generated by sustained public debate, most of it will be irrelevant at best, misleading and manipulative at worst. Increasingly, information is generated by those who wish to promote something or someone without arguing their case on its merits or explicitly advertising it as self-interested material. Much of the press, in its eagerness to inform the public, has become a conduit for the equivalent of junk mail. When words are used merely as instruments of publicity or propaganda, they lose their power to persuade.

Soon they cease to mean anything at all. People lose the capacity to use language precisely and expressively, or even to distinguish one word from another. The spoken word models itself on the written word instead of the other way around, and ordinary speech begins to sound like the clotted jargon we see in print. Ordinary speech begins to sound like "information"—a disaster from which the English language may never recover.

# 17

# Cotton Candy Journalism

## *by* James V. Risser

*Editor's Note:* The irresponsibility of journalism today is mainly due to giving people what they want, charges the author of this article: For all its apparent appeal, the "fluff that's passing for journalism is bad news for all of us. . . . We're not in this business to lick the public's hand; we're here to tell people what they need to know."

The author is James V. Risser, two-time winner of the Pulitzer Prize for journalism and now director of Stanford University's John S. Knight Fellowships for Professional Journalists. This article was originally published in the *Stanford* magazine, December 1990.

"It is the duty of a newspaper to print the news and raise hell," was the proud and feisty slogan that adorned each day's issue of the *Chicago Times.* But the *Times,* like many of the old-time, big-city newspapers, is now defunct. And in some ways, so is the slogan and sentiment it represented.

For many of today's American newspapers, a more appropriate slogan might be "All the news that's not too upsetting" or perhaps "The newspaper that's reader-friendly."

Of course, the country's best papers continue to do distinguished work: watchdogging government, examining businesses, and shedding light on such complex subjects as economics, science, and the environment.

But at too many newspapers, the serious and important side of journalism is in danger of being overwhelmed by the frivolous, the trivial, and the bland. Across the country, newspapers are beginning to look more and more alike, and it is a look that has more to do with design and color than it does with substance.

To the extent that the accepted look does deal with substance, it involves a greater reliance on easy-to-do local news, feature stories, celebrity profiles, and so-called "lifestyle" pieces. Lost in the shuffle are the tougher local stories, national and international news, and in-depth coverage.

Why has this happened, and what difference does it make?

The primary reason for the change is that newspaper editors and publishers are desperately trying to cope with the alarming and steady decline in per capita readership of their product—from 90 percent of U.S. households in the early 1960s to fewer than 70 percent today. Project this trend line out a ways and, sometime in the next century, newspapers disappear altogether.

Erwin Potts, the chief executive of the respected Sacramento-based Mc-Clatchy Newspapers, says that among his colleagues "there are lots of dooms-day predictions about the future of newspapers." Still, he believes that "there will always be a core of people who will want a daily newspaper." The unanswered question, though, is just how large that core will be.

A study completed this year by the Times Mirror Center for the People & the Press came up with the alarming finding that younger Americans, under the age of 30, "know less and care less about news and public affairs than any other generation of Americans in the past fifty years." Compared to their parents and grandparents, they read newspapers less, are more ignorant of major events, and are much less likely to vote.

As media analyst Anthony Casale has pointed out, "Over 60 percent of all Americans were not alive the last time newspaper readership was on the upturn nationally." For both editors and publishers, that's an especially sobering statistic.

And it should be sobering to the rest of us, as well, simply because newspapers have played such a critical role in both government and public affairs, a role that cannot be filled by any other news medium.

*New York Times* columnist Tom Wicker has written that the plain meaning of the free press clause in the First Amendment "is that the American press has a constitutional obligation to act as a check on and a balance against the power of government and other institutions." It is precisely that kind of performance by the press that comes to mind when we think about the proudest moments in American newspapering: the *Washington Post*'s coverage of the Watergate scandal, the *New York Times*'s publication of the Pentagon Papers, and the less known but crucial reporting that the best newspapers do, day in and day out, to keep government and other prominent institutions honest and on track.

Such journalism has an important, beneficial impact on U.S., and sometimes world, history. It often is journalism that cannot be done by magazines, which are too slow, or by commercial television, which is too superficial.

Yet many of those in charge of newspapers today are abandoning their business' proud heritage in a rush to compete with television to "give the readers what they want." The "readership survey" has become a favorite tool in this regard, a tool that has led newspapers away from what they do best.

The prototypical example of this is *USA Today*, the paper that is sold in a coin box that looks most like a television set. This is no accident. From concept to execution, *USA Today* is meant to be as close as possible to a television-watching experience.

On the positive side, this has meant an imaginative use of color and graphics, quick and bright writing, features tailored to people's leisure and cultural interests. On the negative side, however, *USA Today* stresses the superficial, glorifies the trivial, oversimplifies the complex, and panders to a certain perceived need among Americans to feel good about themselves.

In short, *USA Today* is emblematic of a growing willingness among today's newspapers to practice what I would call "cotton candy journalism"—journalism that's bright, attractive, and pleasantly sweet, yet so devoid of substance that it dissolves as soon as you bite into it.

It is a strategy that cannot work over the long haul, and even those surveys that poll readers suggest as much. Over the past thirty years, for example, Leo Bogart has conducted numerous readership surveys for the Newspaper Advertising Bureau, and they show both a consistent and strong preference among readers for news over features—although the strength of that preference has certainly decreased over time.

Is it possible for newspapers to survive and remain faithful to their best traditions? There are reasons to be hopeful. After all, those with vigorous news coverage have almost always done well and have attracted strong reader loyalty—from longtime industry leaders like the *Des Moines Register,* with its uncommonly enterprising reporting of Iowa government and politics, to upstarts like the *San Jose Mercury News,* which has become the best paper in the Bay Area on the strength of its public affairs coverage.

Papers that have failed have generally been of poorer journalistic quality, have been metropolitan papers unable to compete with television, or have been caught in economic and demographic problems peculiar to their community. Their failure is not an argument for changing newspapers into magazines or into a print version of broadcasting news. Better that they fade from the scene.

But those that do survive will have to sink or swim by doing a better job at what newspapers do best: serious, substantive news coverage and commentary. Television newsman John Chancellor put it well, arguing that "the biggest advantage print has over broadcasting is in the reporting of fact," while broadcasting is best at transmitting experience. "Being more like television won't help," he said. But if newspapers go with their basic strengths, "they have a bright future."

We lose our way and mistake our mission if we think our business is only to give the public what it wants," says Eugene Patterson, the former editor of the *St. Petersburg Times.* "We're not in this business to lick the public's hand: we're here to tell people what they need to know."

Newspapers can and need to act as a check on government and on those individuals, both public and private, who hold power. They must inform the public of things it *needs* to know, as well as what it wants to know. Newspapers can and should investigate and report on societal conditions, especially those that need correction or change. And newspapers must find ways to anticipate future trends rather than react to events that have already occurred.

In other words, they should go back to printing the news and raising hell.

# V

# Ethical Values

It is important to say at the outset of any discussion about ethical values that these are matters of social norms, not of laws. One isn't obligated by law to comply with a social norm; to do so is a voluntary and personal matter. Since there aren't many laws governing mass media, given the First Amendment guaranteeing press freedom, most of our legitimate concerns about media deal with ethics. For example, there is no law against telling a lie by mass media, but it would be unethical to do so. There is no law against doctoring a photograph, but that would be unethical as well.

Of course, mass communications cannot violate normal laws (murder, theft, bribery, etc.) in doing their work. Yet some of their legal activities may strike some people as unethical because they might seem to be violations of social norms. Nevertheless, communicators are free to violate such norms because they are only voluntary.

There is probably a difference between the social norms accepted by journalists and those of some of their critics. Most journalists in American society seem to be motivated by the idea that the public has a right to know what is going on in any sphere of activity. There are others (perhaps even some journalists, too) who feel that the public shouldn't know everything. Journalists frequently believe that whatever they do is justified if the end result is to inform the public. For example, using stolen documents might be justified if the information they contain is essential to the public. Some would call this behavior unethical, but it is not illegal.

However, there are journalistic behaviors that society in general, including journalists, would consider unethical. Such behavior can be divided into two categories. First, there is exploitation of others for one's own gain. Sensationalizing news, not for the purpose of keeping people informed but to sell media, would be unethical to most journalists. Invading a person's privacy, not to reveal some essential information but to sell that information, would also be unethical to most journalists. Causing persons embarrassment or even harm by identifying them publicly when it is not essential to do so, such as in a rape case, would be considered unethical, particularly if the motive for the revelation is to attract an audience and thus make a greater profit from the information. For the press or mass media to do these things is not illegal, but many would rightly question the ethics of such behavior.

Second, there is the problem of allowing outsiders to exploit for their own gain or purposes the mass media. Journalists who allow themselves to be used so that others can influence the public have broken an unwritten contract with the latter. They have not broken any laws, but we would certainly question their ethics. Conflict of interest is one of the most frequent problems here. Journalists might put forth information as if it were balanced, fair, accurate, and objective when in reality it represents a biased point of view because of the journalists' own involvement with one side of an issue. Again they have not broken any laws, but they have committed what many would regard as unethical behavior.

Journalists who allow others with special interests to influence their work, whether deliberately or out of laziness and inattention to their job, have not violated a law, but we should question their ethics. If an item released by some PR office is published or broadcast as if it were a balanced and objective account, no law would be broken but we could legitimately question the ethics of such behavior.

Most American news media today have codes of conduct for their own employees that deal with ethical standards. An organization might discipline its employees for violating its code of conduct, but the employee could not be charged with breaking any law. Many journalistic associations, such as the Society of Professional Journalists and the Radio Television News Directors Association, maintain codes of conduct. These are not laws by which communicators must live; they are voluntary guidelines. Even so, there are growing concerns about the ethical behavior of mass media, and the articles in this section describe some of the current problems.

# 18

# Private Grief, Public Exposure

## *by* Saul E. Wisnia

*Editor's Note:* Where should the line be drawn by the news media in reporting on a disaster? Is it appropriate to tell the public intimate details
about those involved? Such details about a moment of intense grief certainly seem to attract attention, perhaps because it is human nature for
us to wonder how we would react in similar circumstances. We put ourselves in the position of the grieving and mourn with them.

But what about those experiencing the grief? Isn't grief a private matter? When is it too intrusive to interview and photograph grieving people? Journalists have sometimes rationalized such news because it
provides a warning to others. A newspaper editor, for example, justified
a front-page picture of a drowning victim by saying the picture would
alert readers to the dangers of unsafe swimming.

There are no easy answers to these questions, but this article provides
a personal point of view. The author, Saul E. Wisnia, was a senior in journalism at Syracuse University when PanAm Flight 103 crashed in Scotland. This article was originally published in *The Quill,* July/August 1989.

Lillian Abbott, a junior at Syracuse University, had just finished her last final
exam of the fall term. As she relaxed in her apartment on the afternoon of December 21, 1988, a TV program was interrupted by a bulletin: a Pan American
jet had crashed while over Lockerbie, Scotland.

Although Abbott was editor-in-chief of the school paper, *The Daily Orange,* she paid little attention to the news at first. But when reports a few minutes later confirmed that the plane had been traveling from London to New
York, she began to take notice. Her best friend, Julliane Kelly, also a junior at
Syracuse, was due home from a semester in London that same afternoon.

The news worsened. As the evening wore on, Abbott would learn that 35
Syracuse students had been among the 270 people killed in the crash—and
Kelly had been among them.

That night and in the weeks that followed, Abbott mourned the loss of her
friend. And she also saw a darker side of journalism as reporters and photographers scrambled to get the story, often oblivious to the emotional turmoil their
sources were experiencing.

"I used to want to be a hard-news reporter," Abbott says today. "But I don't think I do any more. I don't want to be the person on the other end of the phone saying, 'Mrs. Kelly, I'm sorry to hear about your daughter. Now, how do you feel?' "

Abbott was not alone in her distress. Many Syracuse communications students and their professors were forced to deal with the loss of the 35 students on Flight 103 while confronting another aspect of the tragedy—the way it was covered by the local and national media.

As intrusive reporters bearing cameras, microphones, and lights descended upon the campus after the crash of Flight 103, at least a few present and future journalists at Syracuse University came to question the ideals and ethics of their chosen field.

Lawrence Mason, an associate professor of communications at the university, was at home preparing to go to work at his second job as a UPI photographer when he got word by telephone that a jet had crashed, and that Syracuse students may have been aboard.

Shortly thereafter, UPI headquarters in Auburn called Mason with verification of the news, and asked him to cover a memorial service for the students that night at Hendricks Chapel, the campus house of worship.

Hanging up the phone, Mason paused. How many of those students had he taught? Although he didn't know it then, eight of his students had been on the plane. With that uncertainty in mind, he called UPI headquarters back. Out of respect for all Syracuse University students, he would not cover the service.

"I just knew I couldn't go and take photos at a memorial service—I just didn't feel it was appropriate," explains Mason, who, after 11 years with UPI, says he feels comfortable with his decision. "A lot of younger people in the media would feel they had to go. I'm just glad I wasn't thrust into that position."

The hastily called memorial service at Hendricks Chapel that Mason chose not to cover teetered on chaos. Photographers jammed the aisles and balconies with bulky TV equipment, and they triggered blinding strobe lights and noisy motor drives on still cameras. The service was more like a press conference than a prayer vigil.

While no one could have been fully prepared for the tragedy that befell Syracuse University that night, one question still lingers: Just how unprepared was the university?

"We were as prepared as you can be," says Sandi Mulconry, director of news services for Syracuse's public relations department. "But obviously, we had never dealt with anything like this before. We were caught off guard."

In any campus crisis, a good deal of organization is left up to the public (or university) relations department. Prepared or not, the PR people have to keep things under control on campus while releasing pertinent information regarding the event as it comes in.

But on the night of December 21, as the magnitude of the crash and its implications for Syracuse grew more apparent, it was clear that the PR department at SU was not in control.

Local television stations had already begun listing names of possible Syracuse victims on their 6 P.M. newscasts, a signal that brought hordes of journalists rushing to the SU campus. But as reporters began to crowd the hall outside the PR office, no official confirmation was forthcoming.

"We were getting conflicting lists (of victims) from conflicting people, and we were not going to release any names until we were sure," said Mulconry. "We ended up not releasing any names until the following morning, and I believe there's no way we could have gone any earlier. Part of the problem was that DIPA [the Division of International Programs Abroad, the group the SU students were traveling in] was calling reporters before they called us."

The department did issue one statement that night—a confirmation of the crash released shortly after 9 P.M. by Robert Hill, vice president of public relations.

That was not enough. Although Mulconry believes that Hill and the staff did the right thing in not confirming names the first night, she concedes that the Public Relations department should have released more than a single statement.

"We should have explained our situation to the media," Mulconry says. "And we should have been more conscious of the need for hourly updates and for keeping the lines of communication open."

But other than Hill's brief statement, the communication lines were closed, and reporters seeking information were forced to look in other places. The grief at Syracuse University was *the* story of the hour, and with no one directing them, reporters ran wild—calling friends and families of the victims, stopping students in the streets, even pelting sorority windows with pebbles to gain the attention of those inside—all in an effort to find details to fit the names on their lists.

Press behavior reached a nadir at the memorial service at Hendricks Chapel, where students were harassed before, after and during their prayers by reporters and photographers. Where were the PR people? Back at the office answering the phones.

"Unfortunately, we didn't know what went on at Hendricks until the next day," explains Mulconry. "We made the mistake of being tied up on the phones all night, and there was nobody who thought of going to the chapel. Maybe if we had been willing to let the phones ring a few more times, we would have had time to think about other things."

But Mulconry and the staff of 10 in news services didn't let the phones ring, and while they provided media all over the world with information specifying the time and place students would be mourning, they failed to stop and think what it might be like at the actual service.

When they did find out—the next morning—matters improved. Reporters and photographers were kept in the balconies at a second memorial service. But by then the damage had been done.

"Younger [reporters and photographers] especially, feel the pressure to go and do it [cover the service]," journalism professor Mason says. "That's why I think the university should have stepped in and said, 'No cameras allowed in Hendricks Chapel.'"

"It would have taken the pressure off those young reporters. I know a lot of the journalists I talked to would have liked to have been asked not to go."

Mason suggests that university officials might have offered alternative methods of coverage, such as having reporters wait outside the chapel for students, or by organizing a pool in which photographers could have sat in fixed positions in the balconies above the mourners.

"Time is an important factor," Mason adds. "I'm sure the university administration had a lot on its mind, but I think one thing they didn't consider was what the media coverage might be like. The university controls press access to a very large extent at graduation—a happy occasion—and here we have one of the most dreadful news stories that has ever hit this city, and nothing was done."

Like Mason, Mark Weiner, a 1984 Syracuse University alumnus and now a city-desk reporter at the *Syracuse Herald-Journal,* was upset by some of the actions of print and broadcast journalists. After working the morning shift the day of the crash, Weiner was kept at the paper all night (along with most of the staff) answering phones and scraping together facts. Much of what he saw amazed him.

"Still early on, before we [at the *Herald-Journal*] had confirmed the crash, I got a call from a woman at a radio station in New York City," Weiner says. "She said, 'I want to know what you know about the crash, and whether there were Syracuse people on board.' I told her what we had confirmed at the time, which was nothing.

"Then she says, 'We need someone to go on the air live with us right now—I'll give you $150 if you go on the air with us.' Again I said no, so she asked if there was anybody else willing to talk. She wouldn't give up, and that was a sign of what was to come the rest of the evening. I was there all night, and I saw a lot of callousness."

Weiner said that long before the crash of Flight 103, he had learned how to handle this type of story the hard way—through experience. As a result of covering other death-related stories, he could better understand and even justify much of what went on at the paper as well as elsewhere that night.

For example, with only the first initials and last names of students scheduled on the flight confirmed, the *Herald-Journal* staff was left with the difficult task of piecing together biographical data on each victim. This meant talking to family members and friends just a few hours after they had learned of the tragedy, a move that upset some Syracuse journalism students.

"The question, 'How do you feel?' makes me crazy," says Shelly Weiss, a senior majoring in advertising whose grief-stricken face seemed to appear on CNN every 30 minutes for two days after the crash. "It's one thing if it's something great, but if 35 of your friends or your son or daughter were just killed by terrorists, how do you *think* you would feel?

"It's an invasion of people's rights," adds Weiss. "After four years of college, I have what to do and not to do ingrained in my head—and now I've seen all that thrown away."

Reporter Weiner agrees that some of the questioning—especially that done at Hendricks Chapel—was not in good taste. But he stands by the *Herald-Journal*'s decision to make phone calls to the victims' families that first night.

"This is one of the dirty jobs in journalism, but you have no choice," Weiner says. "People want the information, and they want it now. Once you've done this type of story a few times and done it right, you develop a certain sensitivity. You learn to be human about it."

Keith Shaw, a senior in journalism who had covered several murders as an intern on the *Herald-Journal*'s city desk, echoes Weiner.

"People are saying they were bothered by the cameras," says Shaw of the Hendricks Chapel coverage. "But it didn't bother me that much. I understand where the journalists were coming from—they have a job to do, and people would have been more mad if [no coverage] was done."

And yet, says Shaw, he *was* bothered by the lack of reverence shown by reporters and photographers toward the sanctity of the service.

Covering the deaths of 35 students—colleagues and friends—was a uniquely difficult emotional task for Syracuse University journalism students.

For *Daily Orange* Editor-in-Chief Abbott—and others—the scars caused by the crash of Flight 103 have diminished, but they have not gone away. The staff of the daily was able to produce a memorial edition that appeared the day after students returned from winter break.

A month later, Abbott was one of two students to sit on a media panel sponsored by the Syracuse University chapter of the Society of Professional Journalists titled "Media Coverage: Where to Draw the Line."

Speaking to a crowd of more than 300, Abbott explained that "in our coverage of the Hendricks Chapel service [for the memorial edition], we didn't show pictures of anybody crying. . . . Our reporters were as sensitive as possible."

Clearly, said Abbott, a line could have been drawn.

Abbott recalls another memorial service that took place after students had returned to campus following the winter break. The service was in the Carrier Dome, a large sports arena on the campus. Photographers were confined to restricted areas away from the students.

Abbott remembers one photographer who shot the students with a telephoto lens.

He "panned over us once and I said, 'Once, OK, it's legitimate.' Then he panned over us a second time, and I said, 'OK, maybe he missed us the first time.' But the third time was too much—it seemed like the guy was just trying to get us all crying at once.

"Well, he succeeded. The next day I opened up *The New York Times*— and there I was, crying on the front page of the B section.

"I'm just glad I was crying with my head in my hands."

# 19

# No Consequences

## *by* Jody Powell

*Editor's Note:* In August 1993, Vincent Foster, Jr., a lawyer in the Clinton White House, committed suicide. Foster had been a close friend of the Clintons, a law partner with Hillary Clinton in Little Rock, Arkansas, and one of the key advisors in the Clinton administration. He was also the subject of several critical news analyses and editorials in the press, especially the *Wall Street Journal.*

Much discussion about the responsibility of the news media followed his death. Many observers suggested that the press blithely destroys people as if it were doing no more than playing a game. Foster himself suggested as much in one of the notes he left behind. Many journalists did much soul-searching as a result.

However, it should be noted that many questions about Foster's suicide have remained unanswered. And since his death, much has been revealed about his role in what has been termed the "cover-up" of the Whitewater scandal, directly involving President Clinton and his wife Hillary. Thus, many journalists feel that probing questions about Foster's suicide were justified and in the public's interest.

In this essay Jody Powell provides a personal touch to the consequences of suicide and the role of the press. He was press secretary to President Jimmy Carter and is now a partner in a Washington PR firm. This is the complete article written by Powell. A shorter version appeared in the *Washington Post*, August 15, 1993.

I confess that I do not come to this subject with anything approaching objectivity. Just over 18 years ago my father took his own life. All of us who loved him were as shocked and grief-stricken and unbelieving as were the family and friends of Vincent Foster.

Fortunately for us and for him, my father was a south Georgia farmer not a public servant. We came to understand, or at least to think that we understood, why he did what he did without the assistance of a ghoulish pack of sensation-crazed journalists.

When Vincent Foster wrote about ruining people as "sport" and about journalists being free to do it without fear of consequences, he spoke the truth.

Were there any doubt of that truth, the despicable conduct of Washington journalism since his death has surely removed it.

Two clear journalistic approaches were well-established within hours of his death. Both could only spring from some fine combination of willful ignorance and callous indifference. A five minute conversation with any two-bit psychiatrist or psychologist could have taken care of the ignorance, but that would have left the indifference factor, so probably nothing would have changed.

The more subtly destructive story line hung from the theory that people must kill themselves because they are really disappointed about some event or series of events. This provided an excuse to publish every conceivable shortcoming, mistake, or weakness in Vincent Foster's life, real or imagined, that any reporter could dream up. After a couple of days of this you would have thought that Vince Foster was singularly responsible for everything that had gone wrong in the White House from day one. It cleared the way for all manner of commentators to slither forth with their uninformed personal opinions on just why this man killed himself. We've heard the "big-pond, small pond" theory and the "you need to experience failure before forty theory" and the "small-town insularity" theory, to mention but a few. They all have at least two things in common: They insult the memory of a decent man; and the people who are spouting them have no idea on God's earth what they are talking about, nor the decency to keep their mouths shut.

The second and more obviously vicious approach is based upon the equally ignorant idea that if someone takes his own life there must be some really big, dark, ugly thing there that we just don't know about. That tawdry exercise began the day after Vincent Foster's death when one network correspondent declared: "Vincent Foster's friends do not want to believe that there is something looming that could bring public pain to the Clinton White House." (To make sure no one could confuse TV journalism with civilized behavior, these words were spoken over footage of Vincent and Lisa Foster walking quietly together in happier times.) There was, of course, no smidgen of evidence in the reporter's "report" to support such outrageous innuendo.

Now, despite weeks of frenzied activity by investigative teams and rumor mongers, there is still no evidence of anything other than a personal tragedy. But that hasn't been a problem for the good sports in the no consequences crowd. On Thursday, the *New York Times* ignored or dismissed with disdain Vincent Foster's criticisms of journalism and decided that everything else he said should be taken seriously enough to warrant the appointment of a special counsel.

(The *Times* also was kind enough to instruct us in how we could "best mourn" Vincent Foster. It was by "understanding that he identified curable defects in the White House." Excuse me, Timespersons, he identified some defects alright, but you didn't have to jump on the shuttle to find them. Unfortunately, the real defects he identified give no evidence of being "curable." And by the way, don't take this personally, but no one who truly mourns Vincent

Foster needs pompous, self-serving advice on how "best" to do it from you or the *Wall Street Journal* or anyone else.)

Intertwined with all this has come an array of familiar journalistic dodges, copouts, and deceits. One of the more despicable has been the repeated use of this tragedy by those with personal and political axes to grind—or those without the wit to come up with anything better to say that day—to bludgeon Vincent Foster's friends and colleagues. Even MacNeil-Lehrer, apparently trying to prove that you don't have to be commercial to be crass, trotted out an essayist who used Foster's death to attack his friend in the Oval Office for avoiding the draft.

The President has been called a liar because he said within hours of his friend's death that he had no idea of the pain he was in or why he did what he did. But, of course, with hindsight, perhaps there were signs, and if someone had seen them all and had interpreted them just right—if presidents and all the rest of us were as smart as journalists. . .

A slightly less obnoxious variant of the above is the time-worn "devil made me do it" excuse for journalistic misconduct. In this case, it takes the form: "If only everyone else were perfect, we wouldn't be so horrible. If only the White House press office or counsel's office [in the midst of great stress and personal trauma] had anticipated every allegation and innuendo we could dream up, we would be acting like responsible adults and decent human beings. Honest, we really would."

Then there is the "how to smear a man and pretend you didn't mean it" ploy. The most infamous and wide spread examples make use of the fact that Vincent Foster chose to end his life in a quiet, dark park, far from friends and family, rather than in his office or bedroom or the "park within walking distance of his house" or wherever else any journalist thinks he should have chosen. All that is needed to perfect the deniable smear is to mention in passing that the park is rumored to be a favorite spot for "assignations." It is not difficult to determine that many people who commit suicide pick out-of-the-way places to make absolutely sure that their bodies are not discovered by a friend or loved one. I believe that is what my father did. That is almost certainly what Vincent Foster did. Thus is a man's final act of kindness toward those he loved twisted into implications of infidelity or worse, contorted beyond all reason and decency to inflict additional pain on already suffering friends and family by people who clearly care not what they do.

Finally, running through it all is the old familiar reporter's trick of avoiding responsibility for one's actions by attributing causation to some inanimate object or event. How many times have we all been told that "this (statement, report, question, or you fill in the blank) can only prolong this painful (insert crocodile tear) controversy."

But things don't act, people do. Washington doesn't do things to people, people do things to people. At the moment a whole host of people who think rather highly of themselves are doing terrible, unforgivable things to a very few people who have done absolutely nothing to deserve it. And, as Vince Foster tried to say, when people do things that are wrong and cruel and unfair, there ought to be retribution, consequences, a price to be paid.

For the journalists involved in the sport of the moment there will be no consequences, no price, no more than there has ever been. That will only change when journalists are willing to apply to each other something like the same standards they so freely impose on everyone else. Any number of reporters with whom I have spoken over the past few weeks have privately expressed their disgust at what is taking place. I have no doubt that there are many others who feel the same way. That is all well and good; but for any real good to come of it, some of those in journalism who enjoy the respect of their peers will have to find the courage to point the finger of public condemnation at the rotten apples and shoddy behavior in their own profession.

But that is not likely to happen, and we all know it. So let the games continue. It's a blood sport, of course, and it's beginning to make a lot of the spectators sick. It's a strange sort of game because one side appears to honor no rules that amount to very much. But Washington, as you gentle folk of the fourth estate are kind enough to inform us when it suits your purposes, is a tough town where you need a thick skin and the ability to take your lumps like a man if you're gonna survive. A lot of truth in that, I suppose, unless you happen to have picked just the right Washington profession.

# 20

# My Truth, Their Consequences

## by Robert H. Williams

*Editor's Note:* Vincent Foster's suicide forced many journalists to examine their consciences to determine how they would respond to the ethical problems raised by the potential damage news media can cause. For Robert H. Williams, it meant looking back at his beginnings as a journalist and his experience in dealing with such dilemmas.

Williams is now an editor for the *Washington Post,* where this article was published on August 15, 1993.

> *"Here, ruining people is considered a sport."*
> —*The late Vincent Foster Jr., in a note.*

Tom Duffy was an admired, if not universally beloved, professor of journalism who had been a splendid editor at the East St. Louis Journal until his career there ended under an ethical cloud. Specifically, the Frank "Buster" Wortman gang he'd fought so hard and so long from the editor's chair turned out to be holding some of Tom's loan papers, acquired by a third-party lender. His ethical quandary followed him to his grave.

Duffy was my first editor, and in our only interview that spring of 1958 he asked me just one question: Why do you think I should hire you to be a reporter here?

Without hesitation and with complete confidence I responded, looking him in the eyes, "Because I am kind."

He hired me on the spot.

I've laughed, somewhat cynically, about that over the years, but eventually I came to realize that I had not lied to him, and that he had seen some truth in what I said that morning. But like the ethics of Tom Duffy, the kindness of my beginnings has faced the tests of harrowing experience, and I have failed myself and others. It hasn't always been easy to recognize that a borrowed C-note here might be called in as payment due from somewhere else next week.

My very first brush with this sort of duality came in that first year in the newspaper business, working for Duffy on what was by then the Metro-East

Journal. I was assigned that fall to cover politics around St. Clair County, and specifically an upcoming election in Cahokia Township. A lot of people told me a lot of things, and from it I concluded that an old-line politician named George Pluff was being dumped so that the party (one of those Southern Illinois coalitions that included everybody white and with money to contribute) could extend itself politically into a new tract housing development, one of those that spent most of this past summer under water.

I wrote the story, and neither I nor anybody on the city desk thought that perhaps I should invest a moment or two to talk to Mr. Pluff. So my first major thumbsucker, while politically on target and amazingly detailed, was a betrayal of the very reason I had been hired.

I was of course astonished to walk into the newsroom the next day and find George Pluff and several supporters waiting for me. He was an old man, white-haired and bent, with pain in his eyes, a lifelong citizen and backwater pol suddenly at the depth of humiliation. I shifted into a defensive crouch and asked if there had been any factual errors in the story, and it was in that precise moment that the ceramic glaze of professional journalism began to harden my soul. It had not been too long, remember, since Harry Truman gave us the Killer's Kreed: If you can't stand the heat, stay out of the kitchen.

After Pluff and his friends left, my city editor, Rube Yelvington, assigned me to write a full-fledged takeout for the front of the Sunday think section, on Cahokia and its history and future and political cast of characters, and in doing this piece I learned how to bury an apology inside column yards of never-ending type. The time had not yet come when a newspaper could or would admit its mistakes in a straightforward manner.

Which brings us into the part of the 20th century where journalism caught ethics and reporters got more or less honest, and to Donald E. Santarelli, who has walked through the mist of my bedroom in the early morning hours more times than I would like to admit over the past 19 years.

According to the ghost, I ruined Donald Santarelli in 1974. In reality, there was no ruin; he is, after all, a successful Washington lawyer and partner in a firm that bears his name. He simply lost his job, and perhaps the opportunity to continue work he had begun in the area of public policy. But I did not let that enter into the picture last Thursday when I made an appointment to see him for the purpose of making an apology. We stood face to face in the foyer of his offices and I told him I was sorry I had done what I did, and he was all his young manhood had promised, gracious, warm and accepting. He told me how bad it had hurt.

The year, as I say, was 1974, and the Nixon administration was hitting bottom, and the president and I were sharing a propensity to drink martinis and toast inanimate objects. On April 8, the Newspaper Guild at The Post went out on strike, a notorious walkout that featured no picket lines and no admonition to any other union to do anything. The Guild's muscle would come simply from "withholding our excellence." After 11 days we all came back and took essentially what The Post had offered before. It cost a couple of paychecks.

Except I was running on empty, as usual, and could not miss any paydays. And so, with strike benefits of something like $35 a week, I called an old friend at the Philadelphia Inquirer and contracted to write some pieces for its Sunday magazine, all nebulously related to a Philadelphia circulation. I completed some of them after I'd been back to work at The Post for several weeks. One was about Donald E. Santarelli, who'd been born in Hershey into an old-line Italian family and who'd become head of the Law Enforcement Assistance Administration here in Washington.

It is important right here to remember that I did not set out to ruin Santarelli. I was not even a player in the Washington scheme of things; I was riding the national copy desk rim and changing "that" to "which" and "which" to "that" wherever those words appeared, and I was out there to find food for my children's bellies and to pay for the roof over my head and the clothes on my wife's back.

In April, Santarelli had released a study showing that the crime rate in the nation's five largest cities was several times higher than reported by the citizens, and that in Philadelphia the figure was five times as high. That and Santarelli's Hershey upbringing were the pegs for this magazine piece. I interviewed Santarelli several times for the article, and I just loved him. My most vivid memory is not of what Santarelli said that was to boomerang on him but where he was standing when he said it—next to his desk on which was a plaque whose words seemed to describe his own life: "Quality and Candor."

I'd asked him how the White House had reacted when he presented the crime report, which put the crime rate on a dizzying upward pace at the end of 1973, when the Nixon machinery was still crowing about 1972 improvements.

He walked toward the window, thrust his hands into his pockets and, to quote my own article, replied:

" 'That's interesting,' or 'Thank you,' or something like that. There is no White House. There is no White House anymore."

At that point, or perhaps it was a sentence or two or three later, he said, "It pains me, but I think he should resign."

He didn't put it off the record, and I wasn't about to suggest that he might want to. He later said he had misunderstood the ground rules, and it is almost certain than I did, too, if there were any.

I finished writing the article on May 6 and mailed it the next day. The story appeared on June 2, and it turned out to be a pretty good one. The headline said "Santarelli the Super-Cop." But it was rather anticlimactic for Santarelli and for me, because late in May the Associated Press had gotten an advance copy of the magazine and had moved a story that contained not a peep about Hershey and Santarelli's fluent Italian, but only about this business of Nixon resigning.

Nixon in fact, accepted Santarelli's resignation two days after publication of the magazine piece. I was able to rationalize Santarelli's downfall as in fact a stroke of good luck for him. I had helped him extricate himself from an administration gone amok.

The Washington Star noted with some satisfaction that this journalistic coup of mine had been staged during the period that we at The Post had been "withholding our excellence"—although in fact claiming credit for such an affair falls more in the category of a terrorist group claiming "credit" for bombing a bus station.

The truth is that I'd simply gone to see Donald Santarelli to take some notes and write a story. But I had been a professional journalist for 16 years, as a reporter and an editor, and I knew a good quote when I saw one—especially with the Watergate drama churning along. I was on a remote fringe of the biggest story The Washington Post has ever had, and nothing would do at that instant but that I would deal myself in.

What had happened here? Is this the essence of classical tragedy, the fall of the mighty and the powerful through a string of simple events chained together in an Aristotelian progression of spiritual DNA?

Well, not very likely.

Perhaps it was an accident. But whatever it was, Donald E. Santarelli was able to stand the heat, with dignity and grace.

On Thursday evening, during a telephone conversation, Santarelli summed up the matter succinctly, and told me that "If you thought you learned a lesson, I learned one too: that in this town to be too free with one's views has its costs, sometimes the ultimate cost. To that end I have that much to thank you for."

# 21

# Privacy and the First Amendment

## *by* Floyd Abrams

---

*Editor's Note:* The growing concern about privacy has caused the enactment of laws protecting people's privacy, especially in certain situations such as rape. But are these laws in violation of the First Amendment to the Constitution?

Author Floyd Abrams is one of America's leading attorneys on issues of freedom of the press and the First Amendment. He is a partner in the New York law firm of Cahill Gordon & Reindell. This article appeared in *NewsInc.*, July/August 1989.

---

Consider the following situation. A woman is raped. A Florida newspaper learns the victim's name from the police. A state law makes it a crime to publish the name of a rape victim. The newspaper nonetheless prints the victim's name.

Question: Is the state law constitutional? Does the First Amendment permit the state to make it a crime to publish truthful information given to a newspaper by a state official? Or, to put it a different way, can the interest of the rape victim in her privacy overcome the right of the press to report accurately?

That the question can even be raised—it now awaits decision by the U.S. Supreme Court—says much about the growth of privacy law in America. It is, as legal doctrine goes, a new area of law with a pedigree less than a hundred years old. In some cases, particularly those involving misconduct by the government, privacy law alone protects what Supreme Court Justice Louis Brandeis called "the right to be left alone." It is a great and uniquely American body of law. In other areas, however, often involving privacy suits against the press, privacy law sometimes seems on a collision course with the First Amendment.

The law has generally been clear that so long as a newspaper tells the truth it can publish freely without fear of criminal or civil punishment. No libel suit, for example, can succeed against a newspaper that publishes a true story. If anything, the law is even clearer that if truthful information is provided the press by the government, the press may not be punished for printing it.

Privacy law is different. Many states permit recovery against a newspaper, even if it publishes information that is true, so long as what is printed is extremely intimate and does not serve the public interest. Criminal laws, such as that in Florida, add special risks to the press as it decides what to print.

The trouble with this is that people—even quite reasonable people—can differ about what the public interest is. Editors may and do, for example, disagree about whether to publish the names of rape victims. The name of the Central Park jogger who was brutally beaten and raped has been withheld by most of the New York press. At least one newspaper and one television station, however, have published her name. Could the state punish them if a New York statute existed similar in scope to the Florida statute?

It is true that in many situations the publication of a rape victim's name serves little useful purpose. That—and the embarrassment of the victim—is why so many newspapers choose not to publish the name of rape victims.

In some situations, however, the accurate description of a rape committed that includes the name of the victim can serve to expose in stark terms a social evil that our society has done far too little to prevent or punish. Florida's statute could have prevented the public from hearing that former Florida senator Paula Hawkins had been the victim of a sexual attack when she was a child, a revelation that greatly served the public.

How, then, can we reconcile the claims of privacy and those of the public to be informed? One way is to acknowledge that editorial decisions about which truths to publish are sometimes difficult. Somebody has to make them. That somebody, for better or worse, should be the press, not the state. Except in the rarest of circumstances, the publication of truthful information should be protected by the law.

That does not mean that the press should not be criticized when it decides wrongly—or we think it has. What the press has the right to do, as Supreme Court Justice Potter Stewart noted, is not always the right thing to do. It does mean that the Florida case should be decided by the Supreme Court (as I believe it will) in favor of the Florida newspaper. And, more broadly, it means that when we hear the word "privacy," we should listen carefully before we cheer too quickly.

# 22

# No Anonymous Accusers

## *by* Nat Hentoff

*Editor's Note:* Suppose a prominent person is charged with rape but the accuser is never publicly identified. The story hits the headlines and the accused suffers the agony of public exposure in the news media while the case is tried in court. Suppose the court finds that the accusation was false; the prominent person is cleared, except for the scars left by all the negative publicity. Meanwhile, the person bringing the false accusation has no wounds or scars. What is the answer to this dilemma?

Nat Hentoff expresses the philosophy that would probably guide most journalists on this issue. He is a nationally syndicated columnist who writes about freedom of speech and press and civil liberties. This article appeared in the *Washington Post* on April 27, 1991.

When all the debates, recriminations and edgy justifications for printing the name of the Palm Beach rape victim are over, what should the press have learned about covering future rape stories?

Largely overlooked—except by Harvard law professor Alan Dershowitz and American Civil Liberties Union President Nadine Strossen—is a basic precept of our system of justice: There should be no anonymous accusers.

If the woman who says she has been raped gives the police the name of the alleged rapist, and that name is printed, so should her name be. Or if the name of the accused gets into print—or on the air—in any other way, so in fairness should the name of the accuser.

The way it is now, only the accused is named in most cases, and even if he is later exonerated, his reputation is not likely ever to be made whole again. Should William Kennedy Smith, for instance, turn out to be innocent, the albatross of the accusation will be with him for the rest of his life.

In a post facto report in the New York Times on how its editors agonized over whether to print the woman's name, we are told that they "discussed whether they could visualize the woman moving to another area of the country and escaping the stigma of being involved in the notorious case."

Did the editors of the Times put William Kennedy Smith in a similar scenario?

Once the name of the alleged victim is public, there is now a standard—set by the Times—of prejudicial reporting on the woman involved that should be avoided by all journalists, and it will surely be avoided henceforth by the Times.

A background story on either the victim or the accused should not have the aftertaste of an indictment. The Times' "biography" of the woman in Palm Beach—by Fox Butterfield and Mary B. W. Tabor—read as if it were from the notebooks of Kennedy family investigators. The woman had a child out of wedlock, a high school friend said she "had a little wild streak," and she actually frequented bars. (Would this last revelation have been printed if the story had been about a man?) And at the very end of the story, one of the reporters, having peeked in the window of the woman's very young daughter's room, discloses to waiting Times readers the titles of two books on the child's shelf: "Babar's Anniversary Album" and "Two Minute Bible Stories."

What could have been the journalistic intent behind that exclusive? To contrast the innocence of the child—not yet aware of what "a little wild streak" can get you into—with the state of her mother?

On the other hand, if in the record there had been reports that the woman had filed false rape charges in the past, that information, of course, would belong in any story about the accusation. It hardly happens that often, but women have filed charges of rape out of revenge, out of momentary rage or because they're emotionally disturbed.

One reason for naming an accuser that not only has no justification but is also rather repellent has to do with removing the stigma of rape by bringing the victim into the light, whether she wants to make that contribution to future victims or not.

This is Pecksniffian utilitarianism—the greatest good for the greatest number as decreed by the great benefactor who is himself immune from being wounded. Michael Gartner, president of NBC news, is a leading advocate of this transformation of journalism into mass psychotherapy.

Moving from Palm Beach, let us take an even more difficult case—although to most people, including most journalists, it is being handled with the requisite sensitivity.

On April 26, the New York Times reported that a 47-year-old gym teacher in the Bronx had been arrested and charged with the rape of a 13-year-old female student in his office. The man's wife told the Times that the charges against her husband were "absolute lies," that in 20 years of teaching, he has never had a problem and that he is the father of three teenagers.

On the other hand, residents in the area of the school told the Times reporter that they were former students of the gym teacher and that he had, said the Times—without checking these reports—"a reputation for touching female students in suggestive ways."

The story noted that "the police did not identify the victim because of her age and the nature of the crime." Not mentioned is that there have been occasion in the past when students have falsely accused their teachers of rape. Not to mention Tawana Brawley's tumultuous fantasy.

Was it necessary, at this point, to mention either name? Does the people's right to know always include the right to know everything right away—even when what is thought to be known so far may be destructively misleading?

# 23

# Do Reporters Have a Right to March?

## *by* Stephanie Saul

*Editor's Note:* Is it conflict of interest for a reporter to take a stand on an issue that he or she is covering? In the past, most journalists would have said yes. In fact, most news organizations have discouraged reporters and editors from even belonging to a political party because it might jeopardize their objectivity. Even if objectivity remains intact, does it jeopardize the public perception of the objectivity of journalists and their organizations if they publicly take part in an event or a cause?

This, too, has been the subject of increasing argument, both publicly and privately within news organizations. Here is a summary of some of the recent debate. Stephanie Saul is a reporter in the Washington bureau of *Newsday,* the Long Island daily. She did not participate in the April 1989 march in Washington, D.C. This article appeared in the *Columbia Journalism Review,* July/August 1989.

In nearly twenty years of writing about abortion for *The New York Times,* Linda Greenhouse frequently thought about taking a public stand on the issue. After what she calls "careful consideration," she finally acted, joining thousands of marchers in a Washington demonstration. Their aim: to fend off a reversal or revision of the Supreme Court's 1973 *Roe* v. *Wade* decision legalizing abortion.

Greenhouse was by no means the only journalist who took part in the April 9 march. Dozens of reporters and editors were there, most of them without the knowledge or approval of their employers. But Greenhouse's participation caused the most controversy because she covers the Supreme Court for the country's most prestigious newspaper. And her dual role has sparked a renewed debate over an old ethical question: To what extent may a journalist become involved in public controversies?

Many editors believed that the issue had been resolved after the 1960s and early '70s, when reporters found it difficult to remain neutral on civil rights and Vietnam and management drew up guidelines prohibiting political activism. Warren Hoge, the *Times*'s assistant managing editor, for instance, says he was surprised when the issue came up again "because I just assume that reporters realize that you forfeit the right to take part in a political demonstration." Now, editors are busy re-educating their staffs, particularly the younger members. "What's been noted here is that there's a generation gap, with younger reporters not seeing this as an issue and older reporters thinking it is terribly obvious," says Boyce Rensberger, science editor of *The Washington Post.*

After the word filtered down that some *Post* reporters and editors had marched, managing editor Leonard Downie, Jr., and executive editor Benjamin C. Bradlee issued a memo ordering anyone who had participated in the march to refrain from further coverage of the abortion debate. Then Downie began a series of ethics discussions with his staff. At some other newspapers, editors issued memos restating or redefining policies regarding political activism. And during an interview for a Nieman Fellowship, *Chicago Tribune* reporter Ann Marie Lipinski was pressed on the ethical dilemma by Harvard professor Helen Vendler. "She was very fascinated with where reporters draw the line," says Lipinski, who believes strongly that reporters should avoid community activism. "She was pressing me on various gradations of where reporters draw the line." (Lipinski was selected for this fall's Nieman class.)

Vendler's question is central to preserving public trust in the media. But, despite its importance, the question has never been definitively resolved.

There seems to be a consensus that it's improper to participate in a public controversy while covering it. Several journalists who cover the high court with Greenhouse were stunned by her action. "There's no way you can explain those two acts, one journalistic and one political, as compatible," says the Baltimore *Sun*'s Supreme Court reporter, Lyle Denniston, who went out of his way to avoid being involved in the demonstration. "On the day of the march, I was sailing on my boat expressly so I wouldn't be associated with it," Denniston says.

But Greenhouse's case is more clearcut than most. Generally, journalists' views of the issue fall somewhere in between agreeing with the action Greenhouse took and that taken by former NBC president Bob Mulholland. While executive producer of *NBC Nightly News* during the early 1970s, Mulholland quit registering to vote.

"Those were very political times. The Nixon administration was going after journalists. Spiro Agnew was loose in the land," recalls Mulholland, now head of broadcast news at Northwestern University's Medill School of Journalism. "I wanted no one to be able to accuse me of being unfair."

"I start out with the presumption that a given individual is going to be a professional and try to present both sides of the issue," says Douglas Johnson, the National Right to Life Committee's legislative director. "But it is hard to operate on that presumption if somebody calls you up who you know has been marching outside the Supreme Court to defend *Roe* v. *Wade.*"

Johnson says he believed Greenhouse was an advocate of legalized abortion even before she chose to join the demonstration. But the anti-abortion group, which occasionally monitors speeches made by reporters who cover the abortion issue, doesn't consider Greenhouse's reporting particularly offensive. "Of people who regularly cover abortion issues, whose stories are consistently unbalanced, she would not be on the short list," says Johnson.

For Greenhouse the decision to march was "not a casual act at all. It's the first public act I've engaged in in the twenty-one years I've been at the *Times*," she says.

Greenhouse adds that she would never sign a petition supporting legalized abortion, making a distinction between placing her name on a written document and marching in a mass demonstration, which she views as an anonymous act. "I honestly thought it was just a few steps removed from the privacy of the voting booth," she says. "It's not as if I was marching under a banner that said 'New York Times Reporter for Choice.' I was just another woman in blue jeans and a down jacket."

"We don't have anonymity," Hoge counters. "I don't have it, Linda Greenhouse doesn't have it."

Those who sympathize with Greenhouse's position say that a professional journalist is capable of setting aside his or her personal beliefs while sitting down to type a story, particularly when covering a formally structured event like the presentation of oral arguments in a court case.

"I think reporters are capable of separating their personal views from what they report," says Tom Goldstein, a former *Times* reporter who is now dean of the Graduate School of Journalism at the University of California at Berkeley.

And many journalists who believe a reporter should not participate in a public controversy while covering related stories have no problem with participating in such an event while not covering the issue. *New York Newsday* reporter Alexis Jetter says she felt free to march because she does not cover abortion-related stories.

Another *Newsday* employee, former state editor Bob Keeler, used the same rationale when he participated in a couple of anti-abortion marches in Washington during the mid-1970s: "At that time, I was covering county government and not writing regularly about abortion. So I decided that my presence among thousands of other people would not affect my ability to be fair or the appearance of my ability to be fair." Later, however, when Keeler became Albany bureau chief and was covering abortion-related issues for *Newsday*, he stopped participating in such marches.

Despite his willingness to participate in a mass demonstration, Keeler registers to vote as an independent so as not to affiliate with a political party.

Others believe that any political expression should be taboo for a journalist. "We have spent the last fifty years trying to achieve a professional status in our society in which we approach the events we write about with what we hope would be the disinterestedness of a scientist," says *Post* ombudsman Richard Harwood. "That's impossible and I recognize it, but that's the attitude of mind we should have and that's the goal we should be after. I don't care if it's an abortion march or writing speeches on the side."

The Society of Professional Journalists' statement on ethics says that "secondary employment, political involvement, holding public office, and service in community organizations should be avoided if it compromises the integrity of journalists and their employers."

Newspaper policies vary.

• *The Philadelphia Inquirer*'s detailed policy, adopted in 1977, says that staff members "should be careful not to offend or give the wrong impressions to members of the public by blatantly espousing or expressing viewpoints on public issues." The policy statement goes on to prohibit staff members from wearing antiwar buttons, signing petitions, or otherwise identifying themselves with public issues.

Gene Foreman, the *Inquirer*'s managing editor, says he can recall only one incident in which the policy had been violated—when a film critic signed a petition complaining about the condition of a theater. Foreman, who says he has heard that at least one member of the *Inquirer* staff participated in the abortion march, adds, "At every opportunity, we're pointing out that our policy is quite clear on the subject."

• *The Washington Post* has a seven-page standards and ethics statement, written in the 1970s by Bradlee. "*Washington Post* reporters and editors are pledged to approach every assignment with the fairness of open minds and without prior judgment," it says. In another section it states: "We avoid active involvement in any partisan causes—politics, community affairs, social action, demonstrations—that could compromise or seem to compromise our ability to report and edit fairly." It also urges reporters to "make every effort to remain in the audience, to stay off the stage, to report the news, not to make the news."

In enforcing the policy, the *Post* has prohibited its reporters from appearing on Voice of America programs. "We don't want anyone in a foreign land to think we're agents of the government," Harwood explains. The newspaper has also prevented its employees from serving on a school board. And op-ed pieces by reporters must not take a stand on an issue, according to Downie.

• The *Times*'s policy requires that "staff members avoid employment or any other undertaking, obligation, relationship, or investment that creates or appears to create a conflict of interest with their professional work for the *Times* or otherwise compromises the *Times*'s independence and reputation."

The *Times*'s policy contains nothing specific about participating in marches. "Maybe no one thought it would ever come up," Hoge says.

So far, it appears that no one at any newspaper has been officially disciplined for participating. Greenhouse, who says she didn't think she was violating *Times* policy when she took part in the march, remains the newspaper's Supreme Court reporter. Just weeks after the demonstration she resumed the role of an observer, covering oral arguments in *Webster* v. *Reproductive Health Services,* the abortion case before the court this year.

"It's just a force of habit that when you sit down to write, you're acting as a *Times* reporter and not as a pro-choice activist," says Greenhouse, who believes that, despite her personal opinions, she can write stories "straight down the middle."

# 24

# Photographs That Lie

## *by* J. D. Lasica

*Editor's Note:* In a free-press system, as we've said, there is no law against telling a lie. Today it is easy to rearrange a photograph so that it has no connection to reality, although people will believe it to be a true representation because it is a photograph. Isn't that telling a lie? Although not illegal, most people would say it is unethical.

This raises a host of issues about the digital retouching of photographs for publication. These same issues also concern the visual representation of reality on TV and motion picture screens. This article explains technological developments in photography and examines the resulting ethical dilemmas.

J. D. Lasica is a features editor and columnist at the *Sacramento Bee.* This article was originally published in the *Washington Journalism Review* (now the *American Journalism Review*) in June 1989.

A few years ago I wandered into a seminar touting the wonders that technology would bring to the photographs of tomorrow. Up on the screen, a surreal slide show was in progress. One slide showed Joan Collins sitting provocatively on President Reagan's lap. *Click.* Joan was now perching, elfishly, on the president's shoulder. *Click.* Reagan had grown a third eye. *Click.* Now he was bald. *Click.* And so on.

A representative from the Scitex Corporation, a Bedford, Massachusetts, company that manufactures digital retouching equipment, said that computers could now alter the content of photographs in virtually any manner. The slides had all been produced electronically—with no trace of tampering.

The audience, clearly dazzled, tossed off a dozen or so questions about whether the machines could do this or that. Finally a hand shot up. "Nobody's said a word about the potential for abuse here. What about the ethics of all this?"

"That's up to you," said the representative.

Welcome to journalism's latest ethical nightmare: photographs that lie.

In the past few years, this razzle-dazzle digital artistry has begun to turn up at the nation's largest newspapers, magazines and book publishing houses. The trend has a lot of people worried.

Consider what has taken place already:

• Through electronic retouching *National Geographic* slightly moved one of the Great Pyramids at Gîza to fit the vertical shape of its cover in 1982.

• An editor at the *Asbury Park Press,* the third-largest newspaper in New Jersey, removed a man from the middle of a news photo and filled in the space by "cloning" part of an adjoining wall. The incident prompted the paper to issue a policy prohibiting electronic tampering with news photos.

• The *Orange County Register,* which won a Pulitzer Prize for its photo coverage of the 1984 Summer Olympics, changed the color of the sky in every one of its outdoor Olympics photos to a smog-free shade of blue.

• The editors of the book *A Day in the Life of America* could not choose a cover photo from the thousands of pictures taken by the world's leading photojournalists. They solved the problem electronically by taking a photo of a cowboy on horseback, moving him up a hillside and, for good measure, enlarging the crescent moon. "I don't know if it's right or wrong," says co-director David Cohen. "All I know is it sells the book better."

• For one of its covers, *Popular Science* used a computer to place an airplane from one photo onto the background of another aerial photo. And a number of magazines have combined images of people photographed at different times, creating composites that give the false appearance of a single cover shot.

• The *St. Louis Post-Dispatch* used a Scitex computer to remove a can of Diet Coke from a photo taken of Ron Olshwanger, winner of the 1989 Pulitzer Prize for photography.

Faster than you can say "visual credibility gap," the 1980s may be the last decade in which photos could be considered evidence of anything.

"The photograph as we know it, as a record of fact, may no longer in fact be that in three or five years," warns George Wedding, director of photography for the *Sacramento Bee.*

Jack Corn, director of photography for the *Chicago Tribune,* one of the first papers to buy a Scitex system, says the stakes are enormous. "People used to be able to look at photographs as depictions of reality," he says. "Now, that's being lost. I think what's happening is just morally, ethically wrong."

Digital technology's impact will be no less dramatic in other areas.

Within a decade, consumers will be able to buy a hand-held digital camera that uses a microchip instead of film, allowing the owner to "edit" photos. Soon you'll be able to remove your mother-in-law from that otherwise perfect vacation snapshot.

In the cinema, some experts are predicting the day when long-dead movie stars will be re-animated and cast in new films. "In 10 years we will be able to bring back Clark Gable and put him in a new show," John D. Goodell, a computer graphics consultant, told the *New York Times.*

Beyond such fanciful applications of digital technology, Goodell raises a dark scenario. Consider what might happen if the KGB or a terrorist group used such technology to broadcast a fabricated news bulletin about a natural disaster or an impending nuclear attack—delivered by a synthetic Dan Rather.

More likely than an assault by the Islamic Jihad on our airwaves will be an assault on our trust in visual images. Will photos be admissible evidence in a courtroom if tampering cannot be detected? Can newspapers rely on the truthfulness of any photo whose authenticity cannot be verified? As the price of these machines comes down, what will happen when the grocery-store tabloids start using—or abusing—them?

In television, too, the potential for abuse is great. Don E. Tomlinson, assistant professor of journalism at Texas A&M University, foresees the day when news producers try to re-create news events that they failed to capture on camera using exotic technology whose use was once confined to cinematic special effects. Airing such a simulation on a nightly newscast could confuse viewers about whether they're watching the real thing.

Tomlinson goes so far as to suggest that an unscrupulous TV reporter might use digital technology to fabricate an entire story because of ratings pressure, for career advancement or simply to jazz up the news on a slow day. A shark lurking near a populated beach, for example, could be manufactured using the file footage and a digital computer.

While digital machinations on television may pose the greatest threat to the credibility of visual images in the long run, today the war is being waged in print.

Ironically, publishers are snapping up these systems not for their photo-altering capabilities but for economic reasons. Newspapers and magazines are using digital computers to achieve huge savings in labor and materials, enhance the quality of color photo reproduction, push back editorial deadlines (because of the time saved) and transmit color separations to remote printing plants via satellite.

Among the publications already employing the technology are *Time, Newsweek, U.S. News & World Report, USA Today, Newsday,* the *Atlanta Journal* and *Constitution,* the *Providence Journal-Bulletin* and, most recently, the *New York Times.* (Incidentally, while Scitex is the industry leader in producing these machines, it is not alone in the field. Crosfield Electronics of East Rutherford, New Jersey, and Hell Graphics Systems of Port Washington, New York, also manufacture digital retouching systems.)

"People have no idea how much alteration is going on," says Michael Morse of the National Press Photographers Association. "When you're looking at that *Redbook* or *Mademoiselle* or *Sports Illustrated* tomorrow, there's a good chance somebody has done something to that picture."

Of course, some of this photo modification is familiar terrain. Pictures have been faked since the earliest days of photography in the 1850s. Retouching photos by hand was once common practice in many newsrooms, and photographers can change the composition of a black-and-white print in the darkroom. But over the years, ethical standards have tightened. Today retouching a news photo is forbidden at most publications, and faking a photo can be grounds for dismissal.

As the tools of the trade change, however, the rules of the game evolve as well. Altering a photo has never been so fast and seamless. Digital systems allow an editor or art director to capture, display, alter, transmit and publish a picture without it ever seeing photographic paper.

A photographer in the field is now able to capture an image on a light-sensitive semiconductor chip and send it to the newsroom via telephone line, microwave or even satellite. The image—a collection of hundreds of thousands of pixels, similar to the makeup of a TV screen—is then reassembled on the video monitor of a picture editing station, or "electronic darkroom," where an editor can size it, crop it, enhance the contrast and tone and correct minor flaws. From there the image is sent to a color laser plotter, which converts the pixels into signals of zeros and ones (representing the densities of magenta, cyan, yellow and black printing inks) and produces a color separation. While conventional processing reads a transparency or photo by exposing it to light, electronic scanning creates an instant digital representation of an image. *Voilà!* A process that would normally take hours is accomplished in minutes. With a plaything this seductive, it's easy to understand the temptation to "improve" a news photo at the stroke of a few keys.

*Rolling Stone* magazine used a digital computer to erase a pistol and holster slung over the arm of "Miami Vice" star Don Johnson after he posed for a 1985 cover shot. Editor Jann Wenner, an ardent foe of handguns, ordered the change; using a computer saved the time and expense of having the cover re-shot.

Unquestionably, this high-tech process is here to stay. The question thus becomes: Where do you draw the line?

"If someone wants to remove a tree from a photo or move two people closer together, that's crossing the line," says Dennis Copeland, director of photography for the *Miami Herald*. "The media's image has been hurt because of those few people who've abused the technology."

While a spot survey of editors, art directors and picture editors at major newspapers nationwide found no one who supported the notion of using digital technology to tamper with the integrity of a documentary news photograph, there was far greater acceptance of using it to create conceptual or illustrative photos.

The distinction is far from academic. Documentary photographs aim to portray real events in true-to-life settings. Conceptual photos are meant to symbolize an idea or evoke a mood. Because a studio shot of, say, a truffle is more akin to a still life than to the hard-edge realism of photojournalism—indeed, because the shot is staged in the first place—art directors and page designers are given wide latitude in altering its content.

What is happening, many photographers and picture editors fear, is that the distinction between the two styles is blurring, partly due to the new technology. Scott Henry, chief photographer for the *Marin County* (California)

*Independent-Journal,* detects in photojournalism "a quiet shift toward pictures as ornamentation or entertainment rather than reportage."

And George Wedding of the *Bee* says of tampered photographs, "Fabricated images that look authentic on first glance sometimes taint the believability of the pictures around them."

Wedding sees a trend toward increased reliance on conceptual photos, caused in part by the recent influx into newsrooms of art directors and designers who take their visual cues from art schools and the advertising field, where manipulation is the name of the game. "These people have not been taught the traditional, classic values and goals of documentary photojournalism," he says.

Joseph Scopin, assistant managing editor for graphics at the *Washington Times* (which uses the Scitex system), thinks those fears are overblown. "If you run a photo of someone holding a 4-foot-tall, 300-pound strawberry, it's pretty obvious to the reader we're playing with the images," he says.

Sometimes, however, the distinction can be lost on the reader.

The *Asbury Park Press* ran into that difficulty in 1987 when it ran a cover story in its "Health and Fitness" section on a new kind of beef with lower cholesterol. Says Nancy Tobin, the paper's design director, "We had a head-on shot of a cow munching hay and a studio shot of a beautiful salad, and [we] combined the two images on Scitex. People came up to us afterward and said, 'How'd you get that cow to eat that salad?' We labeled it *composite photo illustration,* but some people were left scratching their heads."

Readers may grow more accustomed to digital photography's use as it spreads from the feature sections to the rest of the paper. Last summer the *Hartford Courant* ran a Page One color photo that showed how the city's skyline will look after several new skyscrapers go up; the feat was accomplished with *Newsday*'s Scitex equipment. Experts say it won't be long before newspapers' real estate pages display computer-created photos, rather than rough "artist's conceptions," of planned developments.

But some observers worry that increased use of digital retouching will make readers skeptical about the integrity of even undoctored images.

"People believe in news photographs. They have more inherent trust in what they see than what they read," says Kenneth Kobre, head of photojournalism studies at San Francisco State University. "Digital manipulation throws all pictures into a questionable light. It's a gradual process of creating doubts in the viewer's mind."

It was precisely that concern that led *National Geographic,* the magazine that moved a pyramid, to rethink its position. Jan Adkins, former associate art director, explains: "At the beginning of our access to Scitex, I think we were seduced by the dictum, 'If it can be done, it must be done.' If there was a soda can next to a bench in a contemplative park scene, we'd have the can removed digitally.

"But there's a danger there. When a photograph becomes synthesis, fantasy rather than reportage, then the whole purpose of the photograph dies. A photographer is a reporter—a photon thief, if you will. He goes and takes, with a delicate instrument, an extremely thin slice of life. When we changed that slice of life, no matter in what small way, we diluted our credibility. If images are altered to suit the editorial purposes of anyone, if soda cans or clutter or blacks or people of ethnic backgrounds are taken out, suddenly you've got a world that's not only unreal but surreal."

Adkins promises that, at *National Geographic* anyway, "the Scitex will never be used again to shift any one of the Seven Wonders of the World, or to delete anything that's unpleasant or add anything that's left out."

But even if other publications begin to show similar self-restraint, critics warn, digital technology is making additional inroads that threaten the credibility of visual images.

Already, there are a half dozen software programs on the market, such as "PhotoMac" or "Digital Darkroom" for the Macintosh, that allow the user to edit photographs digitally. The programs retail for about $700.

And then there is the digital camera, a sort of hand-held freeze-frame video camera that should be in stores within a decade, at a price within reach of the average buyer. What disturbs many people about this device is that the original image exists in an electronic limbo that can be almost endlessly manipulated. The camera differs from Scitex digital retouching equipment, which works with an original photo or negative.

"The term *photographic proof* may already be an archaic term," says the *Bee*'s Wedding. "You used to be able to hold up a negative and see that the image is real. With the advent of digital technology, you're going to hold up a floppy disk and you're not going to see anything."

Adds Tobin of the *Asbury Park Press*: "This is scaring everyone, because there's no original print, no hard copy. From the moment the shutter is snapped, it exists only as a digitized electronic impulse. Talk about the ability to rewrite history! It literally will be possible to purge information, to alter a historic event that occurred five years ago because no original exists. There's enormous potential for great wrong and great misuse."

Scitex spokesperson Ned Boudreau says the digital industry addressed such concerns long ago. "To hear the critics tell it," he says, "it's like we've unleashed Joe McCarthy all over again. We haven't."

He says safeguards, such as an archiving system that stores originals where no one can get at them, can be built into the digital equipment. At present, however, manufacturers do not provide such options unless requested.

John Derry, director of graphic services for Chromaset, a San Francisco creative-effects studio that has used digital retouching for dozens of corporations' advertising campaigns, thinks Americans will learn to accept the technology as it becomes pervasive. "Maybe it's generational," he says. "My mother could never tell the difference between videotape and movies, between the hard, sharp edge of Johnny Carson and the soft look of motion picture film.

"As we move into this new technology, perhaps there will be people who won't be able to discern electronically manipulated images from undoctored images. But I think most of us are already pretty savvy about this stuff. If you show someone a picture of Reagan punching Gorbachev, most people won't think it's real. They'll think, Oh, look at this doctored photo. How'd they do that?"

None of this assuages the critics of digital technology, but even its detractors concede this much: It's not the technology itself that's the culprit. Machines aren't ethical or unethical; people are.

"You've got to rely on people's ethics," says Brian Steffans, a top graphics photography editor at the *Los Angeles Times*. "That's not much different from relying on the reporter's words. You don't cheat just because the technology is available."

Wedding of the *Bee* is less sanguine about the future of news photography: "I hope that 10 years from now readers will be able to pick up a newspaper and magazine and believe what they read and see. Whether we are embarking on a course which will make that impossible, I don't know. I'm afraid we have."

# 25

# Truth, Lies, and Videotape

## *by* Russ W. Baker

*Editor's Note:* Is it ethical for journalists to deceive news sources to get the real truth? Is deception justified if it results in necessary information that cannot be obtained in any other manner? Lately, these questions have been raised by some TV news programs in which hidden cameras or staged situations were used to make an effective news story.

The Society of Professional Journalists (SPJ) says hidden cameras and other forms of misrepresentation should be used only for these reasons: (1) The information obtained is of profound importance. It must be of vital public interest, such as revealing great "system failure" at the top levels, or it must prevent profound harm to individuals. (2) All other alternatives for obtaining the same information have been exhausted. (3) The journalists involved are willing to disclose the nature of the deception and the reason for it. (4) The individuals involved and their news organizations apply excellence through outstanding craftsmanship as well as the commitment of time and funding needed to pursue the story fully. (5) The harm prevented by the information revealed through deception outweighs any harm caused by the act of deception. (6) The journalists involved have conducted a meaningful, collaborative, and deliberative decision-making process.

The SPJ guidelines discuss criteria that do *not* justify deception, such as (1) winning a prize, (2) beating the competition, (3) getting the story with less expense of time and resources, (4) doing it because others did it, and (5) knowing that the subjects of the story are themselves unethical.

After reading this article, determine for yourself what was ethical and what wasn't. Author Russ W. Baker is a freelance writer who lives in New York City. This article appeared in the *Columbia Journalism Review*, July/August 1993.

They're like Hugh Hefner's rabbits: by turns fluffy, then aggressive, then sexy, but always profitable—and multiplying. In 1969 there was one television newsmagazine—*60 Minutes.* By 1989, *20/20* and *48 Hours* had joined the nest. Though some succumbed to the cruelties of nature, today there are seven, with more on the way. By fall, ABC will have three, CBS three, and NBC two. Even

Fox is getting in on the act, introducing *Front Page*, with correspondent Ron Reagan, the ex-president's son.

As the genre grows, each show seeks a distinguishing trait. For ABC's *PrimeTime Live,* the effort has proven wildly successful. Now finishing its fourth season, it is one of television's top-ranked shows, and likely to be with us to a ripe old age.

But it wasn't always that healthy. Despite voluminous hype, *PrimeTime Live* was practically born *PrimeTime Dead.* "It was supposed to be the second coming of broadcast news," recalls Eric Mink, TV critic for the *St. Louis Post-Dispatch.* "Instead, it was a laughingstock."

On August 3, 1989, *PrimeTime Live* debuted, emphasizing the "live" aspect: "Why did Thomas Root wind up on the ocean with a bullet wound? His first television interview, live. The American hostages in Lebanon: Can they be rescued? How do you punish their captors? Secretary of State Baker joins us live as military experts develop a plan." Plus: "Can men and women be just friends? . . . An electronic prison, worn on the body, monitored by computer, for one of the world's richest men. And Roseanne Barr, who says she's been dissected and critiqued, and she's ready to sound off. . . . Roseanne joins us live tonight."

The show tried to do too much. The anchors, Diane Sawyer and Sam Donaldson, wandered the studio, shoving mikes in the face of a live studio audience, facing the camera or each other, often sounding geeky, a bit like George Bush. Here's Donaldson on that first show: "Diane, going live without a script, you know, is exciting, but it's also a little scary. It's a little bit like Evel Knievel getting on his motorbike, trying to jump the Grand Canyon. If he makes it, it's terrific. If he doesn't make it, it's a long way down." Sawyer: "No parachutes here, no parachutes."

No one felt more like bailing out than Sawyer when a live remote from a playground on a later show revealed . . . a playground, with nobody there. An interview with a Chinese student dissident fell apart on-air, under the weight of technical difficulties and language barriers. *Saturday Night Live* found the show an easy target.

More trouble: Diane and Sam just didn't seem to get along. Then again, everybody and Sam didn't seem to get along. And that live studio audience—well, this wasn't quite David Letterman.

Instead of canceling, ABC started shifting. The "live" aspect faded out. By 1990, Diane and Sam were separated, she to stay in New York, he back to his Washington turf. But it wasn't star management that did the trick.

Instead, *PrimeTime* concentrated on investigations, partly by exploiting a device most of its subjects can't see and wouldn't like if they could: a hidden camera. Under the direction of investigative whiz and senior producer Ira Rosen, a *60 Minutes* veteran, and prolific hidden-camera producers like Robbie Gordon, the show has gone seriously undercover.

We've watched from the inside of a refrigerator as dishonest repairmen did nothing for a lot of money, witnessed televangelists faking miracle cures, watched day-care workers slap their charges and crooked doctors line up to buy and sell fraudulent workers' compensation claimants.

Although *PrimeTime* is hardly the first television show to employ the technology, it airs more secret-camera episodes than any other TV newsmagazine. "They seem to want to use a hidden camera every week," says Esther Kartiganer, a senior editor who vets shows for *60 Minutes* and likes to keep an eye on the competition. Actually, over the past twelve months there have been eight such pieces, but each packs such a wallop that they stick in the viewer's mind. And the impact of *PrimeTime*'s hidden-camera work is likely to spur its competitors further into the act.

Television newsmagazines have an insatiable hunger for the kind of documentation that looks good on screen. Palatial homes, incriminating memos, revealing audiotape—these have always been the truffles of the producer on the hunt. But secretly recorded video, where the viewers see the action with their own eyes, may be the tastiest delicacy of all. (It is an expensive delicacy, however: *PrimeTime* often spends twice as much on such stories as on regular pieces, because of extra labor and research.)

The raw power of such clandestine filming was well demonstrated in *PrimeTime*'s November 1992 segment on racism, called "True Colors." The show sent out two investigators, one white and one black, and watched how they were treated. From the employment agency that was courteous to the white but lectured the black, to the employees at a drycleaner who told the black that all jobs in the shop were filled, then moments later said the opposite to the white, to the auto salesman who quoted the black a higher price and stiffer terms than the white on the identical car—the show was a powerful evocation of the stalled civil rights march. By the time Diane Sawyer walked in and confronted the bigots, all they could do was sputter.

In the tradition of the *Chicago Sun-Times,* with its famed Mirage Bar sting of corrupt city inspectors (see "The Mirage Takes Shape," CJR, September/October 1979), *PrimeTime* set up a phony medical clinic in Los Angeles and filmed middlemen offering to supply doctors with patients whose ailments were bogus. The suppliers would get kickbacks; the doctors would collect on improper insurance claims. As the show made evident, rampant operations like this contribute to excessively high health care and insurance costs. The hard-hitting segment prompted California authorities to crack down.

*PrimeTime* has pointed a hidden camera into the London hotel room of Malawi's president, documenting the shopping binge of the leader of one of the world's poorest countries. It has shown Wichita students selling guns, Peruvians defrauding adoption-minded Americans by selling them unexportable babies, doctors who repeatedly misread mammograms, and a quadriplegic patient crying out amid filthy conditions at a veterans hospital, "Don't leave me, please! They're trying to kill me out there!" This April the show followed members of Congress to a lobbyist-funded vacation in Florida.

While *PrimeTime*'s reliance on this sexy but intrusive technology has not become a matter of public discussion, several aspects of hidden-camera journalism have triggered serious debate within ABC's walls. "There's a certain general unease at ABC News on what constitutes misrepresenting who you are," says a news division veteran. All hidden-camera shoots for the show must be pre-approved by the network's news division, which in turn gets an okay from ABC's legal department (state laws vary greatly in their tolerance of the practice; Texas, for example, is relatively easy, while Illinois is tough). ABC is rewriting its guidelines on the technique, incorporating lessons learned in recent years. Meanwhile, they rely on the guidelines developed by the Society of Professional Journalists.

Perhaps no story better illustrates the strengths and weaknesses of the medium than *PrimeTime*'s story on the Food Lion supermarket chain. On November 5, 1992, millions of Americans watched through the lens of a well-camouflaged camera as store employees took old meat and chicken, then relabeled and sold it as fresh. Former employees from several stores talked of managers retrieving food from dumpsters and dipping putrid ham in bleach instead of discarding it—all to reach departmental profit levels.

The program, shades of Upton Sinclair's 1906 *The Jungle,* shocked an enormous audience and jolted an industry. Food Lion's stock dropped about 15 percent the next day. The company, which calls itself America's fastest-growing supermarket chain, with almost 1,000 stores throughout the South, is still struggling to turn around poor employee morale and worse public perceptions.

The Food Lion story began with a tip from the United Food and Commercial Workers Union (Food Lion is nonunion) and documentation by the Washington-based Government Accountability Project (GAP regularly supplies reporters with massive research from its staff, which includes attorneys and law student volunteers). *PrimeTime* followed up with some seventy interviews of Food Lion employees.

Scrambling for visuals, the show sent in a field producer, Lynne Nuefer Litt, to get the goods. Litt secured a job in the meat department of two Food Lions in North Carolina and stayed two weeks—all it took to get the disturbing evidence.

The piece came out punching, with an interview with a woman from a Food Lion meat department: "I've seen my supervisor take chicken out of the bone can, make us wash it, and put it back out. And it was rotten."

Food Lion didn't exactly whimper. It launched a massive and aggressive p.r. effort, charging that *PrimeTime* had distorted the truth, exaggerated, and used manipulative, selective footage to back a pre-established point of view.

The company also filed a lawsuit, an odd one. Food Lion is asking the court to rule that undercover investigative reporting be actionable under the RICO (Racketeer-Influenced Corrupt Organization) statute. The case is pending, and the implications for the news industry, if any, are unclear.

Litt, the *PrimeTime* producer/Food Lion meat wrapper, was certainly undercover. She rigged references and wrote on her application: "I really miss working in a grocery store, and I love meat wrapping. . . . I would like to make a career with the company." She told a co-worker, Linda Anglin, who is about the same age and warmed quickly to her, that she had been recently divorced after ten years of marriage, which was true, and had moved down to North Carolina for a change, which wasn't. She explained her abrupt departure by saying a grandfather had just died.

Television is not alone with the subterfuge issue—print reporters have been known to go undercover and to debate the ethical considerations (see "To Sting or Not To Sting," cjr, May/June 1991). Besides, as Janet Malcolm pointed out in her famous *New Yorker* essay, even plain old interview journalism can involve betrayal (see "Dangerous Liaisons," cjr, July/August 1989). But hidden-camera journalism is unique in that its very nature requires lies or, at least, a lack of candor—and that seems to make some print ethicists crazy. One was the syndicated *Washington Post* columnist Colman McCarthy, who once studied to be a Trappist monk. After sardonically calling the Food Lion segment "really bold journalism," he added: "It's possible to uncover the truth by being untruthful, but where do television newspeople secure the right to legitimize their deceits? How about some truth-in-packaging as the program begins: 'We lied to get this story.' "

On the other hand, *60 Minutes* producer Don Hewitt contends that "People committing malfeasance don't have any right to privacy. . . . What are we saying—that Upton Sinclair shouldn't have smuggled his pencil in?"

However, Sinclair did not have to deal with television's thirst for pictures and its insistence on brevity, which sometimes means that context gets left on the cutting room floor. In one Food Lion sequence, Anglin is heard saying that she doesn't know how to clean the meat saw; the implication is that no one is bothering to maintain the equipment. But according to Anglin, *PrimeTime* didn't show the other part—in which she explains that she doesn't even *do* cleaning—it's not in her job description. In fact, Anglin says, it was Litt's job, and Litt had asked Anglin to stay late and help her. "She was fully aware that I didn't do that," Anglin says. "So she set me up on that one." On the other hand, Litt apparently hadn't been trained either, and never observed *anyone* cleaning the saw. *PrimeTime* seems to have made a fair point in an unfair manner.

This raises another question: Are the on-camera Food Lion workers victims or perpetrators? On the show, Sawyer declares that most of the Food Lion employees shown are hard workers, that *PrimeTime* meant no harm to them. "If so, they shouldn't even have showed our faces," says Anglin.

Sometimes the hidden pictures failed to prove anything. At one point the narrator described workers relabeling old chicken, as *PrimeTime*'s reporting indeed indicated; but on close inspection, viewers would note that the supporting before-and-after shots were of different parts of a bird.

Yet in the final analysis, *PrimeTime*'s evidence appears sound, especially as it is supported by the Government Accountability Project's volumes of affidavits from Food Lion workers. Hence, the show did its job—successfully illustrating a serious problem.

Or at least a piece of it. It is hard not to wonder whether the tight focus of the hidden camera leads journalists further into a typical trap—zeroing in on a villain when the problem is systemic. *PrimeTime* clearly explained that Food Lion's harsh labor policies encouraged employees to cut corners. But while *PrimeTime* was focusing on Food Lion, Atlanta's WAGA-TV was in the midst of a six-week hidden-camera investigation that documented alleged violations in every one of the twenty metro Atlanta supermarkets it surveyed. Many were offering for sale meats more than two weeks after the original expiration date. The station found trouble at Bruno's, Ingles Markets, A&P, Big Star, Kroger, and Winn-Dixie.

Viewers of hidden-camera journalism serve as their own eyewitnesses. "Seeing is believing," says NBC field producer Bob Windrem, who spent a dozen years each in TV and print. "That's why television has higher credibility with the public than print."

Not that aiming a hidden camera at someone is inherently worthwhile. For example, take this fairly recent *PrimeTime* promo: "Coming up: Is fraud in the cards? Behind the scenes of a tele-psychic scam, when *PrimeTime* continues." Given that standard, one might imagine another piece—with *PrimeTime* itself as a target: "Coming up: A dressing down at *PrimeTime Live!*" The subject: tensions between Sam and Diane, Diane and executive producer Rick Kaplan, and Kaplan and ABC News president Roone Arledge, widely reported in the press. Might we one day see *Hard Copy* airing secret footage of Arledge arguing with Kaplan in a mid-show call, as he did on April 29 while *PrimeTime* rolled a hard-hitting piece about congressmen frolicking on Captiva Island, courtesy of electronics industry lobbyists? Donaldson himself had received speaking fees from the same lobbyists and, according to *The Washington Post,* Arledge, over Kaplan's objection, angrily demanded a fuller on-air disclosure.

Clearly, a thin line separates substantive footage from voyeurism. Watching someone do virtually anything without their knowing can be titillating. Daydreaming on the job, licking an envelope while looking around nervously—innocent acts can seem dubious, even nefarious. Practitioners know this. "It's no secret to anyone that this hidden-camera stuff intrigues the viewers," says Kelly Ogle, investigative reporter at KWTV, a CBS affiliate in Oklahoma City. "They like to see people doing things when they don't know they're being watched."

Some veteran producers argue that hidden-camera journalism can be a sort of souped-up event, a contrivance that with too frequent use will make their craft look cheesy. Don Hewitt, for one, uses it only occasionally. "Taste and integrity and ethics—a lot of things go into this," he says. *60 Minutes* employed a hidden camera in preparing its much-acclaimed piece on how the U.S. government encourages U.S. firms to export jobs to Latin America. But, says Hewitt, "I cut out all the hidden-camera stuff—it would have looked like we were doing it for the sake of doing it."

However, the tabloid TV shows, less tortured over philosophical issues and desperate to supply five days a week of shockers, have taken eagerly to the practice. Local stations, too, are shooting away with this equipment, sometimes swatting flies with sledgehammers. KWTV bought a minicamera early this year and immediately used it to show minors buying beer at a hockey game. New York's WNBC smuggled one into a coffee shop meeting of an alleged pedophile group, the North American Man/Boy Love Association.

While a hidden camera in the locker room, the boiler room, or the conference room can be a powerful journalistic implement—witness *PrimeTime's* exposés on everything from crooked mechanisms to racism—it can cheapen the craft when misused. Abuse could also lead to calls for regulation.

What *PrimeTime Live* is wrestling with, and what an increasing number of TV journalists are likely to confront, are questions that boil down to this: Where is the threshold? When does investigating become spying? And is spying always wrong?

# VI

# Profit versus Service

One of the most uncomfortable developments in mass media in America over the past decade has been the move toward centralized ownership. Thomas Jefferson, James Madison, and other Founding Fathers of our system envisaged a journalism of competition. They believed truth would emerge from an open marketplace of ideas, but only if there were competing ideas. If only one voice were heard, we could not judge the truth of what was being said. Many different newspapers, each with their own perspectives, are necessary for us to get all the facts so we can make up our own minds.

Throughout American history we have feared the concentration of power that made our forebears flee their native lands. They came here to avoid religious, political, economic, or cultural domination. They fled from despotic kingdoms and religions, and they set up a political system that would minimize the chances for any one person or group to become all-powerful. The three branches of government that were devised—executive, legislative, and judicial—were to provide checks and balances on one another, lest any one become too strong. A free press was essential as a watchdog of all three branches of government.

The Founding Fathers also believed that newspapers should be published because their owners had something important to say. Only then would such publication perform a valuable service to the health and freedom of the community. The Founding Fathers without doubt did not ratify the First Amendment to give the press the freedom to make money. Freedom was to allow the press to publish the truth needed by the community, a service that only a competitive press could provide.

That notion still prevails among many mass media, but not all. An increasing number seem to be motivated not by public service but by profit. In the rush to profit, mass media businesses have increasingly joined forces, merged their operations to be more efficient, and catered to the largest common denominator.

Corporate journalism, however, has not come about simply because of greed. It is also the product of economic forces over which media owners have little control. Costs of everything have skyrocketed, from paper and equipment to salaries and benefits. A case can be made that without mergers and conglomerations, even more small media would be forced to go out of business.

News media, rather than entertainment media, have been most affected by corporate journalism and economic recession. Throughout the world of journalism, news staffs and news bureaus have been "down-sized," to use a 1990s corporate word, and news has been turned into entertainment to attract larger audiences to replenish the owner's dwindling coffers.

Fortunately, as we can learn elsewhere in this book, new technologies in print and broadcasting are making the process less expensive and more easily accessible to a larger number of people. This may to some extent help to offset the rise of corporate journalism and the decline of competition among mass media.

# 26

# The Empire Strikes

## *by* Ben Bagdikian

*Editor's Note:* "It is quite possible," writes Ben Bagdikian, " . . . that by the 1990s a half-dozen large corporations will own all the most powerful media outlets in the United States." In this article, taken from *The Media Monopoly,* Bagdikian describes what happens when fewer and fewer owners take over more mass media channels. He says that America has become a game show: "Winning is all that matters . . . cash prizes . . . get rich quick. We are turning the commonweal into the commonwheel of fortune."

And we are not alone. Bagdikian points out in his book that in Canada, three chains now control 90 percent of French-language daily newspaper circulation, and three other chains control two-thirds of all English-language newspaper circulation. In seven provinces, two-thirds or more of provincial circulation is controlled by a single chain.

Bagdikian, former dean of the Graduate School of Journalism at the University of California at Berkeley, was for many years a newspaper editor and reporter. This article originally appeared in *The Media Monopoly* (New York: Beacon Press, 1983, 1987). This version was published in *Media & Values,* Summer 1989.

If all major media in the United States—every daily newspaper, magazine, broadcasting station, book publishing house and motion picture studio—were controlled by one "czar," the American public would have reason to fear for its democracy.

The danger is not that this single controller would necessarily be evil, though this kind of extravagant power has a grim history. Whether evil or benevolent, centralized control over information, be it governmental or private, is incompatible with freedom. Modern democracies need a choice of politics and ideas, and that choice requires access to truly diverse and competing sources of news, literature, entertainment and popular culture.

Fortunately, no single corporation controls all the mass media in the United States. But something is happening that points in that direction. If mergers and acquisitions by large corporations continue at the present rate, one massive firm will be in virtual control of all major media by the 1990s. Given the complexities of social and economic trends, that is not inevitable. It is, however, quite possible—and serious corporate leaders predict—that by the 1990s a half-dozen large corporations will own all the most powerful media outlets in the United States.

The predictions are not groundless. They are based on extraordinary changes in recent years. At the end of World War II, for example, more than 80 percent of the daily newspapers in the United States were independently owned, but by 1986 the proportion was almost reversed: 72 percent were owned by outside corporations and 15 of those corporations had most of the business. The pace of takeovers by large national and multinational corporations is increasing. In 1981, 20 corporations controlled most of the business of the country's 11,000 magazines, but only five years later that number had shrunk to six corporations.

Today, despite 25,000 media outlets in the United States, 29 corporations control most of the business in daily newspapers, magazines, television, books and motion pictures.

But there is something strange about leaders of the media acquisition drive. Most would agree that one "czar" in control would be disastrous for democracy, yet they praise the march toward that unhealthy end. The media they control take every opportunity to report the beauties of corporate bigness. And while there is much news and commentary about media mergers and acquisitions, it is reported almost exclusively as a financial game without social consequences. The general public is told almost nothing of the dangers.

Compounding the trend has been the practice of companies already dominant in one medium, like newspapers, investing in a formerly competitive medium, like television. Ownership in every major medium now includes investors from other media—owners of newspapers, magazines, broadcasting, cable systems, books and movies mixed together. In the past, each medium used to act like a watchdog over the behavior of its competing media. The newspaper industry watched magazines, and both kept a public eye on the broadcasting industry. Each was vigilant against the other industries' lobbying for unfair government concessions or against questionable business practices. But now the watchdogs have been cross-bred into an amiable hybrid, with seldom an embarrassing bark.

Corporations do not purchase local newspapers and broadcast stations for sentimental reasons. They buy them as investments that will yield a maximum return as quickly as possible. When they buy a local monopoly, which is typical of newspapers, or an assured share of the market, typical of television, few investors can resist the spectacular profits that can be made by cutting quality and raising prices. The magnitude of this temptation is not what media executives talk about in public. But in private they and their acquisition agents are unequivocal. Christopher Shaw, the merger expert, for example, speaking at a session of potential media investors in October 1986, said that a daily monopoly newspaper with a 15 percent annual operating profit can, within two years of purchase, be making a 40 percent profit by cutting costs and raising advertising and subscription prices. The investors were told, "No one will buy a 15 percent margin paper without a plan to create a 25–45 percent margin."

## No Public Accounting

During most of this century the process of media consolidation remained quiescent, but beginning in the mid-1960s large corporations suddenly began buying media companies. The financial trigger was Wall Street's discovery of the best-kept secret in the business of American newspapers.

For decades American newspaper publishers cultivated the impression that they presided over an impoverished institution maintained only through sacrificial devotion to the First Amendment. This image helped reduce demand from advertisers for lower rates and agitation by media employees for higher wages. The truth was that most daily papers were highly profitable. But that was easy to conceal when newspapers were privately owned and no public reports were required.

The golden secret was disclosed by an odd combination: the fertility of founding families and the inheritance taxes.

Most of the country's established newspapers were founded or began major growth in the late 19th Century, including *The New York Times,* the *Washington Post,* and the *Los Angeles Times.* At the time they were modest operations. But by the 1960s, thanks to the country's population growth, affluence and heightened literacy, as well as to mass advertising and local monopolies, they had become substantial enterprises. Papers that once represented small investments (Adolph Ochs bought *The New York Times* in 1896 with only $75,000 of his own money) were now worth millions.

Inheritance taxes for family owners can be avoided for about three generations; a person could leave the estate in trust to someone alive at the time the will takes effect, often a grandchild, plus 21 years. By the end of the 1960s, the grace period for hundreds of papers was about to end and owners looked for a way to avoid overwhelming taxes (and possible forced sale of the papers) on the death of the heirs and the imposition of postponed estate taxes. One answer was to spread the ownership by trading shares on the stock market, thereby relieving family members of inheritance taxes on the entire property. Or the family could sell the paper outright to an outside corporation.

Major papers began offering their stock publicly in the early 1960s, thus opening their financial records to scrutiny by the Securities and Exchange Commission and Wall Street. So, suddenly, in the 1960s the investing world discovered that the newspaper industry was fabulously wealthy. The media race was on.

Television in the 1960s was already concentrated in ownership, but was to become even more so. Television, in the jargon of Wall Street, is a "semimonopoly," not only because of the limited number of owners, but because in most cities the dominant stations have virtually guaranteed high profits; the ratings simply determine which company gets the most.

Recent events in broadcasting have further concentrated ownership in television. Initially, no company was permitted to own more than seven radio and seven television stations. Under the political drive for deregulation, the FCC in 1984 permitted each company to expand its holdings to 12 AM and 12 FM radio stations and 12 television stations, and said it would lift all restrictions in 1990.

In the past decade, magazine groups, book companies, even Hollywood studios, were added to the corporate mix when conglomerates came to appreciate the power to create national styles and celebrities (and extra profits) when combinations of different media reinforced each other in unified corporate promotional campaigns.

Magazine articles could become books, which could become television programs that could become movies from which a novelized version could join the parade of accompanying T-shirts, posters, cosmetics and stylized clothing. Owning properties in all the media concentrated the profits from them all.

## Public Trust

It is possible that large corporations are gaining control of the American media because the public wants it that way. But there is another possibility: the public, almost totally dependent on the media to alert them to public problems, has seldom seen in their standard newspapers, magazines or broadcasts anything to suggest the political and economic dangers of concentrated corporate control. On the contrary, for years the media have treated mergers and acquisitions as an exciting game that poses no threat to the national pattern of news and information.

Most owners and editors no longer brutalize the news with the heavy hand dramatized in movies like *Citizen Kane* or *The Front Page*. Only a few bosses still storm into the newsroom to order outrageous lies into the headlines. Most of the time, professional journalistic standards and public sophistications are high enough to make gross suppression of dramatic developments ineffective.

Far more effective in creating public opinion is the pursuit of events or ideas until they are displayed in depth over a period of time, until they form a coherent picture and become integrated into public thinking. It is this continuous repetition and emphasis that create high priorities among the general public and in government. It is in that power—to treat some subjects briefly and obscurely but others repetitively and in depth, or to take initiatives unrelated to external events—that ownership interests most effectively influence the news they create.

As media conglomerates have become larger, they have been integrated into the higher levels of American banking and industrial life as subsidiaries and interlocks within their boards of directors. Half the dominant firms are members of the Fortune 500 largest corporations in the country. They are heavy investors in, among other things, agribusiness, airlines, coal and oil, banking, insurance defense contracts, automobile sales, rocket engineering, nuclear power and nuclear weapons. Many have heavy foreign investments affected by American foreign policy decisions.

It is normal for all large businesses to make serious efforts to influence the news, to avoid embarrassing publicity, and to maximize sympathetic public opinion and government policies. Now they own most of the news media that they wish to influence.

# 27

# Whatever Happened to the News?

## *by* Daniel Hallin

*Editor's Note:* News is not only being manipulated by public relations and advertising. It is also being manipulated by news media themselves to make it more entertaining. Of course, news must have some entertainment value if it is to attract an audience. People do not usually turn to news for functional information, but they have been informed by what they have read, watched, or heard, regardless of their motives, when the information quotient of news has been high.

Now, says Daniel Hallin, hard news is going soft, and entertainment is taking over. Hallin is associate professor of communication at the University of California at San Diego. This article was originally published in *Media & Values,* Spring 1990.

News has always mixed the serious and the entertaining. The tension between journalism and commercialism goes back long before television, but it is felt with special intensity in television news today. In the early 1960s the networks, hugely profitable but worried about their images and about regulatory pressures, expanded their news operations and largely freed them from the pressures of commercial television. The "church" of news was to be separated from the "state" of entertainment.

In the 1970s and '80s, however, the barrier between news and entertainment has been increasingly eroded. Not all the changes of these years have been for the worse. But taken together, they raise serious questions about the future of journalism in an entertainment-dominated medium. A recent edition of the news "tabloid" *A Current Affair,* for example, ended with the "tease," "Coming up—sex, murder and videotape, that's next!" It may be that this is indeed the future of television news.

It was the local stations that first discovered, late in the 1960s, that news could make money—lots of money. By the end of the '70s, news was frequently producing 60 percent of a station's profits. With numbers like that, news was much "too important" to leave to journalists, and a heavily entertainment-oriented form of programming began to evolve. Often it was contrasted directly with the network news. "Feel like you're getting a bad deal from poker-faced

TV news reporters?" asked San Francisco's KGO in one ad. "Then let the Channel 17 Gang deal you in. They're not afraid to be friendly."

Competitive pressures began to impinge on network news in a serious way in the late 1970s. In 1976 ABC began a successful drive to make its news division competitive with CBS and NBC. Its successful move into news was followed by the growth of cable, which began to erode the networks' audience share. . . . This new source of competition, combined with other economic conditions, put a significant squeeze on network profits that has since come home to the news divisions in the form of an unprecedented concern with the bottom line.

### Free-market Journalism

In Washington, meanwhile, the FCC was dismantling most of the regulatory framework that had been imposed on the television industry since its beginnings, especially the obligation—vague, to be sure—to provide some minimum of serious public affairs programming.

Proponents of deregulation assumed that the free market would bring forth an age of diversity in television programming. In fact, there is a lot more news on television now than ever before. In a sense, there is also greater diversity. The last few years have seen a proliferation of new forms of "reality-based programming."

If we set aside live programming and the Sunday interview shows, there were basically only two forms of public affairs television in the 1960s: the evening news and the documentary. In the '70s new forms appeared: the news magazine, represented first by *60 Minutes,* and local news in its modern, fast-paced "happy talk" form. Each breached the barrier between news and entertainment in important ways. The decade also saw the consolidation of morning news as a strongly entertainment-oriented form of programming. NBC's *Today* show had pioneered such a form in the 1950s. In the '70s, ABC joined the field with *Good Morning America,* produced by the entertainment division, and CBS abandoned hard news in the morning to try and imitate *Today.*

The 1980s gave us two significant additions to public affairs programming, *Nightline* and CNN. The latter, it might be added, is itself a complex mix of the serious and the trivial. CNN has taken up slack from the established networks in live public affairs programming, covering, for example, much of the Iran-Contra hearings ABC, CBS, and NBC declined to carry and providing electrifying live coverage of the massacre at Tiananmen Square. But day in and day out, CNN news offerings resemble local news more than anything else, mixing short reports on political affairs with large doses of weather and human interest.

The '80s also saw a proliferation of *60 Minutes* imitators, often with a particularly fast-paced, glitzy style. And they have seen the demise of one important form of public affairs programming: the documentary. More than any other public affairs programming, the documentary unit *CBS Reports,* established in that period in the early '60s when the networks were moving to head off regulatory pressures, stood apart from commercial constraints. The works produced—"Harvest of Shame," for instance, or "The Selling of the Pentagon"—were hour-long statements about serious issues. Often a year or more in production and featuring a clear point of view, they provided a unique perspective on many problems, policies and controversial issues. Thanks to corporate scruples and bottom-line consciousness, their day in commercial television is definitely over.

Most of today's growth, meanwhile, has been at the "low end" in a proliferation of shows that practice what might be called "parajournalism." The most important new form is the "tabloid" news magazine, including such shows as *A Current Affair, Inside Edition, Hard Copy* and *The Reporters.*

In a way, these shows represent something very new. They are not news shows that borrow conventions from entertainment television, but the other way around—entertainment programs that borrow the aura of news. The forms and the "look" are news—the opening sequences frequently feature typewriter keys and newsroom-like sets with monitors in the background. The content, however, has little of the substance of journalism; above all, little about public affairs.

In another sense, these shows are nothing new at all. What they have done is to take the approach pioneered by the hybrid forms of the 1970s and push it to extremes. Local news is typically concerned with crime, accidents and disasters, children lost and found and new animals born at zoos; morning news with celebrities, health and "life styles." What all these stories have in common is that they are about everyday life—and about its disruptions and exaltations (crime, illness, the hero, the celebrity, the rescue). They are about private, not public, life. The "softer" news shows have always traded heavily in this kind of material. But they have mixed it with a measure of genuine journalism. Their origins in the older tradition of public affairs reporting have also imposed some limits on what they will stoop to in the way of sensationalism.

With the new "tabloids" these scruples are mostly out the window. Their appeal is to the emotions, with no apologies; their interest in public affairs is not quite nil but very close (issues with sufficient emotional content, like crime and AIDS, can still bring it out). They have had great success with this model, and the rest of television news is sure to be sorely tempted to compete with them.

## New Agenda

The main vehicle for serious public affairs coverage, meanwhile, remains the network evening news, which is widely seen as having betrayed the values of the so-called Golden Age of Cronkite, Huntley and Brinkley. This view is not entirely accurate: like many "golden" ages, television's early years have been very much romanticized.

In many ways the evening news is better now than it was in the '60s and early '70s. There is nothing wrong with learning to use the medium effectively. The truth is that much of television news 15 or 20 years ago was both dull and difficult to understand. There is nothing wrong, either, with shifting the news agenda toward the kinds of stories more meaningful to the average audience member. If television does more stories about health or child care, up to a point that's a change for the better.

But the drive for ratings has produced many troubling practices, from the furious pace of modern news to a tendency for journalists to scramble like politicians onto the bandwagon of the latest wave of popular sentiment. In the mid-1980s the fashionable emotion was patriotism. Today it is often the evils of drugs. Poker-faced objectivity gives way to breathless moralism, as long as the issue is safe. The danger is both that passion will be inflated at the expense of understanding and that the public agenda will be distorted, with emotional issues blown up larger than life and less dramatic but equally serious ones diminished.

In the long run, there is reason for concern not only about the quality of the evening news, but even its survival. The networks expanded news programs to 30 minutes to begin with, and affiliate stations carried them, not because it was profitable but because they were a regulated industry and wanted the prestige of belonging to the Fourth Estate. But the regulatory pressure is gone now, and the temptation for local stations to drop the network news is increased by the fact that technology has made it possible for local stations to cover many of the national and international events the networks have covered, albeit usually in a sporadic and superficial way. Technology can transfer pictures from Panama or Eastern Europe quickly and cheaply, while understanding of their context is harder to come by.

Even now the amount of time American television devotes to the affairs of public life is tiny. Most industrialized countries, for instance, have at least a full half-hour of national news in prime time; the United States has 22-23 minutes (the length of an evening news broadcast when commercials are eliminated) in "early fringe" time, with even the slots at 6 or 6:30 p.m. increasingly going to game shows and tabloids. Some form of serious television journalism will surely survive. But it could well be reduced to serving a specialized audience, while most of the public watches nothing but the softest form of "infotainment." With most of the public getting its news from television already and newspaper readership declining, the danger of creating a public that knows and cares little about public life is very real.

# 28

# Profit and Quality Are Inseparable

## *by* Leading Newspaper CEOs

*Editor's Note:* In June 1990, the *Washington Journalism Review* (now the *American Journalism Review*) published a lengthy special report by Jonathan Kwitny entitled "The High Cost of Profits." Highly critical, it said that "corporate newspapers lay golden eggs for Wall Street. And CEOs pressure editors, sometimes with bonuses, to cut news staffs and keep dividends rising." It asked whether the constant pressure to increase profits focused newspapers too much on the short term, and was that threatening news coverage and journalistic quality?

The *Washington Journalism Review* sent advance copies of the articles to more than a dozen of the nation's top newspaper company executives with a request for their comments.

The executives, seven of whom responded, were asked the following questions:

1. Kwitny describes economic conditions—including monopoly status, stockholder expectations and high newspaper acquisition prices—that pressure management to increase profits. Do you see any changes ahead that could ease the severity of the profit pressure?
2. Various editors and reporters told Kwitny that emphasis on short-term profits is forcing news cuts and lowering newspaper quality. Under these conditions, will newspapers be able to maintain the quality and the sense of public service that journalists traditionally feel to be part of their calling?

Here are the answers, allowing the CEOs to speak for themselves. This article is reprinted from the *Washington Journalism Review*, July/August 1990.

*James K. Batten*
*Chairman and CEO,*
*Knight-Ridder, Inc.*

Newspapers, not unlike other American businesses these days, do indeed face significant economic pressures. But to suggest that profit-crazed infidels from the countinghouse are massing at the newsroom door is a little farfetched.

Through my more than 30 years in this business, conscientious editors, publishers and corporate people have struggled to strike a wise and proper balance between obligations to readers and communities, and to their newspapers' owners. It's not a perfect or painless process, but in Knight-Ridder at least, it works. Over the years we have become ever more convinced of this article of faith: Ultimately, journalistic quality and financial success go hand in hand.

Finding the right balance at any newspaper in any given year is rarely simple. That job gets tougher when business is sluggish, as it has been for much of the last three years. In 1989, due mainly to a soft retail economy, newspaper revenues did not even keep up with the cost of living. That generates stress for all concerned.

But contrary to Jonathan Kwitny's implication, Knight-Ridder is controlling costs without harming the quality of our newspapers. In fact, newsroom spending will be up more than 5 percent company-wide this year—and more than 23 percent over the last four years, above the rate of inflation and the rate of newspaper revenue growth. News spending as a percent of total revenue has been steady over that period. Full-run news space, despite careful trimming at some papers, is up about 5 percent compared to 1986.

*WJR* readers unfortunately did not get this picture from Mr. Kwitny's article, even though we tried to explain it to him.

None of this is to suggest that life is easy at the moment, or that every decision is unanimous. But we don't simply resolve things by business-side fiat. We encourage honest debate, and because we have excellent and deeply caring people, we usually get it. That makes for better final decisions.

When the U.S. economy becomes healthier, as it will, newspapers' health will follow suit. That will help, but the pressures will not disappear. Profit growth is important if newspapers are to remain an attractive investment and, ultimately, retain their vitality and independence. Financially stagnant newspapers are at best uncertain guardians of a free press. In addition, another set of pressures—for improved performance on behalf of newspapers' customers—will continue to escalate. Readers and advertisers are more demanding than they were a generation ago. Longer term, newspapers' prosperity—and First Amendment vigor—will depend heavily on the editors' and reporters' ability to hold the attention of an American audience increasingly distracted from public affairs, the traditional centerpiece of excellent journalism.

Newspapers whose journalists disdain that challenge—feeling their high calling *entitles* them to reader attention and respect—will not do well. Such papers inevitably will erode both in public-service effectiveness and in profitability.

Our profession in the 1990s needs editors and reporters with talent and relish for *communicating* with busy and easily diverted Americans already awash in news and information—even before they reach for a newspaper. Wafting earnest journalistic messages into the air is not enough. They have to land somewhere to matter to anybody.

The choice is not between fluff and substance, as some believe. Our need is for newspapers so compelling, so varied, so enlightening, so well-written and designed, that they maintain daily print journalism's invaluable role in American life and public discourse.

I see heartening examples of that kind of newspapering increasingly around the country. Even in these tough times.

**John J. Curley**
**Chairman, President and CEO,**
**Gannett Company**

You must consider the nation's economic climate when you pose this question [about the possibility of profit pressures easing]. We see little evidence that the economy continues its endless expansion, despite the rosy government data. The imperative to control cost derives less from ownership status or stockholder expectations than it does from the deteriorating consumer economy and restructuring in the retail industry. These two factors have combined to produce the poorest advertising environment in almost 20 years, and we're feeling its effects on the revenue side.

To counter this, we're prudently spending money, not socking it away. We put a lot of money into appropriate programs in circulation and advertising, and the result is that we've been successful in stemming the slide of household penetration at our newspapers. We expect to see the returns on that down the road.

I said this to stockholders at our annual meeting in April, and I'll say it again here: We're building for the year 2000, not the short-term fixes. We continue to be very frugal at corporate headquarters, but we've spent more on salaries and news holes to hire and retain quality people and improve the newspapers. There's no question that today's economic conditions require editors to be more strategic in their allocation of newsroom resources. But doing things differently doesn't mean doing them less well, and I believe news executives throughout Gannett understand that.

Through ANPA's circulation and readership steering group, which I've chaired, we are working to develop ways in increase public interest in coverage of public affairs and vital issues. This is, of course, the heart and soul of news coverage and our responsibility under the First Amendment.

*Michael Johnston*
*President and CEO, Thomson*
*Newspaper Corporation*

Very few journalists work for nonprofit newspapers. It is important for everyone to realize that we are in a business, and it's called the newspaper business. As in any other business, the purpose of the stockholder's investment is to make a profit. It seems obvious to us at Thomson Newspapers that it is in every employee's best interest that the enterprise be profitable, as that is the only way employment can be maintained, and also to understand that profit and quality are not at odds but complement each other. It is also important to keep in mind that the best way to increase profit is by increasing market share and penetration. That comes about only through better newspapers, which seems to us to mean that high standards must be maintained if the market is going to let the newspaper grow.

A good newspaper holds up a mirror to the community it serves, not to the face of a single reporter or journalist, although a good reporter can become that mirror. Where the conflict always develops is when the journalist determines that he knows, by some divine right, what that community needs to know. Journalism prizes awarded by peers represent only one of many measures of quality. Newspapers have an obligation to present to their subscribers a balanced report, but they must develop a product their market wants to read and is willing to buy. Those two interests can be, and often are, in conflict. At Thomson Newspapers, we feel strongly that, over the long term, the market is the arbiter of quality standards, and success in the marketplace is a genuine award of merit.

*Jim Kennedy*
*Chairman and CEO, Cox Enterprises*

Our newspapers are businesses and, as such, I don't see any prospects for the reduction in emphasis on profitability. In the case of newspapers with adequate profit margins, I would suspect management to be more concerned with maintaining those margins while at the same time seeking new ways to grow revenue. In newspapers with unsatisfactory margins, I suspect the focus would be in eventually improving those margins to satisfactory levels. I do believe, though, that both public and private newspaper companies are willing to accept short-term reductions in profit to better position themselves to achieve long-term goals.

In fact, most of us will have to do just that in order to reclaim some of the circulation penetration we have lost over the past two decades. As we try to rebuild the basic foundation of our business, circulation (hopefully the goal of both editors and publishers), we must also contend with a much more complex business environment. Not only do we face increased competition from shoppers, weeklies, direct mail, radio and television but also from new businesses that seem to surface daily. Addressing the issue of quality is a terribly subjective enterprise. How do you define quality in a daily newspaper? Certainly a newspaper that isn't profitable, and therefore unlikely to survive, could not be considered a good newspaper. Also a newspaper that continues to lose market share, in my opinion, should not be considered a good newspaper.

We must find effective ways to reach the mass audience and at the same time tailor our newspaper to smaller, highly targeted audiences. The zoning of news and advertising copy is an obvious example. In my opinion, newspapers will have to get better to do all this, and when I say "better," in many cases that's going to mean doing things in different ways than they have been done before. Our society is changing, and so must our newspapers.

Editors must continue to shoulder the historic responsibility of journalism to serve a free people and safeguard the workings of our democracy. Journalists must continue to honor the sense of public service that they feel is their calling. They must also be men and women who are open-minded and willing to listen to what their readers say they want from a newspaper. Editors who understand both their "Fourth Estate" obligations and the realities of the marketplace will be the successful leaders of our newspapers as we go into the new century. Those who refuse to change with the public they serve and who don't master the totality of their responsibilities will fail, as might their newspapers.

*Phillip J. Meek*
*President, Publishing Group,*
*Capital Cities/ABC*

Management's obligation is to balance profit optimization, franchise strengthening, community service and employee development within the context of whatever external conditions exist. Excessive multiples [ratios of newspaper purchase prices to revenue and cash flow], which are coming down, require a shorter-term view and more emphasis on profits near term. Otherwise, use of the word "pressure" twice in the question is about as subjective as Kwitny's inescapable point of view—and terribly unfair.

Too many journalists are driven by, but vehemently deny, acceptance and recognition by their peers. When times are good, it is easier, but not necessarily right, for publishers to accommodate those desires. Witness the increasingly absurd assemblage of professionals at the World Series, Super Bowl and political conventions. One's presence assures acceptance in the fraternity. Declining market penetration, not profit levels, is forcing an analysis of priorities. What information readers want to cope with—with the increasing demands on their daily lives—must be the constant objective of any newspaper, not what the newsroom professionals think the readers need and the newsroom wants!

### D. R. Segal
### President and CEO,
### Freedom Newspapers, Inc.

Until we overhaul the human race and delete the greed chromosome, I suspect there will be unremitting pressure to increase all profits. Of course, greed being the engine that drives progress, when we eliminate cupidity we can go back to trading stone axes for flint knives, and who is to say we wouldn't enjoy all that?

I do not think there is anything on the subject of profits that is particular to owners of newspapers. Most of them have a nice sense of self but so do the owners of shoe stores and practitioners of medicine. I don't think I caught the name of the newspaper CEO who was rewarded with a substantial raise when he announced the winning of a Pulitzer Prize and the diminution of the operating net by 25 percent, especially if his company was highly leveraged.

Of course, it's not fair. I mean, my situation is far different from, say, Jim Batten's or John Curley's. They have thousands of investors, some of them little widow women in Boise and teachers' pension funds. (The latter, to quote an investment banker I know, "don't buy stocks, they rent them.") These passive and even transient investors might not read newspapers nor even like them. Very likely few of them hold voting stock, but they vote with their feet, and when their computers tell them to. I don't think the element of quality or responsibility to the Republic figure in the computer software. The CEOs of the huge public companies live their lives in three-month increments, and I venture to guess that they reach for a Tums every morning when they turn to the stock pages. My God, it's down a point. Maybe I can call in sick.

My company is family-owned. We think in terms of generations, not quarters. The pressure on management is there, but apparently more benign and kinder. I think we are structured to react cautiously to downturns. What's best for the grandkids? Go for the buck now or build value for the long term? Usually the verdict comes down for the latter.

What a luxury! And what motivation to keep up the quality of products and services for a very selfish reason: It's good business for the grandchildren.

Those are the realities. Whether by attrition or the Saturday Night Unpleasantness, we'll all try to tighten up. Except for that company whose name escapes me, that is going at 100 percent efficiency, certain economies might not substantially reduce quality. And on Sunday we can take flowers over to Boot Hill and put them so solemnly on the graves of such heroes as the old *Herald-Tribune*, which died of an excess of devotion.

### W. Dean Singleton
### Vice Chairman and CEO,
### MediaNews Group

Upon reading Jonathan Kwitny's provocative piece on modern newspaper economics vis-a-vis editorial quality, I was somehow reminded of the man who loved the taste of sausage until he found out how it was made.

In this day and time, when you scrutinize profitability and the myriad parts of newspaper economics, there is, I suppose, something suddenly distasteful about a profession we all prefer to believe is noble, compassionate and critical to the democratic process.

Clearly something is wrong when newspaper profits in many places—but certainly not everywhere—are soaring while the number of daily newspapers is dwindling, readership is falling at an alarming rate and credibility in the public's eye is said to be at an all-time low.

I, for one, am not ready to lay the blame for these dismaying trends entirely at the feet of profit-taking, although in the industry some of us—perhaps all of us—may indeed have some soul-searching to do with respect to the profit question.

There is a Catch-22 at work here, certainly so for those publicly held media companies. With growing profit, you cannot reinvest—without investors, you cannot grow—and without attractive earnings, you cannot dazzle the Wall Street analysts who push the stocks.

I have some problems with that last part, It is the main reason why I am glad our newspapers are privately held. We aren't under any analysts' guns. But we are in business just the same and we begin each day mindful that there simply is no way to be an artistic success without first being a financial success.

Mr. Kwitny's piece does not address some tough realities that every publisher faces today.

1. Newspapers and newspaper groups must be profitable enough to handle the huge capital expenditures needed to modernize, especially in the larger markets. Advertisers want perfect color, for example, and readers are now dead set against having inky newspapers in their homes. Readers also want full-time, on-time delivery. Adult carriers are paid more than teens.

2. Today's publishers, to compete for readers and advertisers with other information sources, namely television, must spend as much as 5 or 6 percent of annual revenues on marketing, promotion and research. That wasn't the case a generation ago when most publishers would have laughed off today's "promote or die" thesis. To some degree, at least, the need to promote cuts heavily into monies that would be put into newsroom staffing and news hole.

One complaint I have with Mr. Kwitny's piece is that I think he makes the age-old mistake commonly seen when our industry tries to cover itself—viewing newspapers strictly from the eyes of reporters and editors. To wit: Never mind *how* the money is spent, never mind *how* good the news staff might be—just *how many* people work in the newsroom and *how much* are they paid?

Also of great concern to me is the arrogance I see in too many newsrooms and among too many editors. "Editorial quality," in my estimation, also has a lot to do with understanding readers and what they say they need, and understanding the hard-for-reporters-to-swallow fact that readers buy newspapers for advertising as well as for news.

There is nothing more odious to me, as a publisher, than the specter of an editor hell-bent for the almighty Pulitzer Prize at the expense of the local news, or a supercilious newsroom that ignores reader-research data that begs for a new direction.

Corporate dividends will not kill our industry—arrogance and history might!

# VII

# Public Relations: Manipulating Mass Media

For a variety of reasons, mass media can be manipulated by outside forces who would seek to use the media for their own purposes, usually to influence the public. Let's examine some of the causes before we look at some of the effects.

One cause is the inequity in personnel. News media can rarely afford to employ enough reporters and editors to cover any situation thoroughly, so they must depend on outsiders for help. At the University of Maryland, for example, only two daily newspapers have large enough staffs and budgets to cover the university full time. Even those two reporters, one for the *Baltimore Sun* and one for the *Washington Post,* cannot keep up with all the news on the campus. Local TV and radio stations and weekly newspapers cannot afford to assign full-time reporters to the university.

At the same time, the university employs several dozen people in its PR office. When something happens on campus, these people provide information to the news media, but because the news media are understaffed, they cannot always determine whether the information provided by the university is fair, accurate, balanced, and objective or whether it has been deliberately or even accidentally shaped to serve the interests of the university.

If the PR people are ethical, of course, that won't happen, and it probably doesn't happen at the University of Maryland. But there is no law to prevent it from happening, and not everyone is ethical.

A second reason for manipulation is inequity in knowledge, experience, and access to information. Fewer than fifty reporters cover the U.S. Defense De-

partment on a regular basis, and that department employs more than a thousand people who deal with the press. Moreover, journalists who cover the Pentagon are usually generalists; a few have covered military affairs long enough to have acquired some expertise in the subject, but none of them could have the skills and knowledge and access to data and information that would characterize the department's PR specialists. Because journalists must often depend on these specialists for the facts and their interpretation, the Defense Department can put out its own interpretation on any matter of national defense. Perhaps the best example of this ability to manipulate the news is the 1991 war in the Persian Gulf. (See Part XII for further details.)

A third reason for mass media manipulation is greed and laziness. It is cheaper for news organizations to let others do their work, and of course it is easier on reporters if they only have to look over someone's press release rather than doing extensive research and writing themselves. The result is that what might seem like an objective and factual news story might instead be only part of the facts told in a way that would serve some special interest.

Another form of manipulation comes from using news to serve the interests of advertisers. In most mass media, news and advertising are separate parts of the organization, and one should not influence the other. But this separation has been breaking down in some organizations, and the lines between news and advertising have been blurred.

The articles in this section develop these problems with specific examples.

# 29

# Green Like Me

## *by* Bill Walker

*Editor's Note:* One of the big problems of the 1990s is the pollution of the environment. We needn't describe these issues here; everyone is surely familiar with them.

Obviously, environmental protection is and will continue to be a costly problem for many corporations. Their profits are being reduced by the laws and the public pressures forcing them to clean up. Because it's easier and more profitable to make the issue go away, many corporations use PR tactics to cover up the problem or to deflect our attention to something else.

This article by Bill Walker discusses the hype and spin that some organizations are using to avoid the real issue of protecting the environment. It was published in *Greenpeace,* May/June 1991.

Green garbage bags. Green gasoline. Computers, hamburgers, compact discs: all here, all green, already. In California, where I live, supermarket chains that refuse to stop selling pesticide-dusted grapes are trying to promote themselves as environmentally correct because their pickle jars are reusable (you know, you can stick flowers in them). They're getting away with it. The chairman of Du Pont has the *New York Times* practically comparing him to John Muir. An oil company is forced by federal regulations to put a few bucks into preserving wildlife habitat, so it spends 10 times that much to buy newspaper ads patting itself on the back for obeying the law. Do people buy it? People do. Me, I buy Natural Brown coffee filters.

Sorry to have to tell you this, but you ain't green nothing yet. Get ready for a brazen new wave of hype, half-truths and plain old lies, as the greenwashers turn their spin-cycling talents to really challenging subjects. Green chlorofluorocarbons. Green nuclear power plants. Green Agent Orange. Oil tankers, toxics incinerators, dolphin steaks—you name it, the PR flacks of America are ready to reassure you that it's green, clean, and using it is one more simple thing you can do to save the Earth.

I learned all of this at the 43rd annual convention of the Public Relations Society of America (PRSA), which met in New York City last November. The theme of the 1990 convention was "Our World in Transition," but when I looked through the program for the first time I thought it was How to Make

Your Corporation Look Like a Friend to the Planet While Reaping Billions in the International Waste Trade. And getting away with it. I signed up.

What I found, I must admit, was more subtle, less cynical, than I expected. Most greenflacks, it appears, believe in what they are flacking. When the cocktail chatter turns to environmental ethics, they tend to say thing like this: "I've always considered myself a child of the sixties—stop the war, save the Earth, corporations are environmental criminals. It wasn't until I started working for this company that I saw for myself how strong their commitment is to the environment."

"What's the company you're working for?"

"Waste Management."

I made a note for my friend Bradley, who works for Greenpeace in San Francisco and is fighting on half a dozen fronts against toxics incinerators proposed by Waste Management Inc., the largest hazardous-waste handler in the country, and among the most frequently fined: "Big news. Inside source says WMI not environmental criminals."

In the interest of full disclosure, I should admit something else. I work for Greenpeace, too, and as much as I hate to admit it, my job there is basically public relations. So I suppose I shared a certain familial guilt with the thousands of legitimate PRSA conventioneers with big plastic "hi-my-name-is" tags who queued earnestly for workshops like "Understanding Activist Publics: Making Allies Out of Enemies." (One of the most intriguing, "Emerging Public Relations Challenges in a Changing Defense Environment," was inexplicably canceled—maybe somebody noticed the world heading toward an oil war and decided that stuff about the changing defense environment was a bit premature.) But I was really there, hanging around the red-carpeted meeting rooms of the Marriott Marquis on Times Square, as a spy: Observe greenwashing, document same, report findings, eat in Manhattan on $20 a day.

The first day, I nearly blew my cover.

Sixty or so of us had been bused over to the Fordham University Graduate School of Business Administration for a symposium called "The *Exxon Valdez* Story: How to Spend a Billion or Two and Still Get a Black Eye in Public." For two hours, communications experts like William J. Small, former president of NBC News and United Press International, argued about the most notorious man-made environmental disaster in U.S. history from what seemed to me a brilliantly novel, if perverse, point of view: that the spilling of 11 million gallons of crude oil into Prince William Sound, the fouling of at least 1,500 miles of pristine Alaskan shoreline and the ensuing deaths of hundreds of thousands of sea birds, otters and salmon, was fundamentally a public relations problem. Small, now professor of communications at Fordham, wore a name tag that said "Bill."

"I won't ask how many of you are environmentalists," he began. "We are not here today to debate environmental or ethical questions. We are, at least for today, not concerned with the fate of sea otters, but with how a huge American corporation spent $2 billion on the cleanup of what was not the worst oil spill ever, yet lost the battle of public relations and more than a year later is still struggling with one of the worst tarnishings of its corporate image in American history."

Oh. Exxon's struggling, not the otters. Bill, it was clear, felt the company had gotten something of a raw deal.

"There are lots of reasons to feel sorry for Exxon," he said. "Joseph Hazelwood [the *Valdez*'s captain] had a terrific reputation. Although the press made much of the fact that the first mate was not officially certified, he had met all of his qualifications to be certified. The judge who sentenced Hazelwood called the spill 'a manmade disaster not seen since the likes of Hiroshima.' Well, let's be realistic: Nobody died at Prince William Sound—no humans, anyway. Exxon failed to tell the best sides of its story."

I was thinking that the only good side of Exxon's story was the fact that the oil the *Valdez* spilled didn't end up as an L.A. smog alert. But Marion Pinsdorf, a professor of communications and media management at Fordham, also took up the company's case: "There were lots of positive Exxon stories that could have been picked up that were not." And what really hurt Exxon, said Professor of Management Systems Falguni Sen, was not immediately sending its chief operating officer to the scene of the disaster to display the company's concern.

"Exxon," declared Sen, "was long ago past the point at which it could no longer afford to have an operations-oriented CEO vs. a public-relations guy. Of course, as the chairman of Union Carbide found out in Bhopal, just as important is how well you manage the perception of why the boss goes to the site." Someone asked: "What happened to the chairman of Union Carbide?"

"He spent his first 24 hours in India in jail," said Sen.

"Lesson learned," I scribbled in my official convention notebook. "Jail time harder to explain than thousands of deaths from toxic chemical leak." But I couldn't let it go at that. Bill Small said there was time for one more question, and I put my hand up. I felt like the one kid in first grade who doesn't believe in Santa Claus, but—and here's where I nearly blew it—managed what I thought was a pretty reasonable sounding hypothetical: "Isn't the, uh, real question here whether a company should continue engaging in actions that are inherently dangerous? Maybe a public relations department's responsibility should include telling the CEO that what the company is doing is not only unpopular but irresponsible, and that if there's an accident, there'll be no way to put a good face on it."

People coughed. People turned to look at me. I wished I'd worn a tie.

"Well," Bill said, finally. "What would you do? Cut off the flow of oil from Alaska?"

This notion also sounded quite reasonable to me. But there was no time left; we were not there, after all, to discuss ethical questions. The buses were leaving for the hotel. I shook Bill's hand on the way out. He assured me that his own daughter used to make the same argument I had, but she had come around to her old man's way of thinking. There was still hope for me.

Back at the Marriott, one of the other participants in the Exxon seminar sought me out. Her name tag said "Kerry," she was from Seattle, and she worked for one of those outdoor clothing companies up there. Kerry just wanted me to know how much she appreciated what I'd said, because someone had to say it, and she was feeling bad because she hadn't said it, and of course she was really into recycling and all, and she couldn't believe the attitudes of these people. Could I?

She told me about a workshop she had attended earlier: "Building Public Support by Resolving Disputes Through Consensus," billed in the program as "a hands-on exercise based on real-life applications in which a company, government agencies, environmentalists, labor and elected officials worked together to develop solutions all could live with." It struck me that the problem was that companies and government agencies were usually not interested in environmental solutions all could live with, but in those only a politically acceptable number would die from, but I had a feeling that wasn't what the people doing the workshop meant. I asked Kerry what she'd learned at the workshop.

"One of the group leaders said when you're dealing with a group of outside agitators—Greenpeace or somebody like that—they usually have a different agenda than the people in the community where you're trying to place your facility," Kerry said. "If you let them rant and rave and foam at the mouth, the community will sometimes get turned off and approach you with a compromise. She said you can short-circuit these outside agitators by letting them disrupt public meetings, then you can arrange a private meeting behind their backs."

"Where was she from?"

"Waste Management, I think."

I drifted from meeting room to meeting room, searching for the soul of the greenwasher.

I got a rather enthusiastic dose of optimism from keynote speaker Patricia Aburdene, collaborator (and wife) of *Megatrends* pop-futurist John Naisbitt. "We now have the opportunity," she said, "to create techno-topia—although we've also got to deal with poverty, homelessness, this Persian Gulf thing and, of course, the environment."

I witnessed an act of bravery by the manager of a big financial services company, who began his seminar ("Managing the Environment: A Business Perspective") by declaring, "I am an environmentalist." He handled the account for Pacific Gas & Electric Co. (PG&E), my hometown utility monopoly, so he talked a lot about "trade-offs" between environmental quality and "continuing to provide an adequate supply of energy for healthy economic growth." He later predicted that, during the '90s, "You're going to see a lot more of this radical activism—people tying themselves to redwood trees, that sort of thing. And that's probably healthy, as long as you don't have social disorder."

I heard Jay Hair, head of the National Wildlife Federation (the only environmentalist, incidentally, quoted in the *Times* piece on the greening of Du Pont who found something good to say about the company), bluntly tell a gang of oil company flacks that fossil fuels had to go, and safe alternatives must be urgently pursued. Perhaps unintentionally, he quickly found a chorus of supporters from the other side of the room: "Nuclear!" they cried.

I tried to put all this together, from a flack's point of view. The future, it seems, will be great, except for war and global warming; we'll save the planet, but not enough to hurt the stock market; the environmental movement is OK because preserving redwoods keeps people from worrying about plutonium. There was a common thread there, but I couldn't put my finger on it. Then I overheard a conversation that made it clear:

A PR manager for a company named ChemLawn complained that the entire city of Columbus, Ohio, its headquarters, hated the company because it makes, you know, chemicals. "But what can you do?" she asked a couple of colleagues. They replied immediately—and in unison—"Change the name."

Of course. What did Reagan's EPA Chief Anne Gorsuch do when Congress threatened to throw her in jail? She got married! Anne Gorsuch might do time, but would Anne Burford? And after Windscale, Britain's notorious nuclear reprocessing plant, reached its fourth decade of pumping plutonium into the Irish Sea, it changed its name to Sellafield. The pollution, of course, continues. What did Exxon do when it got ready to put the *Valdez* back into service? Change the name. It hasn't worked—"ex-*Valdez*" is still shorter in a headline than "*Mediterranean*"—but you had to admire the thought behind it, because it was the very spirit of greenwashing: Things are whatever you say they are.

You can say that a new brand of gasoline will "drive away pollution" because it's not as dirty as the stuff you were selling before. You can say that your tuna is guaranteed dolphin safe when you've got all of nine certified observers working the entire North Pacific fishing fleet. You can say that nuclear energy is a safe alternative to fossil fuels if you ignore Chernobyl and Three Mile Island. You can say whatever you want, because if you send out enough press releases on brown paper, sponsor enough nature series on public television and hire enough flacks for your Department of Marketing and Publicity, you might get away with it. Just change the name: Now it's the Office of Environmental Affairs.

I was still thinking about this on the final afternoon of the conference. I was waiting for an elevator when I recognized someone from the opening night cocktail party—the same woman from Waste Management who told me she was a child of the sixties. We said hello, and she tried to recall what company I was with.

"None," I confessed. Since I was practically on my way to the airport, I dropped my cover and told her the whole scam. "Greenpeace," she said. "What's Waste Management going to have to do to get you off our back?"

"Well," I said. "You could change the name."

# 30

# Is the Press Any Match for Powerhouse PR?

## *by* Alicia Mundy

*Editor's Note:* Public relations firms seem to be getting much more so-phisticated about managing the news media. This article analyzes the "new and improved" devices that big PR firms in Washington, D.C., are using to manipulate journalism and thus control the public agenda.

Alicia Mundy was national correspondent for *Regardie's,* and is now contributing editor of *The Washingtonian.* This article appeared in the *Columbia Journalism Review,* September/October 1992.

The use and abuse of journalists by p.r. flacks and lobbyists has long been a fact of life in Washington. In the past couple of years, though, media manipulation has been taken to a new level. How have the spinmeisters come to play such an important part in our political life, and why do the media go along with them?

Media manipulation has evolved considerably since the days when a well-connected flack could place a story simply by calling up a columnist or editor. Power has been diluted among the government and lobbyists, GOP and Demo-cratic factions, and an array of interest groups. And the rise of new media out-lets, together with increased competition among Washington bureaus of many papers, has made it almost impossible for a single media connection to decide whether a story lives or dies. As a high-ranking Hill and Knowlton executive said, "You can't just show up with a bottle of Wild Turkey and get your topic on the hearing schedule anymore. You have to work with staffers, and you have to be more aware of alliances and petty fights on the Hill. It's just not easy." To which a former H&K media specialist adds, "You can't just pick up a phone and call Scotty Reston and get a story out, because there *are* no Scotty Restons."

The '90s bag of tricks includes such time-honored ploys as using media foibles and competition to keep a story alive, as well as "media assistance" and "image enhancement"—slicker versions of the apocryphal call to Reston. It also includes a new emphasis on keeping a client's name *out* of the news.

And then there's the New Aggressiveness, consisting of threats veiled and unveiled. Hill and Knowlton's Bob Gray began advising controversial clients several years ago that they should "Go after the little lies in a big way." In other words, attack any and all flaws in a reporter's story, then use them to discredit the whole piece. His philosophy, as summed up by clients, is: if you get them to back down on the minor details they've screwed up on, they're unlikely to fight you on the major ones.

There's also a new and worrisome emphasis on official forums to jump-start a news story when you can't get it launched independently in the media. Though reporters interviewed insisted that no one can create a story if it isn't genuine "news," a good lobbyist can make news happen by putting it in the right mouths. At least one crucial congressional hearing on Kuwait in the fall of 1990 was prompted by H&K, according to Gray, because of concerns within the Kuwaiti royal family that Americans just weren't "upset enough" by the invasion by Iraq. As foreign countries keep hiring American lobbyists to handle diplomatic issues in Washington, you can expect to see more "official stories" on the front page and the evening news that have a hidden agenda.

And there's the latest wrinkle in p.r.—"De-Keatingization," a combination of vaccination and crop dusting that allows a public official to do what he wants to do (such as voting his conscience on an issue), without appearing to be contaminated by impure motives (such as money).

Oh, a few p.r. firms say they're trying something completely different: the New Honesty. "It's something we recommend to corporate clients, especially on environmental and health issues," says a media consultant, as though suggesting a new hem length or hair color. "In some cases, we really push directness with the media, openness. And," he adds, "it sometimes disarms them. When they think you're being up front, they'll let you tell your story your way."

It's a minefield out there for reporters, and the good news is that many of the lobbyists interviewed insisted that we Washington reporters have gradually become sophisticated, less likely to fall for a spin. But if that's really true, a hell of a lot of flacks are making a hell of a lot of money in Washington for doing nothing.

Hill and Knowlton is not the biggest firm spin-doctoring in the capital these days, but it's the first company that comes to mind when media practitioners and observers discuss how news is shaped and how the Washington press corps helps out. The bookends at H&K's Washington operation (the main office is in New York) are Bob Gray and Frank Mankiewicz.

Perhaps the most successful campaign Gray has run is the Richard Nixon Rehabilitation Campaign, on which he's left as many fingerprints as a five-year-old on a jelly jar. It's no accident that Nixon the Monster has become Nixon the Elder Statesman, appearing in your living room in the Sunday op-ed pages, on *Nightline*, before the American Newspaper Publishers Association, and at a dinner at the liberal Carnegie Endowment for International Peace in Washington. Ask Gray who got 500 foreign affairs writers to believe they were among the "50" elites selected to receive Nixon's comments on aid to the Soviet Union, and he will only smile. Ask who helped arrange the Washington affair at which President George Bush gave his imprimatur to the Nixon resurrection, and Gray's smile grows wider.

An inside look at a "classic propaganda campaign" by Hill and Knowlton was recently provided by *The Daily Record,* a business and legal newspaper in Maryland, in the form of a memorandum—one of several confidential documents released in court as the result of a lawsuit over the installation of asbestos in public buildings in Baltimore. The memo was drawn up in 1983, but the p.r. strategy outlined in it is timeless.

Representing U.S. Gypsum, which for years had used asbestos in some products, H&K advised Gypsum that "the spread of media coverage must be stopped at the local level and as soon as possible." One focus of this strategy was to plant stories on op-ed pages "by experts sympathetic to the company's point of view." The plan included placing articles attesting to the safety of asbestos.

Although a Gypsum spokesman told *The Daily Record* that the company did not implement the advice, court papers show that Gypsum planted op-ed pieces in papers in Baltimore and Detroit. An interoffice Gypsum memo reads: "Attached is an excellent series run over four days, beginning March 3 [1985] in the Detroit News. Our consultant, Jack Kinney, very actively fed much of this information to the special writer, Michael Bennett. SBA is exploring ways of more widely circulating these articles." (As recently as June 30, 1991, the Baltimore *Sun* published an article by Bennett which claimed that the risk of asbestos exposure was comparable to "smoking one half a cigarette in a lifetime.")

The memo further recommended that Gypsum set up an industry group to handle media inquiries and "take the heat from the press and industry critics," and suggested that Gypsum should enlist scientists and doctors as "independent experts" to counter claims that asbestos is a health risk. "It can then position the problem as a side issue that is being seized on by special interests and those out to further their own causes," the twenty-five-page memo continued.

"The media and other audiences important to U.S. Gypsum should ideally say, 'Why is all this furor being raised about this product? We have a non-story here.' "

Ideally, such articles would not only have influenced the public, but would also have worked their way into court exhibits in the lawsuit and swayed the jury. But this past May, U.S. Gypsum and the Asbestospray Corporation were ordered to pay the City of Baltimore $23 million for compensatory and punitive damages.

H&K executives call the strategy outlined in the 1983 memo "old-fashioned," but recent H&K blitzkreigs show it's still state of the art.

## Talking Frankly

Asked for a success story to demonstrate the effectiveness of H&K, Mankiewicz proferred two: the packaging of the movie *JFK,* and the repackaging of the Wall Street law firm Kaye, Scholer. In this case, there's no memo; just Mankiewicz.

As director Oliver Stone was finishing filming *JFK* last spring, an article by *Washington Post* reporter George Lardner, Jr., appeared, fiercely attacking Stone's adaptation of history for his movie. That fall, a *New York Times* piece by Bernard Weinraub reported that "Warner Brothers . . . has taken the unusual step of hiring Frank Mankiewicz, the Washington press-relations executive and former campaign manager for Robert F. Kennedy, to promote the film and seek support in the news media for Mr. Stone. Last week," the November 7, 1991, piece continued, "Mr. Stone flew to Washington and had dinner with representatives from *The New York Times, The Washington Post, People* magazine, and CBS." Mankiewicz coached Stone in writing and, suddenly, thoughtful pieces by Stone began springing up like dandelions in bluegrass all over the nation's op-ed pages. (Sound familiar?)

Did Stone himself pen those pieces? "Sure, he did," Mankiewicz hrrmmpps. Then he winks. "Most of them."

If a journalist had the gall to question a scene from the upcoming movie (versions of the script were floating around the country), Stone pounced on him with a full-fledged attack, out of proportion to the comment by the reporter ("Go after the little lies in a big way"). He and Mankiewicz fought back on every negative article, even threatening to take out a full-page ad in *The Washington Post* if the paper wouldn't print Stone's rebuttal to an unfavorable article—a concession executive editor Benjamin Bradlee had opposed. Ultimately the *Post* printed an edited form of the rebuttal. "We couldn't let anything go unchallenged," Mankiewicz explains.

Then he pitted *Newsweek* and *Time* against each other, convincing each magazine that it had an exclusive. Both responded with overkill—arranging cover stories, historical perspectives by veteran reporters, and later, in the case of *Time*, a contempo essay by Ron Rosenbaum on America's fascination with JFK assassination theories. The ploy worked beautifully up to the last minute, when *Time* had to change its cover for its exclusive Gorbachev interview. "But they gave it a big line on the cover anyway," Mankiewicz says, smiling.

When the film was about to premiere, Mankiewicz arranged meetings with influential congressmen such as Lee Hamilton of Indiana and Louis Stokes of Ohio. He also arranged a few cozy dinners in Georgetown for friends in politics and movies. After screenings of the film for selected journalists and others, he made the legendary recluse Stone available for questions. Finally, he helped to get Stone invited as a speaker at the National Press Club.

"Frank just knows how Washington works," Stone says. "He got us into the right audience, got the movie presented as a serious historical statement. He knows how to work the press establishment here, and got us a fair hearing with the right congressmen. I think he's a genius."

The second success story cited by Mankiewicz in an interview in May was what he saw as the repositioning of the Wall Street firm Kaye, Scholer as victim, not perpetrator, in the S&L scandal. Kaye, Scholer had represented Charles Keating in his S&L dealings with the Lincoln thrift in Arizona. Earlier this year, Kaye, Scholer was forced by the Office of Thrift Supervision to pay $41 million and to bench its senior partner because the firm had allegedly helped Keating conceal his financial dealings from Lincoln's shareholders. Kaye, Scholer called in Hill and Knowlton, and soon pieces contending that the firm had been wronged began to crop up in legal journals and on newspaper op-ed pages.

"Kaye, Scholer was a mugging. We have shown that they have been unfairly attacked by the Justice Department and victimized by the threat of publicity," says Mankiewicz, handing me a two-inch stack of articles defending the law firm.

All this is designed to "target our audience," which he defines as other law firms, accounting firms, and potential clients.

It's not a bad scheme, says media reporter Howard Kurtz of *The Washington Post.* "All these op-ed pieces may not save the day at the time, but they can change the debate or raise the possibility of another side of the story, which may come back later to a client's benefit."

Meanwhile, Mankiewicz tells me, there's more on the way. "And there's a piece coming out in *The American Lawyer* soon," he says, smiling.

Weeks later, the new issue of *The American Lawyer* hits the stands. On the cover, inch-high red type declares: U.S. V. KAYE, SCHOLER: THEY GOT WHAT THEY DESERVED.

Asked about this unexpected setback, "So what?" Mankiewicz snarls. "I hear they've got an article coming out saying the Rodney King verdict was justified. Here's my quote: '*The American Lawyer* supports police brutality in all forms—from the Justice Department to the Los Angeles police.' "

## Making a Federal Case

"Op-ed plants are bullshit," say a chorus of Hill and Knowlton competitors, many of whom cut their teeth working with Mankiewicz. The "new" media management doesn't waste time with opinion articles read by "five people drinking coffee in a newsroom," as one consultant puts it.

"The real work today is done behind the scenes on issues," says a former H&K executive. "You have people of substance going to regulators and assistant secretaries," he explains. "Then you notify the press in advance that the government is taking a certain action, and why, and who you represent, and why your client deserved to have this regulation changed.

"You make your client's story a *government* story, showing how the government's action—by now a quiet fait accompli—has not only helped your client, but is good for the people. That's how you get the story out the right way in the media," he says, smiling, before going on to cite several environmentally incorrect clients who, thanks to adept manipulation, survived encounters with the feds, the media, the "greenies," even a sing-in by aging rocker Jackson Browne.

The executive reviewed the Gypsum asbestos situation. "Listen, the client's alibi was that asbestos isn't bad. Asbestos is one product that is uniformly feared, maybe more than cigarettes. You don't do the op-ed drill."

What he would have recommended would have included more elements of lobbying: "Admit the error. Talk to city officials privately. Explain your financial situation and offer the cheapest way out to remove the stuff. This avoids the costly suit. Then tell the world what a good-neighbor company you are and come back for another contract."

H&K, like other large firms, has tried to adjust to the differences between the two functions—p.r. and lobbying—as they are defined in Washington. On such controversial issues as Kuwait and *JFK*, for example, it was faced with the choice between targeting the media directly or using official channels to spin the story and *then*—as in the case of Kuwait—going after the media. The choice will determine how the press will play the story. Meanwhile, with Washington firms now pushing foreign policy agendas for China, Italy, Haiti, and many other countries, the Capitol Hill approach has gained more acceptance.

"Using Congress is an old tack, but I've never seen it done so openly as I did with H&K and Kuwait," says a former White House official who lobbies, but does not flack, in Washington. "What astounds me is that the press just went along with it. In this case, it was a legitimate story. But it makes you wonder about the other stories that get built up the same way."

The press often has little choice. When a representative or senator calls a press conference or a hearing, somebody has to cover it.

## De-Keatingization

As Mankiewicz recalls, "A member of Congress told me he'd support me on [business legislation that would benefit a client] if I'd de-Keatingize him first. I didn't know what he meant, but he explained he didn't want his constituents, especially the press, saying he was supporting it just because he'd gotten contributions from one of the parties involved."

The object of "de-Keatingizing" someone, Mankiewicz explains, is to make your target, the person you want to support your issue publicly, invulnerable to negative press coverage. "You have to make the issue bomb-proof. 'De-Keatingize,' meaning Get rid of any taint. You have to give your guy the ammunition to show the press that the issue he's backing is inherently something the public—specifically your target's constituents—wants." An easy way to do that, Mankiewicz says, is to produce a favorable poll on the issue. The best recent example of this tactic, says a key member of the White House team that oversaw the Clarence Thomas nomination, was the handling of the Senate Judiciary Committee. The senators found it a lot easier to support Thomas once they'd seen *USA Today* polls showing that a majority of African-Americans approved of Thomas's nomination. "We used media polls—which appear unbiased—to give the senators their out on the matter. And the senators used the polls to explain their vote to the media," this source says.

"The polls de-Keatingized Thomas," Mankiewicz sums up.

## The Hernia Stratagem

This is a new technique not currently taught in p.r. texts. Mankiewicz has used it to considerable effect in response to questions about H&K's representation of Kuwait and BCCI. If you interview him in person about such issues he will chase you with a six-inch-thick pile of clips, rebuttals, and op-ed pieces showing what a bum rap H&K took—and he won't let you leave until you've promised to take the clips and read them all.

Don't knock this. This past May, Daniel Schorr found himself on the receiving end of a Mankiewicz missive on Kuwait. In a lengthy piece for *The Washington Post* titled "See It Not: True Confessions of a Lifetime in TV Journalism," Schorr had referred—in a single sentence—to "public relations 'video releases' or outright hoaxes, like the tearful recital of atrocities in Kuwait by the carefully coached daughter of the Kuwaiti ambassador in Washington"—whose appearance at a congressional hearing was arranged by Hill and Knowlton. Mankiewicz responded by sending a pile of clips that persuaded Schorr that he was in error in using the word "hoax."

"I sent a letter to the *Post* correcting myself, and a copy to Frank," Schorr says. "He called and asked if he could circulate it." Shortly thereafter (and well before the *Post* ran it), the letter became a lead story in a p.r. newsletter, which benefitted Hill and Knowlton if no one else. "I think it was cheap," says Schorr.

By forcing the journalist to retreat on one detail, the counterattack served to blunt the point of Schorr's original article—the lack of suspicion among the media about staged "news."

## Lobbing Back the Lobby Charge

In its handling of the Bank of Commerce and Credit International, Hill and Knowlton had more at stake than the bank's reputation; it had its own. After former Customs Commissioner William von Raab testified in 1991 that "influence peddlers" had prevented federal regulators and prosecutors from moving in on BCCI, H&K went on the offensive. The firm was registered at the Justice Department as a lobbyist for BCCI from 1988 to March 1990 and had taken charge of blocking any negative publicity about an affiliated institution, First American Bank of Washington.

In response to charges that H&K had "lobbied" for BCCI, Mankiewicz resorted to the hoary ploy "The Public Testimonial"; he wrung from von Raab a carefully phrased letter (which now hangs behind his desk) stating, "I do not have any information that Mr. Gray or you spoke to any official in either our federal government's executive or legislative branch on behalf of BCCI."

True. According to Mankiewicz, all of the work on behalf of BCCI done by H&K was handled by offices in London and Tampa. True, too, lobbying, in the technical Washington sense, means that someone officially registered as a firm's representative officially visited a member of Congress on behalf of that client. Of course, if the p.r. person mentioned the client over dinner, got a few pieces placed in the *Post,* or placed a few calls to the White House, that wouldn't officially count as lobbying.

In fact, when *Regardie's* magazine, my employer, was going to press in April 1990 with a cover story called "Who Really Owns First American Bank" (about BCCI, Clark Clifford, and First American), we were deluged with calls from Mankiewicz on behalf of First American and copies of letters to congressmen denouncing the story. Still, he can legitimately wave von Raab's letter like a vaccination certificate to ward off an outbreak of skeptical reporters.

## The Preemptive Strike

"It's more common now for p.r. firms to try to stop a negative story *before* it's in print," says *The Washington Post*'s Howard Kurtz. "Correcting a story afterwards is rarely as effective as shutting it down, or turning it around a little."

One increasingly popular way of aborting a story is to launch an ad hominum attack on the reporter. An H&K executive who insisted on anonymity confirmed that one of the standard procedures these days when a client anticipates negative press involves digging up the reporter's previous stories, then alleging that the reporter has already shown malice towards the subject. A former H&K executive provides an example. He says that when *Time* was preparing its cover story on the Church of Scientology, H&K employees dug up the reporter's previous work, trying to document disputes between the reporter and church leaders. In April, the church filed a $416 million libel suit against *Time,* Time Warner, and reporter Richard Behar, claiming among other things that *Time* had assigned a biased reporter to write the story.

Other tactics include dredging up the number of corrections that can be traced to a reporter as proof of negligence-to-be. Or alleging that the reporter has some conflict of interest in connection with the subject.

"Like the little-lies approach, the anti-reporter tactics are all red herrings," says the former H&K media specialist, who insisted on anonymity. "But if you make enough noise about them, you can make an editor in Washington think twice about how hard he'll let the reporter write the story. And that's your goal."

## The New Honesty

Public relations firms "always say, It could have been worse without our help, when a p.r. problem blows up in their faces," says an H&K competitor. "And that way you can never call their bluff and say, Prove it."

But in the case of United Way of America, failure to accept Hill and Knowlton's advice clearly did make matters worse. Last December, Washington reporters began calling to ask about the UWA president's travel, expenses, subsidiary commercial for-profit ventures, and his personal liaisons. United Way hired Mankiewicz to field "inquiries." He in turn urged UWA to hire a respected D.C. investigative firm to look into UWA itself. The investigators looked, gasped, and gave Mankiewicz the bad news: the allegations were true. The top echelon of UWA had been living in the lap of luxury on donors' dollars.

Mankiewicz urged the board of directors and UWA president William Aramony to follow the simplest rule of p.r.: Tell the Truth. Tell it All. Tell it Now.

But, informed sources says, Mankiewicz was overruled by the board and Aramony, who weren't prepared to let the public know what was happening. The result was that when the UWA stories broke in February, affiliates across the country responded with devastating effect by withholding their dues.

"We could have controlled the story, given it our spin, if they'd let us," says Mankiewicz.

## "There's No Such Thing as a Bad Client"

It's fine for Alan Dershowitz to insist on the innocence of some of his more notorious clients, but media types wonder how lobbyists and flacks justify plugging the causes of some of theirs.

It wasn't always like this. Loet Velmans, president of Hill and Knowlton from 1978 to 1986, remembers when the firm had the "luxury" of turning down clients. "Let's call it pragmatism," he says. "But we wouldn't take on clients who would upset our most important people—our employees—or other clients." He cited the tobacco industry, which H&K dropped as a client in the 1960s. "We couldn't do anything for them because they wouldn't take our advice—to research what smoking would do to you, and to invest in cancer research. They couldn't publicly do anything to suggest the link between cigarettes and cancer, and it was useless to represent them."

Velmans also recalls an era when H&K refused unsavory political clients: Ferdinand Marcos, South Africa.

Nowadays the list of foreign clients of prominent firms such as H&K; Black, Manafort, Stone and Kelly; Van Kloberg & Associates; Neill & Company; and Sawyer/Miller includes Zaire, Peru, El Salvador, Colombia, Kenya, and Saddam Hussein. With a good spin, Eva Peron could have been packaged as a victim of sexual harassment.

"Things have changed now. The competition is so fierce, hardly anyone turns away paying customers," Velmans says. Mankiewicz wishes that some *had* been turned away. He was infuriated when he learned in 1990 that H&K had been hired by the Catholic bishops to push the church's anti-abortion position. "That's what they have priests for," he says. The controversy briefly raised the issues of legitimacy in clientele, but last year an executive told the Washington staff at H&K, "We'd represent Satan if he paid."

Maybe, but they may have to be careful what they say about him. Last year, H&K was sued by investors in BCCI; plaintiffs claimed H&K had portrayed the bank as pure. The suit was dismissed, but it raised questions of how far a p.r. firm can go with a controversial client.

"If asbestos is safe, China is a democracy, and BCCI is clean, how can you believe these guys on anything?" asks a fierce-featured news show host who doesn't like H&K but often goes along with its spin, like the rest of us. "There should be more backlash."

What steps can the media take to, if not lash back, at least make it clear that the emergence of certain issues reflects the handiwork of a spinmeister? Kurtz of *The Washington Post* believes that more stories exposing how a p.r. firm has been brought in to effect policy on a grand scale will help to alert the public to possible manipulation.

It's a warm and fuzzy sentiment. But as long as we need stories, and as long as we rely on outsiders to do the legwork, and as long as we're afraid of being beaten, says a newsmagazine editor in Washington, we are going to give spin-meisters more credence than we should.

There's some good news: "You won't get a story placed by having a flack call a reporter anymore," says Kurtz. "Most reporters would prefer to hear from the source or subject themselves."

"You are your best spokesperson," says Mankiewicz. "There's an American prejudice against having someone else field your questions. That's starting to come into it more."

So how can Mankiewicz charge $350 an hour for doing what he does? "*Some*body has to do it," he says.

As for the bottom line: "Can you manipulate the Washington media?" Mankiewicz muses, "Can I? Well, if I could I wouldn't tell you."

"And I can't," he hrrmmpps. And winks.

# 31

# The CEO and the Reporter

## *by* Harold Burson

*Editor's Note:* Of course, not all PR workers are devious, and not all reporters are free from their own biases and special interests and ignorance. Often PR consultants are necessary because the press isn't doing a good job.

This is the view of Harold Burson, founder and chair of one of the world's largest PR firms, Burson-Marsteller Ltd. This article originally appeared in the *Emory Business Magazine,* Spring 1989, and this version was published in *Across the Board,* July/August 1989.

Today's typical *Fortune*-500 chief executive officer is, at best, suspicious of the motives of reporters covering him, his company, his industry, or business in general. At worst, he has a deep-seated antagonism that keeps him removed from or inaccessible to the press.

Horror stories that have the media as centerpiece abound among CEOs. Regrettably, some of these stories have a basis in fact: a reporter's biased point of view reinforced by selective out-of-context quotes, ill-prepared reporters writing on complex business issues for which they lack even rudimentary grounding, a predilection for the controversial and "sensationalizing the trivial."

True enough, it's not always the reporter who's at fault when an article contains information the CEO considers better left unsaid or unwritten. More frequently than most CEOs want to admit, they themselves are the sources or otherwise bear responsibility for less-than-favorable articles. Some (fewer today than in years past) arrive for interviews without having thought through what they want to say; others simply talk too much—they say things, forgetful of the reality that a reporter's job is to report.

Talk to business reporters and you'll find the suspicions are not one-sided. They have their own versions of the relationship: CEOs talk with reporters only when they have something positive to say; in times of adversity, they simply cannot be reached; you can't get a straight answer—and when you do, it's too late.

There is truth to both points of view. Yet CEOs and business reporters need one another. Business today requires all of the understanding it can muster. And who better to help create and promote that understanding than the media, both print and electronic, that report the news?

My observation is that, during the past decade, progress has been made on both sides of the equation. And this bodes well for a public better informed about business and the workings of the private sector.

Increasingly, CEOs have come to recognize both the needs of the reporter and the process that moves news from the reporter's notebook to the printed page or the television screen. Many have come to appreciate the need for speed in responding to questions posed late in the afternoon; there's better understanding of deadlines. Many have even taught themselves to respond in quotable terms, in terms of television's 10-second sound bite.

More significant, some CEOs have begun to look at the press as a communications vehicle that is available to help them achieve their own corporate objectives. After all, the media, individually and certainly collectively, have a wide audience. What better vehicle to reach customers, employees, shareholders, or government leaders with a specific message? A few CEOs now view the media as potential partners in their own communications process. And they are learning how to work with the media to better advantage.

Speaking for the media, today's business reporters are better equipped for their jobs than their eager counterparts of the decade of the '70s. Many, if not most, have broad general knowledge of business; many have become specialists in the industries and business disciplines they cover.

Most important, the media have made a major commitment to business news coverage. Each of the network evening news shows now has a segment on business; each of the networks has set aside time and committed resources for business news shows. Newspapers are devoting more space to business news coverage; a lot of it has moved from the business page to the front page.

All of this is for the good. Our free market economy requires the underpinning that only the public can give it—as consumers, as employees, as investors, and as voters. Anything that contributes knowledge and understanding of how business operates in a democratic society is worth working for.

# VIII

# Advertising:
# Manipulating the Public

News should be accurate, fair, balanced, and objective, but as we learned in the previous section, it is often loaded or slanted by those inside and outside the media to influence rather than to inform. Advertising is something we expect to be more manipulative, but we don't expect it to be misleading or false.

In the 1990s, misleading advertising appears to be increasing in mass media. Federal government efforts to police standards diminished during the Reagan and Bush years, causing a number of consumer groups to express growing concern about deceptive advertising.

Reporting on this issue in the *Washington Post*, Paul Farhi said that the debate is "rarely over flagrantly fraudulent practices like selling snake oil as medicine; rather, the most frequent complaints concern potentially misleading information or lack of information." He points out that health organizations, for example, "decry such common practices as touting reduced-calorie products as 'lite' because there are no generally accepted standards for making such a claim. There is also much debate over nutritional claims such as cereal advertising that proclaims to reduce cancer." Car rental and airfare advertisers have been accused of not fully disclosing additional charges and restrictions. Auto ads cram detailed information about safety features, options, and prices into fine print.

Of course the debate has two sides. According to Farhi, the advertising industry's self-regulatory group claims that the perceptions of increased deceptive ads are just perceptions, not supported by real evidence. In the advertising business, says William V. Weithes, chair of a large, worldwide agency, "If you're not on the up and up, your competitors will jump all over you."[1]

Perhaps a bigger problem than deceptive advertising is the misuse and abuse of human needs and emotions to sell a product, or advertisements that appeal to children and youths who are particularly vulnerable to such appeals. Cigarette advertising has been especially guilty, according to consumer and feminist groups.

"Bored? Lonely? Restless?" What you need, says a four-page R. J. Reynolds Tobacco Company ad campaign, is a Camel cigarette. It features a sexy blonde on the cover and the face of Camel's mascot, Old Joe, inside. It offers tips on "how to impress someone at the beach," including a suggestion to "run into the water, grab someone and drag her back to shore, as if you've saved her from drowning. The more she kicks and screams, the better." The ad includes a coupon for a free pack of cigarettes and urges the would-be coupon users to "ask a kind-looking stranger to redeem it." A Reynolds company spokesperson said the ad series was intended to be tongue-in-cheek, but the company's CEO apologized and said it would never run again.[2]

Advertising aimed at children is a special problem. According to *Adweek*, there were about 160 children's magazines in 1990, almost twice as many as in 1986. Most of them carried advertising, much of which blurs the line between editorial and product pitch. One example is an Instant Quaker Oatmeal ad that appears to be a full-page Popeye comic strip. Popeye proclaims, "Can the spinach. I want me Instant Quaker Oatmeal."

Product-related TV programs are also proliferating. Syndicated programs such as "G.I. Joe" and "Transformers" are "toy-driven," and the entire program is a commercial for the product.

These ads have an impact on children. A survey of 1500 children aged eight to fifteen by the Yankelovich Youth Monitor asked what influenced them the most to buy a product: 41 percent said TV commercials; 41 percent said a peer who owned the product; parent suggestions only influenced 20 percent.[3]

Following are a few examples of some of the issues being raised in the 1990s about advertising's manipulation of the public.

**Notes**

1. Paul Farhi, "Misleading Ads Seen on Rise as Federal Policing Efforts Diminish," *Washington Post*, 23 May 1989, p. C-5.
2. Brooke A. Masters, "Camel Ad Ignites Opposition," *Washington Post*, 26 July 1989, p. C-1.
3. Daniel M. Gold, "The Backlash Over Clutter in Kidland," *Adweek*, 8 October 1990, p. 4.

# 32

# Cigarettes under Fire

## *by* Richard W. Pollay

*Editor's Note:* Cigarette advertising usually provides glowing visions of the good life. Everyone is young and healthy, the women are thin and sexy, the men are virile and strong, and the setting is usually the clean outdoors.

This vision, says George Gerbner, former dean of the Annenberg School of Communication at the University of Pennsylvania, "counters and overwhelms all other information about an addiction that kills more than a thousand people a day, more than heroin, crack, alcohol, fire, car accidents, homicides, and AIDS combined."

Richard W. Pollay is a teaching and research professor at the business school of the University of British Columbia and curator of its History of Advertising Archives. This article originally appeared in *Media & Values*, Spring/Summer 1991.

Although inseparable from the act of smoking, cigarette smoke is one substance that is hardly ever seen in ads and commercials for cigarettes. Evidently, its haze would obscure the illusion of youth and vigor advertisers attempt to project with healthy models and pure and pristine environments.

In a way that's ironic, because the "PR smokescreen" the industry has been producing for decades has been highly effective in camouflaging the pernicious nature of its activities. Even in these days of anti-smoking awareness, tobacco producers have been fighting a highly effective rear guard action aimed at reassuring and retaining concerned smokers and recruiting new ones to replace an increasing number of quitters. The industry's own records show how it's done. A closer look at 50 years of ads shows how good they have been at turning a pernicious product into a symbol of health and good times.

## Smokescreens

"Tobacco industry says it wants to halt kids' smoke," say headlines reporting public relations from the Tobacco Institute. Don't believe it. No matter how privileged or persuasive, this cigarette smokescreen is totally contradicted by facts emerging from archives and trials. The facts show that cigarette firms research the starting process and preferences of kids as young as 15 extensively, design ads to appeal to their emotional needs and are well aware of teen nicotine addiction.

For every dollar spent on PR activities denying an interest in kids, many hundreds more will advertise cigarettes and recruit starters. More millions are spent to support a decades-long effort to minimize and obscure consumer judgments about smoking risks, reach new markets by appealing to women and minorities and reassure troubled "pre-quitters."

Thanks to recent ground-breaking suits seeking liability compensation for cancer victims, records of the industry's public relations firm, Hill & Knowlton, are now open at the Wisconsin State Historical Society. In addition, boxes of incriminating corporate records for virtually all cigarette makers and affiliates have been subpoenaed and reviewed by experts. They expose in detail what the cigarette firms seek to accomplish and how they go about it.

Since smoking dropouts from quitting—and dying—are high, continued success depends on a steady flow of recruits. The industry is dominated by the companies who recruit the most new, young smokers. "Young smokers represent the major opportunity group for the cigarette industry," said Canada's Imperial Tobacco Limited. A marketing executive quoted by the FTC said: "Market expansion in this industry means two things—kids and women. I think that governs the thinking of all the companies."

Much research and marketing effort is aimed at teenagers beginning at age 15. Memos about industry plans bear titles like "Youth Target Study" or "Project 16." Hidden camera interviews and surveys gather data on demographics (e.g. age, sex, family size), lifestyle (taste in music, clothes, movies, hobbies, etc.), health (knowledge, rationalizations and concerns), and personality. The psychological research is highly sophisticated, measuring factors like ego strength, submissiveness, shrewdness, tendency toward guilty feelings and self-discipline. Different personality types are targeted, like Dakota's current efforts to reach "virile females."

## Molding the Image

One of the purposes of cigarette advertising is to shape how others perceive the nicotine user, and his or her own social and self image. Advertisers know that peer group pressure is an important factor in kids' decision making. Thus they work consciously to use ads to shape group, as well as individual, perceptions.

According to corporate studies, adolescents' urge to display symbols of their desired independence can be turned into a motivation for smoking. Ads for Marlboro fit this model, since the cowboy is self-sufficient with no boss (parent/teacher). Selling a drug like nicotine—documented by the Surgeon General as addictive as well as lethal—as a symbol of independence is ironic and tragically deceptive.

Many studies have shown that media that carry cigarette ads do a poor job with the health story. Editors are naturally reluctant to bite the hands that feed them, and the cigarette firms don't hesitate to use their clout if necessary. The world's largest ad agency, Saatchi & Saatchi, offended R. J. Reynolds Nabisco in 1989 by writing an ad for Northwest Airlines announcing a no smoking policy. The ad agency lost $84 million dollars of business, not from cigarettes, but from Nabisco Brands, owned by RJR. Cigarette firms also own all brands made by Kraft, Miller Beer and General Foods, keeping them among the top 10 advertisers, even on TV.

Promotional spending by U.S. cigarette manufacturers has more than tripled in the two decades since cigarette ads were banned on American radio and television—perhaps the clearest evidence of advertising's importance to these corporations. Instead of adding their TV advertising budgets to their profits they chose to invest instead in free sample distribution, billboards, magazine ads and sport and concert promotion.

## Underestimating the Risks

The addictiveness and health risks of smoking are underestimated by even the well educated, thanks to advertising and the relative lack of media exposure to the medical catastrophe represented by lung cancer and other smoking-related illnesses. About 90 percent of today's college students, for example, underestimate the risks of smoking. Corporate research finds that starters "almost universally assume these risks will not apply to themselves because they will not become addicted." R. J. Reynolds found that: "However intriguing smoking was at 11, 12 or 13, by the age of 16 or 17 many regretted their use of cigarettes for health reasons and because they felt unable to stop smoking when they want to." Other research documents discuss how teens become "slaves to their cigarettes."

Firms also know that warnings are little noticed by kids and, if and when seen, go unheeded. But it's ironic that the 1964 U.S. law requiring warning labels on cigarette packages is seen as a triumph for consumer advocates.

Of the 15 proposals considered by Congress at the time, only the industry-sponsored bill passed. Even *Advertising Age* called the legislation that finally emerged—a version of the industry-sponsored proposal—"a shocking piece of special interest legislation." It weakened the warning wording, let the industry decide placement and type, did *not* apply to ads until the next decade (1972), handcuffed the FTC's regulatory powers for many years and blocked cities or states from passing more stringent laws. Political astuteness, media contacts and lobbying experience helped tobacco producers work a "damage control" victory.

Despite Congressional intentions, the warning formula that finally emerged from the legislative process is far from effective. The placement and printing of warnings on tobacco packages and ads minimizes the attention they get. Research shows that the warnings are rarely noticed and poorly recalled. Recent changes require a rotation of four different warnings and less ambiguous language but even these are all but illegible in billboards or transit ads, and are totally absent in sponsored sports events, like Virginia Slim-sponsored tennis. They actually do have one unintended effect—helping firms avoid lawsuits because they can tell courts and grieving families that smokers were warned.

Not all ads are aimed at kids, of course. Women have been targeted since the 1920s, when Marlboros were called "Mild as May" in an attempt to position them as a product for the growing women's market. Public relations photos from the era identified women smoking in public as lighting a "torch of liberty." As in many modern ads, some brands were portrayed as symbols of fashionable slimness. Virginia Slims tells today's women that "You've Come a Long Way Baby!" But in truth things have changed very little. Women, like men, are sold addiction and death by ads positioning cigarettes as symbols of freedom and style. Blacks, too, have long been targeted, but were years late in being offered filter products as an appeal to safety concerns.

Now ads from Philip Morris Companies Inc. feature endorsements from prominent African Americans for "Free Speech" ads. The company poses as a defender of freedom and liberty, while in reality protecting its record profits as a promoter of nicotine addiction.

## A Leaky Pail

Frequent industry claims that cigarette advertising is merely intended to promote brand switching also don't stand up to analysis. Switchers are a small and unattractive market segment. Only about 10 percent or less of smokers are switchers in any given year, and these are mostly fickle "pre-quitters." Corporate documents identify efforts aimed at switchers as third in their priority list, behind advertising designed to attract new starters and reassure existing smokers. This is exactly what might be expected. If you had a leaky pail (business) and wanted to hold as much water (dollars spent on cigarettes) as possible, you would try to stop the leaks (block quitting) and/or open the taps to fill the pail faster (recruit starters). Stirring the water (promoting switching) would do you no good at all.

Ads are developed and carefully tested to insure that viewers get the intended message of an image, such as "self-reliance," "intelligent choice," or "no need to quit." Pictures in this case are worth far more than a thousand words. Because seeing is believing, they are experienced, not analyzed. Regulatory laws, which deal with the meanings of words, are ill-prepared to deal with the consequences of visual persuasion. Thus, pictures of healthy smokers are permissible and potent in a context in which verbal health claims would be regulated or ridiculed.

## Ads Aimed at Health Concerns

Ads aimed at smokers concerned about health risks, a vast majority of adult smokers, appeal to their fears, offering reassurances about health and safety. The majority show pure, pristine environments with healthy, robust smokers fit for athletic challenges because "positive life-style images . . . effect the continued social acceptability of smoking." Most ads for filtered products imply relative safety, an idea sometimes ludicrously false. Kent filters were initially made from asbestos, trade named "micronite." The 1954 ads implied an American Medical Association endorsement that the AMA called "outrageous huckster-ism." The tar and nicotine levels for filtered Pall Mall, Chesterfield and Lucky Strikes were once higher, not lower, than the unfiltered versions of the very same brands.

Cigarette firms complain that they are heavily regulated. In truth, they need *not* comply with the Consumer Products Safety Commission, the Controlled Substances Act, the Federal Hazardous Substances Act, the Food and Drug Administration, or the Toxic Substances Act. Only the Federal Trade Commission has had periodic and limited authority over the years, and it has been frustrated, defeated and handcuffed. Well-meaning Congressional initiatives over the years rarely get out of committee, or survive the lobbying counter-attack.

Other countries are taking far more substantial initiatives to control the ads and other promotional inducements to smoke. Partial or nearly total bans of cigarette promotion already exist or are now before legislatures in Canada, New Zealand, Norway, France, Italy and the entire European Common Market to name a few.

As a Canadian, I have direct experience with Canada's cigarette advertising ban, which became effective in January 1989. Canada's initiative to ban tobacco advertising could be a model for the United States because of the two countries' similar smoking history, shared tobacco suppliers, related cultures and free trade relationship. But at the moment, unfortunately, the Canadian ad ban is locked in controversy.

As soon as it took effect it was instantly challenged by separate suits from each and every cigarette firm. Legal challenges alleged that the ban violates freedom of commercial speech, grounds that would likely be used in the U.S. to fight similar restrictions. A trial spanned nearly a year and a decision from the Quebec Superior Court is pending.

The decision is uncertain, in part because the judge and lawyers are themselves addicted smokers, but no matter what the outcome, the case is certain to go to the nation's Supreme Court. The stakes are enormous both for cigarette firms enjoying record profits, and the Canadian public, currently experiencing 40,000 smoking-related deaths a year, according to statistics from the Canadian Health and Welfare Department. Canada's cigarette sales dropped seven percent during the first year of the ban. A comparable drop in the smoking-related death rate would represent a savings of 2,800 lives a year.

## Ad Bans

Ad bans work, because advertising works. As long as advertising continues to be part of tobacco industry policy, they should be a necessary part of public policy, if only because of the message of warning they send. Unfortunately, many American residents, especially smokers, think that the U.S. would ban cigarette ads if smoking were highly hazardous, and that the lack of a ban implies that the product's hazards are not all that great. This faith in the U.S. government is sadly misplaced to date.

Unlike other products, cigarettes are deadly when used exactly as intended. The advertising images, and their intended meanings, are inherently false. Media need to develop a sense of responsibility for disseminating them. Western society needs to re-examine the commercial ethos that made them possible for so many decades—and is still keeping them going in the United States.

# 33

# When the Walls Come Tumbling Down

## *by* Michael Hoyt

*Editor's Note:* Traditionally walls have been fairly high between the advertising and editorial staffs at the average magazine. Editors edited and advertisers advertised. But that is changing.

"As journalism becomes more marketing oriented, the task of a journalist and an advertiser becomes more and more similar," says Stuart Ewen, author of *All Consuming Images*, a book about advertising. "At one time marketers viewed magazines as a place in which they could rent space for advertising. Today they view them as real estate holdings. Once you own real estate, you begin to think about the neighborhood . . . changing the shrubbery. . . ."

Michael Hoyt agrees that the advertiser now wants to have some say about what goes into the nonadvertising part of the magazine. Hoyt is associate editor of the *Columbia Journalism Review*, where this article appeared in March/April 1990.

The cover of the November issue of *Lear's* is graced with the face of a woman with stunning blue-gray eyes. We turn the page to a red and luscious two-page spread for Samsara, a new perfume by Guerlain of Paris that delivers, the ad suggests, "a sense of serenity."

Four pages later comes the table of contents where, in the credit lines, we learn that the woman on the cover wears makeup from Guerlain and that "her fragrance is Samsara."

In a paragraph at the top of the same page we learn more: the cover person is Lois Doherty-Mander, who lives in Manhattan with her insurance-company vice-president husband and her two children. We also learn—*Lear's* is positively upfront about it—that she is director of public relations for . . . Guerlain. What has she been working on lately? Doherty-Mander's "most recent project has been the launch of Guerlain's new perfume, Samsara."

This is surely a thing of beauty from the advertiser's perspective—a striking advertisement supplemented by the very cover of the magazine, a new fragrance product with the essence of editorial credibility tastefully misted all over it. Guerlain, it is worth noting, bought two and two-thirds ad pages inside the

November *Lear's* (for anti-wrinkle products) as well as the sumptuous Samsara spread in the premium inside-the-cover position, for a total bill that surely contributed to the publisher's sense of serenity. Frances Lear, the magazine's editor-in-chief, calls the plethora of plugs a "terrible mistake." *Lear's* would not normally push any beauty product in the cover credits, she says, but Doherty-Mander insisted and "we had no backup that month." And Lear says she did not know until too late that the Samsara ad was inside the cover. As for the idea of using a major advertiser as a cover subject in the first place, Lear first said it was a mistake that would not be repeated, but after a few minutes of conversation, in which she mentioned the number of fashion designers who appear on the covers of magazines where they advertise these days, she reconsidered—"strike all that"—arguing that "this kind of thing is done all the time."

True but sad. From a reader's perspective this confluence of advertising and editorial is confusing: Where does the sales pitch end? Where does the editor take over?

The ad/edit duet continues inside the November *Lear's*, although in a somewhat less pioneering vein. On page forty-two, a left-hand page in the Money & Worth section of the magazine, for example, is an assessment of Chrysler's new Eagle Talon that is at least as excited about the sports car as the full-page Eagle Talon advertisement on page forty-three, just opposite. Another mistake, says Lear.

But why pick on *Lear's?* Magazines of all stripes are suddenly competing to give advertisers something extra—"value added" in ad-world lingo—in return for their business. Many of these extras are perfectly legitimate and have little or nothing to do with editorial content; others fall into a gray and foggy area; still others involve the selling of pieces of editorial integrity, from slivers to chunks to truckloads.

Pressure from advertisers is not new, of course; magazine professionals say it was always there, particularly in the women's and the trade magazine fields. What's new is the intensity of the demands, the extension of certain kinds of demands to the kind of magazines whose reputations once kept them immune, and the snowball effect that results when too many magazines suddenly relax their standards. What makes the situation worse is the fact that, at many magazines, the great wall that once separated the business side from the editorial side and protected editors and publishers from temptation is, like today's Berlin Wall, more monument than barrier.

"In private conversations among editors that [advertiser pressure] is talked about all the time," says Daniel Okrent, the founding editor of *New England Monthly* magazine, now a writer and consultant. "Get them up on a panel at the MPA/*Folio* convention [the Magazine Publishers of America and *Folio* magazine] and it doesn't exist. It's hilarious." Still, in the December *Folio*, more than 40 percent of the 250 editors who had responded to the magazine's survey said they had been told by their ad director or publisher "to do something that you felt seriously compromised editorial." (More than 70 percent of the consumer magazine part of that group said they had refused, as did nearly 50 percent of trade magazine editors.)

"Is there pressure? You bet there's pressure. There is huge pressure," says David Long, advertising director for *People* magazine. "Not only is there pressure, but it's been successful. It's 'If you do this, we'll do that.' The whole world is softening, and it's cheapening the whole business."

"I hope we see that this is horrifying," says Samir A. Husni, a well-known magazine watcher and a journalism teacher at the University of Mississippi. "I hope we step back from it."

Stuart Ewen, chairman of the communications department at Hunter College and author of a recent book on advertising, *All Consuming Images*, sums up the recent change in the relationship between magazines and advertisers this way: "At one time marketers viewed magazines as a place in which they could rent space for advertising. Today they view them as real estate holdings. Once you own real estate, you begin to think about the neighborhood, the surroundings, changing the shrubbery and so forth."

Part of the reason for this power shift is the revolution in marketing in the '70s and '80s: as advertisers feared that consumers were growing resistant to their generalized mass advertising they began to aim at market segments—specific groups of people with spending money. Niche marketing led to niche magazines, many of them centered on specific activities—decorating, investing, computing, boating, etc.—or at least around the tastes and sensibilities of the target group. These days many magazines are hatched more as marketing concepts than as editorial ideas; at their core they are advertising delivery vehicles.

Ewen fears that these developments have exerted a gravitational tug on all the media, creating a degree of confusion about the role of journalism in the minds of journalists, advertisers, and the public. "As journalism becomes more marketing oriented, the task of what it is to be a journalist and what it is to be an advertiser becomes more and more similar," Ewen says. "The task becomes keeping people interested in a certain range of goods or activities."

Such a shift does not happen all at once, but in increments, collections of seemingly small and innocuous decisions. *The New York Times* adds another boutique section; *Rolling Stone* starts covering fashion; *U.S. News & World Report* adds another ad-building annual "Guide" on fitness or investing or home ownership, displacing who knows what; *Lear's* adds another product-mentioning article, such as the one on perfumes in November (one of five product-mentioning pieces in that issue), which manages to mention twenty-four perfumes by name, five of them advertised in the same issue.

Accelerating this trend is a supply-and-demand dilemma. Advertising expenditures have been fairly flat since the mid-1980s and, although magazines as a group have held their own in competition with other media, they are in ferocious competition with each other. They keep dividing the ad-dollar pie into more and more pieces. Husni, who has tracked the birth of new magazines for years, estimates that about 100 new ones appeared in the year 1968. During 1988 he counted 491, and approximately 580 last year. "There are too many publications and a limited number of advertising dollars," says Don E. Schultz, a professor of advertising at Northwestern University's Medill School of Journalism.

The scramble for ad dollars led to rate cutting—rate-card discounts for heavy advertisers. But rate cutting is profits cutting. The keynote speaker at the MPA/*Folio* convention last fall, George V. Grune of the Reader's Digest Association, called it "a plague on our business" that is "spreading like a virus gone wild." As a defense against this virus, publishers developed the notion of value-added advertising—giving the advertiser something more than just a page. "I wouldn't blame it all on the advertiser," says Schultz. "The advertiser says, 'We are going to buy thirty-six pages somewhere, but your rates are too high. You want X, we can pay Y.' So the publisher says, 'You pay X, and we can do this and this and this.' "

What *this* and *this* and *this* is depends on the magazine. *Good Housekeeping*'s Seal of Approval is an ancient ancestor of value added advertising. More recently, *The New Yorker* lent its name to a luxury car road rally. *TV Guide* is offering free bonus ads and a free telephone listing to advertisers who buy a certain number of pages in special editorial packages, such as "celebrity diet and exercise tips." *Parenting* co-sponsors "baby fairs," where advertiser products are displayed. *People* offers new advertisers, or old ones who increase their spending by half a million dollars, space on the monthly health club posters created by Whittle Communications (and recently acquired by Time Warner), and for select advertisers who are interested, *People* is now even in a position to help set up sponsored entertainment tours, along the lines of last year's Budweiser/Rolling Stones concert series.

These kinds of extras would seem to have little or no effect on the editorial part of the magazines. But there is another kind of added value that magazines can offer for sale—their own editorial content. Consider a former publisher for a major retail trade publication. Since he is job hunting and asked that his name not be printed, let's call him X. Like most trade magazines, X's routinely covered products made by advertisers. But X says he kept his ad sales staff and his editors and writers apart from each other and strictly avoided the quid pro quo. Under that system, the magazine was profitable, despite some belt-tightening in the industry it covered, but not profitable enough for X's boss. The boss began selling big, long-term advertising packages "and promising cover stories as a sweetener to close the deal," says X. "It wasn't in the contract, of course, but he'd do it with me standing right there."

It became X's job to order editors to drum up stories on subjects that were sometimes not legitimate, upbeat cover stories on companies that were actually fading, for example. Two editors quit over ethics. In January, X quit, leaving behind a $100,000-plus salary. "I asked myself if I could do this anymore, and the answer was no," he says. X thinks the magazine will increase profits for a while under the new system, but will begin to sink in tandem with the magazine's reputation. Once the editorial content is devalued, he figures, the magazine becomes less valuable to advertisers.

We are less shocked, perhaps, at such a story in a trade magazine than we would be about compromises at top consumer magazines, but it is clear that the pressure to sell out can be just as strong in the consumer field these days. According to a former editor at *Manhattan, inc.*, when the magazine approached fashion designer/potential advertiser Ralph Lauren for a story a few years ago, his organization attached certain conditions: the cover, approval of the writer (Lauren's people had two specific writers in mind, as the editor recalls), and a guaranteed minimum number of pages. Lauren's representatives even wanted to pick the photographer and the photographs, the former editor says, but *Manhattan, inc.* turned down the deal. It is hard to know whether other magazines have struck such deals, but there are cases that invite scrutiny. *Vanity Fair's* puffy profile of Lauren in February 1988, for example, was illustrated by the same photographer who shoots Lauren's ads. As Daniel Lazare noted in this magazine (see "Vanity Fare," CJR May/June 1989), *Vanity Fair* is apparently addicted to obsequious stories about fashion designers who, in turn, purchase many ad pages in the magazine. André Leon Talley, who wrote *Vanity Fair's* cover piece on Calvin and Kelly Klein, explained to Lazare that a fashion writer's job is not to probe or investigate but "to seduce a consumer into a store."

Sometimes an advertising/editorial connection is right out front. *Family Circle*, the nation's largest women's magazine (owned by The New York Times Magazine Group), joined forces with mega-retailer K Mart last year with the aid of style and entertainment author Martha Stewart, who is a *Family Circle* contributing editor as well as K Mart's "life-style and entertaining consultant." According to a fascinating article by Randall Rothenberg in the January 18, 1989, *New York Times*, K Mart helped to finance the reconstruction of one of Stewart's country houses. *Family Circle* then covered the reconstruction in three articles, starting in February 1989. K Mart, in turn, purchased more than sixty pages of advertising in the magazine—worth some $4 million, according to the *Times*—including three eight-to-twelve-page advertorial sections that include descriptions of K Mart products useful for renovating homes. The advertorials were also to be distributed at K Marts, which were to introduce a Martha Stewart line of products. K Mart, in short, got quite a lot of value added—editorial support from a magazine with a readership of twenty-one million.

Rule 4 of the "Guidelines for Special Advertising Sections" promulgated by the American Society of Magazine Editors states that "editors and other editorial staff members should not prepare advertising sections for their own publications." Advertorials are designed to give ads an aura of editorial credibility, and ASME tries to keep them within certain bounds. ASME's enforcement tool is a polite letter of reprimand to the magazine.

Its guidelines seem to be widely ignored. Rule 2b, for example, says that "the layout, design, and type" of special ad sections should be distinctly different from the publication's editorial look, but the November *Elle* includes a fifteen-page advertorial section that mimics the look of the magazine. The January 15 *U.S. News & World Report* contains three advertorials—on Brazil, Zimbabwe, and Indonesia—which might be mistaken for editorial matter and which, although they carry disclaimers at the bottom of every other page, do not identify the section as advertising at the top, as rule 1A requires.

Rule 2c says special advertising sections should not be slugged on the cover, but the top cover line of November's *Popular Photography* announces a "Special Advertorial Section" about video filmmaking and equipment. Rule 3 says that "the editors' names and titles should not appear on, or be associated with, special advertising sections," but in November's *Automobile Magazine* we find a thirty-four-page "special supplement" all about Volkswagen. All the advertisements in the supplement are also about Volkswagen. The insert has its own masthead—a condensed version of the magazine's masthead—and the editorial valentines about Volkswagen products and Volkswagen history are written and illustrated by *Automobile* staff members, including the editor.

*Esquire* sailed at least close to the edge of rule number 4, the one about editors not preparing advertorials, with its Absolut Vodka short story contest, sponsored by Absolut's distributors, Carillon Importers. The stories had to include the words "Absolut Vodka" to be eligible and, according to both the original rules in the magazine and the introduction to the winning story, which ran in the December *Esquire*, they were judged by "a panel of *Esquire* editors and Carillon officials" under the supervision of Smiley Promotion Inc., an independent judging organization. *Esquire* editor-in-chief Lee Eisenberg says that once he learned about the contest, hatched by *Esquire*'s marketing staff, he ruled out the participation of his editors. "No *Esquire* editor was involved in any way," he says, adding that the fact that the introduction to the winning story says otherwise is a mistake "that slipped by me."

In any event, the perception that a magazine of *Esquire*'s stature had crossed the line gave the publisher of another major magazine a nervous moment. Carillon invites magazine representatives to its Teaneck, New Jersey, offices each year, and last spring the publisher, who asked not to be identified, says the company was all abuzz about *Esquire*'s innovation. "They said, 'Isn't this a great idea? Could you come up with something similar?' They wanted something that would use our editorial reputation as a way of promoting liquor sales. Fortunately, I was able to steer the conversation in another direction." When one magazine bends the rules, or even appears to bend the rules, it creates a little more pressure on the next one.

The advertorial battle is earnestly fought but it's really only a police action along the frontier, where the main rule is fairly clear: advertising copy ought not to pretend to be editorial material. The real war is being waged not on the border, but deep within the editorial interior. The issue is to what degree should editorial content be shaped for the purpose of attracting or keeping advertising.

The old doctrine—strict church/state separation of editorial and advertising—remains strong at many reputable magazines. "We take the old-fashioned view that in the long run you'll be the most successful in the commercial sense if you are successful in the editorial sense," says Stephen Shephard, editor of *Business Week*.

But there is a competing doctrine these days. "This is not the 1950s any more; this is a very, very competitive world," says magazine consultant Robert Cohen, whose clients include CJR. "Readers and advertisers are having to pay more to keep these magazines alive. I believe in editorial integrity, but a lot of people have old-fashioned ideas of what integrity means. There is not one standard definition that applies to everyone." He notes that magazines are integrated businesses that require the cooperation of editors and publishers. As for the decline of the church/state doctrine, "Thank God," says Cohen.

Cohen, a former publisher of *The New Republic*, would give advertisers the "compatible, friendly editorial environment" they want, up to the point of "serious editorial damage: Are readers harmed?" Daniel Okrent, the former editor of *New England Monthly*, fashions a strikingly different guideline. "Am I really serving my readers?"

Still, editors who operate without that church/state wall are susceptible to a variety of subtle pressures. Once they are made part of the business team they become reluctant to make decisions that might lower the score.

"The ad sales people would say, 'Gosh, you've got this depressing stuff here that makes it hard to sell,'" says Okrent. "Editors and publishers do an elaborate dance." Another magazine consultant, this one a former publisher, describes one of the dance steps: "A publisher will say, 'I hear you are doing a story on, say, John Deere. Don't let this affect you, but John Deere is buying forty-eight pages of advertising.' At one time it was unthinkable that a publisher would ever say that to an editor. Now it happens all the time."

Since cigarette companies are heavy advertisers, developments in the tobacco and health story is a classic and fairly obvious example of the kind of issue many magazines are reluctant to light up (see "The Magazines' Smoking Habit," CJR, January/February 1978). In a four-year study of tobacco and health coverage in major women's magazines—including *Ms., McCall's, Cosmopolitan, Mademoiselle,* and *Woman's Day*—Lauren Kessler noted recently in *Journalism Quarterly* that "none of the magazines covered one of the more significant women's health stories of the decade: the ascendance of lung cancer as the number one cancer killer of women."

Abortion is another topic known not to thrill some advertisers. But the topics advertisers dislike are not always so obviously controversial. Mary Kay Blakely, who writes frequently for women's magazines and has long gray hair, remembers a conversation with an editor of a leading women's magazine who also has long gray hair, telling her that an article about the glories of gray hair once cost her magazine the Clairol account for six months. James Fallows, *The Atlantic*'s Washington editor, says that when he was writing from Japan recently some major Japanese advertisers told him that, while their first instinct is to advertise wherever it is effective, they are disinclined to advertise in publications critical of their country. Fallows did not want to say whether he felt these comments were directed at *The Atlantic*, for whom he was writing a series of tough articles on Japan's trade policies. These are the kinds of sensitivities that, when conveyed to editors who are not protected by the editorial/advertising wall, lead to self-censorship, if not to censorship.

The fear of controversy has a flip side—the attraction to articles that tend to generate ads. It is easy to tilt, just a little, perhaps, to a story about Disney World, European travel, or whatever—articles that might help sell ads—and to convince yourself that you have done so for strictly editorial reasons. Most editors, presumably, would rule out commissioning laudatory articles on heavy advertisers, such as fashion designers. But most decisions are not so clear cut. What about starting a regular fashion section to attract ad dollars? "Is it great journalism? Is it a crime? No, it's neither," says an editor turned consultant. "Most editors can justify that: 'A good idea is a good idea; fashion is of interest to my readers, so why not?' That's the top of the slippery slope. The way I would try to view it is, Does it make sense editorially? If it does, I wouldn't care if it derived out of an advertising imperative.

"Editors are always thinking of advertising categories," he adds, "although they'll deny it." This accelerates the proliferation of articles and sections on such subjects as travel, home design, investing, automobiles, health, and fashion, along with such women's-magazine staples as food and beauty. Deciding whether or not to run such sections is not the only decision, of course: How puffy are they to be? Should they mention products by name? Only advertised products? And how much of the magazine is to be surrendered? What do they crowd out? Valerie Muller, vice-president and media director for the ad agency Pedone & Partners, says that these sections have proliferated to such a degree that some clients complain about them, contending that they are out of character with the rest of a magazine's personality.

"We live in a real world, where advertising is a matter of survival," says *Esquire*'s Eisenberg. "It behooves me to find that intersecting point between what a reader wants and expects and what advertisers want and expect. The only pressure I feel is the pressure I impose upon myself to make sure that *Esquire* does have revenues from advertising to the optimum amount we can and still preserve editorial. If there isn't a discernible reader value to something, I won't do it."

As a case in point, Eisenberg cites *Esquire*'s "Express Traveler," a foldout guide for the tourist in a rush. "I knew that our readers travel a lot. What could we do that is valuable to them? It dawned on me that they probably travel like I do, on short trips," he says. "There was no doubt in my mind that as I was formulating these things they were conducive to travel advertising.

That's fine. No one told me to do more travel coverage; it just so happens that both ends were served."

But *Harper's Magazine* publisher John R. MacArthur, something of a purist on these matters, cites *Esquire* as "the classic case of a fine magazine going to seed with this stuff. Take a look at the editorial," he says. "You wouldn't need all those articles about what to drink, what to wear, or whatever without advertisers in mind, would you?" The February *Esquire*, it should be noted, carries seventy-seven and two-thirds pages of advertising, compared with twenty-nine in the February *Harper's*. Still, editing for advertisers, MacArthur believes, will eventually destroy what advertisers want in magazines in the first place—an environment of quality and trust. At the bottom of this slippery slope he sees Christopher Whittle, whose Whittle Communications specializes in creating slick and bland editorial products to justify advertising aimed at captive audiences in places like doctors' offices, health clubs, and schools.

"It's ass-backwards," MacArthur says. "You are supposed to edit for the reader and sell the advertisers."

Blaming the advertisers for all these trends in the magazine world also seems ass-backwards. "Advertisers are not evil," says Robin Wolaner, publisher of *Parenting* and a former publisher of *Mother Jones*. "If they're being allowed that kind of power, they'd be stupid not to take it. What I found about advertisers is that when you've got an editorial policy, they respect it. The publishers who have problems have created them themselves." MacArthur agrees. "Advertisers are supposed to extract all the value from you that they can. Publishers are supposed to draw the line."

And editors. What if they don't? Let's check the crystal ball. Cross my palm with silver. Stare deeply. Behold: we see more magazines filled with more ersatz journalism, more blurry advertorials. We see more editors tossing in their beds, haunted by the ghosts of controversial and thoughtful stories that should have been assigned instead of this month's Caribbean travel or holiday drink-recipe feature.

Stare deeper, deeper into the crystal, my friend, where we see a sort of editorial environmental crisis—advertisers and magazine people beginning to realize that credibility, like petroleum or the ozone, is a fragile, limited resource. Listen. A major advertiser is talking to his media buyers in some futuristic teleconference. "Who needs magazines?" he says from the big screen. "Let's get Chris Whittle to come up with something projected on the ceilings over dentists' chairs."

# 34

# Deadly Persuasion

## *by* Jean Kilbourne

*Editor's Note: Advertising Age,* a publication serving the ad industry, says, "The trick for marketers is to project the right message in their advertisements to motivate those often motionless consumers to march down to the store or bar and exchange their money for a sip of image."

In this article Jean Kilbourne analyzes seven myths that alcohol advertisers want consumers to believe, hoping that these messages will motivate consumption of their products. Kilbourne is a visiting scholar at Wellesley College and a member of the board of directors of the National Council on Alcoholism and Drug Dependence. This article appeared in *Media & Values,* Spring/Summer 1991.

"Absolut Magic" proclaims a print ad for a popular vodka. "Paradise found," headlines another. "Fairy tales can come true" says a third.

All these ads illustrate the major premise of alcohol advertising's mythology: Alcohol is magic, a magic carpet that can take you away. It can make you successful, sophisticated, sexy. Without it, your life would be dull, mediocre and ordinary.

Everyone wants to believe in happy endings. But as most of us know, the reality of alcohol for many people in our society is more like a horror story than a fairy tale. The liquid in the glass is definitely not a magic potion.

We are surrounded by the message that alcohol is fun, sexy, desirable and harmless. We get this message many times a day. We get it from the ads and, far more insidiously, we get it from the media, which depend upon alcohol advertising for a large share of their profits. Thanks to this connection, alcohol use tends to be glorified throughout the media and alcohol-related problems are routinely dismissed.

Alcohol is related to parties, good times, celebrations and fun, but it is also related to murder, suicide, unemployment and child abuse. These connections are never made in the ads. Of course, one would not expect them to be. The advertisers are selling their product and it is their job to erase any negative aspects as well as to enhance the positive ones. However, when the product is the nation's number one drug, there are consequences that go far beyond product sales.

Most people know that alcohol can cause problems. But how many realize that 10 percent of all deaths in the United States—including half of all homicides and at least one quarter of all suicides—are related to alcohol? The economic cost to the nation exceeds $100 billion a year. At least 13,000,000 Americans, about one out of 10 drinkers, are alcoholic—the personal cost to them and their families is incalculable.

The tab for alcohol use doesn't end there. More than $2 billion a year—a sizable chunk of the over $90 billion the industry takes in annually—goes to prime the advertising and promotion pump and keep drinkers' money flowing freely. Problem drinkers and young people are the primary targets of these advertisers.

Of course, industry spokespeople disagree with this claim. Over and over again, their public statements assert that they are not trying to create new or heavier drinkers. Instead, they say they only want people who already drink to switch to another brand and to drink it in moderation. However, the most basic analysis of alcohol advertising reveals an emphasis on both recruiting new, young users and pushing heavy consumption of their products.

Indeed, advertising that encouraged only moderate drinking would be an economic failure. This becomes clear when you know that only 10 percent of the drinking-age population consumes over half of all alcoholic beverages sold. According to Robert Hammond, director of the Alcohol Research Information Service, if all 105 million drinkers of legal age consumed the official maximum "moderate" amount of alcohol—.99 ounces per day, the equivalent of about two drinks—the industry would suffer "a whopping 40 percent decrease in the sale of beer, wine and distilled spirits."

## Young Prospects

These figures make it clear that if alcoholics were to recover—i.e., stop drinking—the alcoholic beverage industry's gross revenue would be cut in half. I can't believe that industry executives want that to happen. On the contrary, my 15-year study of alcohol advertising makes me certain that advertisers deliberately target the heavy drinker and devise ads designed to appeal to him or her. As with any product, the heavy user is the best customer. However, when the product is a drug, the heavy user is often an addict.

Not all problem drinkers are alcoholics. Youthful drinking is frequently characterized by binges and episodes of drunkenness, making young people a lucrative market for alcohol producers. According to the 1989 National Institute on Drug Abuse survey of high school seniors, 33 percent of students reported that they had consumed five or more drinks on one occasion within the previous two weeks. This group is vulnerable to ad campaigns that present heavy drinking as fun and normal.

Media sell target audiences to the alcohol industry on a cost-per-drinker basis. "*Cosmopolitan* readers drank 21,794,000 glasses of beer in the last week. . . . Isn't it time you gave *Cosmopolitan* a shot?" proclaims an ad aimed at the alcohol industry.

The primary purpose of the mass media is to deliver audiences to advertisers. It's worthwhile taking a closer look at how some of the common myths alcohol advertisers have created do this.

### #1. Drinking Is a Risk-free Activity

Ads featuring copy like "The Joy of Six" imply that it is all right to consume large quantities of alcohol. Light beer ("great taste") has been developed and heavily promoted not for the dieter but for the heavy drinker. It is "less filling," and therefore one can drink more.

Ads like these tell the alcoholic and those around him or her that it is all right, indeed splendid, to be obsessed by alcohol, to consume large amounts of it on a daily basis and to have it be a part of all one's activities. At the same time, all signs of trouble and any hint of addiction are erased.

Every instance of use seems spontaneous, unique. The daily drinking takes place on yachts at sunset, not at kitchen tables in the morning. Bottles are magically unopened even when drinks have been poured. All signs of trouble and any hint of addiction are conspicuously avoided. There is no unpleasant drunkenness, only high spirits. Certainly alcohol-related problems such as alcohol-impaired driving, broken marriages, abused children, lost jobs, illness and premature death—are never even hinted at.

### #2. You Can't Survive without Drinking

"It separates the exceptional from the merely ordinary," is how a Piper champagne ad puts it. By displaying a vibrant, imbibing couple against a black and white nondrinking background crowd, the advertiser contrasts the supposedly alive and colorful world of the drinker with dull reality. The alcohol has resurrected the couple, restored them to life.

In general, such advertising is expert at making the celebration of *drinking itself*—not a holiday, festivity or family event—a reason for imbibing ("Pour a Party," "Holidays were made for Michelob").

At the heart of the alcoholic's dilemma and denial is this belief, this certainty, that alcohol is essential for life, that without it he or she will literally die—or at best be condemned to a gray and two-dimensional wasteland, a half-life. These ads, and many others like them, present that nightmare as true, thus affirming and even glorifying one of the symptoms of the illness.

### #3. Problem Drinking Behaviors Are Normal

A shot of a sunset-lit bridge, captioned "At the end of the day, even a bridge seems to be heading home for Red," is actually advertising not just Scotch, but daily drinking. Often symptoms of alcohol, such as the need for a daily drink, are portrayed as not only normal, but desirable. A Smirnoff ad captioned "Hurry Sundown" features a vampirish lady immobilized in a coffinlike setting awaiting the revivifying effects of a vodka gimlet.

Slogans presenting drinking as "your own special island," and "your mountain hideaway" capitalize on the feelings of alienation and loneliness most alcoholics experience. Such ads seem to encourage solitary drinking, often one of the classic indicators of trouble with alcohol. They also distort the tragic reality that problem drinking increases—rather than alleviates—those feelings of isolation.

Alcohol lies at the center of these ads, just as it is at the center of the alcoholic's life.

### #4. *Alcohol Is a Magic Potion That Can Transform You*

Alcohol advertising often spuriously links alcohol with precisely those attributes and qualities—happiness, wealth, prestige, sophistication, success, maturity, athletic ability, virility and sexual satisfaction—that the misuse of alcohol destroys.

For example, alcohol is linked with romance and sexual fulfillment, yet it is common knowledge that drunkenness often leads to sexual dysfunction. Less well known is the fact that people with drinking problems are seven times more likely to be separated or divorced.

Such ads often target young people, women and people of color, since members of these groups often feel powerless and are eager to identify with "successful" groups in our society. These ads sometimes connect "prestige" beverages with the aura of the rich and powerful or the goals of women's liberation.

Ads and products aimed at young people deserve special mention in these days when many preteens start drinking in junior high school. Cartoon and animal characters such as Spuds MacKenzie, Anheuser-Busch's canine mascot, are not as innocent as they appear. In one Christmas campaign, Spuds appeared in a Santa Claus suit, promoting 12-packs of Bud Light beer. In the summer of 1990 he was cavorting with ninjas, drawing on the popularity of the *Teenage Mutant Ninja Turtles* movie, a big hit with younger children.

Ads that portray drinking as a passport to adulthood, coupled with transitional products such as high-proof milkshakes and chocolate sodas, can be very successful lures for young drinkers.

### #5. *Sports and Alcohol Go Together*

Alcohol consumption actually decreases athletic performance. However, numerous ads, like a Pabst Blue Ribbon poster showing a speeding bicyclist with a bottle of beer on her basket, wrongly imply that sports and alcohol are safely complementary activities. Others feature sponsorship of a wide range of sporting events or endorsements by sports stars.

### #6. *If These Products Were Truly Dangerous, the Media Would Tell Us*

Most media are reluctant to bite the hand that feeds them by spending $2 billion annually on advertising and promotion. Media coverage of the "war on drugs" seldom mentions the two major killers, alcohol and nicotine. From the coverage, one would assume that cocaine was the United States' most dangerous drug. However, while cocaine, heroin and other illegal drugs are linked with about 20,000 deaths a year, alcohol contributes to at least 100,000 and cigarettes more than 450,000—or more than 1,000 a day.

Although many media feature occasional stories about alcoholism, they usually treat it as a personal problem and focus on individual treatment solutions. Reports that probe alcohol's role in violence and other chronic problems are rare, while the role advertising plays in encouraging its use is almost never discussed.

### #7. *Alcoholic Beverage Companies Promote Moderation in Drinking*

The current Budweiser "moderation" campaign says, "Know when to say when," as opposed to "Know when to say no." In the guise of a moderation message, this slogan actually suggests to young people that drinking beer is one way to demonstrate their control. It also perpetuates the myth that alcoholics are simply people who "don't know when to say when," irresponsibly engaging in willful misconduct, rather than people who are suffering from a disease that afflicts at least one in 10 drinkers.

Most of these programs are designed to encourage young people not to drive drunk. Although this is a laudable goal, it is interesting to note that few of the alcohol industry programs discourage or even question drunkenness *per se*. The tragic result is that many young people feel it is perfectly all right to get drunk, as long as they do not get behind the wheel of a car.

In any case, we might be better off without programs designed by the alcohol industry to promote ideas about "responsible" drinking that in fact subtly promote myths and damaging attitudes. For example, one program by Miller beer defines moderate drinking as up to four drinks a day. Copy for a Budweiser program called "The Buddy System" defines drunkenness as having "too much of a good time." Doesn't this imply that being sober is having a bad time, that being drunk and having a good time go together? Even the industry's "moderation" messages imply the advantages of heavy drinking.

One of the chief symptoms of the disease of alcoholism is the denial that there is a problem. In general, as a society we tend to deny the illness and to support the alibi system of the alcoholic. Advertising encourages this denial.

It may be impossible to prove conclusively that alcohol advertising affects consumption, but it clearly affects attitudes about drinking. The ads contribute to an environment of social acceptance of high-risk drinking and denial of related problems. In addition, media dependence on alcohol advertising discourages full and open discussion of the many problems associated with alcohol.

A major comprehensive effort is needed to prevent alcohol-related problems. Such an effort must include education, mass media campaigns, increased availability of treatment programs and more effective deterrence policies. It must also include public policy changes that take into account that the individual acts within a social, economic and cultural environment that profoundly influences his or her choices. Such changes would include raising taxes on alcohol, putting clearly legible warning labels on the bottles and regulating the advertising.

Above all, we must become fully engaged in the struggle to solve alcohol-related problems. We must stop supporting the denial that is at the heart of the illness that alcohol advertising both perpetuates and depends upon both in the individual and in society as a whole.

What can be done? We can investigate the extent to which the media are influenced by their dependence on alcohol advertising. We can consider the possibility of further restricting or banning all alcohol advertising, as some other countries have done. We can insist on equal time for information commercials in the broadcast media. We can raise the taxes on alcohol and use the extra revenue to fund programs to prevent and treat the illness and educate the public. We can become more aware of the real messages in the ads and work to teach their implications and consequences to those we love and care for.

# 35

# Fantasy, Not Flesh

## *by* Joshua Levine

*Editor's Note:* Sex sells. That's true for newspapers, magazines, paperback books, movies, television—all mass media—and of course it's true for advertising as well. Perhaps sex has always been used in ads, to some degree, although it was most explicit in the 1980s. Now in the 1990s, sex still sells, but it's being used in advertising in a way that reflects contemporary attitudes. Gauzy, erotic fantasies are now elbowing out the more explicit, peep-show approach.

Joshua Levine is marketing editor of *Forbes* magazine, where this article appeared on January 22, 1990.

In advertising, a funny thing is happening on the way to the boudoir. The raw sex advertisements typified by Georges Marciano's Guess Jeans and Calvin Klein's Obsession are losing their impact. No more angry, pouting black-jacketed males all but raping lubricious adolescent girls wearing skin-tight jeans. No more grainy tableaux of tangled limbs and group sex.

The decency decade? Not quite. Sex isn't going out in advertising, but it is lightening up, softening up. "It's more playful, more subtle than it was four years ago," says Paul Marciano, Georges' brother and director of advertising at Guess Jeans, among the pioneers of the steamy sell. In one two-part ad for Guess four years ago, for instance, a close-to-adolescent girl is carried off, seemingly kicking and screaming. On the following page, she reappears in the back seat of a car, looking dazed and worked over. "We were trying to suggest passion, but some of the images got borderline aggressive," admits Marciano. "Now, it's calmer."

More noticeable and already well established is the trend in advertising toward reflecting contemporary attitudes toward sex roles. Advertisments today frequently picture women as sexual aggressors, or at least equal sparring partners, rather than available sex objects.

The pioneer here may well have been Revlon. Three years ago Revlon's Charlie girl bestowed a memorable pat on her male companion's rump both in print and in a TV commercial. "It was meant as an asexual gesture, the same kind of thing a quarterback does to a lineman," says Mal MacDougall, who wrote the ad for agency Hill, Holliday, Connors, Cosmopulos and is now vice chairman of Jordan, McGrath, Case & Taylor.

MacDougall is being a bit disingenuous, but, no question, the Charlie girl launched a powerful trend. Take the new advertising for Sansabelt, the pants made by Hartmarx subsidiary Jaymar-Ruby. In 1989 Sansabelt introduced a line of more expensive, fashionable slacks. Since most slacks in television commercials look pretty much alike, agency Berenter Greenhouse & Webster took another tack. Commercials and print ads that ran last summer and fall feature four female models commenting drily about what they look for in men's slacks. "I always lower my eyes when a man passes," says one winsome model, a wry smile playing at the corner of her mouth. "To see if he's worth following."

"I don't think it's a dirty joke. I think it's a witty remark by a secure woman," says Berenter Greenhouse & Webster's Martin Greenhouse. "It tells men they can feel confident about wearing them, and that women will like them. It's tongue-in-cheek."

Not everyone agreed. Sansabelt retailers in Chicago, for instance, demanded that a tag at the end of the commercial identifying their stores be removed. Nevertheless, Sansabelt says it will rerun the ads this spring.

Along the same male-ogling lines, consider one of the latest Johnnie Walker scotch ads running in major national magazines. Two fashionably sporty showstoppers on a ski lift have just passed a great-looking guy going the other way. "I just saw what I want for Christmas," one woman announces confidently to her pal. "And I bet he drinks Johnnie Walker."

In short, while girl-watching seems here to stay, guy-watching is also. The latest commercials for Fruit of the Loom underwear, for example, would probably not have made it past the network censors just three years ago. The commercials ask the musical question "Whose underwear is under there?" The answer is provided by beefy TV celebrities Ed Marinaro, Patrick Duffy and James DePaiva. Marinaro reveals himself in his Fruit of the Looms and nothing else.

Yes, Calvin Klein showed much more skin four years ago when he posed a perfectly sculpted male model in skivvies. But those ads appeared mainly in magazines, where a degree of risque advertising has long been acceptable. The Fruit of the Loom campaign airs on national television, which has always tried to keep advertising on the prim and proper side.

Three years ago, for instance, the networks would let viewers see men's underwear, but only if there were no men standing in them. Thus, when Grey Advertising fielded a commercial for Fruit of the Loom in 1986, it showed a lingerie-clad female model holding a pair of Fruit of the Loom briefs across her bare-chested beau's midriff. He was wearing pajama bottoms. For another, more recent Fruit of the Loom commercial, Grey Advertising lawyers spent two weeks wrangling with one of the networks, which had withheld approval because the commercial's male character had too much hair on his legs.

Madison Avenue is also getting even more skillful at marketing with erotic imagery and sensual fantasy—steamy without being crudely explicit. In part, fear of AIDS has given overt sexual imagery menacing overtones. As important, however, advertising is reflecting the changing tastes of an aging generation of baby boomers, rapidly pairing off and hunkering down at home. "There's a sadness that the days of casual sex are gone," says Judith Langer, a market researcher who recently conducted focus groups on the subject in Kansas City. "We miss it, and that tends to make everyone fantasize about it more."

And fantasy can be most potent when least pornographic. "It's like the old Hedy Lamarr movie *Ecstasy*," says Sidney Levy, chairman of the marketing department at Northwestern University's Kellogg School. "If you know what that leaf moving on the water means, the rest is beside the point."

Coty's most recent campaign for its new Iron cologne for men illustrates the moving-leaf technique, 1990s style. It is a mass-market brand bought primarily by blue-collar women. Opening shot: a gorgeous hunk, pulling on a T shirt, musing and preening in an empty room. Moonlight shines through the French doors, while the rest of the room is bathed in a blue sheen not found in nature. A woman in a simple dress, her shoulders bare, appears in another room. He sprays himself with the stuff, she glides in and kisses his neck.

Explicit? Not very. Sexy? Very. Says Elizabeth Nickles Murray, executive creative director at Ketchum Advertising, New York, which has the account: "A few years ago the guy would have met up with three different women, and we would have shown breasts, not neck. And, of course, there's that blue sheen, a clear tip-off that we're in fantasyland." She adds: "There are two ways to go when so little is allowed in life—commitment or fantasy. In focus groups, people say they want commitment, but that's not really what they want. I think you're going to see some real mind trips when fantasy kicks into high gear."

But there are limits. For now at least, Americans won't accept the amount of nudity that is frequently featured in European advertising. Nivea moisturizing lotion, from Germany's Beiersdorf A.G., recently posed a striking nude model in profile against a cloud-puffed blue sky, billing itself as "the perfect climate for your skin." The advertisement wouldn't have raised an eyebrow in Europe, and did run here in women's magazines like *Vogue, Ladies Home Journal* and *Harper's Bazaar* but after it ran in the U.S., Nivea had to modify the advertisement in response to reader protests. "You know, I'm not a prude," said one woman in a focus group, "but I was really offended. My brother-in-law knows the exact page the ad's on. He likes it!" Nivea substituted a more demure photograph.

Europeans also have a far higher tolerance for erotic imagery, even when it has no apparent connection to the advertised product. Take this spot for K Shoes, which sells stylish pumps to women in the U.K. In the vignette, a woman makes an unannounced visit to her lover's apartment only to discover him in a romantic tête-à-tête with another woman. Our heroine dumps a bowl of pasta on her boyfriend's head, and—slowly and silently—takes the cigarette from her rival's mouth and grinds it out on the floor. Intermittent flashes of type spell out the commercial's message: "Have you noticed the softest leather never creaks?"

Far-out fantasy, to be sure, but it would never play here. Americans still bridle when they see no connection between the sexual setup and the advertised product. Kraft General Foods found that out when it tried out a new approach for Maxwell House coffee. A man is addressing his significant other, unseen in bed, after he's prepared and delivered the morning coffee. The dialog is shot through with double entendre: "Was it good for you?" he asks innocently. Phooey, said viewers. The commercial was pulled after a few showings.

Which isn't to say Americans aren't as easily suckered by the age-old sexual promise in advertising as everyone else. They just require their own, homegrown come-on. Says Kellogg School's Sidney Levy, "If an ad implies an enhancement of our desirability, part of our minds may say, 'Baloney!' The other part will always say, 'It couldn't hurt.'"

# IX

# Sex, Crime, and Violence

On June 17, 1989, *Time* magazine published a special section called "7 Deadly Days." It contained twenty-five pages of individual pictures of the people in America who in the week before had died violently from gunfire—464 altogether. In 1989, more than 30,000 Americans were killed by guns, including murders and suicides. More people are being killed each year with handguns in the schools of Detroit than in some entire European countries. And the numbers continue to rise.

In 1986, there were more than 13,000 murders in the United States; in 1991 there were nearly 25,000. In the decade from 1981 to 1991, violent crimes increased 33 percent, the juvenile arrest rate for violent crime jumped 27 percent, and the number of juveniles who shot a victim to death increased 79 percent.

What is wrong with America? Why are there so many more violent deaths by handguns in this country than in any other society on this planet? Is it because handguns are so readily available? Is it because we've had a history of the violent use of guns going back to the settlement of a new continent and a lawless frontier? Or is it because of mass media, especially television and motion pictures? Most experts would say it is some combination of these factors, plus the stress of modern, fast, harried, and competitive society.

Yet statistics on crime and violence show a dramatic rise since the advent of television. Is television more to be blamed than the other factors? A University of Washington study concluded that without television, there would be half the number of homicides each year in America. The study was based on a comparison of homicide rates in Canada, the United States, and South Africa, both before and after the introduction of television. Homicide rates doubled in Canada and in the United States in the first twenty years of televi-

219

sion. During the same twenty-year period in South Africa, before television was available, homicide rates increased only 7 percent. In the first ten years of television in South Africa, from 1974 to 1984, homicides increased 56 percent.[1]

One thing is certain: U.S. mass media are full of violence. A study by the National Coalition of Television Violence showed that 37 percent of all programming on American cable and network television features themes high in violence; on HBO it was 86 percent; on USA Network, 85 percent. Hollywood movies make up the majority of the most violent programming, although violent TV series were prominent on the major networks.

Why should television be so taken with violence? Perhaps the answer lies in the nature of the medium itself. Television isn't made up of letters and words and sentences that must have an internal logic. It is made up of images to which we are more apt to respond emotionally than rationally. Those images must move, especially on a tiny screen, to attract our attention, and the more violent the movement, the more we are compelled to watch.

Crime and violence are not only major themes of entertainment media; they are also an essential part of news, and part of advertising, too. Moreover, they are not limited to the small screen of television. The movies have become more violent since the advent of television (compare current movies to those that were made prior to television), perhaps to keep up with the competition. Newspapers and magazines deal with more violent issues than they used to, especially crime, accident, and disaster stories, again perhaps to compete with television.

The murder of Nicole Simpson and Ron Goldman and the subsequent trial of O. J. Simpson in the summer and fall of 1994 further underlined the public's intense interest in violent crime, especially when celebrities are involved. That murder case received newspaper headlines of a size usually reserved for a declaration of war, while network television gave it nearly round-the-clock coverage and even pre-empted the president of the United States and world sports events. Some said more people viewed the O. J. Simpson hearings than had watched the moon landing in 1969.

Even video games may be part of the problem. About a third of all American homes now have some kind of video game, and children are spending up to forty hours a week playing such games, according to *Computer Magazine.* Roughly 80 percent of the games have violence as a theme. "When a kid plays a violent video game, he is getting trained to pull the trigger," says Carole Lieberman, a media consultant at the University of California at Los Angeles.[2]

Sex, which is often combined with violence, is more explicit on television and in all mass media now than ever before. Is it because we have become less puritanical, and the media are reflecting this? Or are we less puritanical because we watch and hear and read more explicit sexual messages than ever before?

In New Zealand, as in much of the world now, young people watch a lot of music television, much of it American, most of it full of sex and violence. A New Zealand woman described it:

> A young black woman, long and lean, wearing a tight miniskirt, sheer bustier, fishnet stockings and stilettos, leans forward and pouts. Then she gyrates her lips and throws back her head, exposing her bare throat and cleavage. A young white man in jeans and T-shirt stands singing and watching the woman. He reaches out to grab her, perhaps he chases her, but she slips from his grasp. Sound familiar? It could be the outline of any one of thousands of popular music videos that screen on TV each year.[3]

Worldwide, MTV is the fastest growing mass medium.

The following articles discuss how and why sex, crime, and violence are so much a part of mass media today.

**Notes**

1. "Study of 3 Countries Links TV and Homicide Rate," *Chronicle of Higher Education,* 17 May 1989, p. A-6.
2. Courtland Milloy, "Video Wars: The Next Generation," *Washington Post,* 20 January 1991, p. D-3.
3. Lisa Sabbage, "Video Vagaries," *Broadsheet,* July 1991, pp. 16–20.

# 36

# America Is Saturated by Violence

## *by* Harry James Cargas

*Editor's Note:* We have become a nation obsessed with guns and power, says the author of this article, and those who say the repetition of media violence has little impact need only speak to advertising executives. "Justice, law, and order values are brushed aside for either a posse-type mentality or the legal rules are seen as a hindrance for justice," he writes.

There are many reasons why America is a violent society. Certainly mass media cause violence as well as reflect it. But mass media frequently fail to deal with this issue, sometimes ignoring or hiding it. Most studies on the issue are reported in books for researchers or in specialized or alternative media, although mass media have occasionally focused on the problem. Public television aired a documentary called "The Violence Factor" in the 1980s, but it wasn't shown on network television. Some newspapers and magazines are now doing a better job of covering the issue.

The author of this article, Harry James Cargas, is a professor of literature and religion at Webster University. The article was originally published in the *St. Louis Journalism Review* (a publication devoted to media criticism), January 1990.

The American emphasis on individualism, competition and capitalism in print, via our air waves and on celluloid can be destructive. Not because individualism, competition or capitalism are evil, but because they are misunderstood by so many in authority, and are represented in the media in their very worst anti-community aspects.

Individualism, competition and capitalism make contributions to our society, but not if they emphasize greed, acquisitiveness, "me-first" and often "me-only" attitudes; then they become devastating.

We must demand accountability for each other. You owe me to be the best human being that you can be, just as I owe you the very same. If we have not absorbed this lesson through our reading and experience, perhaps we can see

**223**

it in the worldwide environmental and ecological interdependence. The Chernobyl disaster in the Soviet Union has an impact on Finland's agriculture, acid rain in Germany affects *at least* 14 other nations, cutting down the Amazon forest will influence oxygen around the world. These lessons the media largely ignore.

The destruction of human beings by other human beings during the Holocaust, while still others looked away, is one of the greatest blots on humanity. When we look at the newspapers and magazines of 1940–1944, we read that the information was all there. We must ask our parents "Why didn't you do something?"

Will the next generation accuse us in the same way? The information is all here: babies are being brutalized and women are being murdered and beaten.

We are a nation built on violence. Our forebears appropriated land that belonged to others and justified it as spreading the Gospel, Manifest Destiny, the White Man's Burden; it all meant "I want it, so I take it."

We are a nation obsessed with guns and with power. *Time* magazine in its July 17 issue lists the 464 names and photos of people shot to death in America in one week: women, men, boys and girls. That number, 464, exceeds by over 40 times the total shot to death in Japan in a year.

Violent crimes are on the increase. In 1988, they were up 5.5 percent according to the Federal Bureau of Investigation. Over 1.5 million violent crimes were reported last year and we do not know how many were unreported. More than 18,000 Americans were murder victims. Ten percent of those were killed in New York City, but if we go by population statistics, in eight other cities you are more likely to be murdered than in New York and St. Louis is among them.

In Los Angeles, of every 100,000 persons, over 20 were killed. In Washington, D.C., 60 of every 100,000 have their lives violently cut short. The fear of sexual assault has become a part of everyday life for a large portion of our population. One of every three females will experience some form of a sexual assault in their lives—one out of nine males will. In New York City alone, 198 children died from abuse last year.

What is the media's role in all this mayhem? Gerald J. Waggett writes in the May 27, 1989 issue of *TV Guide,* "The emergence of the rapist as hero began a decade ago on ABC's 'General Hospital' when Luke raped Laura. Laura not only refused to name Luke as her attacker, she eventually fell in love with and married him. For a rape victim to fall in love with her assailant contradicts the fact that rape is an act of violence. 'General Hospital' made rape look like an act of love. At one point, Laura herself referred to the incident as 'the first time we made love.' "

Waggert shows how on ABC's now defunct "Ryan's Hope," Roger tried unsuccessfully to force Maggie into bed with him and two years later the pair married. On "Dynasty," Adam raped Kirby and later proposed to her. These male characters have been turned into heroes, into sex symbols by writers. The rapist in "General Hospital," we are told, has become a women's TV idol as Ross of "All My Children," who raped his father's fiance, a crime for which he was sent to prison, then was portrayed as a sympathetic character. A similar kind of transformation occurred with Josh on CBS's "As The World Turns," He raped his cousin, Iva, impregnated her, then had a love affair with her sister.

Acceptable violence is portrayed not only by the soaps. Rock video shows are replete with acts and threats of violence in the visual portion and the song lyrics. The "concept" videos contain violence of a somewhat different variety. On these, older adults are more likely to be aggressors rather than victims; the same is true of non-whites as well as of women according to a study in *The Journal of Communication.*

Researchers Barry L. Sherman and Joseph R. Dominick found about a quarter of all characters on videos are presented in suggestive or provocative dress. Three-fourths of all ethnic characters are lower class. Children are twice as likely to be the targets of aggression as they are to be agents of violence. Non-whites are far more likely to use weapons in committing video mayhem. Four sexual activities per video is the average and the emphasis is on titillation and physical activity of a very adolescent nature: devoid of emotional involvement.

When we treat people as things instead of human beings, as objects instead of persons, we can do just about anything to them that we want.

Martin Buber expounded on this in his epic work titled *I-Thou.* In it, he taught how dehumanizing it is to treat another as a thing, as an "it." What we owe each other as human beings is the recognition of each other's spirit. Or we can learn from the Buddhist form of respect, the bow. When the followers of Buddha bend at the waist as a mark of honor to another person, they bow to the God who is in all.

In literature, we teach the technique known as "personification," the attribution of human qualities to non-human entities. But television and other media often take us in the reverse direction into *reification.* This comes from the Latin word "res" which means thing. This is the tactic of the military. The commanders would have us believe that in the field we are fighting Communists or gooks or imperialists or capitalists instead of fathers and brothers and sons. It is much easier to kill a fanatic than someone's father, an infidel rather than a man, a demon instead of someone's beloved.

The power of advertising is enormous. Those who say that the repetition of media violence has little impact need only speak to advertising executives—whose technique of repetition of messages for their clients earn billions of dollars.

Advertising is most effective where it can generalize while appealing to our individualism, where it can keep us from certain realizations in order to make its message more appealing, and where it can convince us that we have a right to expensive possessions. It appeals to instincts of greed, self-gratification, instant success, and lack of responsibility. Such conditioning facilitates the acceptance of values associated with violence.

A favorite example of mine is the promotion that was used for Schlitz beer. The ad told us that "You only go around once in life." This message was not spiritual but epicurean: Life is short and a one-time experience, so enjoy it. The best way to enjoy it is to purchase beer (and make our stockholders wealthy). Never mind if too much of it is bad for your health or dangerous, or makes you violent or makes you lose control of your faculties. Life is for pleasure and Schlitz sells pleasure by the bottle. It is only a step from advocating that anything—or anyone—standing in the way of your pleasure is to be swept aside, not tolerated. The individualism, the self-gratification, and the ensuing violence is all suggested here.

The values that advertising depends on and encourages have to do with acquiring, with owning, with obliterating frustrations, with pleasure now. These indoctrinations, when thwarted, can lead to a sense of failure, to disappointment, to revenge and physical violence.

Exposed to hundreds of thousands of commercials in a lifetime, we can hardly be blamed for developing some envy, some sense of deprivation, some impulse towards getting. Commercialism, enhanced by advertising, brings out the material instinct in us. In children it is that much more damaging. Children are easier to brainwash, and ad companies have made a science out of it.

In the Christian scriptures, we are warned not to scandalize little children. It would be better, we are advised, to have a millstone hung around our necks and be thrown into the water than to abuse the minds of the young. Profiteers from the persuasion industry are doing just that when they convince our boys and girls that it is not enough just to wear clean, neat jeans but they must be *this* brand; or that the tennis shoes they purchase must be of a special kind; or the treats to which they are entitled have to be of that particular high calorie, unhealthful variety. And an entire industry is making huge profits seducing people into smoking. Some live in luxury by poisoning others.

In 1969, the National Commission on the Causes and Prevention of Violence issued a lengthy report on its findings. Some 14 years later, in their important book *Milestones in Mass Communication Research*, Shearon Lowery and Melvin L. DeFleur lament the fact that the public received only a superficial coverage of the report's conclusions noting that, "The media chose not to make this book and its contents a subject of public discussion."

Chairman of the Commission, Dr. Milton S. Eisenhower, said that his group was charged to "go as far as man's knowledge takes" in attempting to find the causes of violence and methods of prevention. In volume IX of their proceedings, this body tells of finding that media aggression stimulated rather than deflected viewer aggression—violence increases rather than decreases a viewer's subsequent aggressiveness. Any theory that such action provides a catharsis is dismissed by the Commission.

For 20 years the data on television violence has been buried and ignored while the atmosphere of killings, abusiveness, fighting and the disregard for other human beings has saturated our psyches. Violent acts were most often performed at close range, primarily with a weapon, about half the time upon strangers and most often upon persons who either could not or did not resist. Most of these actions were committed out of self-interest rather than for any other reason. Most of the violence was in the context of a good versus evil conflict. The so called "good guys" inflicted as much violence as the "bad guys." When the "good guys" triumphed, their violence was justified.

Violent episodes ranged from three to five per comedy to a high of 24 per cartoon. In 70 percent of these actions the characters were close enough to speak to each other suggesting violence of a very personal nature. Half of the violent episodes showed no witnesses and where there were witnesses they were generally passive. At least half of all characters in all dramas were violent and at least one out of every ten was a killer. And here is a statistic especially appropriate for those considering the impact of media on family violence— male violence overwhelmingly dominates the screen.

The Commission went on to report that there seems to be little evidence that children can differentiate between fantasy and reality in TV programs, and that many children have their first contact with violence via video.

Justice, law, and order values are brushed aside for either a posse-type mentality or the legal rules are seen as a hindrance for justice—the Ollie North types go their own way because they know in their hearts they are right.

An article in a recent issue of *Criminology* based on research funded by the Hubert Humphrey Institute of Public Affairs at the University of Minnesota insists, "The link between exposure to mass media violence and aggressive behavior has been demonstrated in various kinds of experiments." It led one researcher to testify before Congress, "There can no longer be any doubt that heavy exposure to televised violence is one of the causes of aggressive behavior, crime, and violence in society."

It should come as no surprise, then, that the *New York Times* reported on August 1 that the House of Representatives agreed with the Senate to waive the Sherman Antitrust Act for the purposes of allowing television networks, cable channel operators and producers of programming to draw up a code to curb violence on TV. U.S. Sen. Paul Simon (D. Ill.) urged the television industry "to forge a partnership with America's families to scale back the atmosphere of violence." The primary motivation for the legislation came from a number of sources including the American Academy of Pediatric Medicine, the Justice Department, The American Psychological Association, the United Church of Christ, and the National Congress of Parents and Teachers.

It is not just the entertainment programs or the Saturday morning cartoons which offer so much violence. Sports programs must be included. Encouragement to hurt others is not restricted to television: radio and the newspapers are equally culpable.

Professional football involves meanness. Players speak openly of intimidation, willingness to injure an opponent and just plain hatred of members of the other team. The contests are filled with violent contact and highlights that are replayed frequently focus on smashing collisions which are appropriately admired by the commentators. Boxing, in spite of its proven brain-damaging effects, contributes immensely to the macho image. The National Hockey League's tolerance, and in some cases sponsoring, of brawling turns graceful performances into brutality. In college hockey and European pro leagues, fighting is prohibited. Finally, there is professional wrestling. It is not a sport at all but a savage dramatic performance where people glorify violence in a most cynical way. The actors—who do take great physical poundings—pretend to choke each other, twist limbs in impossible ways and smash one another senseless, in order to appeal to what is base in human nature for the purpose of making heaps of dollars. One has only to be in an audience to hear how revved up the easily fooled can become. The violence committed in the ring, the rule-breaking punishment administered by the combatants, is dosed out equally by the so-called good as well as by the bad guys. The fans eat it up. The ends justify the means.

Radio and newspaper accounts of athletic events contribute to the exalting of violence. One has only to listen to the gleeful tone of voice of the announcer who enjoys reporting that in the encounter between a linebacker and a ball carrier "he literally tore his head off."

If we can dehumanize the opposition, we can do anything to them. That is part of the media's message. A story from the *St. Louis Post-Dispatch* two basketball seasons ago began, "Thank goodness for bad blood. It produces such juicy sports rivalries as the Blues and the Blackhawks, the Cardinals and the Cubs, the Dallas Cowboys and the Washington Redskins. And in high school basketball it produces Vashon against DeSmet. Tuesday night at DeSmet High, the bad blood couldn't have been better." The writer is describing a children's game and evaluating it like a war.

The lead of a *West County Journal* story on girl's track reads, "The tale of the gunslinger riding into town and challenging the established champion to a duel on Main Street is one which is firmly entrenched in Western lore." The journalist goes on to describe a kind of shoot out between two of the girls, one he labels "the established gun." This under a heading that reads "Lindbergh's Lorenz Guns Down Hotshot." Violence becomes the value.

The aura of violence is also part of the news. Dan Rather, Tom Brokaw and Peter Jennings keep filling our homes with stories about wars and murders and kidnappings and child abuse and disasters of every kind. NBC, ABC and CBS radio news do the same. Front-page news stories do likewise. Violence and tragedy are everywhere.

Brokaw and Rather and Jennings and our local casters and many of our editors and radio people do not know what good news is. It is unfashionable to proclaim the value of the arts, of the spiritual life, of those areas of creativity where the very best of humanity is expressed. Our true fulfillment is not found in war, in profitmaking, in advertising, in materialism. It is found in the Beethovens, the Dantes, the Homers, the Martin Luther Kings, the Garcia

Marquezes, the Wiesels, the Panikkars, the Mother Theresas—the list is so very long and so very neglected by our media.

The real heroes of society are overlooked because the image makers have so decided. So our job is one of education—ballet is more beautiful than football; classical music is more satisfying than rock video; good literature does more for humanity than pornography; our children are more valuable as spiritual beings than as consumers; the RAVEN self help group for men performs a greater service than stag clubs; responsibility is to be admired and irresponsibility is to be shamed.

What we do must be done not just for money, or fame, or status, but because it is right. This is true for me, this is true for you, this is true for media representatives, sports figures, business people, politicians, homemakers, fathers, the entire gamut of the human family. The challenge is there. If we fail to meet it, shame on us.

# 37

# How Much Violence Is There?

## by Neil Hickey

*Editor's Note:* A new study commissioned by *TV Guide* shows that there's more violence pouring through our TV screens—and it's coming from more sources—than in past years.

Neil Hickey is editor of *TV Guide,* and this article appeared in a special edition of that publication on August 22, 1992.

More televised violence than at any time in the medium's history is flowing into American homes. It's coming from many more sources than ever before—home video, pay-per-view, and cable, as well as from broadcast networks and stations. The overwhelming weight of scientific opinion now holds that televised violence is indeed responsible for a percentage of the real violence in our society. What is new is that psychologists, child experts, and the medical community are just now beginning to treat televised violence as a serious public health issue—like smoking and drunk driving—about which the public needs to be educated for its own safety and well-being.

How much violence is there on American television? Is it more virulent now than in recent years? Where is it coming from? What are its effects? What can parents, educators, the industry, and public officials do about it?

To attack those questions systematically, we commissioned a study of one day in the life of television. We also mustered the best experts we could find for a symposium—titled "The New Face of Television Violence"—to explore the import and the seriousness of what seems a burgeoning crisis. To snap our day-in-the-life-of-TV photo, we enlisted the Center for Media and Public Affairs, a nonprofit monitoring company whose business is fashioning statistical portraits of how American society is depicted in the media. We asked for and received a nonjudgmental, bias-neutral content analysis of one typical day. Thursday, April 2, 1992, was chosen for several reasons: Thursday is a heavily-viewed night of television by a wide cross section of America; the prime-time shows on that evening tend to be popular, well-known series. We wanted a weekday rather than a weekend, to avoid sporting events. And April is not a sweeps month.

Thus, during 18 hours (6 A.M.-midnight) on that day in Washington, D.C., the Center taped, tabulated, computerized, and analyzed the programs on 10 channels: the affiliates of ABC, CBS, NBC, Fox, and PBS; one non-affiliated station, WDCA; plus the cable channels WTBS, the USA Network, MTV, and HBO. The program schedules, it turned out, were notable only for their ordinariness: no untypically violent movies like "Rambo" or "Scarface" were shown; even the news on that date was light on violent events such as wars, civil disorders, and local crime.

The results of the study were an eye-opener. In those 180 hours of programming, we observed:

- 1846 individual acts of violence—purposeful, overt, deliberate behavior involving physical force against other individuals.
- 175 scenes in which violence resulted in one or more fatalities.
- 389 scenes depicting serious assaults.
- 362 scenes involving gunplay.
- 673 depictions of punching, pushing, slapping, dragging, and other physically hostile acts.
- 226 scenes of menacing threats with a weapon.

Newer program forms, such as music videos and reality shows, we discovered, are significantly increasing the amount of violence on our screens. And commercials for violent theatrical movies and TV series have become a major source of televised violence. News broadcasts, in their heightened competitive fervor, are peddling strong doses of murder, muggings, and mayhem as ratings-getters. In fictional programming alone—which accounted for 95 percent of the total—we found an average of 185 scenes of violence per channel. That works out to more than 100 per hour across the 10 channels we monitored.

Well over a third of all the violence (751 scenes) involved some sort of life-threatening assault. Many scenes showed attacks with knives, clubs, bombs, and other weapons. Victims were terrorized and traumatized by all manner of assailants. And violence came in a wide variety of program forms. Cartoons were the most violent, with 471 scenes. (A note: child experts agree that violent cartoons are inadvisable for children 2 to 5, who may not distinguish between animated violence and the real thing, so they were included in our tabulations. Also, our study shows a glut of super-hero-style cartoons that feature more "human" characters than earlier Tom & Jerry-type fare; these realistic cartoons may have an even stronger influence on children.) Promos for TV shows were next (265); then movies (221); toy commercials (188); music videos (123); commercials for theatrical movies (121); TV dramas (69); news (62); reality shows like *Top Cops* and *Hard Copy* (58); sitcoms (52); and soap operas (34). The outlet purveying the most violence that particular spring day was the unaffiliated station: 376 scenes, or one every three minutes.

The rest: WTBS—321 scenes (18 per hour); HBO—257 scenes (14 per hour); USA Network—209 scenes (12 per hour); MTV—202 scenes (11 per hour); Fox—182 scenes (10 per hour); CBS—175 scenes (10 per hour); ABC—48 scenes (3 per hour); NBC—39 scenes (2 per hour); PBS—37 scenes (2 per hour). (WTBS's high total is partly explained by a high incidence of Tom & Jerry-type cartoons and old movies and TV series.) HBO showed "Paint It Black," "To Sleep with Anger," "Tales from the Crypt," and other films.

An important finding of the study is that music videos are a far more fecund source of TV violence than previously imagined. The 144 videos that MTV showed in those 18 hours bore as much violence as the Big Three commercial networks combined, and they came from such youth heroes as Guns N' Roses ("Live and Let Die," "Don't Cry"), Jon Bon Jovi ("Blaze of Glory"), Bruce Springsteen ("Human Touch"), Aerosmith ("Janie's Got a Gun"), Van Halen ("Right Now"), Ugly Kid Joe ("Everything About You"), and Metallica ("Enter Sandman").

CBS was the most violent of the major networks—much of the difference between it and the other two coming from *Top Cops,* with its re-creations of violent crimes. An afternoon slate of cartoons and an unusually violent string of prime-time plot lines in series such as *Drexell's Class* and *Beverly Hills, 90210* boosted Fox's total. By far, more violent incidents took place in fiction rather than non-fiction shows, but newer program forms such as reality-based series are now beginning to contribute significantly to television's freight of violence. *Top Cops, Street Stories, Inside Edition, Hard Copy,* and *A Current Affair* accounted for 58 violent moments; the news programs added 62 more.

The makers of commercials and promotional announcements for theatrical movies and TV shows, it now appears, have clearly adopted the tactic of utilizing the most action-packed moments of their entertainments to grab viewers' attention. Thus, we observed 386 scenes—containing violence—in ads for movies such as "Thunderheart," "The Power of One," "McBain," "Newsies," and "The People Under the Stairs," and in promos for TV series like *The Commish, Columbo, Knots Landing, Mann & Machine, Hunter, Mystery!, MacGyver, Counterstrike,* and *Dallas.* Serious forms of violence topped the list of the most frequently presented modes of violent behavior:

|  | Number of Scenes | Percent of Total |
|---|---|---|
| Serious assaults (excluding use of guns) | 389 | 21 |
| Gunplay | 362 | 20 |
| Isolated punches | 273 | 15 |
| Pushing/Dragging | 272 | 15 |
| Menacing threat with weapon | 226 | 12 |
| Slaps | 128 | 7 |
| Deliberate property destruction | 95 | 5 |
| Simple assaults | 73 | 4 |
| All other types | 28 | 1 |
| *Total* | *1846* | *100%* |

Since most of the programming in our one-day snapshot of television went out nationally via broadcast and cable networks, we deem it generally representative of what the country as a whole saw on that day. One reason for conducting the study on District Cablevision in Washington, D.C.: it's the hometown TV supplier to such major lobbying groups as the National Association of Broadcasters, the National Cable Television Association, the Association of Independent Television Stations, and the Radio-Television News Directors Association, as well as the Corporation for Public Broadcasting, the Federal Communications Commission, Congress, and the White House. We now have a fair and documented idea of the violence quotient that those influentials are seeing every day on their TV screens.

Unmeasured in our survey, of course, were the many hundreds of hours of VCR-watching that went on in that city on that day—much of it devoted to theatrical films with violent content. Thus, the study's conclusion: Violence remains a pervasive, major feature of contemporary television programming; and it's coming from more sources and in greater volume than ever before.

# 38

# Growing Up Violent

## by David S. Barry

*Editor's Note:* For several decades, social and behavioral scientists have been studying the relationship between mass media and human behavior, especially violent and abnormal behavior. This article reviews that research and concludes that there is a link between "screen mayhem" and an increase in aggressive behavior.

Author David S. Barry is a journalist and freelance writer as well as a TV screenwriter. This article first appeared in the *Journal of the Writers Guild of America West,* and the version reprinted here appeared in slightly condensed form in *Media & Values,* Summer 1993.

If you were a teenager in the 1950s, you remember the shock effect of news headlines about the new specter of juvenile delinquency. The book *The Amboy Dukes* and the movies *Blackboard Jungle* and *Rebel Without a Cause* were deeply alarming in their portrayal of teenagers willing to defy their school teachers and beat up other students. The violence portrayed in those stories, terrifying as it was, consisted almost entirely of assaults with fists and weapons which left victims injured, but alive. It was nonlethal violence. The notion of American teenagers as killers was beyond the threshold of credibility.

Since the 1950s, America has [become] almost unrecognizable in terms of the level of criminal violence reported in everyday news stories. In looking for a root cause, one of the most obvious differences in the social and cultural fabric between postwar and prewar America is the massive and pervasive exposure of American youth to television. Behavioral scientists and medical researchers have been examining screen violence as a causative element in America's crime rate since the 1950s. Study after study has been published showing clear evidence of a link. And researchers say that the evidence continues to be ignored as the violence steadily worsens.

The statistics about children and screen violence—particularly that shown on television—are grim. You've probably seen figures that show an average of 28 hours of weekly TV watching by children from ages two to 11. For prime-time programming, which contains an average of five violent acts per hour, that works out to 100 acts of violence each week, 5,000 a year. But children also watch cartoons, which contain far more violence than adult programming. For

Saturday morning cartoon shows, the violence rate spikes up to 25 acts per hour, the highest rate on TV. With children's programming added to the mix, the average child is likely to have watched 8,000 screen murders and more than 100,000 acts of violence by the end of elementary school. By the end of the teenage years, that figure will double. Those numbers are not mere statistics. They do not occur in a social vacuum, but in a culture and society with a murder rate increasing six times faster than the population. Whether we like to acknowledge it or not, America is in the grip of an epidemic of violence so severe that homicide has become the second leading cause of death of all persons 15 to 24 years old (auto crashes are the first)—and the leading cause among African-American youth. In 1992, the U.S. Surgeon General cited violence as the leading cause of injury to women ages 15 to 44, and the U.S. Center for Disease control considers violence a leading public health issue, to be treated as an epidemic.

## A Hostile America

From the 1950s to now, America has gone from being one of the safest to one of the most violent countries on earth. Here are some numbers: In 1951, with a population of 150 million, federal crime reports showed a national total of 6,820 homicides, 16,800 rapes and 52,090 robberies. For 1980, with a population of 220 million, (a 47 percent increase) the numbers were 23,000 murders, 78,920 rapes and 548,220 robberies.

In big cities, changes were more drastic. In Detroit, for instance, the 1953 murder total was 130, with 321 in New York and 82 in Los Angeles. Thirty years later, the Detroit murder tally was up to 726, the New York toll 1,665—and the Los Angeles murder total was 1,126. The fastest climbing sector of the rising crime rate is youth, with the past 10 years showing a 55 percent increase in the number of children under 18 arrested for murder. America now loses more adolescents to death by violence—especially gun violence—than to illness.

The reason these numbers belong in this discussion is that the medical community sees a direct link between screen violence and criminal behavior of viewers. In panel discussions on this subject, we usually hear claims from TV and movie industry spokespersons that opinion is divided in the medical community. Different conclusions can be drawn from different studies, so the arguments go, and no clear consensus exists. Yet, the American medical establishment is clear—in print—on the subject of just such a consensus. The American Medical Association, the National Institute of Mental Health, the U.S. Surgeon General's Office, the U.S. Center for Disease Control and the American Psychological Association have concluded that study after study shows a direct causal link between screen violence and violent criminal behavior.

## Causal Links

The research goes back decades. The 1968 National Commission on the Causes and Prevention of Violence cited screen violence as a major component of the problem. The 1972 *Surgeon General's Report on TV and Behavior* cited clear evidence of a causal link between televised violence and aggressive behavior by viewers. A 10-year followup to the Surgeon General's Report by the National Institute of Mental Health added far more data in support of the causal link. The NIMH report, a massive study covering an additional 10 years of research, was clear and unequivocal in stating: "The consensus among most of the research community is that violence on television does lead to aggressive behavior by children and teenagers who watch the programs."

A 1985 task force for the American Psychological Association Commission on Youth on Violence came to the same conclusion. A 1992 study for the APA Commission on Youth and Violence took the issue further, examining research evidence in light of its effects or implementation. The finding was that the research evidence is widely ignored. The APA report was authored by Edward Donnerstein, Ph.D., chair of the Department of Communications, University of California Santa Barbara, by Leonard Eron, Ph.D., University of Chicago and Ron Slaby of the Education Development Center, Harvard University. Their 39-page report, about to be published, states definitively that, contrary to arguments of people in the TV and motion picture industry, there is consistency and agreement in the conclusions drawn by the major medical organizations' studies of media violence.

After discussing a massive number of studies and an extensive body of research material, Donnerstein's study quotes from the 1982 NIMH report: "In magnitude, television violence is as strongly correlated with aggressive behavior as any other behavioral variable that has been measured."

Specifically, the report noted the agreement by the NIMH, the APA and the Center for Disease Control that research data confirms that childhood watching of TV violence is directly related to criminally violent behavior later on.

## Daily Assault

Adding scope to the APA report is a study recently conducted for the nonprofit Center for Media and Public Affairs in Washington, D.C. The CMPA tabulated all the violence encountered during an 18-hour broadcasting day (a Thursday) in Washington, including cable TV. The tally showed an overall average of 100 acts of violence per hour for a total of nearly 2,000 acts of violence in the 18-hour period. Most of the violence involved a gun, with murder making up one-tenth of the violent acts recorded. A breakdown by channel, or network, showed cable to be far more violent then network broadcasting. WTBS was clocked at 19 violent acts per hour, HBO at 15 per hour, USA at 14 and MTV, the youth-oriented music video channel, at 13 violent acts per hour.

The networks (except for CBS, whose violence content was skewed by the reality show *Top Cops*) were as low in violence content as PBS, which showed two violent acts per hour. ABC showed three violent acts per hour and NBC two. CBS, because of *Top Cops*, was tallied at 11 violent acts per hour. But only one-eighth of the violence occurred in adult-oriented TV entertainment. The bulk of the violence occurred in children's TV programming, with cartoons registering 25 violent incidents per hour—six times the rate of episodic TV drama. Toy commercials ranked with cartoons in violent content. Next were promos for TV shows and movies, which were four times as violent as episodic drama.

The most violent period of daily TV programming was mornings from 6 to 9 A.M. where 497 scenes of violence were recorded for an hourly rate of 165.7. Next was the 2 P.M. to 5 P.M. afternoon slot with 609 violent scenes, or 203 per hour. The morning and afternoon slots compared to 320 violent scenes in prime time, from 8 P.M. to 11 P.M. or 106 per hour, and a late-night rate (from 11 P.M. to 12 A.M.) of 114.

## No Consequences

In addition to recording totals, the CMPA examined the context in which the screen violence occurred. The finding was that most TV violence was shown with no visible consequences, nor any critical judgment. A significant amount of the violence occurred in movie promos, where it was shown out of context. Music videos generally present violence without comment or judgment. Similarly, violence in cartoons and toy commercials usually occurs without consequences or comment. More than 75 percent of the violence tallied in the study (1,640 of the nearly 2,000 violent acts) was presented with no judgment as to its acceptability as behavior. Violence was judged criminal in fewer than one-tenth of the incidents. And, ironically, while violence in episodic TV drama and TV movies for adults viewers is subject to close scrutiny for context and suitability, the bulk of the screen violence viewed by children is not.

The studies mentioned above make a compelling argument, particularly when looked at as a group. But a new study, by Dr. Brandon Centerwall of the University of Washington Department of Epidemiology and Psychiatry, takes the discussion much farther. In a study published in the June, 1992 Journal of the American Medical Association, Centerwall looked for statistical connections between the change in violent crime rates following the introduction of TV in the United States.

Centerwall found this: murder rates in Canada and the U.S. increased almost 100 percent (92 percent in Canada, 93 percent in the U.S. corrected for population increase) between 1945 and 1970. In both countries, the ownership of TV sets increased in almost the same proportion as the homicide rate.

Centerwall's stark and unmistakable conclusion is this: white homicide rates in Canada, the U.S. and South Africa were stable or declining until the advent of television. Then, in the course of a generation, the murder rates doubled.

The APA study by Donnerstein, Slaby and Eron also makes the point that research evidence of TV violence effects has "for decades been actively ignored, denied, attacked and even misrepresented in presentations to the American public, and popular myths regarding the effects have been perpetuated." Consequently, Donnerstein says, a major education gap exists regarding television's contribution to the problem of violence in America.

The discouraging point made in both studies is that, despite the massive research evidence of screen violence as a direct contributing factor to America's homicide rate, the screen violence level continues to rise.

As a writer deeply committed to the Constitutional guarantees against censorship, I don't like to hear the suggestion of government regulation of movies or TV. But it's time we at least face the evidence of what screen violence is doing to our children, and come to some sober conclusions about our responsibilities to the common good.

# 39

# Yes, TV Violence Is Awful, But What's the Cure?

## *by* Kenneth R. Clark

*Editor's Note:* Not everyone sees a cause-and-effect relationship between media violence and violent behavior. The author of this article claims that the kind of research discussed in the previous article was usually done in a laboratory, not in real life. Thus it does not provide conclusive answers.

Kenneth R. Clark writes about media issues for the *Chicago Tribune*, where this article was published on October 25, 1992.

History tells us homo sapiens never really liked each other very much, even before television came along to reflect and, some say, to engender increasing acts of violence we perpetrate upon each other. But is television really a prime factor behind the rising tide of murder, mayhem and rape now plaguing the nation?

A growing cadre of critics, armed with evidence from several scientifically conducted studies, says it is, because youngsters who soak up hour after hour of TV violence become desensitized to pain and death and are taught that a brass-knuckles approach is the best problem-solver.

The studies, reported in such scientific publications as the Journal of the American Medical Association and the American Journal of Epidemiology, arrive at some disturbing conclusions.

In one study, researchers singled out a remote Canadian town, identified only as "Notel," which first got television in 1973. Using two nearby communities that previously had television as control groups, the scholars studied 45 1st- and 2nd-graders and reported that after two years of watching the new medium, aggressive behavior in the group increased by 160 percent over pretelevision levels.

A 1990 study by the American Psychological Association estimated that by the time the average child is 12, he or she will have witnessed 8,000 murders and 10,000 acts of non-lethal violence on television.

The critics cite such studies as proof that less violence on television would mean less violence in our streets, schoolrooms and homes. They want television violence, if not eliminated, sharply muted and structured to show that violence does not pay.

But for all the scientific method brought to bear on the subject, not all scholars agree that real-life violence can be curbed with a return to "Ozzie and Harriet" fare. Peter Stearns, social historian and dean of the department of humanities and social sciences at Carnegie-Mellon University, is a doubter.

"It's very difficult to nail this thing down," he said. "Most of the studies that have demonstrated correlation have done so in laboratory settings, and one of the uncertainties is how a lab setting relates to real life. If television violence promotes unfortunate behavior, it does so very differentially, depending on the individual. There are lots and lots of Americans who can watch TV violence and not have it impact their lives in any meaningful way."

Debate on the issue is nothing new; it has been raging off and on since the 1950s when the public appetite for Westerns and action-adventure series on network prime time guaranteed a fairly respectable body count. After all, the gun that won the West is deeply imbued in the American psyche, and it is difficult to make a "Hill Street Blues" without shooting someone.

But network television today actually may be less violent than in past decades when top ratings went to "Have Gun, Will Travel" (1957–1963), "The Life and Legend of Wyatt Earp" (1955–1961) and "The Untouchables" (1959–1963), which was possibly the most egregiously violent television series ever created.

By comparison, there isn't enough violence in this fall's slate of network sitcoms to crack an egg. It is dominated by the likes of "Murphy Brown," "Roseanne," "Life Goes On," "Evening Shade," "Seinfeld" and "Melrose Place."

Of 103 new and returning series for ABC, CBS, NBC and Fox, only a third have the potential for violence, and that includes such news magazines as "48 Hours," "20/20" and "Street Stories" that rarely are graphic, even in pursuit of a crime story.

Cable is another matter. Some cable channels routinely run uncut Hollywood movies that can leave blood and body tissue on the living room rug. They do so with impunity because their customers, like those who go to the movie box office, are paying for it. It does not come into the home uninvited.

A recent survey of 10 stations in Washington, D.C., commissioned by TV Guide, found that the channels showing the greatest number of violent scenes were—in descending order—WTBS (for its huge slate of ultraviolent cartoons), HBO, USA Network and MTV. They had a combined total of 55 violent scenes per hour. In comparison, the networks practically were operating in "Mr. Rogers' Neighborhood," with Fox and CBS tied for the highest violence count, at 10 scenes per hour, followed by ABC at three and NBC at two.

Even news—especially local news where competition for ratings runs at a feverish pace—is not held blameless.

"I recall being horrified and upset for quite some time some years back when I was watching a newscast and saw a person being shot, up close," says Brian Wilcox, director of public policy at the American Psychological Association. "I watched, literally, this guy getting his head blown off. That was just one incident, but it was one incident too many."

There can be no doubt that we are becoming a society increasingly besieged by violence. The Centers for Disease Control have declared it an epidemic, to be treated as a public health problem. The FBI says juvenile violence has gone up 25 percent in 10 years.

A lot of people want something done, but nobody seems to be sure what should, or even can, be done where television is concerned. In their zeal to do something, they overlook one very real danger. If television becomes a scapegoat for violence in America, attention may be diverted from the deadlier causes: drugs, underclass rage, unemployment and availability of weaponry.

Americans haven't won more than a skirmish or two in the drug war, and no one has been able to remove the short-fused powderkegs of race and class hatred from the nation's major cities. Against problems of this magnitude, television is a tempting target simply because it can be hit.

Sen. Paul Simon (D-Ill.) two years ago introduced and Congress passed a bill enabling television programmers to draft common anti-violence guidelines without fear of prosecution under federal anti-trust laws. It expires in December 1993.

ABC, CBS and NBC, all of which have nearly identical standards and practices guidelines that do keep a lid on the most gratuitous violence, have discussed the matter, but cable programmers have not joined them. Since cable does not use "the public airwaves," it was immune to content control by the Federal Communications Commission.

Fox Broadcasting and independent stations also are ignoring Simon's call. Their lawyers say that while this bill exempts them from federal collusion charges, it does not immunize them from similar charges at the state level, where they operate. They also fear they would be open to lawsuits on 1st Amendment grounds.

In fact, censorship, which never has withstood a freedom of speech challenge in Congress or the courts, would seem to be the sole, futile choice of those bent on purging the medium of mayhem.

Simon is among those who tend to open a discussion of the topic with, "I don't believe in censorship, but . . ."

"The answer is not censorship, but if they don't voluntarily do something, I think there will be attempts by the FCC or the Congress to do it for them," he says of the networks, independent stations and cable networks.

Leonard Eron, professor of psychology at the University of Illinois and architect of several field studies on the impact of television violence, says governments in Scandinavia, Belgium, Luxembourg, France and England always have forbidden depictions of violence during hours in which children are likely to be watching.

"I've never heard complaints by citizens of those countries that their rights have been violated," he says.

But Tim Duncan, executive director of the Advertiser Syndicated Television Association, says government intervention in the programming process never would be tolerated by American viewers.

"American producers are only interested in giving American audiences what they want to see," Duncan says. "If what they want to see is violence, that's a pity. You can decry that, but that's why it's on the air. That television set is a voting booth, and what's on the air is the result of the most democratic process there is."

Although most of the academics who study television violence specifically deplore "happy violence," in which the perpetrator pays no price and the results are not seen as tragic, the actual incidence rate is taken with no regard to context. Any scene in which someone hurts or kills someone, or threatens to do so, is counted as an act of violence, whether the act stems from a "Tom and Jerry" cartoon on Saturday morning or a rerun of "Hamlet."

George Gerbner, of the Annenberg School of Communications at the University of Pennsylvania, a contributor to the APA study and author of an as yet unreleased survey of violence in cable-generated fare, says the role of television must change.

"For the first time in history, a child is born into a home in which the television is on an average of seven hours a day," Gerbner says. "It's no longer the parent who tells the stories and it's no longer the school or the church; it's television."

Because of that, Gerbner says television now should act more as a responsible parent than an entertainer, an unlikely role for an audience-seeking medium.

However sincere the motives of those who would tame television, it just won't work. Even if, as Simon urges, every television set were equipped with a channel lock to preclude unsupervised viewing by youngsters, what legislation would force parents to use it? And even if all of television cleaned up its act, or labeled its fare the way movies are labeled, any kid with $2 and a VCR can rent a videotape of "Basic Instinct" or "Die Hard" at the local mall.

It may be a sad commentary, but activist H. Rap Brown was on target in 1967, after a race riot in Detroit left 40 dead, 2,000 injured and 5,000 homeless.

"Violence," he said, "is as American as cherry pie."

It will take much more now than simply sanitizing the television schedule to get cherry pie off the menu.

# 40

# What You See Is What You Think

## *by* Diana Workman

---

*Editor's Note:* More and more, prime-time television uses sex to draw viewers. But rather than enlightening the audience, television serves to entrench discomfort about sex more deeply and contributes to continued ignorance in society about love, sex, and responsibility, according to the author of this article.

Diana Workman, M.P.H., is a health education and family planning specialist. She is president of Family Planning Alternatives in Sunnyvale, California. This article was originally published in *Media & Values,* Spring 1989.

---

A 12-year-old caught spreading a telephone sex number around school can expect a lecture from his parents.

So it isn't surprising that that's what happened to Ben, a leading character on the show *Growing Pains,* during one of the sitcom's 1986 programs.

But the episode featuring his crime and punishment should strike other chords among television viewers. Its storyline provides a good example of television's increasing tendency to present sexual themes—many of them involving young people—without fully facing the consequences.

Intensive analysis of three weeks of 10 top prime-time shows from late 1986 as part of a study sponsored by the Center for Population Options and the University of California/Berkeley led my co-researcher Kim Bloomfield and myself to some uncomfortable conclusions about television sex.

Our months of laboriously counting and then decoding sexual references and behavior during our sample time made one thing perfectly clear: there is a tremendous amount of sexual activity and innuendo on television. And its pervasiveness as a means of drawing viewers, which began to accelerate in the late 1970s, has continued and even increased.

## How Much Sex?

Our focused viewing of 10 popular shows tallied physical, verbal and implied acts or references to sex, before further analyzing them according to the program type, network and time frame. Age and gender of initiators were also recorded.

The following brief summaries represent the frequency of many types of sexual behavior:

- "Touching behaviors," including kissing, hugging, and other affectionate touching were presented at the rate of 24.5 acts per hour.
- "Suggestions and innuendo" involving flirtatious behavior or general allusions to sexual behavior appeared at a rate of 16.5 times per hour.
- Sexual intercourse was suggested 2.5 times per hour.
- A range of "discouraged sexual practices" such as sadomasochism and exhibitionism were suggested at a rate of 6.2 times per hour.
- On the other hand, educational information about sex was infrequently presented, occurring at a rate of 1.6 times per hour.

Although portrayal of sexual intercourse is still taboo, virtually every program in our sample contained at least one sexual reference. We also found more sexual content than one might expect in programming that aired during the supposedly family-oriented, mid-evening viewing hour (8-9 P.M./Eastern and Pacific and 7-8 P.M./Central and Mountain time). Some of the emphasis in this time frame was explained by the heavy use of sexual references and innuendo on sitcoms, where they seem to be regarded as a sure-fire laugh. The sitcom format tends to distort the treatment of serious issues even when shows are brave enough to attempt serious themes.

In the *Growing Pains* example, Ben was ahead of many of TV's sexually confused young people in one way: he did talk to his Dad about the phone-sex incident. And even when meting out punishment, his father, Jason, appeared very supportive. But in other ways the show matched our profile of television's sexual references, which were clear enough to enable us to map their characteristics and identify several recurring themes.

## Five Problems with TV Sex

**1.** *Children, especially young boys, are often "straight men" in jokes about sex and sexuality. Either they lead in to an adult's joke or they make it themselves.*

The "phone sex" show, in which one adolescent not only participates in, but underpins, a kinky sex episode, is not unusual. More typical, perhaps, is a joke that arises on *Who's the Boss*, when eight-year-old Jonathan breaks his arm.

"I broke my toe and couldn't walk," says his sister. When his grandmother, Mona, portrayed as very sexually active, says "I broke my pelvis. . . . " "She couldn't walk!" interrupts Tony, Jonathan's embarrassed father. In this case, the eight-year-old's broken arm sets the stage, the 13-year-old sister provides the lead-in, and the adults deliver the punchline to this sexual joke.

**2.** *TV children avoid discussing problems with their parents, and they discuss sex least of all.*

Very few shows in our sample feature parent-child sexual discussion. When it does occur, it is only because an incident or problem forced the issue, as in the phone-sex segment. Interestingly, although father Jason of *Growing Pains* is a psychiatrist and he and his wife appear very understanding, the young characters usually try to prevent their parents from discovering what they're going through. As a result, the parents have a minimal role in solving their children's problems. An episode of *Family Ties* in which Mallory is prevented from eloping by brother Alex provides another example. Although faced with a serious life issue and blessed with understanding, low-key parents, she discusses her motivation and feelings with them only after the incident is closed.

No interaction is one-sided, and TV's parents are often equally uncomfortable. Although on *Who's the Boss?* father Tony is upset to hear his daughter got a C, he's *relieved* to learn it was in sex education. The message here is twofold. As a father, Tony is uncomfortable about his daughter taking sex education. He also concludes that the better she does in sex education class, the more likely she is to be or become sexually active. Thus, the program reinforces the misconception that sex education causes promiscuity and implies that most parents are uncomfortable with it.

Unlike most TV families, *The Cosby Show*'s Huxtables were approached by their children before, not after, a crisis in their relationships with boy and girlfriends. Although the problems were perhaps not as serious as in some other shows, the parents were able to contribute their experience and play an active role in their resolution. Unfortunately, this seems to be the exception, not the rule, on prime-time television.

**3.** *Sex and sexual issues are usually presented in an exploitative way, rather than a loving and meaningful one.*

Of the six implied acts of intercourse in our sample, four were described as "lustful," one "routine" or involving sex out of habit, and only one was clearly "loving." In only one case, involving impotence, did any sort of sexual discussion take place before or after intercourse.

**4.** *Tender, loving sexual behavior is rarely portrayed between people in committed relationships. Instead, sexual references are presented in a context that makes even normal sexual practices appear extreme.*

Relationships on recent shows like *thirtysomething* have made loving sex between committed couples more common. In our sample, an episode of *Murder, She Wrote* in which a young husband picks up his wife and lovingly carries her into the bedroom and shuts the door was about as graphic as most television intercourse gets (and more loving and committed than most).

By contrast, most of the few references to intercourse we observed were made among friends, co-workers and strangers, demonstrating a focus on sexuality not preceded, protected or sustained by a loving relationship.

Even more problematic were the large numbers of sexual references to a variety of sexual practices besides intercourse, including some usually considered to be socially discouraged. Shows like *Night Court, Golden Girls, Moonlighting* and *Murder, She Wrote* refer with relative frequency to masturbation, voyeurism, transvestitism, transsexualism, homosexuality, sadomasochism, oral sex, prostitution and pornography.

In our sample, the farcical *Night Court* features the largest number of sexual references of this type. In almost every episode, Dan, the prosecuting attorney, searches relentlessly for sexual partners. When a woman asks him if he ever has sex at work, he replies, "Well, never with another person." In one scene, an offstage sexual episode ends with him bound and gagged in a closet, implying a sadomasochistic encounter. Such references fail to separate the kinky from the normal; instead, they tend to view all sexual behavior with a leer.

**5.** *If sexual intercourse is implied, precautions or discussions of birth control are avoided. Unintended pregnancies almost never occur, and sexually-transmitted diseases and contraception are seldom discussed or portrayed.*

Maddie's pregnancy on *Moonlighting*, ending in a miscarriage, is typical of TV's unwillingness to focus on the consequences of sexual behavior. Rare as they are, TV pregnancies are apt to end in miscarriages and stillbirths, leaving the characters apparently unchanged by the experience. Even more common are sexual relationships untroubled by worries about pregnancy and sexually transmitted diseases, even though safe sex, contraception and sex education are rarely discussed.

In our sample, a reference by *Moonlighting*'s David Addison to a pregnancy resulting from his first sexual experience (once again, "the kid didn't make it"), and a fantasy pregnancy arising from *Growing Pains'* father Jason's fears about his son's first car are the only acknowledgment that sex can have consequences. The first did not result in a real baby, and the second wasn't real at all!

In the shows we watched, sexually transmitted diseases were never mentioned and contraceptive use was neither depicted nor discussed. Pressures to be sexually active and issues related to it (self-esteem, peer pressure, boy/girlfriend anxieties) were never addressed. Although fears about AIDS have recently broken the taboo against discussion of condoms and safe sex practices, such instructive programming remains an exception rather than the rule.

## Sex and Consequences

Our study confirms that prime-time television has created a market for itself by taking shocking, often humorous sexual material and packaging it as family entertainment. But what children learn from TV sex is still open to discussion.

That they are learning something seems indisputable. Most children spend more time with television than they do in school. The screen inevitably becomes a classroom for lessons about life.

Perhaps TV's most profound lesson is its reflection of the continuing sexual discomfort of our society. Thus, today's frequent, but veiled, sexual references become the flip side of the sexless TV of the '50s and early '60s. It just makes one wonder what's in store for the '90s.

# X

# Politics

Politicians seem to have won the war against mass media. It used to be a pretty even match, although politicians usually were winners in the long run, with the exception, perhaps, of Richard Nixon. Yet even Nixon was elected twice to the vice presidency and twice to the presidency before his own troubles with Watergate brought him down.

In many ways television has become absolutely essential to American politics and has changed the whole nature of the process. It took awhile for politicians to discover how to use and control the medium. By the 1980s, the lessons had been well learned. By the 1990s, it no longer seems to be a contest.

First, television requires politicians to have certain kinds of physical characteristics and personality traits. Abraham Lincoln probably would not have been elected in an age of television; he may have been too ugly. Theodore Roosevelt was probably too boisterous; television requires a low-key, cool approach. Franklin D. Roosevelt could project a strong image on radio because of his booming voice, but as a paraplegic his disability probably would have been overwhelmingly negative on television. Ronald Reagan, however, was just right. By the 1980s it seemed as though one should be a movie star, or at least comfortable in front of cameras, to win high political office in the United States.

Second, television requires a lot of money. In nominating candidates to run in elections, political parties have learned not only how to choose those who are reasonably telegenic but also to pick nominees who can raise money. Fund-raising has become a major part of campaigning because television costs so much. Those who are already wealthy have a great advantage. Where the party stands seems less important than how much money it has raised to make an issue of its policies in campaign advertising. Money itself determines the issues; if money can't be raised to push a particular issue, it probably won't get into the party's platform.

Television is a medium that can be more thoroughly controlled than most other media. The industry is more concentrated, with fewer reporters than newspapers and fewer stations than radio; in fact, three major networks still count the majority of Americans in their audiences each evening. Thus television is easier to deal with. There is also the subtle problem that TV stations must be licensed by government and subject to FCC (Federal Communications Commission) regulations, which some critics say have been chilling factors for bold and blunt political reporting.

Politicians have learned how to control political dialogue. They no longer have to answer tough questions from reporters. All they have to do is craft speeches containing a few snippets, TV-designed thirty seconds long, which is all that can appear on the nightly news. When these sound bites are used on national television, they dictate the coverage of print media as well, especially if the candidate has been "too busy" to meet with reporters during the campaign day. All the candidate has had time for are some photo opportunities for television and the front pages. An entire campaign can be conducted with sound bites and "photo ops," without the intrusion of fact, argument, policy, or answers to hard questions about a candidate's stand.

Television deals with impressions rather than facts. Politicians don't have to have a lot of reason on their side, but they must make a good impression. By the same logic, they can more easily smear and damage their opponents before there is a demand for the facts. Indeed, negative advertising has become a staple in contemporary politics.

In his analysis of such advertising, Victor Kamber writes about the ad for Lyndon Johnson in 1964 known as "The Little Girl and the Daisy," which "ushered in a whole new set of rules for the old game of political mudslinging." A little girl stands in a field picking the petals off a flower. As she counts her petals, an adult voice begins counting down to a nuclear explosion. The announcer tells viewers they must love their neighbors or risk "going into the darkness," and then he reminds them to vote for Johnson. According to Kamber,

"The Little Girl and the Daisy" had all the elements of modern negative political advertising. It appealed on an emotional, gut level to a widely-held concern of the American electorate. The spot was ingenious in its attack on Johnson's Republican opponent, Barry Goldwater, because it never mentioned his name. Rather, it played on fears that Goldwater's hawkish stand on nuclear weapons could lead him to "push the button" if elected president.[1]

The man who created that ad, Tony Schwartz—who has become the guru of political TV spots—later wrote, "The question of truth is largely irrelevant when dealing with the electronic media. The best political commercials are like Rorschach patterns. They do not tell the viewer anything. They surface his feelings and provide a context for him to express those feelings."[2]

In the elections of 1988, 1990, and 1992, negative advertising, especially on television, became a staple of the political process. The radio talk show has become another way to bypass the tough questions of reporters. And the line between journalist and political consultant, as the line between news and advertising and entertainment, has become blurred. All of this raises questions about the future of the political process as a major mass media issue.

**Notes**

1. Victor Kamber, *Trivial Pursuit: Negative Advertising and the Decay of Political Discourse* (Washington, DC: Kamber Group, 1990), p. 4.
2. Robert Spiro, *The Duping of the American Voter* (New York: Lippincott & Cromwell, 1980), p. 160.

# 41

# Television and the Changed Political Process

## *by* Diane Mermigas

*Editor's Note:* Almost every presidential election since Eisenhower's in the 1950s has brought another dimension to the problem of elections in a society dominated by television.

In some ways the 1988 election was the most important because it used the sound bite and the photo op more than ever before and showed that negative advertising in politics was here to stay. This is even more meaningful because the winner, George Bush, was not the great communicator that his predecessor was; he was not a particularly good speaker nor particularly telegenic nor the low-keyed, cool character television needs. But he was able to win by using all of the other new tools of politicking in an electronic age, changing basic campaign strategies, perhaps permanently.

Diane Mermigas is a senior reporter for *Electronic Media,* which published this article on November 28, 1988, immediately following the national elections.

Television coverage of presidential politics may never be the same again, thanks to the election of 1988.

The day after the Nov. 7 election, politicians and the press began what will probably be one of the most intense scrutinies of election-year campaigning and coverage to date.

Both sides now admit there was too much character assassination—the outgrowth, some say, of Ronald Reagan's eight successful years of press manipulation—and too little attention focused on the issues.

Critics say the candidates' heavy reliance on negative advertising and the media's excessive reliance on voter polls contributed to low voter turnout.

One of the more serious questions being raised, however, is whether television itself became too prominent a part of the story this election year, inspiring candidates and their parties to cater to the medium.

The candidates' media managers and image makers decided daily which sound bites would play best on the evening news, following their belief that controlling exposure was a means of controlling news content.

And they were right.

"I think more and more, things are packaged for television. And it is not us who are doing the packaging and it's not us who want to be packaged that way," said ABC News President Roone Arledge, echoing the sentiments of executives at CBS News and NBC News alike.

"There's no question that people have photo ops and they have staged opportunities, and they aim things for the evening news programs," he says.

"They carefully control the content of the conventions. They speak to people through commercials and sound bites, and they don't want it any different."

Mr. Arledge says it is very difficult to cover the political process in a meaningful way on television if the people controlling the candidates "don't want the American people to know what the issues are."

ABC media critic Jeff Greenfield insists that, next time around, the networks will have to resist being used by savvy political forces.

"The candidates really do set the agenda. The media can only be a catalyst for change. The politicians have to make it happen," Mr. Greenfield said.

But it's the networks in particular that have anxiously started their own election post-mortem.

They began their critical retrospection Nov. 8, in a provocative, 90-minute live "Viewpoint" telecast on ABC.

Since then, their self-analysis has continued primarily as part of internal reviews by the major news organizations.

ABC News executives say they may even use an outside research firm to help break down the different types of election-year coverage the network provided compared to its competition.

Already, ABC has addressed some of its own election-year frustrations by launching a new evening news feature. "American Agenda," a segment of the network's "World News Tonight," now provides at least three minutes of in-depth reporting on a major national issue each night.

The week before the elections, "World News Tonight" went on the road in an attempt to find out what was on the minds of the electorate.

Since September, ABC had been devoting every Monday broadcast of "Nightline" to a close examination of an issue or aspect of the election.

Lengthy news forums for in-depth interviews and analysis should be supplied in greater number next election year, most TV news professionals say.

"World News Tonight" anchorman Peter Jennings contends it also will be more important in the next presidential election year to assign correspondents to closely examine the way candidates are campaigning on the medium, with a look at paid advertising and orchestrated news coverage.

"I think there also is reason to examine the whole question of whether networks and their stations should be accepting political advertising that includes known falsehoods," Mr. Jennings says.

"I think one of the best things that can happen is for all of us to spend some time trying to figure out whether anything we did contributed to lower voter turnout, and what we can do about it. I think people should cool the rhetoric and engage in some hard-core soul searching."

At NBC, "Nightly News" anchorman Tom Brokaw has suggested that in addition to paying more attention to campaign advertising, the networks' news organizations should seek a change in the debate formats before agreeing to broadcast them in 1992.

He wants to see more follow-up questioning and examination of the issues.

In addition, a more discriminate use of polls might also be worth pursuing, he said, as well as shortening the length of the campaign year.

"However, I think the candidates' focus, inaccessibility and absence of discussion of the important issues contributes more to low voter turnout than the polls we take," Mr. Brokaw said.

In addition to doing more original reporting in 1992 and possibly dropping the requirement for sound bites from their daily campaign coverage, executives at all three broadcast networks say they will seriously consider giving less live coverage to the made-for-television conventions.

Ed Turner, executive vice president of the 24-hour Cable News Network, said that despite all of the media's pitfalls, television coverage of the year's election activities "went about as well as it was going to work."

To rely less on polls and focus more on grass-root issues in its coverage, CNN on election night took many of its cameras out into the field, where it picked up voter reaction as the returns trickled in.

"I think in the future, we are going to use the technology we have to bring a different viewpoint to our coverage from out there," Mr. Turner said.

But the press and the politicians aren't the only ones assessing election-year performance.

Various third-party groups, outraged by this year's election coverage, have already begun conducting their own reviews, leveling criticism at the media and the candidates.

The Center for Media and Public Affairs has criticized the media for failing to create the "public dialogue" with candidates that forces more thoughtful debate of important issues.

"It's my conviction that television coverage of a presidential campaign is inherently flawed simply because it must be compressed in only 22 minutes on the evening news," says ABC News correspondent James Wooten.

"What we have here is a headline operation that is very vulnerable to the skillful manipulation of a political candidate or party who knows how to feed us just what we need—sound bites, staging and a single theme of the day."

Although elongated news programs such as "Nightline" and "This Week With David Brinkley" try to offset the brevity factor, they do not draw large audiences, Mr. Wooten said.

However, television news executives and correspondents interviewed by *Electronic Media* agreed that it is not appropriate for the media to insist that political campaigns be conducted as high-minded philosophical forums.

All agree that it will be up to politicians and their parties to change the way in which campaigns, debates and conventions are conducted.

"But somewhere along the way, a bold network will deny a candidate air-time on their evening news unless they have something important to say," Mr. Wooten said.

That process may have gotten its start in the critiques Mr. Wooten filed following each of the three televised debates, in which we pointed out factual errors made by the candidates.

"The candidates this time around were more willing to color or twist the facts to their own advantage, especially in the case of Mr. Bush and Mr. Quayle," Mr. Wooten said.

However, the networks came under fire again this year for their own interpretation of the facts through the controversial practice of exit polling.

They were blasted the day after the election for rushing to call the national presidential race before many of the nation's polls were closed.

"I think they ought to stop the practice of exit polling and find some other way of evaluating voter responses," said Bob Smith, vice president and general manager of WCYB-TV, Bristol, Va., and co-chairman of NBC's affiliate news committee.

In fact, most network affiliate and news executives interviewed by *Electronic Media* agreed that the practice of exit polling should be refined, not eliminated.

Network news and station executives insist they are obliged to report information when it becomes available.

They say that it's up to Congress to legislate uniform poll closings instead.

Affiliates of all three commercial networks also shared a frustration with the length of live prime-time coverage ABC, CBS and NBC devoted to the lackluster nominating conventions last summer.

Veteran affiliate executives such as James Babb, executive vice president of Jefferson-Pilot Communications Co., contend that the networks have a right to seek some reforms of the political process.

"The networks and their stations didn't determine these formats, but they sure have been victimized by them," Mr. Babb said.

Just what type of election reform might occur is largely out of broadcasters' hands, however.

"I think a lot will depend on the mood Congress is in," said Phil Jones, former chairman of the CBS affiliate board of governors.

"But I think there is support for change on both sides. Many of these issues will be examined seriously over the next four years, and I think we'll see some changes made."

# 42

# The Talk-show Campaign

## *by* Gary Griffith

*Editor's Note:* If 1988 was the year of the sound bite and photo op, 1992 was the year of the radio talk show, yet another way for political candidates to take their message directly to the public without interference from the mass media gatekeepers. There were no reporters to question the candidates' answers or to put into context what was being said.

The talk show has become a popular format on radio, and in 1992 it was found to work for political candidates. Gary Griffith is the Washington bureau chief for Hearst Broadcasting. This article, written while the 1992 campaign was still running, was published in the *Communicator,* the magazine of the Radio-Television News Directors Association, August 1992.

The talk-show campaign that has been waged by the presidential candidates during the spring and early summer will no doubt continue in some form after the political conventions, as journalists and campaign strategists alike try to determine its place and its importance.

The early opinions of this unconventional phase of the campaign have divided into two camps. The journalism elite has largely determined that it is a dangerous end run around the legitimate questions of informed correspondents.

As Harvard professor Gary Orren put it recently in an interview with *The Wall Street Journal,* "The name of the game has become: Bypass Sam Donaldson."

The politicians rather agree with that assessment, although they tend to explain it more positively as "going directly to the voters" without what they call "the filter of the press."

Exactly when the 1992 talk-show campaign began is open to argument. Bill Clinton and Jerry Brown certainly gave it some credence when they appeared on the "Donahue" program during the New York primary. But it was Ross Perot who escalated it with his appearance on "Larry King Live." And it clearly got another big boost on June 3, when Bill Clinton played the saxophone on "The Arsenio Hall Show."

The unifying element of these appearances has been a lengthy interview, as long as two hours, and often including questions phoned in or asked by members of the studio audience.

Because it is not conducted by network news correspondents or members of the national press corps, the questioning is believed to be "softer," with few follow-ups on specifics. Thus, for example, Ross Perot was able to claim, as he did on the "Today" show, that he grew up in a modest family, without being challenged in a follow-up about his parents' membership in a country club.

As *Newsweek's* Jonathan Alter has observed, "It's very hard to follow up when you're sitting in your kitchen, trying to challenge a candidate."

President Bush referred to this difference in the nature of the questioning when he scolded co-anchor Paula Zahn for asking a somewhat "hard" one during his appearance on "CBS This Morning." "Why is it," he asked, "that it's the correspondents that have the controversy about Iraq or the polls or what I want to say about Ross Perot, when the American people want to know what I'm doing about the problems?"

One answer was posed by columnist Michael Kinsley. He compared the first ten questions asked by correspondents at the most recent Bush prime-time news conference with the first ten questions asked by callers on Ross Perot's first "Today" show appearance. Kinsley concluded, "The pros are obsessed with process while the amateurs are obsessed with substance." The pros, he also noted, seemed interested in making "news" or extracting the next day's headline.

Such an assessment plays right into the beliefs of many campaign strategists, who have become disenchanted with normal network news coverage, which they have come to view as increasingly unfriendly and unsympathetic.

"Presidential politics is about controlling the message," says Bob Beckel, the Democratic analyst and former Mondale campaign manager. "When you allow the press to control that message, you are taking a chance."

Spurring on an even more compelling argument for avoiding network reporting and their newscasts has been an influential 1990 study by Harvard sociologist Kiku Adatto. Adatto found that the average sound bite from a presidential candidate used on network newscasts had shrunk from 42.3 seconds in 1968 to 9.8 seconds in 1988.

Her study appears to have given the world of political handlers the scientific proof it needed to show that the network reporters they had learned to hate were not only self-important and sanctimonious, but also a hindrance to the democratic process. As Adatto put it in her report, "Television's growing impatience with political speech raises serious questions: What becomes of democracy when political discourse is reduced to sound bites, one-liners and potent visuals?"

Not surprisingly, this 9.8-second sound bite often gets shaved a bit when discussed by the political pros. Bill Carrick, Richard Gephardt's campaign manager in the last campaign, and now a spokesman for the Bill Clinton campaign, had this to say recently in a discussion on "The McNeil-Lehrer News Hour": "If we look at '88, the problem for the electorate was the candidates basically were spending their entire day positioning themselves for an eight-second sound bite on the nightly news."

James Carville, Clinton's main strategist, when asked about the strategy of having his candidate appearing on talk shows, explained that the campaign was not avoiding the hard questions, but "just going where the voters are."

This may be true to some extent. But only by grouping a number of talk programs can the candidates find a larger audience than on the evening newscasts that used to get so much attention.

Network newscasts are delivering a smaller percentage of households than they did during the 1964 through 1988 campaigns, but they still have a combined audience of about 30 million people a night. Morning talk shows have less than a third of that.

But when Bill Clinton appeared on the "Today" program the first time, its audience was roughly 3.8 million. That is no small change, particularly when the candidate is given an hour or more of time. And the talk shows have found to their delight that they can do more than just public service by inviting the candidates aboard.

The "Today" show audience for Clinton was higher than its average audience of about 3.5 million. And Perot, who was hot at the time, brought "Today" an audience of about 5.4 million. Whether political talk will have the same draw after the conventions remains to be seen, but those who have called the talk-show campaign "the latest fad" may have used the right term.

Two things seem certain to continue, however. One is that the campaigns will remain hungry for big blocks of air time for their "unfiltered" messages. Another is that the campaigns will continue to want their freedom from what they view as the tyranny of network news.

Local newscasts may be able to learn something from the current situation and use it to their advantage. Indeed, one station, Atlanta's WSB-TV, has already held its own voter-to-candidate program, and was able to provide the Clinton campaign with something the networks are not as anxious to give them—prime time. WSB produced a one-hour town meeting entitled "Ask Bill Clinton" from 8 to 9 pm on Sunday, June 21.

Just as the network talk shows have found merit in the format, journalists from local TV do not appear to be overly concerned about letting the voters ask the questions.

"The insiders are upset because they claim the candidates are by-passing the process," says Bill Nigut, WSB's well-traveled political correspondent, "but I don't feel threatened by it, and I think it's a good thing for the candidates to answer questions from the voters."

Emily Rooney, news director at Boston's WCVB-TV, agrees. "I think it is an arrogance among traditional journalists that this is somehow inappropriate," she says. The longer-form questioning, she adds, helps to balance normal news coverage and gives the viewer another opportunity to get to know the candidate. "People will see what they need to see in any format. In the end, they're going to see the same person."

And Marty Haag, VP for news of the broadcast division of A.H. Belo at Dallas's WFAA-TV, feels the inclusion of the audience's questioning in these talk shows' formats adds an important element, and may in fact improve the public's declining opinion of the media.

"People are irritated with us because they see us as an impediment in the communication between the candidate and the public," he says. "I think we ought to use people's questions and people's attitudes for part of our database in deciding what the issues are."

While the voter-to-candidate forum is easily extended to state and local candidates, local stations usually get their best access to presidential candidates during the primaries, which, of course, have passed for 1992. But several opportunities may still lie ahead for the post-convention presidential campaign. As WSB has shown, large local stations may become participants by arranging programs at advantageous times.

Smaller stations may also have some access as the race narrows in certain states. The end-game of the 1992 election will no doubt follow the pattern of previous years, when much of the emphasis turns to the states that are considered toss-ups or too close to call. Missouri, Ohio, and Texas, for example, were among the states that got a great deal of attention in October 1988.

For all the anticipation of high-tech campaigning this year, and the possibilities raised by developments in satellite technology, the talk-show campaign has been a relatively low-tech affair. It is well within the means of even the smallest stations. For the most part, the candidate comes to the studio, sits on the set, and perhaps takes a few phone calls.

Historians will no doubt argue that the talk-show campaign isn't really that new, and that Richard Nixon and John F. Kennedy started it with appearances on "The Tonight Show" in 1960. But it is clearly going to be one of the interesting developments of the 1992 campaign, even if it proves to be a pre-convention phenomenon.

One of its weaknesses is that most of the talk-show appearances to date have not made much "news" or generated additional coverage on other news programs and in newspapers. Due to the softness of the questions, few of the shows have had much excitement, or drama, or any reason to remember them. Howard Kurtz, a media critic for *The Washington Post*, recently offered a suggestion: "The lesson may be," he wrote, "that a candidate needs an occasional fastball to hit a home run."

So perhaps after a few months of listening to questions from the kitchen, the candidates—and the public—will want a change of pitchers.

# 43

# Too Much Talk, Not Enough Action

## *by* Marvin Kalb

*Editor's Note:* In the 1992 election campaign, competitive pressures nearly put network broadcast news out of serious contention as a journalistic medium. The networks devoted far less time to in-depth political coverage of important issues and more time to rumor, gossip, and horse-race journalism. Even the candidates took their serious discussions to non-network broadcasts, such as talk radio and C-SPAN.

Even before the campaign was over, Marvin Kalb analyzed the situation and suggested ways in which the networks could improve. His suggestions weren't taken. Kalb was a news correspondent at NBC and CBS for thirty years. He is director of the Barone Center on the Press, Politics, and Public Policy at Harvard's Kennedy School of Government. This article was originally published in the *Washington Journalism Review* (now the *American Journalism Review*), September 1992.

It was a highly unusual event. A day before the opening of the Democratic National Convention in New York last July, five anchormen gathered to critique television coverage of the 1992 presidential campaign. ABC was represented by Peter Jennings, CBS by Dan Rather, CNN by Bernard Shaw, NBC by Tom Brokaw and PBS by Jim Lehrer. Rarely if ever had so much talent and ego come together publicly for such a soul-searching session. C-SPAN taped it, and, within a week, broadcast it time and again.

Although the networks spent months in heroic efforts to improve coverage, enthusiasm for the '92 product was in short supply. None of the anchors raved about it. A few found pockets for praise. Rather, for example, thought reporters were asking tougher questions than in 1988.

What was surprising was that each of the anchors, acting out of a refreshing sense of candor, leveled criticism at one aspect or another of their product, none more bluntly than Lehrer. "I think we're in trouble," he said. "We are losing our credibility." Jennings thought the coverage started impressively but then suddenly, in February, was "derailed" by press preoccupation with scandal, while the public was concerned about pocketbook issues. "Everybody in the press seemed to be interested in Gennifer Flowers." the ABC anchor asserted, "and everybody in New Hampshire wanted to know about the economy." For Brokaw, television news had become so intrusive that it was driving good people out of politics and attracting only those of superficial quality. "I think we've made it almost unbearable," NBC's anchor concluded, "[for candidates] to enter into the public arena."

Never before has so much been expected of television news, and never before has the spotlight of criticism—from viewers, newspapers, universities, even their own bookkeepers—been so relentlessly riveted upon the networks. Were they acting responsibly when they drastically cut convention coverage? (Sixteen hours of network coverage of the 1992 Democratic convention, compared with 34 hours in 1988.) How did they explain the fact that sound bites were down to an average of 8.8 seconds during the primary season? How could they have spent so little time on health care? (In March, only 9.1 percent of 220 TV stories—20 in all—were devoted to the subject; by May, only 3.2 percent.) Has the pooling of political polling made any sense in other than a budgetary way?

These anchors are journalists of enormous power and influence, tested and intelligent people capable of transforming the news agenda. Yet they only seem able to identify the problems and, after a nibble here and a nibble there, demonstrate sadly that they are unable to solve them. "They are captains in a storm," observes Andrew Glass, Washington bureau chief for Cox Newspapers. "They are lashed to the wheel and able to move it only 5 or 10 degrees in one direction or another."

The fact is they are caught in cruel crosscurrents: between a genuine desire to do the right thing, and, as Rather put it, "brutal competitive pressures" that drive them toward happy, user-friendly news; between a relentless requirement to be objective, cool and detached, and the reality of their increasing intrusion into the political process.

With the demise of political parties and "bosses," the press has moved into a commanding position as arbiter of American presidential politics—a position for which it is not prepared, emotionally, professionally or constitutionally. The press has become a player. Now there are unsettling calls for press responsibility. Some academics and many politicians raise a question: If other institutions, such as the White House and Congress, are held accountable for their actions, then why shouldn't the press be held accountable?

In addition, in this campaign, Jennings, Rather and Brokaw have been transmogrified into the "old news" or "old media." The term was coined by Jon Katz, a former executive producer of "CBS This Morning," and it was intended to be contrasted with the "new news" or "new media" that has risen to stunning importance in recent months. First Ross Perot announced his availability for presidential coronation on the "Larry King Show." Then Bill Clinton, in danger of becoming marginalized in campaign coverage in May and June, lunged for exposure on such unorthodox venues as the "Arsenio Hall Show," saxophone and all, on MTV, on the "Today" show and on morning radio call-ins. Even President

Bush, who had at first belittled such shows as "weird," yielded to the new trend as his polls slipped, and suddenly began appearing on "CBS This Morning," MacNeil/Lehrer, CNN and Pat Robertson's Christian Broadcasting Network.

Although each candidate moved to the new media for different reasons, they had one thing in common: They wanted to leapfrog the elite corps of Washington-based political reporters, who were considered to be interested mostly in process, polls and "character," and instead take questions from "the people," who were quickly demonstrating their interest in substantive issues such as health care, day care, education, crime and taxes.

How did it happen?

The ground rules for campaigning on TV changed. The candidates became fed up with sound-bite journalism. Just about every academic study showed that most people were invidiously linking the old media with the old politics—and, in their minds, a plague on both! The TV market was no longer dominated by just ABC, CBS and NBC. CNN, C-SPAN and other cable outlets, plus PBS, Fox, and the rise of local news, added strong competitive pressures, forcing the old media off center stage.

By no means have ABC, CBS and NBC been pushed to the periphery, but it is unlikely that they will ever again dominate the center. If people expected a shift of this magnitude to force the networks to readjust their strategic thinking, they were to be disappointed. The network attitude toward the twin challenges of social responsibility and profit-uber-alles remained frozen.

For example, CBS rocketed to first place in prime-time ratings this past year but refused to increase its news budget. Why? Did it have no obligation to the public? As the presidential campaign became more unpredictable with the rise and collapse of Ross Perot, why was there no allowance for boosting the budget to meet this increased need?

In fairness, CBS was no better or worse than ABC or NBC. The networks are filled with extraordinarily talented, educated and committed journalists, none better than the anchors on whose shoulders lies so much of the responsibility for fair and accurate coverage. But because the executive suites are more concerned with profits than public policy, even the journalists have had to adjust their editorial compasses to accommodate the blind corporate obsession with ratings. When questions were raised during the Democratic convention about why the networks had cut back on their coverage, CBS Chairman Laurence Tisch said, in effect, go elsewhere. "It's enough," he said. "No one wants to see people just milling around the floor for hours. If they want more, they can go to CNN."

Can anyone imagine William Paley or Frank Stanton suggesting that viewers go elsewhere for the news?

When the ratings emerged after the Democratic convention, the networks felt vindicated. The ratings were terrible. Together, ABC, CBS and NBC averaged 17.3 percent of the television audience for each of the four evenings of the convention. In 1988, they had averaged 20.8 percent.

Clearly the political parties could produce a better show. But even if the parties failed in this effort, the networks would still have a fundamental responsibility to cover this quadrennial marker in the lengthy process of selecting a president. Not everything is dramatic. Some Super Bowls are 45–14 blowouts. But television covers the entire game. It does not prejudge the outcome. It does not intrude on the viewer's pleasure or boredom. Robert MacNeil of PBS once said that it takes courage to be dull on television. Yes.

As the general election campaign of 1992 opens this month, there is still time for television to make the right decisions—and not be dull. Here are some suggestions:

**1.** *Resist rumor.* 1992 may go down in journalistic history as the year when rumor rose to the level of presumed fact. Clinton suffered most from this pitiful decline in professional standards, but so too did Perot and Bush. "I've covered every presidential campaign since 1968," says Jack Nelson, Washington bureau chief for the Los Angeles Times. "I have never before seen a campaign where rumors, and I mean strictly rumors, have been used so much to undermine a candidate. I have seen mainstream media lower its standards down to tabloid journalism."

The remainder of this campaign is likely to be a dirty brawl. The American people want, and deserve, careful confirmation of charges and counter-charges.

**2.** *Beware of polls.* Polls are powerful narcotics in campaign coverage, often conveying the illusion of serious legwork. What is clear so far is that positive coverage produces positive polls and negative coverage produces negative polls. When Clinton was being lambasted for alleged faults of "character," his polls were down and his "negatives" were up. When the coverage changed and began to focus on his message, his polls went up and his "negatives" went down. The networks have a moral and public responsibility to be balanced, honest, fair, and always mindful of the poll-coverage link.

**3.** *If possible, allow viewers to see and judge the event for themselves.* During the Democratic convention, C-SPAN broadcast the speeches and provided occasional commentary when necessary for comprehension. Conversely, ABC and NBC showed virtually no live coverage. During the one hour they allotted nightly to coverage, they felt obliged to highlight their anchors, commentators and reporters, and run occasional snippets of taped speeches. It is a sad day when media reporter Howard Kurtz of the Washington Post observes that "the media's interpretation, it seems, is now more important than the event itself."

**4.** *Keep up the good fight on debates.* They will never be more important than during this general election campaign. The networks have been bold in proposing one vice-presidential and three presidential debates.

Ideally, the debates, each 90 minutes in length, should be broadcast at 9 P.M. on Sunday. That's where the viewers are. What with "60 Minutes," football and baseball, it's harder for NBC and CBS to juggle schedules than it is for ABC, but they should be able to manage. If not, ABC should move its political coverage to Sunday evenings, joining CNN and C-SPAN, which already offer this imaginative programming.

**5.** *Between Labor Day and Election Day, the seven major television networks—ABC, CBS, CNN, C-SPAN, Fox, NBC and PBS—should rotate the responsibility and set aside an hour a week for each candidate to discuss one substantive issue.*

Better than most other journalists, the anchors can appreciate the hunger for information in what has been an extraordinary election year. They are the most powerful people in broadcasting—or, given their positions, they should be. Why wait until after November to promise that next time, in 1996, the process will be improved? Is this not the moment to take the lead and set an example of creative coverage that meets the needs of an exceptional moment in American history? Is it not their responsibility? And if not theirs, whose? Is this not the time for them to test not only their skill and judgment but their courage? If not now, when?

# 44

# The Press and Campaign '92: A Self-Assessment

## *by* Andrew Kohut, Donald S. Kellermann, Carol Bowman

*Editor's Note:* In a study of bias in the 1992 presidential campaign, the Times Mirror Center for the People & the Press undertook a telephone survey of journalists. It concluded that media leaders themselves saw news coverage of the campaign as damaging to Bush's reelection.

The experiment used a complex sample design, yielding a total of 290 responses, including the following media types: 37 national television, top level; 104 national television, middle level; 57 national newspaper, wire and news service, magazine, and radio, top level; 69 national newspaper, wire and news service, magazine, middle level; and 23 radio talk-show hosts.

Andrew Kohut is director of the Times Mirror Center, Donald S. Kellermann is senior fellow, and Carol Bowman is research director. This article was published as a special supplement to the *Columbia Journalism Review*, March/April 1993.

A substantial majority (55%) of the American journalists who followed the 1992 presidential campaign believe that George Bush's candidacy was damaged by the way the press covered him. Only 11% feel that Gov. Bill Clinton's campaign was harmed by the way the press covered his drive to the presidency. Moreover, one out of three journalists (36%) think that media coverage helped the Arkansan win the presidency while a mere 3% believed that the press coverage helped the Bush effort.

Despite reservations about the fairness of the coverage, eight in ten journalists rated press coverage of Campaign '92 as excellent or good. Fewer than one out of five (18%) judged press performance as only fair or poor. The survey also found the press thinking it did a good job on most of the major elements of the campaign coverage.

These are the principal findings of a Times Mirror Center for The People & The Press survey of more than 250 members of the press community, conducted in the final weeks of the election campaign. The polling included both top and middle level print and broadcast journalists, who were either directly or ultimately responsible for election coverage. Among the sample were 48 members of the media elite—newspaper editors and columnists, network anchors and producers, and the senior newspaper, news magazine and television executives—who the Times Mirror Center, with a nod to author David Halberstam, calls "The Powers That Be."

This second Times Mirror survey of the press found the media judging the impact of its coverage quite differently than did the first press survey completed in May of 1992 during the final stages of the presidential primary campaign. The earlier polling found most journalists (50%) thinking that campaign coverage was having a neutral effect on George Bush's campaign, as he turned back the challenge of an insurgent Pat Buchanan. At that time, a 64% majority thought that Bill Clinton was being hurt by the way the media covered him during his struggle with the "character" problems that plagued his primary campaign.

Although the conclusions about who was helped and who was hurt changed over the course of the year, both surveys found journalists lauding press coverage generally, despite their widespread belief that the coverage was having a negative impact on one of the campaigns. In-depth interviews with top media executives conducted as part of this project reflected a widespread view within the media community that the press bore no responsibility for the impact of its campaign coverage. By and large journalists believe that media campaign coverage was either neutral in intent or neutral in effect.

The complex response to the question of responsibility may also reflect a tendency revealed in many of the interviews to confuse the impact of coverage with the intent of the reporting. Robert C. Toth, Los Angeles Times correspondent, who conducted the in-depth interviews found some top editors and news producers thinking that "negative coverage" had a "neutral effect" because the media was "fair and objective," and reflected reality. Others looked at that same coverage and acknowledged that it hurt the candidate.

The quantitative survey bears out these twin aspects of the press community's belief about the tone and substance of its campaign coverage. "Negative coverage was due to his (Bush's) record" was the main reason (45%) given by journalists who nevertheless judged the effect of the coverage on Bush as neutral. But even respondents who said Bush was hurt by the coverage explained that the harm was the result of either reporting "Bush's record" (38%) or "the focus on the economy" (23%). In short, very similar reasons were given for reaching very different conclusions about press performance and responsibility.

Media reluctance to accept responsibility for its impact on the campaign is one of the most important findings to emerge from Times Mirror's in-depth interviews with top media executives. In many of these interviews there was evidence of a new defensiveness in the press this fall. "We are more aware of our public image and trying harder not to be seen destroying people by investigative reporting and dishy stories," said a senior editor. The emergence of talk shows this year, as a chastening sign that politics can work well without the press an interlocutor may have further induced the media to lower its profile. So may have the many indications that the public is turned off by "the cult of toughness" that sought to embarrass and demean candidates.

Whatever the reasons of the media's new stance, one editor accurately predicted that "it is unimaginable that in the debates one of the candidates will be asked what he'd do if his wife was raped." Michael Dukakis stumbled badly over that question in 1988. Despite the "convulsive" coverage of Gennifer Flowers in the primary campaign this spring—or perhaps because it recalled the extremes to which the press went for exposés of Gary Hart's philandering in 1988—a number of media respondents saw Clinton getting off easier this year than Dukakis or Hart did four years ago.

## The People and the Press Differ

The public rendered a more critical judgment of the presidential campaign coverage than did journalists. However, both the press and the public see improvements in press performance over 1988.

While 80% of the news media sample rated the '92 coverage as either good or excellent, surveys of the public throughout the campaign found fewer than six in ten rating press coverage of the campaign positively and *more than one in three voters feeling that the press was doing only a fair or poor job.*

The public also became sensitive to differences in the way the press covered Bush and Clinton over the course of the campaign. The percentage of voters who thought that the press was unfair in the way it covered George Bush steadily increased throughout the year. In March, only 13% of voters believed the press was being unfair to the President. By mid-September that sentiment grew to 22%. In Times Mirror's postelection survey, 35% took the view that the press was unfair to Bush in its coverage while 61% saw the press as fair in its coverage. (Comparatively, 77% believed the press was fair to Clinton and 67% believed the press was fair to Ross Perot.)

**TABLE 1.  RATING OF 1992 PRESS COVERAGE**

| | Press | | Voters | | |
|---|---|---|---|---|---|
| *Rating* | *Nov 92* | *Sept 92* | *May 92* | *Mar 92* | *Feb 92* |
| Excellent | 10 | 12 | 10 | 12 | 11 |
| Good | 70 | 45 | 44 | 51 | 45 |
| Only Fair | 16 | 27 | 33 | 28 | 32 |
| Poor | 2 | 11 | 10 | 6 | 7 |
| DK/No answer | 2 | 5 | 3 | 3 | 5 |
| | 100 | 100 | 100 | 100 | 100 |

Both the public and press agreed, however, that the media improved on its 1988 effort. Times Mirror's post-election follow-up survey of voters found 36% rated the press "A" or "B" for its campaign coverage, compared to 30% who gave the press good grades after the '88 campaign. However, the percentage giving the press a "D" or "F" for its campaign performance remained relatively high (31% in '92, 35% in '88).

Similarly, many of the top media people, after grading themselves good, volunteered that the coverage was "excellent if compared with 1988." "We were determined not to ignore the issues this time, not to get caught up in the horse race (polls) and 10-second sound bites," explained one senior editor. Added a network anchor: "We had much more content analysis, much more issue reportage, this year."[1]

## Coverage of Issues and Economy Praised

Reflecting these views, members of the national press and the top media executives interviewed were positive about specific aspects of campaign coverage. Overall, more than 70% gave good or excellent ratings to coverage of Clinton's Vietnam draft status, the candidates' positions on issues, and the economy. There was little difference of opinion within the media community about press performance, as most elements of the press lauded both overall coverage and the media's handling of several specific aspects of the campaign.

The press gave itself a somewhat lower grade (63% rating it good or excellent) for coverage of Ross Perot's candidacy. But many of the Powers That Be group were nonetheless critical. "We've given Perot a free ride since he reentered the race," complained one senior editor. "We were all on the verge of carrying very critical stories about his temperament and his personal life

**TABLE 2. PRESS RATING OF COVERAGE IN GENERAL AND OF SPECIFIC ISSUES (PERCENT RATING EXCELLENT OR GOOD)**

|  | *Overall Coverage* | *Clinton's VN Draft Status* | *The Economy* | *Candidate's Positions On Issues* | *N* |
|---|---|---|---|---|---|
| *Total* | 80 | 72 | 73 | 76 | (267) |
| *TV* | 82 | 70 | 74 | 78 | (141) |
| *Print/Other* | 79 | 74 | 73 | 73 | (126) |
| *Top* | 84 | 70 | 81 | 79 | (94) |
| *Middle* | 79 | 73 | 69 | 74 | (173) |
| *Powers* | 83 | 71 | 75 | 77 | (48) |
| *Male* | 80 | 70 | 73 | 75 | (213) |
| *Female* | 82 | 78 | 74 | 78 | (54) |
| *18–34* | 84 | 84 | 89 | 79 | (19) |
| *35–49* | 83 | 67 | 71 | 78 | (152) |
| *50+* | 76 | 78 | 73 | 71 | (94) |

when he pulled out. Since he reentered, we've treated him as an eccentric." Observed one television newsman wryly: "We may have been soft on Perot because he was good for ratings."

Times Mirror's media respondents were more self critical about coverage of the campaign's entanglement with TV's fictional character "Murphy Brown." Only 50% rated coverage good or excellent and many offered a strong dose of self criticism. Sitcom's unmarried television newswoman character became a cause celebre after she bore a child on prime time and was criticized by Vice President Dan Quayle for flouting "family values." Most members of the Powers That Be group felt the underlying issue deserved more serious attention than it got. "Quayle's intrusion made it almost impossible for us to examine Murphy Brown in the broader social context of young, unmarried, inner city girls who are having most of the babies," admitted a television newsman. Several of the Times Mirror Center interviewees felt that, as another broadcast journalist put it, "Murphy Brown was actually good for Quayle. We instinctively lined up against him, disdainful of him, saying he's a fool. But he tapped into something." Observed a television producer: "Maybe the moral question for us is how many headlines Iran Contra got compared to Murphy Brown. I'll bet it was 7 or 8 times more about her."

Coverage of Bush's relation to the Iran-Contra scandal received the harshest judgment. Over 70% said it was only fair (48%) or poor (23%); only one-fourth (24%) said it was good. The main excuse was the complexity of the story. "Only programs with lots of time, and papers with lots of space, could treat it adequately," said one television executive. Other excuses were that the story was old, and there was "no smoking gun" to prove that the President lied about his knowledge of the arms-for-hostages. "Besides," said a television newsman, "the polls showed most of the public believed the President lied." "Only the three serious newspapers have done a good job of explaining this issue," said a television executive, citing the *Los Angeles Times, Washington Post* and *New York Times.*

## Press Approves Talk Shows; Feeling Not Reciprocated

Television and radio talk shows emerged not only as a new platform in political campaigns in 1992, but as the dominant mode of discourse between candidates and voters. Twenty-three talk show hosts surveyed by Times Mirror expressed views that were almost always different, certainly more outspoken, than the traditional press. The broad community overwhelmingly approved the effect of the shows on the campaign (68% said positive), but the shows' moderators did not return the compliment.

Nearly four in ten (39%) rated overall press performance as only fair or poor, which was twice more critical than was the press community at large (18%). Similarly, while seven in ten journalists gave the press good grades for the coverage of issues, the economy and Bill Clinton's draft record, more than 50% of talk show moderators gave only fair or poor grades to coverage of these issues.

But almost perversely, the talk show hosts were also more critical of themselves than was the general press community. One in four (26%) of the hosts said the shows had a negative effect on the campaign process. "The format doesn't really allow for exposition on the whole issue," explained one host. "A talk show host has an agenda—part of that agenda is entertainment and securing advertising revenue. I'm just not sure that is the ultimate and valued forum for educating the American public on political issues." Other media critics of this new phenomenon took aim at the cheerleading like atmosphere of some talk show political interviews. Questions are soft, with no follow ups, as many Powers That Be people complained. "It's a free-fire zone," said one TV executive in dismissing the new forum, "with soft-ball questions and no follow-up to keep them honest." A senior editor said: "(Larry) King is atrocious as a journalist, but if viewers had no other source of news, bad journalism is better than nothing." Said another editor: "Anytime you air issues, you have to say it's a good thing. At the same time, the quality of the shows makes me cringe."

Talks' moderators were far more likely to acknowledge that Bush was hurt by coverage than was the larger press community (74% vs. 55%), and also more certain that Clinton was helped (52% vs. 36%). Of the various community segments, they were least approving of press assessments of political commercials (only 48% vs. 77% for the community) and twice as disapproving (74% negative) of media-sponsored opinion polling compared to the rest of the press (36%). "I'm starting to think polls don't reflect public thinking," said a show host. Moderators were also more critical on coverage of issues than the community as a whole. More than half gave fair or poor marks to coverage of Clinton's draft status, of candidates' positions on issues, and of the economy, as mentioned above. But they were also more critical than the larger community on Murphy Brown coverage, and extremely critical (87% fair or poor) on Bush and Iran Contra.

"Until Perot's plan came out, for example," complained one talk show anchor on economic coverage, "there was not enough clear delineation of where Bush and Clinton stood. It should have come earlier. We (the media) thought the issue was too complicated, that people didn't care, but they did. The public began demanding more, and press responded. The public was ahead of us on such things. It has done a first rate job this year."

## Print vs. Broadcast

Print and broadcast journalists judged press performance in Campaign '92 much the same, with some notable exceptions. Television newspersons were more positive about talk shows' impact than their print colleagues (75% vs. 62%), for example, but among The Powers That Be, print Powers were more positive toward the shows than broadcasters.

Print bosses were often quite critical of their broadcast colleagues. "Television got outmaneuvered by the candidates and the radio talk shows this year," said one senior editor. "It decided not to be victimized by 10-second sound bites and political commercials, but it offered no substitutes. Where was the hour of prime time in the campaign explaining the issues? Why was there no hour on Clinton and Bush? I think the written press was pretty good compared to television." Another editor complained that television, unlike the print media, has avoided coverage of the press performance, particularly its own. "Being scrutinized is salutary, but there is clearly less scrutiny of TV by TV, than of print by print," he said.

In comparison, broadcast journalists were often generous in their praise of the written media, singling out specific newspapers and even individual reporters for credit on campaign stories.

These comments notwithstanding, the in-depth interviews with top print executives often revealed a very insular view of campaign coverage. As one senior editor commented on several issues: "I know how well we (his newspaper) did, and generally how well other papers did, but I can't answer about all the media."

Broadcasters were more critical than print newspersons about coverage of Bush and Iran Contra. This was an issue to which the broadcasters clearly gave less attention because it was complicated, old and unresolved. Talk show moderators were particularly critical of opinion polling, perhaps because they found it of little use on their programs and even counter productive if horse race results turned off callers by suggesting prematurely that the race was over.

## Thumbs Up to Policing Ads, Polling Divides Media

Times Mirror's press respondents were for the most part positive about press coverage of political advertising and the press covering its own campaign performance. But journalists were ambivalent, at best, about opinion polling.

The press community barely gave a positive plurality to media-sponsored polls (41%), with 36% negative, 12% saying neither negative or positive and 8% saying not much effect. Print respondents were marginally more favorable toward polling compared to the average. But talk show moderators were far more hostile (74% negative). Familiar arguments were given for and against. "The voter gets to know what the candidate knows, so he can better evaluate why the candidates are doing this or that," said one editor; "polls add insight and understanding." Said another: "It is a horse race, and people want to know who's ahead." But opponents complained that polls can be treated as "self-reinforcing prophecies," and that respondents may give "politically correct" answers that reflect who is ahead in polls rather than their own views. One television executive complained that polls, like Dow Jones averages, "make you think you know what's happening when you don't." And a television newsman observed that polls are often used as a substitute for reporting. "Polls are still a work in progress," said a columnist.

Most of the community (60%) applauded media-coverage of media coverage. Aside from improving accuracy and quality, the consensus view was that media policing contributes to greater public understanding of the diversity within the press. "The public needs to know that we in the media are among the most vigorous critics of the media," said an editor. But critics, particularly among the broadcasting Powers That Be, dismissed media coverage with such words as "incest" and "masturbation." This may reflect the fact that the electronic media did the least self-examination. Only CNN regularly airs a media affairs program, a condition which one print editor called "a great shortcoming of television." On the other hand, a television newsman pointed out that newspapers often use their TV entertainment editors to critique television news, producing misinformed and frequently fatuous copy.

Most applause was given to press assessments of candidates' commercials during the campaign (77% positive). Such propaganda debunking, said one television newsman, "is the primary reason why no Willie Horton ads or their cousins have appeared in this campaign. Our coverage is keeping the bastards honest." Others were less sanguine about the coverage's impact. "They still lie," said a television executive; "we're slowing them down a bit, but they run an ad 400 times while we do one news report once that says the ad is misleading." And an editor noted a downside to such coverage: "Some candidates have used our stories against their opponents, saying (media name) judged the opposition ads to be misleading. So it's not a cure, not a panacea."

"We'll need a Teddy White to come along later to see if those who planned commercials really sat around worrying about whether we'd criticize them or not," observed an editor, in a comment that could well embrace all of the innovative aspects of Campaign '92.

## NOTE

1. When asked in the Spring to compare '92 and '88 coverage, 49% of Times Mirror's press respondents said they felt that coverage had improved.

# 45

## No, the Press Was Not Biased in 1992

### *by* Jeffrey L. Katz

*Editor's Note:* In the previous article, the 290 media people surveyed, who were not quoted by name, stated that the press was biased in the 1992 election. For this article, journalists were interviewed on the record, and their reactions were somewhat different.

Howard Kurtz, media writer for the *Washington Post,* says, "Clinton got some of the best and worst coverage. He got kicked around mercilessly during the primaries, but then we got caught up in the bus trips and the baby boomer theme and didn't hold him to the harsh standard we were applying to Bush. But Bush was also running an inept and eventually losing campaign. . . . "

Cokie Roberts, commentator for National Public Radio and ABC, says, "The losing party always whines . . . as for Clinton's coverage, I do think there was some excitement at the concept of change. And when you say the Bush campaign was a disaster, it's simply a fact. . . . "

The author concludes that most voters in 1992 felt that the Democratic candidates "best embodied their hopes. . . . The campaign coverage reflected that."

Jeffrey L. Katz is a reporter for *Congressional Quarterly.* Ellen Lyon, a news aide for the *Washington Journalism Review,* provided research assistance. This article was published in the *Washington Journalism Review* (now the *American Journalism Review*), January/February 1993.

The aftermath of the second presidential debate in mid-October seemed to produce a coast-to-coast journalistic consensus. A full two weeks before Americans voted, the news media declared Bill Clinton the winner.

"Little Time Left For Any October Surprise," read a St. Louis Post-Dispatch headline. "Stick a fork in George; he's done," said a column in the Denver Post. Newsweek made a big splash with its cover headline: "President Clinton? How He Would Govern."

Most journalists insist they were simply reflecting public sentiment, acknowledging the inevitability of Clinton's election and looking ahead to the consequences. To some supporters of George Bush and Ross Perot, though, the coverage then—and throughout the campaign—simply reflected the media's liberal bias.

Some of the complaints undoubtedly come from Republicans, still shell-shocked at having lost the presidency. But even some journalists suggest that the collective veil of objectivity was raised during the campaign's last two months.

"No one denies the press tilted toward Clinton during the campaign and was hostile to Bush," Fred Barnes wrote in the New Republic. "In pre-1992 days, journalists insisted they didn't really favor one candidate over another. . . . This year the restraint was gone. Instead of denials, reporters offered explanations for their cheerleading for Clinton."

Added William A. Henry III in Time: "It is widely admitted in private that many journalists covering Bill Clinton feel generational affinity and unusual warmth toward him—and that much of the White House press corps disdains President Bush and all his works."

Veteran Clinton critic Paul Greenberg, editorial page editor of the Arkansas Democrat-Gazette, agrees that there used to be "a kind of formal objectivity exercised. This year, the press seemed to be not quite as concerned with the impressions that it made. It would just regurgitate Clinton's lines or defend Clinton before [the campaign] had to."

Studies seem to back up the charges. The conservative Center for Media and Public Affairs analyzed network evening newscasts during the fall campaign and characterized 71 percent of the comments about Bush on the network evening newscasts as "negative." That compared to 48 percent negative comments about Clinton and 55 percent about Perot.

The Washington Post's ombudsman, Joann Byrd, examined the newspaper's photos, stories and headlines during the last 73 days of the campaign and concluded they were "very lopsided" in Clinton's favor. Executive Editor Leonard Downie Jr. says the newspaper should have run more stories toward the campaign's end summarizing earlier scrutiny of Clinton's gubernatorial record.

Many voters also sensed that there was favoritism. A November poll by the Times Mirror Center for the People and the Press found that 35 percent of voters surveyed nationwide felt that the press had been unfair to Bush. Another 27 percent felt Perot was treated unfairly while 19 percent thought Clinton was treated unfairly.

Other surveys—the most recent released in November by the Freedom Forum—concluded that journalists are more likely to identify with the Democratic Party than the public at large does.

Regardless of whether or not journalists were rooting for Clinton, it was only natural that Bush received tougher coverage in 1992 than he had four years earlier. The economy was lagging. Voters were restive. Bush's campaign was in disarray.

Reporters, meanwhile, seemed to develop a certain attraction for Clinton, or at least for his campaign, interviews with journalists, political observers and media critics suggest. Perhaps it was his ideology, or a generational pull, or that a prospective Clinton administration was a better story. Some thought the media were misguided in declaring him the winner weeks before the election.

Nevertheless, only the most conservative and conspiratorial media critics would suggest that journalists threw the election. Journalists are generally too cynical about politicians and too competitive with one another to take sides that easily. Besides, if they were that biased and that powerful, how did Republicans win five of the six previous presidential campaigns?

Yet widespread doubts about the coverage persist. Why did so many readers, viewers and journalists perceive a tilt, especially in the campaign's last two months?

There were some critical facts no good reporter could ignore.

The first, and most obvious, was that nothing affected Bush's reelection bid more than the public's perception of his presidency. Two years ago he was riding high in the wake of the Persian Gulf War, pumped up by the national media's portrait of the president as a courageous and decisive leader respected worldwide. The Democrats who lined up to run against him were largely derided as second-tier candidates.

But Bush's popularity plummeted, largely because of growing concerns about the recession and doubts about his ability to spur economic growth. Far from leading this effort, the media seemed to be as unprepared for voter disenchantment as Bush was when it first appeared in New Hampshire.

By the fall, unemployment hovered at about 7.5 percent and voters were anxious about the future. Many of the formulas designed by political scientists to measure the economy's effect on a presidential election presaged a Bush defeat.

Bush repeatedly cited a two-year study by the Center for Media and Public Affairs that found 91 percent of comments about the economy on the networks' evening news were "negative." The implication was that voters were being brainwashed. But it seems unlikely that viewers could subscribe to any economic outlook that didn't make sense in light of their own experiences. A majority of voters wouldn't have believed Ronald Reagan's "It's morning again in America" in 1984 if it hadn't reflected the optimism of the time.

"Voters are not empty vessels," says Richard Harwood, a former deputy managing editor and one-time ombudsman for the Washington Post. "They know what is happening in their own lives." Adds Thomas Patterson, a Syracuse University political science professor: "What cost Bush reelection was the same thing that cost Jimmy Carter reelection in 1980. You don't want to be the incumbent when the economy is sour and the immediate outlook isn't good. Almost always that means change."

While Clinton generally fared well during the fall, it can hardly be said that he enjoyed a free ride throughout the year. All three candidates rode a media roller coaster.

After being anointed—prematurely, in the eyes of some—as the early Democratic front-runner, Clinton was pounded for his alleged affair with Gennifer Flowers, avoiding the draft and shiftily answering questions about smoking marijuana. Hillary Clinton was portrayed as a radical. A Time cover story in April—later featured in a Bush ad—set out to explain "Why voters don't trust Clinton."

Characterizations of all three candidates often were shaped by their standings in the polls. This amplified rather than led public opinion. When Bush appeared to be losing, journalists "took it to be their mission to explain why this guy was such an irredeemable schlub as to be trailing in the polls," observes Richard Ben Cramer, author of "What It Takes: The Way to the White House," a chronicle of the 1988 primaries. When a Gallup poll in the campaign's final week indicated that Bush might be catching up, "the mission [was] to explain what sterling qualities have enabled this sterling character to fight back."

Perot also rode the poll-driven roller coaster. He was a phenomenon when he had 30 percent support in late spring, a fake when he dropped out of the race in July, an egomaniac when he returned in September and paranoid when he searched for his base in October.

For a while Bush seemed stuck at the bottom. Between September 21 and October 19, Newsweek used the words "desperate" and "desperation" four times to describe his campaign.

Regardless of how they were characterized, Bush's charges against Clinton were widely aired. Thomas B. Rosenstiel, a media writer for the Los Angeles Times, says network coverage during the fall often showed Bush on the attack. Clinton's environmental record, draft avoidance, Moscow trip, lack of foreign policy experience and alleged propensity to waffle on issues were played prominently. It wasn't that Bush wasn't being heard, Rosenstiel says. "He never changed the dynamics of the race even though he was driving the press agenda."

"The main reason the president has received a bad press," Newsweek media critic Jonathan Alter concluded, "is that he's done badly."

Bush showed all the marks of a losing candidate, including serious division within his own ranks. "Republicans were constantly complaining that Bush is losing, running a bad campaign," the Post's Downie says. Moreover, conservative columnists William Safire and George Will were among Bush's harshest critics.

Media analysts couldn't miss the fact that Bush's campaign was failing. "I think the press was one-sided," Reed Irvine, chairman of the arch-conservative Accuracy in Media, told the New York Times. "But Bush had just as many opportunities to get his message across and he did a lousy job."

Even so, journalists are now questioning whether Clinton got better coverage than he deserved.

Reporters who covered Clinton were attracted to his informal style, love of politics, optimism and command of policy. They found it more exciting to write about Clinton's ideas, his aides, his family and friends, and his quest for a moderate Democratic ideology than to rehash stories about Bush.

"Reporters are biased in favor of a good story; it's their bread and butter," says Stephen Hess, a Brookings Institution senior fellow who focuses on the press. "An administration in office 12 years was no longer as interesting a story as a new administration would be."

Four years after following around dour Michael Dukakis, reporters' hopes for a more interesting campaign crystallized with Clinton's and Al Gore's bus trips. Downie found reporters getting so caught up in the hoopla that he spiked one story on a bus trip and ordered that another be toned down. But, he adds, "It wasn't just us, it was the country that was euphoric about change."

Much was made of the generational appeal the Clinton-Gore ticket had on voters, but it held sway with some baby boomers who covered the campaign, too. From agonizing over the Vietnam War to experimenting with marijuana, journalists who came of age in the 1960s found a kindred spirit in Clinton, says Larry J. Sabato, a University of Virginia political science professor. "His problems were their problems in a way they could never relate to Bush."

Perhaps the public detects more of a media bias because it is receiving more analysis and less straight recitation of the day's events. Journalists believe that is the only way to deliver indepth coverage and avoid being manipulated by the campaigns. They are therefore more likely to cover issues, strategy and ads than what the candidates say.

Paul Friedman, executive producer of ABC's "World News Tonight," says the network aired 30 "American Agenda" pieces, spending four minutes at a time analyzing candidates' positions on issues. Correspondents also focused on trends and the campaign process, Friedman says, "in an effort not to be caught falling for a canned sound bite or a visual image that the campaign wanted us to have."

NBC Political Director Bill Wheatley says the network concentrated more on issues and the character of the candidates than the "here they come, there they go" approach of summarizing life on the campaign trail. He says the network ended up doing more "truth-telling" than it had anticipated about statements made on the campaign trail and in ads.

Many hailed the media for analyzing television commercials, given the ads' importance and potential to mislead voters. However, Sabato and some conservative groups question whether it's right for the media to act as a referee. They assert that the "truth-telling" often was overstated and tended to be tougher on Bush than Clinton. Others argue that could be because the Bush campaign ads were actually more misleading.

Providing daily analysis without being colored by one's own prejudices has long been a difficult balancing act for journalists. "There's a thin line between point of view and bias," says Deborah Howell, Newhouse News Service Washington bureau chief.

Readers and viewers are more likely to think that line has been crossed than reporters. "They tell us they want analysis, background, interpretation, and when we do that and it's not entirely keeping with their view of the world, they say we're biased," says Ellen Debenport, the St. Petersburg Times political editor who once covered Clinton from Little Rock for UPI. By traveling with the candidates, listening to their speeches and combing through issue papers, Debenport says, "I'm probably one of the best informed voters in America, and yet when I say the slightest thing someone disagrees with, I'm the one who's biased."

Political reporters take it as a matter of faith that their insight qualifies them to fairly analyze campaigns, but some readers and viewers disagree. One of the disenchanted is Marina Ein, president of the Washington public relations firm Ein Communications and a self-described moderate Republican, who chafed at the Washington Post's campaign coverage.

"That is exactly the extraordinary arrogance of the media today," Ein says when Debenport's remarks are repeated to her. "Who in God's name cares that this woman feels as though she's well informed? . . . The press is literally a very small group of voices with a very, very narrow frame of reference."

Ein wants to get more of her political news straight from the candidates, without the filter of analysis. Sabato, on the other hand, recognizes the importance of political analysis. But he thinks newsrooms ought to be more diversified and include more conservative voices.

Once the debates began, the focus on Clinton's fortunes intensified. During the weekend of October 17, after the second presidential debate, the outcome seemed sealed. Or so the media reported.

"Analysis—Denial, anger and acceptance: The Bush campaign is moving through the classic stages of loss," the San Jose Mercury News told its readers. "Perot seems to accept role as noncontender," the Boston Globe concluded.

Wasn't this a bit premature two weeks before Election Day? Ellen Hume, senior fellow at the Joan Shorenstein Barone Center on the Press, Politics and Public Policy at Harvard University, thinks so. "They should have exercised more discretion," she says, "and held back more from making it seem that the election was over already."

Alan Ehrenhalt, executive editor of Governing magazine, doesn't see how that would work. "It was not the job of the media," he says, "to suppress the fact that Bush was about to lose the election."

The way viewers and candidates embraced the "new media," speaking directly to one another without journalistic intervention, was unsettling to some reporters. "We can certainly learn that we're not as needed as we would like to think we are," Howell says. Candidates "can bypass us and go directly to Larry King, and not pass go."

But no matter how enlightening a call-in show may be, it doesn't substitute for a challenging round with journalists—assuming journalists can move beyond campaign strategy to talk about issues.

The problem is that many readers and viewers do not understand—or accept—the role of a political reporter. They are not buying the notion that reporters are objective, or even fair.

Jon Katz, media writer for Rolling Stone, says people resent journalists not for having opinions, but for pretending that they don't. He says the public sensed that "journalists despise Bush and were dying for someone like Clinton to defeat him." Katz suggests that the media provide a greater diversity of opinions and re-examine the intense focus on candidates' personal lives that blurs the line between "Washington reporters and FBI agents."

Hume, who covered the 1988 presidential campaign for the Wall Street Journal, would like to see campaign analyses periodically linked with stories on the backgrounds and beliefs of the reporters who cover campaigns, as well as occasional explanations of what constitutes straight news stories, analyses and editorial endorsements.

Some journalists wonder if the propensity for analysis gives an overly negative cast to the coverage, portraying all of the candidates as conniving manipulators. In doing so, the media may be seen as responsible as elected officials for the gridlock and cynicism in Washington.

Wheatley finds this especially troubling. Despite the fact that the media did a better job covering the presidential campaign than in 1988, he says, it may be that "the public considers the media part of the power structure, part of what's not working in this country, and holds us responsible for the fact that there's a great many problems."

Even ABC's Friedman, who is wary of self-flagellation over campaign coverage, says, "I worry about whether our seemingly relentless criticism of the process adds to the cynicism."

The tone of coverage also leads to a fractured view of candidates, unconnected to their past and to the electorate, Cramer says. "All of the candidates end up depersonalized and dehumanized in the view of the press because there's never a chance to make them human beings whose stories we can identify with. . . . We voters get the sense that the candidates are great manipulators. And because we have no full or fleshy sense of their lives that came before then, we get the feeling they are kind of empty suits into which this transcontinental manipulation has been poured."

Perhaps the media did go overboard in their determination not to be manipulated by the campaigns, as many thought they were in 1988. The tendency to describe candidates as cynically and desperately plotting to woo voters may have fallen disproportionately on Bush and Perot. Clinton quite likely did come across better to readers and viewers. Generational, ideological and journalistic reasons all played a part.

And yet, it is hardly the case that the media seriously and consciously distorted the fall coverage in Clinton's favor.

A plurality of voters in 1992 felt that the Democratic candidate best embodied their hopes for the future and was best prepared to improve the economy. The campaign coverage reflected that. Ignoring this critical element would have been a distortion indeed.

# 46

# The Media May Devour Democracy

## *by* George J. Mitchell

*Editor's Note:* Of course, politicians and journalists are frequently at war
with each other. Journalists believe that the First Amendment guarantees them the freedom to pursue the truth. Some use that to defend
their rights to be critical of politicians in the interests of the public; others use it for the pursuit of political ends, or profit, or fame.

But whatever their motives, journalists often come into conflict with
politicians and sometimes even the best of politicians cannot hold back
their anger at the press and mass media. George J. Mitchell, Democratic
senator from Maine and majority leader in the U.S. Senate, in this article
accuses the press of unnecessarily raising public doubts and thereby
damaging the political process.

These remarks by Senator Mitchell were adapted from a statement
made on the "MacNeil/Lehrer NewsHour" on public television in March
1994 and reprinted here from the *Los Angeles Times*, March 13, 1994.

There is a culture of disbelief in America. I actually had a reporter say to me
this past weekend, "I don't believe anything any politician says at any time, including you."

If you are an elected official in our society, for a very large number of people anything you say must be untrue on its face. This is a reversal of what I think
ought to be the proper standard.

The presumption of disbelief is caused by a combination of things. For
one, there exists in this country an enormous news machine. There is a huge
demand for news that's 24 hours a day and into it must be fed something on a
daily basis. If something doesn't exist to be fed in, then it must be made up. And
the reality is that much of the commentary, analysis, criticism is highly speculative, often false, usually tinged with sensationalism.

This is a sad commentary on the state of the current coverage of the political process, but I believe that increasingly in America what is news is defined
by what is or is not controversial. If it's not controversial, it's not news. If it lends
itself to sensationalism, it achieves a high level of attention.

We bear a lot of the responsibility, we elected officials, who make mistakes and create the kind of unfortunate attitude that exists. So I don't think it's any one individual or group.

But let me give an example. In the last two years, we've passed significant legislation involving federal assistance to young people who want to go on to college. This is a very important aspect of our society—the education of young people, the opening up of higher education to people of all backgrounds. Nobody knows about the legislation—because it wasn't controversial, it wasn't news.

I'll never forget, two weeks after we passed the bill in the Senate, I went home to Maine and held a series of town meetings. I was at a school and people asked, "Senator, when are you guys going to do something about the student-aid program?"

I said, "well, we just did two weeks ago, but you don't know about it because it literally didn't—it literally was not reported because it was not controversial." On the other hand, something like, dare I say the word *Whitewater*—it's now every night on the news, dominating the news. Why is that? Because, of course, it's controversial and sensational.

I'm not suggesting that all this is made up by the press; there are errors. I don't think there's much malice, frankly.

We use the words *press* and *media* to describe what we know not to be a monolith, but, in fact, thousands of people making millions of decisions in a highly competitive atmosphere, in which you'd better go with the story even though you've only got 6% of the facts, because if you don't, the other guy might go, so you can't wait till you get 60% of the facts.

We ought not to suspend the critical faculties, the sense of judgment and fairness, that exist in all of life outside of politics when we deal with politics, because it is, in fact, a part of our society, and it's part of the process. Not all the problems can be blamed on the press. But it is *a* contributing factor to this culture of disbelief.

# XI

# Government

The Founding Fathers of America tried to establish a government in which no one person nor any one office could ever become all-powerful. They were reacting primarily to the absolute power of the monarchs of Europe, from which they and their families had fled to the new world. To prevent the concentration of power, they pursued the principle of balance of powers among various government entities. That is, they divided government into different parts, each with separate responsibilities. Local, state, and federal governments each had their own jurisdictions. Each was divided further into three branches, executive, legislative, and judicial, with various checks and balances built into the system to keep any one branch from becoming too powerful.

The Founding Fathers also realized that citizens needed information about government, and only with an informed vote at the ballot box could people turn out of office a government that had become corrupt, despotic, or too powerful. Only a free press could provide this information, and then only if there was no government censorship or interference with the press, only if there were competing voices in the marketplace, and only if government did not itself have a voice in that marketplace.

On these basic notions rest the foundation of all American journalism, at least for our first 200 years. Throughout our history, the press has viewed itself as the watchdog of government. Journalists are supposed to bark if the government does anything wrong. Furthermore, the news media are not supposed to support the government in any way; journalists are supposed to be neutral, just as they are in politics. Often, over the past 200 years, the press and mass media have actually seemed to many people to be unpatriotic; some have even called them treasonous in pursuing a policy of being neutral informers and critics of government.

At the same time, of course, government offices and officials must communicate with citizens. In fact, leadership requires the ability to communicate, and much of the government's responsibilities revolve around the collection, interpretation, and communication of information people need. Today we need more information than ever before to survive in a complicated society.

Increasingly, especially in the twentieth century, the government and the press have clashed over these roles. The government has tried to get information to the people or to keep information from them, sometimes for reasonable, and other times for questionable, motives. The press has felt a responsibility to question government motives and actions, to dig out all the information, to uncover all secrets, to ask tough and embarrassing questions, to go into any office, to look through any file—in the name of keeping the people informed.

The power of the press as a watchdog of government probably reached its peak in the 1960s and 1970s, especially with regard to the war in Vietnam and the Nixon administration. In Vietnam, news media had the absolute freedom to report anything and everything that happened. The judicial branch of government, in the Pentagon Papers decision, upheld the right of the press to be such a watchdog, even when it harmed government interests. What was reported was not always in the interests of the government, and many regarded the journalists as unpatriotic in the war effort.

During the Nixon administration, the press doggedly pursued the strange events one night in the Watergate office building until the facts led to the Oval Office and the involvement of President Nixon in unlawful activity and its cover-up. The result was the first and only resignation of a sitting American president.

Although the media war between the press and the government has been going on for 200 years, there are increasing signs that the government is winning. Today it can keep more things secret than ever before. The Freedom of Information laws, first passed in 1967, require the government to reveal much information, but these laws also establish areas where the government can legitimately withhold news from the public. The government is also getting much more sophisticated about using the techniques of public relations to present information with its own spin or to stage situations to make the kind of news it wishes to be communicated by mass media.

Congress passed a law in 1913 supposedly preventing the federal government from employing publicity or PR agents. But the American government today, at all levels and in every department or agency, employs tens of thousands of people who do the work of publicity or PR agents, even if they don't use those titles. Congress itself has become one of the branches of government best able to promote itself.

All of this leaves us with some doubts about the balance of powers and the role of mass media as the "fourth branch of government."

# 47

# The Art of Bulldogging Presidents

## *by* Sam Donaldson

*Editor's Note:* In the White House, rooms have been provided specifically for the news media. Some reporters work there full time, all year around. Their job is to keep an eye on the American president, to tell the people what that executive is doing, and why. Each day the president's press secretary gives White House reporters a briefing on events. Occasionally the president holds a press conference at which reporters can ask questions.

There is no law requiring the president to provide reporters with office space, to give them daily briefings, or to allow them to meet with the president. These things are done as a matter of tradition, but probably also because they serve the president's interests as much as the media's.

When Sam Donaldson was the White House correspondent for ABC News, he gained much national visibility and a reputation as the reporter with the tough (sometimes seemingly rude) questions. Here he tells why. This article was originally published in the book *Hold on, Mr. President,* by Samuel A. Donaldson, Jr. (New York: Random House, 1987). The excerpt here was published by *The Quill,* May 1987.

Many people find it extremely difficult to talk to presidents. They get nervous. They are tongue-tied, intimidated by the larger-than-life quality we've built up around presidents, particularly, I think, in this television age. Jimmy Carter once told me he found it strange and disconcerting to have people from his hometown whom he'd known all his life stammer with awestruck admiration when they visited him in the Oval Office.

But reporters can't afford to remain in awe of those they cover. People expect the press to hold the mayor's feet to the fire and to bore in on the city council and to make sure the governor doesn't get away with a thing. It doesn't make any sense to let up on the one public servant whose official conduct affects us all the most. Presidents have a greater responsibility than other public servants and deserve a compassionate understanding of the difficulty of discharging that responsibility. But they are not due worship.

I know that's easier said than done. I trembled with nervousness when I met my first president, John F. Kennedy. But you get over it and come to realize that presidents put their pants on one leg at a time like everyone else. I think you talk to presidents just the way you talk to anyone else. And reporters can't be timid about it.

Nine months into his administration, I asked Jimmy Carter to defend himself against charges that "your administration is inept" and to comment on the recurring Washington undercurrent that "as a Georgian, you don't belong here."

Two years into his administration, I asked Ronald Reagan to comment on the perception that "disarray is here in the White House, that you have been out of touch, that you have had to be dragged back by your staff and friends on Capitol Hill to make realistic decisions on the budget. There was even a newspaper column saying that your presidency is failing."

I suppose neither man liked hearing those things. But those things were being said about them, and it was legitimate to ask them to respond.

A lot of people want to know what I'm after when I ask questions of the president. Well, it's simple. I'm looking for straight answers on topics the public has an interest in, most of them important, some of them not. With a nod to Will Rogers, I've never heard a question I didn't like. Sure, some were more relevant, important, interesting, more artfully or tactfully phrased than others. But I don't believe there's any such thing as a bad question, only bad answers.

So when I ask questions, I think it's important to challenge the president, challenge him to explain policy, justify decisions, defend mistakes, reveal intentions for the future, and comment on a host of matters about which his views are of general concern. I try to put my questions in a courteous manner, but I try also to make them specific, and pointed.

"Mr. President," I asked Ronald Reagan in October 1983, "Senator [Jesse] Helms has been saying on the Senate floor that Martin Luther King, Jr., had communist associations, was a communist sympathizer. Do you agree?" The president replied, "We'll know in about 35 years, won't we?" (That was a reference to the fact that certain records that might shed light on the subject would be sealed for that length of time.) In the same answer, the president went on to defend Senator Helms's sincerity for wanting to unseal the records. He had not delivered a direct reply to my question "Do you agree?" But he had nevertheless spoken volumes about his feelings.

Reagan later called Dr. King's widow, Coretta Scott King, to apologize for what he said was the press's distortion of his remark. There was no distortion, just an embarrassing insensitivity, and that was his, not the press's.

The wording of questions is very important. If you say to a president, "Would you care to comment on X," he can always answer, "No, thanks," or he can say anything he wants to and call it a comment. As Reagan mounted the stairway of *Air Force One* in Texas one day in July 1986, we tried to get his reaction to the razor-thin victory he'd won that day in the Senate on confirmation of one of his judicial nominees.

"What about [Daniel] Manion?" someone yelled.

"He's going to be judge," replied Reagan with a smile, which was hardly a reaction, only a statement of fact. But having established that he could hear us above the noise, I sang out, "What about Tutu?" an obvious reference to Bishop Desmond Tutu's criticism the day before that "the West, for my part, can go to hell" because of its reluctance to embrace economic sanctions against the white minority government of South Africa.

"He's not going to be a judge," replied the president solemnly as he disappeared through the doorway of his plane. All right, pretty funny, but then in neither case had we asked the president a specific question, so it's fair to say we had only ourselves to blame.

Once I cried out in exasperation as Reagan retreated across the White House lawn, "What about the Russians?"

"What about them?" he shot back. As he ducked into his helicopter, I could only stammer that I'd ask the questions around here.

To be effective, questions must be specific and, preferably, short. They should invite a direct answer. I once asked Jimmy Carter, referring to former CIA director Richard Helms, "Mr. President, Mr. Helms's attorney says that his client will wear his conviction on charges of failing to testify fully before Congress as a badge of honor. Do you think it's a badge of honor, and do you think a public official has a right to lie in public about his business under any circumstances?"

Carter replied, "No, it is not a badge of honor, and a public official does not have a right to lie. . . . " Direct question. Direct answer.

Of course, presidents don't always agree with the way questions are framed, as Carter did in that one. But when they don't, that too can be most revealing.

In March 1985, I asked Reagan about the death of 17 South African blacks who were shot by government authorities the day before, in what I said "appears to be a continuing wave of violence by the white military government against the black majority population." Reagan was having none of my characterization. " . . . I think to put it that way—that they were simply killed and that violence was coming totally from the law-and-order side—ignores the fact that there was rioting going on in behalf of others there," he corrected me, making it perfectly clear who he thought was right and who was wrong in South Africa.

Reagan is always looking for a way to support existing authority, no matter whose, unless, of course, it is communist authority. So his attitude about the unrest in South Africa may not spring from racism. But, of course, to blacks the effect is the same as if Reagan meant it personally.

Occasionally, I'm told I ask mean questions, that I'm always trying to "trap the president," and trying to make him "look bad." Not so. Consider the question I asked Reagan at his first press conference as president; there were no barbs, no hooks: I said, "Mr. President, what do you see as the long-range intentions of the Soviet Union? Do you think, for instance, that the Kremlin is bent on world domination that might lead to a continuation of the cold war, or do you think that under other circumstances détente is possible?"

And out came his view that the Soviets "reserve unto themselves the right to commit any crime, to lie, to cheat, in order to attain" their goal of world revolution. That answer created an uproar, not matched until his speech two years later in which he called the Soviet Union an "evil empire."

And why did I ask him the question in the first place? After all, there was nothing startling about hearing such a view from Ronald Reagan. He had been offering it for years. But he hadn't been president then, and now that he was, it was important for people to know where the president stood. In fact, one of the main objectives in questioning a president is to put him on the record. Of course, sometimes presidents don't want their views on the record. Let me give you an example:

In February 1985, I asked Ronald Reagan at one of his infrequent news conferences, "Mr. President, on Capitol Hill . . . Secretary Shultz suggested that a goal of your policy now is to remove the Sandinista government in Nicaragua. Is that your goal?"

From the beginning of his presidency, Reagan has been working to overthrow the Sandinista government—officials of his administration freely admit it when they know their names will not be used—but for reasons of international law, foreign relations, and domestic policies, no one wants to admit it on the record. Following the advice of his aides, Reagan had always publicly denied any intention of "overthrowing" the Sandinistas.

But when I asked Reagan that night about "removing" the Sandinista government, he replied, "Well, remove in the sense of its present structure, in which it is a totalitarian state and it is not a government chosen by the people. . . . " Ah, I thought: It's out at last! The word *remove* had not triggered the same warning bell in Reagan's mind that the word *overthrow* would have, and he had delivered the unvarnished truth about his policy.

I pursued it.

"Well, sir," I followed up. "When you say *remove* . . . aren't you then saying that you advocate the overthrow of the present government of Nicaragua?" Now, the alarm bells went off in Reagan's head. He threw up a massive barrage of familiar rhetoric about the Sandinistas having betrayed the original revolution.

I pressed on, violating the one follow-up rule.

"Is the answer yes, sir?" I asked.

"To what?" replied the president.

"To the question 'Aren't you advocating the overthrow of the present government if you substitute another form of what you say was the revolution,' " I answered.

Cornered. But when Ronald Reagan is cornered, he stands and fights. "Not if the present government would turn around and say, 'All right,' if they'd say 'uncle.' . . . " he replied.

That seemed clear enough to me. The choice for Nicaragua was on the record: surrender or die. Reagan's zealous pursuit of the Sandinistas led to the illegal diversion of funds from his Iranian arms sales to supply the anti-Sandinista *contra* rebels. Presidents set direction for those who serve under them through many channels. Sometimes they give direct orders; other times subordinates get the message by simply listening to their public declarations. "Cry uncle," indeed!

Getting presidents to put their policy on the record is very important. Lyndon Johnson increased U.S. participation in Vietnam from a military advisory force of 16,000 to a full-scale battlefield force of about 542,000 men while maintaining throughout that there had been no change in policy. Given that reminder, reporters now try very hard to get presidents to keep the record straight about policy changes and the reasons for those changes.

Take the case of the U.S. Marines and Lebanon. In the fall of 1983, with U.S. Marines dying in Lebanon, Reagan declared that the "credibility of the United States would suffer on a worldwide scale" if the U.S. peace-keeping force of marines were withdrawn.

And one Friday in early 1984, *The Wall Street Journal* published an interview with Reagan in which he told the paper's Washington bureau chief, Albert Hunt, when asked about House Speaker Thomas P. "Tip" O'Neill's call for the Marines to be brought home, " . . . he may be ready to surrender [in Lebanon], but I'm not."

You can imagine the consternation in some quarters when the *very next* Tuesday, Reagan announced the withdrawal from Lebanon of the U.S. Marines.

At his April press conference, I asked him about it.

"Mr. President," I said, "last October you said the presence of U.S. Marines in Lebanon was central to our credibility on a global scale. And now you've withdrawn them. . . . To what extent have we lost credibility?"

"We may have lost some with some people," replied the president, " . . . but situations change, Sam. . . . I can, I think, explain." And off he went with the patented Ronald Reagan version of the history of the Middle East conflict. It always takes him several minutes to recite it, and he tells it differently each time.

When the recitation was over, I pressed him.

"You began your answer by saying we lost some credibility. Are you to blame for that? Or, like Secretary Shultz, do you blame Congress?"

I had made a tactical mistake. I had given him an out instead of simply asking, "Are you to blame for that?"

He seized it. " . . . they must take a responsibility . . . with the Congress demanding—'Oh, take our, bring our men home. Take them away'—all this can do is stimulate the terrorists and urge them on to further attacks because they see a possibility of success in getting the force out which is keeping them from having their way . . . " said the president, thus shifting all blame, escaping my question, but at the price of provoking a fearful row with Congress.

Sometimes, people say that my questions reflect a political bias. It may seem hard to believe, but reporters' questions are not necessarily indicative of their own point of view.

A lot of people thought I was personally opposed to Jimmy Carter because of the questions I asked him, and a lot of people think I'm opposed to Ronald Reagan because of the questions I ask him. It's a reporter's job to challenge a president—every president—to explain and defend his policies whether you agree with them or not. Still, a lot of people, including presidents, seem to think the questions are personal.

In the summer of 1980, at a news conference devoted to Billy Carter's business relationship with the Libyan government, I asked President Carter to respond to an underlying widespread criticism "that this Billy Carter case is another example of a general aura of incompetence that hangs over your presidency. . . . " Carter began his response by saying, "I've heard you mention that on television a few times, but I don't agree with it. . . . "

If he had heard me mention that on television, it was because I had often reported what *others* were saying. As a rule, critics should be named when asking for a response, which helps to make it clear the reporter isn't expressing a personal view. But if I had tried that day to name all the people who were accusing the Carter administration of being incompetent, there would not have been a 1980 election; we would all still be in that room listening to me recite names.

Loyal admirers of the chief executive in office frequently demand that I stop asking critical questions and "support our president." Well, if I ever do decide to try to "get" a president, one way to do it would be to stand up and inquire, "Sir, please tell us why you are such a great man," and then watch the "great man" try desperately to keep from making a fool of himself as he tried to handle that softball. Good politicians, like any good batter, want something they can swing at.

Consider the hardball from House Speaker Tip O'Neill I tossed at Reagan in June 1981. "Tip O'Neill says you don't know anything about the working people, that you have just a bunch of wealthy and selfish advisers," I told him.

Reagan, who had already started from the room because the press conference had officially ended, turned back to the microphone with relish. "I'm trying to find out something about [Tip's] boyhood," said Reagan. " . . . I grew up in poverty and got what education I got all by myself and so forth, and I think it's sheer demagoguery to pretend that this economic program which we've submitted is not aimed at helping the great cross-section of people in this country. . . . "

Now you may or may not agree with O'Neill's assessment of Ronald Reagan, but it's hard not to agree that Reagan took that question and hit it out of the ball park.

Not only do good politicians like to swing at tough questions, but they also use them for their own purposes. Reagan did this once in Tokyo even before any questions had been asked.

He and leaders of other industrialized non-communist nations meeting at one of their yearly economic summits were trying to hammer out a statement on terrorism in May of 1986. Everyone was against state-sponsored terrorism, but some of the leaders did not want to specifically identify Libya as one of the chief culprits. Reagan told them that if Libya wasn't named, the very first question the press would ask would be, Why not? And in light of Libya's highly spotlighted activities, that would be a hard question to answer. Reagan's argument carried the day. Libya was put in but, of course, those of us waiting outside didn't know it.

Sure enough, when the leaders emerged, I sang out as if on cue, "Mr. President, your statement on terrorism does not mention Libya by name. Why not?" Reagan's face lit up in a wide smile. "Read the final statement," he said triumphantly, and, I was told later, once out of earshot of the press he turned to the other leaders and crowed, "See, didn't I tell you, the very first question!" Oh, well. I'm always glad to be of service.

No matter how such questions are handled, getting the president to respond to the criticism of others is one of our main jobs in the White House press room. And sometimes, not often enough in my view, reporters ask questions that zero in on people who are not important figures but are still deserving of his attention. The champion of this calling is the legendary Sarah McClendon, who has been badgering, some would say terrorizing, presidents for 40 years.

Once, Sarah sharply berated Reagan for pulling back a promised appointment because the candidate for the job had criticized cutting the budget for an agency that protects consumers. " . . . Did you mean to give a signal to other Republicans that if they don't conform, that off would go their heads?" asked Sarah.

Reagan, looking properly chastened, began his reply, "How can you say that about a sweet fellow like me?" That drew a laugh, but then, he had to go on and answer the question. Sarah, more power to her, is always sticking up for the underdog and asking presidents to explain why they are not.

That seems to me the right approach for a reporter. It's the people who don't have the power or whose thinking isn't in the mainstream who most need help in being heard.

When I said earlier that you ought to talk to presidents the way you talk to anyone else, I wasn't referring only to asking questions. I think that also applies to light banter at appropriate times.

Once, in the Oval Office, Ronald Reagan signed a congressional spending resolution and thanked senators Baker and Hatfield and congressmen Conte and "Michelle" for their "strong leadership" on this.

There is no Congressman Michelle. Reagan was clearly referring to Bob Michel of Illinois, the Republican leader in the House. So I said to the president, "That's Michel, sir, Michel."

"Oh, Michel, yes," he said. "Don't tell anyone, will you?" This while five television cameras were shooting away.

"No deals, Mr. President," I replied sternly.

"Now, Sam, haven't you ever made a mistake?" he pleaded.

"Sir," said I, "The last time I called someone Michelle, she was a blond." He laughed.

Later, I was told one of the VIPs present from Capitol Hill thought it outrageous that a mere reporter had dared to banter with the president of the United States. To his credit, Reagan doesn't seem to share this attitude. Whereas others around Reagan often seem to be striving to put him on some kind of imperial pedestal, he seems to have his feet on the ground. In fact, he can even be a little pixieish. Once, as he stood on the pavement at Checkpoint Charlie looking into communist East Berlin, I yelled out to him to be careful not to cross the line. "You don't want to get captured by the commies," I admonished with a grin.

On hearing this, Reagan lifted his leg and, with a devilish smile on his face, swung it in the air across the line. Fortunately for the safety of the free world, he didn't fall over.

And he laughed loudly at himself when, having fulminated to newspaper editors against the Shiite Muslim leader he identified as Nabih Berra, I later told him out of their earshot, "Listen here, Berra was a catcher for the New York Yankees. The man you're after is named Berri."

Reagan spars better with reporters than Carter did, because of this ability to laugh at himself. Carter preferred to laugh at the other fellow. We noticed this trait early in the Carter campaign. Curtis Wilkie, a reporter for *The Boston Globe,* brought it up on the press plane one day, "Why don't you ever engage in any self-deprecating humor?" Wilkie asked.

The next day, Carter tried to poke fun at himself at every stop. Somehow, he didn't manage to sound convincing. But Carter does have a quick wit when it comes to casting humor in an outward direction. And one day in the Rose Garden he got me good. As I sat relaxing on one of the lawn chairs at the back of the garden, waiting for a scheduled presidential appearance, Carter, suddenly and early, came out of the Oval Office, walked up to the rope line behind which other reporters were waiting, and started talking.

I ran up as quickly as I could, but by the time I got there, Carter had turned away and headed back inside. "What did he say, what did he say?" I asked a little frantically.

"He said," replied one of the reporters, "he just wanted to see if he could get Donaldson off his lawn chair."

On another occasion, Carter hit home in a brief exchange in India. We had been taken to a small village near New Delhi (renamed Carterpuri by the Indians for the occasion) to see how the village solved its energy problem. This was at the height of concern over the energy crisis. Carterpuri solved its energy problem by throwing all the cow manure from its herds into a large pit, then siphoning off the methane gas to light the village lamps. So it came to pass that we all stood on the lip of the manure pit inspecting the process.

"If I fell in, you'd pull me out wouldn't you, Mr. President?" I joked.

"Certainly," Carter replied—pause—"after a suitable interval."

It's not every day that presidents take reporters to the lip of a manure pit (literally, that is), but when they do, that's all right: It's our job to follow them wherever they go. And when presidents try to give us the slip, it's war.

A week or so after Jimmy Carter took office, he let it be known that he didn't see the need to take along a press pool in his motorcade every time he left the White House grounds, as had been the custom for years. We in the press were alarmed. We think there is a great, overriding public interest in covering the president when he's out and about, including in motorcades and on airplane rides.

Consider the day James Salamites, a young man out on the town, accidentally drove through an unguarded intersection in Hartford, Connecticut, and slammed into the side of the limousine carrying President Gerald R. Ford. Fortunately, no one was seriously hurt (one of Ford's aides suffered a broken finger), but it was one of those unplanned events that make the case for full-time press coverage of the president.

Jody Powell, Carter's press secretary, set up a meeting in the cabinet room, and I was chosen by lot as one of the press representatives to argue the case with Carter. The president opened by saying he understood the public interest in his activities, but he saw no need to take the press along on purely personal outings, such as taking his daughter, Amy, to the Washington zoo, for instance.

The headline flashed through my mind: "President Mauled by Runaway Lion, *It Is Suspected.*"

So I told him in so many words that he was wrong; that he no longer could expect to be left alone as an ordinary citizen might, because of the overriding interest in him as president, a position, I reminded him politely, no one had forced him to seek.

"You can take us along in your motorcade or we can stake out every one of the gates 24 hours a day and chase you through the streets, but we're going to cover you one way or the other," I told him. After all, no one dragged Carter or Reagan to the Oval Office and made them serve in the presidency. They fought long and hard for that job and the publicity glare that goes with it. Presidents must understand they live in a glass house when they move into the White House. Carter took the point and agreed to continue the motorcade press pool.

The fact is, the public is curious about everything presidents do, even when no great public issues are involved. A reporter once asked John F. Kennedy why he had a bandage on his finger, and Kennedy replied he had cut it with a knife down in the White House kitchen the night before as he was slicing sandwich bread. People found it fascinating.

During the Carter presidency, much of the copy turned out by news organizations and avidly gobbled up by readers had to do with Carter's family—his mother, Lillian, his sister, Gloria, who rode a motorcycle, his sister, Ruth, who was a faith healer, and of course his brother, Billy. And the comings and goings of young Amy Carter were chronicled and commented on unrelentingly. The same goes, of course, for Reagan's family.

One morning after the serious questioning at one of Reagan's mini-press conferences in the White House briefing room had ended and he was leaving the podium, I asked him, "Are you and your son Michael closer to resolving your differences?" He ducked the question by replying that he would give me the same answer his wife, Nancy, had given me the day before, when I had put the question to her during a Christmas tree photo opportunity: "Merry Christmas."

Well, you would have thought by the outrage registered in some quarters that I had inquired as to the First Couple's sex life—something *Los Angeles Times* reporter George Skelton once did in an interview with Reagan (more power to you, George). A Nixon appointee on the Federal Communications Commission, James Quello, thundered that I had asked the nastiest, most underhanded, most vicious question ever heard. I thought Quello's nomination of my humble effort a little too generous, as well as ham-handed, coming from the FCC.

But balanced against Quello's blast came a flood of letters from ordinary citizens wanting more information on the first family's domestic dispute. They said they had been reading about the dispute (it was in all the papers and news magazines) and wondered why the president hadn't answered the question.

And when Patti Davis, the Reagans' daughter, wrote a novel that reflected an unflattering view of her parents, it was natural for me to ask Reagan if he had read his daughter's book and what he thought about it. Reagan replied that he found it "interesting fiction." Quello has yet to weigh in on that exchange.

I have a reputation for putting uncomfortable questions to presidents, but I am certainly not alone. One of the most relentless interrogators is the White House bureau chief for United Press International, Helen Thomas, the dean of the White House press corps. Helen has been taking dead aim at the first magistrate of the land since Kennedy's days. Two of my favorite examples of Helen's techniques are: to Jimmy Carter, " . . . was it worth it to you to cause some destabilization of the dollar and demoralization of the federal government, spreading doubt through the land, in order to repudiate much of your Cabinet?"; and to Ronald Reagan, " . . . how high does unemployment have to go and how much does the economy have to deteriorate before you are willing to accept cuts in the defense budget?"

Thomas is particularly effective because she is always working. I found that out one day early in the Carter administration, when I stumbled onto a birthday party for deputy press secretary Rex Granum in Granum's office, right off the press room. Carter himself was there having a piece of cake with Rex and other staff members. A moment later, Ed Bradley of CBS discovered the group.

Bradley and I began reminiscing with Carter about his presidential campaign, which we had both covered. Suddenly, Thomas appeared. And after the polite hellos, she immediately whipped out her notebook and began asking Carter about the details of his forthcoming energy program. Carter fled. At first, I was unhappy that Thomas had ruined the light conversation. But upon reflection, I realized she was absolutely right to do it. Reporters are there to get information and do it at every opportunity.

That principle, noble though it may be, once almost cost me my job, however. It came about this way.

In November 1981, the ABC News Washington bureau moved into a new building, and Reagan came to dedicate it. All the top executives of the company were there, led by ABC board chairman Leonard Goldenson. Roone Arledge, president of ABC News, presided at the ceremony in our newsroom. President Reagan delivered a short speech, after which I started shooting questions at him. I'm sure it came as no surprise to him, because he had seen me standing 10 feet away with a microphone in my hand.

"Can David Stockman continue to be effective after saying such damaging things about your economic program?" I asked, referring to the Office of Management and Budget director's famous admission to William Greider in *The Atlantic* that the administration had cooked the budget figures and really didn't know what it was doing.

The president began dodging and weaving in his answers but did reveal that he would be seeing budget director Stockman right after he returned to the White House—it turned out to be the famous meeting in which Stockman said Reagan had taken him to the "woodshed."

I kept on, and Helen Thomas joined me in popping questions.

"I was only joking when I said the first question would be by Sam Donaldson," Roone Arledge snapped in a decidedly non-joking voice, aware that the majesty of the dedication ceremony was rapidly disappearing.

"So, fire me," I interjected in what I hoped was a lighthearted tone.

"You know, that's not a bad idea," replied Arledge in a tone he may have meant to be similarly lighthearted but somehow sounded more like the whistle of a Katyusha rocket about to crash through the roof.

The official party moved backstage. I am told that Michael Deaver, then White House deputy chief of staff, immediately turned on Arledge. "You mouse-trapped us," said Deaver. "We agreed to come here to dedicate the building, and you tried to turn this into a press conference." It was a terribly embarrassing moment for the top management of the American Broadcasting Company and a terribly dangerous moment for me.

Before Arledge could reply—thank God, before he could reply—another voice interrupted. "Oh, that's all right, that's just the way Sam is," said Ronald Reagan with a chuckle.

Reagan may regret that moment of generosity. The give and take of years of intense and often critical press coverage can change a president's feeling toward the press. Carter, whose national career was made possible by early favorable press coverage, left the presidency convinced that many Washington reporters had been viciously unfair to him.

By early 1986, Reagan publicly spoke of reporters as "sons of bitches," and by the end of the year, as his Iranian arms sale policy collapsed about him, he complained that we were circling like "sharks . . . with blood in the water." Such reactions are regrettable but understandable. No one likes to be criticized, especially presidents, who are surrounded by people telling them they are beyond reproach.

Let me sum up my philosophy on covering presidents. It's important work, and it never stops. Neither the press nor the president is ever off duty. I want to put questions to presidents directly, not just to their press secretaries and other aides. As to what questions are appropriate and how they should be asked, well, let's put it this way: If you send me to cover a pie-baking contest on Mother's Day, I'm going to ask dear old Mom whether she used artificial sweetener in violation of the rules, and while she's at it, could I see the receipt for the apples to prove she didn't steal them.

I maintain that if Mom has nothing to hide, no harm will have been done. But the questions should be asked. Too often, Mom, and presidents—behind those sweet faces—turn out to have stuffed a few rotten apples into the public barrel.

So when I cover the president, I try to remember two things: First, if you don't ask, you don't find out; and second, the questions don't do the damage. Only the answers do.

# 48

# Has the Press Reverted to Reverence?

## by Anthony Lewis

*Editor's Note:* Ronald Reagan was particularly good at getting his way with news media, and since the Reagan years, it seems, the government has had the winning hand in its fencing with journalists. Reagan almost seemed to be revered by the press, an attitude that had not been typical in the White House since Franklin Roosevelt, or maybe to a lesser degree, Jack Kennedy. Has that reverence continued?

Anthony Lewis is in a good position to answer this question. For many years he was a Washington correspondent for the *New York Times,* covering the Supreme Court among other assignments, and more lately an editorial columnist. This article was originally part of his Frank E. Gannett Lecture, sponsored by the Washington Journalism Center. This version was printed in the *ASNE Bulletin,* January 1989.

Seventeen years ago the New York Times and then the Washington Post published the Pentagon Papers—and fought off the Nixon administration's attempt to stop further publication. Examining that episode afterward, a law review article by Professors Harold Edgar and Benno Schmidt Jr. of the Columbia Law School said it marked "the passing of an era" for the American press. It was an era, they said, in which there was a "symbiotic relationship between politicians and the press." But now, by printing the secret history of the Vietnam War over strenuous official objections, establishment newspapers had "demonstrated that much of the press was no longer willing to be merely an occasionally critical associate (of the government), devoted to common aims, but intended to become an adversary. . . ."

A year after the Pentagon Papers, the Washington Post began looking into Watergate. What it published, in defiance of administration pressures, set in motion a process of law and politics that ended in the resignation of the president. That surely seemed to confirm what Edgar and Schmidt had said. The symbiotic relationship was over. We now had an independently critical press.

I thought about Edgar and Schmidt this past September when I read an editorial in the Washington Post. It was about the statement by the Speaker of the House, Jim Wright, that the Central Intelligence Agency had admitted, in secret testimony, helping arouse anti-government protests in Nicaragua in order to provoke repression that would harm the image of the Sandinistas. The editorial was critical—of Speaker Wright, not the CIA.

The speaker's statement was harmful to the Nicaraguan opposition, the Post said. It noted Wright's claim that what he said had already appeared in other news reports. But that explanation, it said sternly, failed to consider "the crucial authority that a Congressional figure can add by his confirmation." Finally, the editorial came to the question whether the CIA had in fact sparked the Nicaraguan protests. That would have been "incredibly stupid" it said, and public testimony in Congress had absolved the CIA of the charge.

The CIA has in fact done some "incredibly stupid" things, in Nicaragua among other places. A genuinely critical press would have taken a hard look at the facts before chastising a Congressional leader for improper leaking or abuse of authority in this case.

But what struck me about the editorial was not so much its factual assumptions as its reverential tone. Its premise was that legitimacy rests in the executive branch of the United States government, not the legislative. Congress, along with the rest of us, owes respect to the secrecy that the executive, with its special knowledge and expertise, deems necessary in the interest of national security.

Those were the very attitudes that the Times and the Post and other newspapers rejected when they published the Pentagon Papers. As a result of the Vietnam War they had come to realize that executive officials did not always have superior knowledge and expertise—and did not always tell the truth. They were not entitled to reverence, from the press or Congress. The country would be better off . . . if policies were subject to unstinting scrutiny, including a good many policies covered up by secrecy.

Of course my point does not lie in the particular editorial; there were reasons to question Speaker Wright's wisdom. . . . But the tone of the editorial reflected a general trend. The established press in this country has to a large extent reverted to the symbiotic relationship with the executive branch. We are an adversary only on the margins, not on the fundamentals that challenge power. We have forgotten the lessons of Vietnam and Watergate.

Think about press treatment of the presidency in the 1970s and, by comparison, in the last eight years. In Ben Bradlee's phrase, there has been "a return to deference." We are all uneasily aware that something like that has happened. We are not sure why it came about. But we can place the change in the Reagan years.

When President Reagan took office in 1981, the press at first reported with gusto on the gaps in his knowledge and interest, the confusion of fact and fancy. The evening television news noted his mistakes at press conferences, and newspapers detailed them the next day. But it turned out that the public did not care about Reagan's flubs. James David Barber, the scholar of the Presidency, said the public treated his contempt for facts "as a charming idiosyncrasy." So the press's gusto for recording Reagan's wanderings from reality waned.

More important, the press did not give the public real insight into the working of the Reagan White House—into the confusion and vacuity that have been described so convincingly now in books by former insiders.

After Reagan had been president for about a year, I wrote a column puzzling over why the press seemed to hold back from giving us an unvarnished picture. . . . I ventured a few guesses on the possible reasons.

One was Reagan's political standing. He had won in a landslide in 1980, and rolled over Congress in the tax and budget battle of 1981. He had the most convincing validation a democracy can give, and the public was not interested in carping at the details. Who was the press to challenge that? Some in the press were subconsciously asking themselves what our critics like to ask: Who elected us?

Second, some in the press may have felt uneasy because they were liberals. If they did tough stories, they might be accused of treating Reagan unfairly for that reason, of being insufficiently "objective."

Third, I guessed that some reporters and editors who watched Reagan were reluctant as citizens to speak out about what they saw. They saw the most powerful of offices occupied by a man with an anecdotal view of the world, giving simplistic answers to complicated questions, or tuning out. They found it upsetting to acknowledge, to the public or to themselves, that American leadership was in such hands.

To those possibilities, I would now add a weightier fourth reason: fear.

For nearly 20 years the political right in this country has been working to intimidate the press and arouse public feeling against it. Spiro Agnew may be taken as the starting point, with his denunciations of the liberal elitist press and the nattering nabobs of negativism. We treat him as a joke figure now; after all, he did leave office under particularly unpleasant circumstances. But the resentments he touched and aroused were not a joke, and they have not gone away. There are a good many Americans who use the phrase "elitist press." We get letters from them.

Watergate fed the resentment, the anger. Nixon had his supporters to the end, and they were enraged at the part played in his fall by an unelected press. There was a Watergate backlash against the press. We felt it, we worried about it and we tried to compensate for it.

Most important of all, in these historical causes, there was Vietnam. Millions of Americans, including some in high office, are convinced that we lost that war because the press showed us the horrors of it in graphic detail—and somehow favored the other side. What the press actually did, in its noblest tradition, was to show the reality that it was an unwinnable war. But the anger remains.

Today intimidation of the press is a standard item on the agenda of the organized political right. There are self-appointed monitors who circulate denunciations of articles and television programs that depart from their view of life. There are groups that support libel suits.

People in our business tend to have more than the usual amount of courage. But we kid ourselves if we think that pressure of that kind has no effect on us, or on the companies that own media institutions. Editors and publishers know that tough journalism that may embarrass conservative interests means trouble.

There were a lot of questions about Sen. Quayle that never got answered in the campaign. His academic records would have told us the answers, but Sen. Quayle refused to let anyone see the records. Some reporters were interested, but somehow the questions were not pressed hard enough or often enough to make the refusal to answer an issue—which it properly was.

The 1988 campaign left some reporters who covered it, and their editors and producers, feeling uncomfortable. One said she thought she had been complicit in a fraud on democracy. Another said, "I feel dirty."

A second problem in this year's coverage was fascination with the process of the modern campaign, and with its manipulators: process, not substance. And not values. We celebrated Roger Ailes for his craft as a maker of television ads that created a picture of Michael Dukakis as a friend of murderers and rapists. There were lots of stories about the superiority of the technicians on that side: value-free stories. One newspaper political analyst even wrote a piece arguing that the inferior quality of Governor Dukakis' television ads had "disturbing implications about Dukakis' leadership."

I wonder how Thomas Jefferson, an introspective man, would rate as a political leader by that standard. Perhaps our democracy has been so corrupted by technology that a sensitive person, a Jefferson, can no longer hope to lead it. That may be. But I do not think the press should be cheering the corrupters for their efficiency. . . .

# 49

# News of the Congress by the Congress

## *by* Mary Collins

---

*Editor's Note:* Congress has been able to put its spin on congressional news to a greater degree than ever before. Television stations and newspapers are increasingly allowing their local House members to cover themselves. It saves money for the press—and the representatives love having their version of the news published and broadcast, unfiltered by journalists.

Mary Collins is an associate editor of the *Washington Journalism Review.* News aides John Murawski and John Stetson provided research for this article, which was published in the *Washington Journalism Review* (now the *American Journalism Review*) in June 1990.

---

Every Wednesday at one o'clock the Democratic and Republican National Congressional Committees haul high-quality television equipment to the "Swamp," a patch of grass on the east side of the Capitol. Against the patriotic backdrop, House members tape short interviews with their press secretaries for the committees to send via satellite to stations in the members' districts.

"And the local stations often run the stuff," says Wesley Pippert, former press secretary for Rep. Paul Henry (R-Mich.) and one-time UPI reporter. "You can ponder the implications of that."

Because of this growing electronic flackery, many newspapers and television stations are dropping their independent political correspondents, choosing instead to get their Washington coverage from press secretaries and understaffed D.C. bureaus run by large parent companies. Some of them don't even bother with bureaus or independent news services. Lured by low costs, convenience and a deceptive patina of journalistic professionalism, an ever-growing portion of the Fourth Estate is relying entirely on canned congressional news.

In the last 20 years the number of House press secretaries has quintupled from 54 in 1970 to more than 250 today. Armed with the latest technology—including fax machines and television equipment—these image-makers have access to more media outlets than ever before. "The P.R. machinery is overwhelming," says Ron Cohen, executive editor of Gannett News Service. So much so that political reporters in all forms of media have been giving ground.

At WJMC-AM, a radio station in Jacksonville, North Carolina, News Director Glenn Hargett often uses tapes and releases prepared by Rep. Martin Lancaster's (D-N.C.) press secretary, Marshall "Skip" Smith. "Skip asks the member the questions himself and then sends us down a response. I see nothing wrong with a press secretary controlling the interview," he says. "I'll tell you, there were times in the past when I had to rely on Skip heavily. He was my only source. I had to trust him."

Smith himself says he uses his releases to "cut off bad publicity—to put our own spin on things."

Like most press secretaries on the Hill, Smith is a former journalist who puts his experience as an editor and news director to good use for his congressmen. He knows how to sell stories to thirsty media outlets. He knows reporters and deadlines. "He knows our operation," says Hargett.

Morgan Broman, press secretary for Rep. Richard Neal (D-Mass.), also makes good use of the connections he developed as a reporter/producer for WWLP-TV, a station in Neal's district in Springfield. "I call my old boss, and they'll generally write it [the press release] into the text" of the evening news, he says. WWLP News Director Keith Silver acknowledges that the station sometimes uses Broman's P.R. "He knows what buttons to press," Silver says. "He knows who to talk to."

The ties are even tighter between Tina Kreischer, press secretary for San Diego's Congressman Bill Lowery (R-Calif.) and the *San Diego Union.* Her husband, Otto, reports on the Pentagon for the *Union* out of the Copley News Service's Washington bureau. Sometimes he works with his wife on stories because Lowery is on the Military Construction Subcommittee.

"When I have to go to them for comments or facts it's weird," he says. "The situation becomes interesting when she and I go to the National Press Club for dinner. She's there in a dual capacity [wife/press secretary]. The [Copley] reporters on her beat get to talk shop with her, so in that sense she is treated differently."

Tina Kreischer believes that at least 75 percent of the stories about Lowery that appear in the *Union* are based on her press releases. Though the paper rarely runs them verbatim, former Copley reporter Mark Ragan, who covered the Hill for the *Union,* says that the bureau does rely on them "heavily." "They're all so busy," he says. "Tina is very helpful."

Steve Green, managing editor of Copley's Washington bureau, describes the Kreischers' situation as an "odd-couple relationship. But I don't know what to do with it," he says. "You can't say he should divorce his wife or leave his job."

Copley's Washington office and other parent company news bureaus say they make a conscious effort not to rely on press secretaries for their congressional coverage. So do such independent bureaus as Potomac News Service and States News Service. Many smaller media outlets, on the other hand, depend almost entirely on press secretaries for Hill news. Case studies abound, particularly in the broadcast media.

One station in Rep. Porter Goss's (R-Fla.) district in Fort Myers, Florida, WINK-TV, gave up on Potomac News Service, an independent agency that provides Capitol Hill news for stations across the country, because "the cost is prohibitive," says Jim McLaughlin, managing editor and anchor. He estimates that one 30-second sound bite can cost as much as $500. "With Senate feeds and House feeds we pretty much have it covered," he says. According to News Director John Emmert the station now links up with news services only on an on-need basis. "It is more reactive," he concedes. "We no longer have a service hounding out a story."

KLBK-TV in Lubbock, Texas, also has a reactive relationship with the House member from its district, Larry Combest (R-Texas). According to News Director Michael Sommermeyer, the fact that Combest's current press secretary, Keith Williams, is a former local reporter makes having a D.C. correspondent or using a news service superfluous. "As a small-market television station, we have to skimp and save and try to convince other people to help us out. That's why it's good to have Keith there. The only problem is the slanted view."

"Capitol Hill press secretaries often send out daily feeds of an hour or more," says Bruce Finland, president and founder of the Potomac News Service. "It's not bad to have that, but more and more it's the *only* thing TV stations are taking out of Washington. That's what bothers me."

Business is booming for television crews at the Republican and Democratic National Committees and at the House's own TV studio in the basement of the Rayburn building. Costs are low—often 60 percent below the commercial rate—and equipment is top quality.

The demand is so high that use of the House studio has quadrupled since 1980, even though the political parties expanded their own television facilities during the same period. The House Administration Subcommittee is currently considering a request for $203,000 for additional personnel at the Hill studio.

This sudden surge in video press releases has put several independent television news services in Washington out of business. Finland says that at least three of a dozen or so services have died in the last five years. "Soon, I expect there will be only one or two left," he says. "Basically, the free satellite feeds have killed an industry. They've supplanted real news coverage."

This is not to say, however, that relying on parent bureaus like Hearst Broadcasting, or on news services like CONUS or Potomac News, is a cure-all. These bureaus provide Hill coverage to countless small stations that can't afford their own Washington correspondents. But most of these bureaus are chronically understaffed, using two general assignment reporters to cover *all* of Washington for six to 10 clients. Congress must compete for attention with the president, the U.S. Supreme Court, demonstrators and more. House coverage in particular gets short shrift.

Potomac News Service, for example, has just seven people in its bureau, only three of whom are full-time reporters. "On any given day," says Bureau Chief Eileen Cleary, "we do anywhere from one to 20 stories."

There is a case to be made that some station budgets just don't permit original Washington coverage. There is also some validity to the argument that tapes made by members of Congress may contain legitimate news. But it's not so easy to justify another aspect of this conveyance of incumbent propaganda: Few of the stations tell their viewers they are dispensing material prepared, not by the station, but by a politician. The viewer is left free to assume that the congressman's words are in response to a reporter's questions when, in fact, they are worked up by the congressman in collusion with his own paid press representative.

This practice is not only ethically suspect, it's potentially unlawful. According to the Federal Communications Commission (FCC), the public should be informed when any "records, transcriptions, talent, scripts, or other material or services of any kind are furnished by a candidate as an inducement to the broadcast of the program. . . . An announcement shall be made both at the beginning and conclusion of such program."

Practically speaking, the law is not enforced, because the FCC depends on complaints to trigger official monitoring, and viewers—unfamiliar with the law and unaware they're viewing congressional hand-outs—don't complain. Uncertainty about when a congressman is a "candidate" also clouds the issue. The FCC is now revising these regulations to include specific guidelines for video news releases (VNR).

But many news directors appear untroubled by either ethical or legal doubts. Based on an informal *WJR* survey of 26 stations, 87 percent say they rarely if ever notify viewers when "news" footage is provided by a congressman's office.

"I find that surprising and disturbing," says David Bartlett, president of the Radio-Television News Directors Association. "It's RTNDA's view—and the [view of a] vast majority of the people in the industry—that identification of a video is vital.

"Failing to identify the source of a VNR is a terrible breach of journalistic practice."

Stations that don't label political VNRs sink into a corrosive coziness with House members. A congressman gets to control his own 15-second appearance on the evening news—all the more effective because viewers consider it straight news. And the news director gets a free clip out of Washington relating to current events—all the more effective because viewers assume it's news coverage by the station, not the transmission of a political message. The only loser in the deal: the public.

The situation among newspapers, while also bleak, contains one bright aspect. According to media critic Ben Bagdikian, professor of journalism at the University of California, Berkeley, the concentration of ownership of print media in the hands of a few companies has improved congressional coverage. Many small papers now have access to Washington reporters via their parent bureaus. "They end up with a certain amount of delegation coverage that they've never had before," he says. And unlike Potomac News Service, business at States News Service has improved, says Managing Editor Rem Rieder.

But newspaper bureaus in Washington are also short staffed. The typical reporter in these bureaus is expected to track eight to 10 House and Senate members for several newspapers.

States News, for example, covers U.S. representatives from more than 30 states with 31 reporters. According to Rieder, a state like California—which has 45 members in its congressional delegation—is assigned three reporters; most others get just one.

High staff turnover and low budgets also constrict the Hill reporting of these news services. Editor David Greenfield of the *Charleston* (West Virginia) *Daily Mail* says that when he was a Washington correspondent from 1979 to 1984 he saw four or five people from States News come and go on the Hill beat for the rival *Charleston Gazette*. "It's so low budget and has such a high staff turnover rate that reporters leave before they get to know the state. There's no continuity," he says.

Rieder, however, feels that things are changing—at least at States News, where the average reporter now stays two years, he says. Other staffers claim the average is closer to a year.

Many bureaus for newspaper parent companies are also stretched thin. At Knight-Ridder Newspapers two reporters provide congressional coverage for 28 dailies in 16 states; Scripps Howard News Service has one Hill reporter for 20 dailies.

"Flacks with faxes have real sway with local dailies," says David Hawkings, a Hill reporter for the Thomson Newspaper Group who covers 14 members for 14 papers. "A fax in the hand of a small local newspaper editor can be better than a bureau story in the bush."

Print reporters from the home districts could easily complement the House news provided by the understaffed D.C. bureaus, or even generate stories on their own, by making a few long distance phone calls. But few do.

A comparison between two dailies in Charleston, West Virginia, with roughly equal circulation, the *Gazette* and *Daily Mail*, dramatizes the difference a paper's own correspondent can make.

The morning *Gazette* (circulation, 55,000) closed down its independent Washington bureau in the 1960s and signed up the States News Service instead. Now it has dropped States News as well and relies on "the national wires and the P.R. people of congressmen for its Hill coverage," says City Editor Rosalie Earle.

The *Gazette's* JOA-partner and rival, the *Daily Mail* (circulation, 51,700), has taken a different approach. This evening paper has had its own full-time political correspondent for 12 years, even though Thomson Newspapers, which owns the paper, has a Washington bureau. "It's difficult to get a pertinent local story out of a bureau," says *Daily Mail* Editor David Greenfield.

When Congress gave itself a pay raise in November, for example, the *Gazette* relied on UPI for its Page One story, which included remarks from Senate Majority Leader Robert Byrd (D-W.Va.) but nothing from Charleston's less renowned House member, Bob Wise. On the same day, the *Daily Mail's* Hill correspondent, John Kimelman, also had a cover story, but it quoted extensively from the entire West Virginia House delegation, which had split its vote on the pay-raise issue.

The *Daily Mail* regularly carries localized front-page stories about such topics as Wise's decision to cut back on press releases, his family's response to the swearing-in ceremonies for the 101st Congress and his latest proposed legislation. The *Gazette,* by contrast, rarely publishes such specific stories on the representative, relying instead on the more generic news that comes over the wire. And even when the *Gazette* does play up congressional stories, it seldom mentions West Virginia's House members, because wire services tend to focus on politicians with national reputations.

Dailies that provide the *Gazette's* type of off-the-shelf House coverage make it difficult for voters to learn about the doings or misdoings of their U.S. representatives. "There's such a lack of interest," says congressional press secretary Morgan Broman, "that opponents must educate the public on the failings of an incumbent at election time."

But the "educational" opportunities for challengers range from slim to none. For two years prior to election day, incumbents shape the flow of "news" from Washington to many of the newspapers and TV stations in their districts. Then at campaign time, incumbents outspend their opponents—on TV spots in particular—by more than three to one. The right question here may not be why 98.5 percent of House members seeking re-election in 1988 retained their seats, but how 1.5 percent managed to lose.

The problem, says Bruce Finland, of the Potomac News Service, is that the media have become accustomed to getting House coverage for free. And news organizations are bothered less and less by the fact that a press secretary's releases do not provide an objective, critical account of a congressman's activities.

"The genie is out of the bottle," Finland says. "I don't know of an instance where someone who gets something for free will suddenly turn around and pay for it."

But the "something for free" amounts to a hidden media contribution to the political welfare and safety of every incumbent U.S. representative, good, bad or indifferent. At a time when the media are concerned about their own credibility, this genie is a good candidate for grabbing, squeezing and stuffing—back into the bottle.

# 50

# Has the White House Press Corps Met Its Match?

## *by* Gary Griffith

*Editor's Note:* The administration of President Bill Clinton seemed to herald a new era in government relations with the press. Clinton's honeymoon with the press was shortlived, however. Early in his administration, the press jumped on him for late appointments, for reneging on campaign promises, and for floundering on the budget and health care.

However, most observers expected that he could take on the "wolves" in the press room, mostly by bypassing them for media in which he could take his message directly to the people without having to answer tough questions from reporters. Clinton had successfully bypassed the traditional media in his election campaign. Certainly, the author here predicts, he could do the same during his stay in the White House.

Gary Griffith is a seasoned president-watcher as the Washington bureau chief of Hearst broadcasting. This article was published in the Radio-Television News Directors Association *Communicator,* December 1992.

Bill Clinton seems likely to take a new approach to White House press relations, based largely on what worked for him during the campaign. The desire to avoid what has become known as "the filter" of the national press was a driving force in the media strategy of all three presidential campaigns in 1992. But Clinton, in particular, showed his ability to connect directly with the voters during his appearances on the talk show circuit.

He has already indicated that he intends to continue to attempt to communicate to the American public through the types of unconventional media that he used during the campaign, even though many of the press regulars may find the idea undignified.

"He did say, God help us all, that he would continue to do a lot of unusual things," Deborah Potter, the CNN correspondent, said at a recent American University forum on Clinton and the media. "The very idea of the President of the United States going on a bus trip is almost more than I can bear."

But the stated desire of the Clinton team to continue to communicate through the unconventional or so-called news media is an indication that the small and elite White House press corps will be somewhat diminished in importance. It is, after all, the very filter that the campaign tried to avoid.

At the same AU forum, Stephen Hess of the Brookings Institution made this prediction: "Bill Clinton will eventually find that the White House press corps is counterproductive to what he wants to do, and perhaps even irrelevant."

Linda Chavez, a Republican analyst, believes Bush erred in not using the other options that were open to him to address the public in his first years as President. "He did not talk directly to the American people," she says. "He would go into the press briefing room and talk to reporters, whom I think he really thought were sort of his pals, and they weren't."

The briefing room crowd, or what has become the permanent White House press corps, is now about 125 people who work full time with desk space on the two floors of the White House press room. Network TV personnel—correspondents, producers, and technicians—make up about a third of the total.

The individuals in the group have remained somewhat stable for the last 12 years, and it did not have a great turnover from Reagan to Bush.

The traditional honeymoon between the new President and the press will no doubt occur. Clinton and the national press will find that their interests intertwine. During the inauguration, and perhaps for the first few weeks, there will be an air of excitement in the Washington press coverage of the new administration and personalities. After that, as programs stall in Congress the reporting will change in tone and so will the relationship.

Expectations for Clinton are quite high. Like any President, he will have trouble keeping all his campaign promises. When that happens, the press will again have a more open ear to his opposition.

As John Ciccone, a Bush campaign operative, predicts, "There will be buyer remorse on the part of the press, not just the public."

It is at that point that Clinton may find it more productive to try to go around the national press, with talk-show appearances, bus tours, and whatever else will help him to avoid the negative stories that an objective press will most certainly find appropriate.

How long Clinton will stay in good graces of the Washington press remains to be seen, but he will come to town with a great deal of good will. He was accessible on a casual level during the campaign and was generally liked by the reporters who covered him. It was his opponent, after all, who campaigned against the press in the final weeks, making much of his "Annoy the Media—Re-elect Bush" bumper stickers.

If the truth be told, much of the Washington press corps will be glad to see Bush go. The Bush press operation was never considered as sophisticated as the Reagan team, and it was much less sensitive to the need for press access both in Washington and on foreign trips.

"The people in the Reagan administration were great," says Leo Meidlinger, a White House producer for ABC during the last two administrations.

"They knew where they were going, and they would fight for access for us. It went 180 degrees the other way with the Bush people."

The wider Washington press corps will be relieved to see Bush go for different reasons.

While there are about 125 journalists and technicians assigned to the White House on a daily basis, there are another 1,500 or so who cover Washington daily for local newspapers, local TV stations, broadcast-group bureaus, and news services. That group was all but cut off by the Bush press operation.

"There was the assumption that if you took care of the networks, nothing else mattered," says Eileen Cleary, VP of Potomac Television Communications, Washington's largest television news service. "We couldn't get the main press office to take our calls."

Under Bush, and Reagan before him, the White House set up a two-tiered press structure, with Marlin Fitzwater's White House Press Office dealing exclusively with the reporters who covered the beat full time, and the Office of Media Relations working with everyone else.

Ironically, the Media Relations Office was set up under the Nixon administration to sell the President's agenda to the heartland by going around the national press, much as the current campaigns tried to avoid what they now call the filter. But under Bush, Media Relations became a roadblock to access and information.

"I don't think they really understood what we do," says Andy Cassells, D.C. bureau chief for Cox Broadcasting. "We would call up and say, 'We know the Mayor of Atlanta is meeting with the President tomorrow,' but they would tell us they didn't know anything about it."

For the non–White House Washington press corps, the Bush Media Relations Office was a nightmare. Dorrance Smith, the former executive producer of ABC's "Nightline," was brought in April 1991 to reorganize the office. He held a meeting with representatives of the wider Washington press corps once and listened to their complaints. But nothing got better.

"I thought when Dorrance came in we had some hope," says Tina Gulland, Washington bureau chief for Post-Newsweek Stations. "Maybe, he'll get these people in shape, I thought, but he absolutely did not."

The average print or broadcast reporter working in Washington rarely ever saw the President except on TV. Bush had only a few prime-time news conferences, preferring instead to drop into the briefing room on 30-minutes' notice during the morning or early afternoon. That practice all but eliminated the wider Washington press corps. Reporters simply did not have time to get to the building between the time the news conferences were announced and the time they began.

In his first years as President, Bush made a genuine attempt to strike up good relationships with the regular White House press corps by inviting individual members to attend state dinners, to play tennis, and to visit in the family quarters. But he had few contacts and virtually no relationships with the non-network press.

Maria Sheehan, who was deputy director of the White House Media Relations Office, defends the way the Bush administration handled the bulk of the non-White House press by stressing the volume of work and staff had to handle. "It's a very small office that serves a massive press corps," she says. "We had to answer questions on everything from what the President had for breakfast that day to incredible details of his health plan."

As to advice for the Clinton administration, Sheehan says, "It would be to put a lot more emphasis on this office in terms of resources, people, and stature."

Clinton might also be advised to abandon the idea of a two-tiered press office entirely and integrate the wider Washington press corps with the day-to-day regulars.

The change to a Democratic administration after 12 years of Republican rule will mean vast changes not only in the White House but in the entire executive branch. There will undoubtedly be a great deal of interest by local newspapers and TV stations about how the changes in administration will affect their areas, and it is certain that those stories will not get done by Larry King and Phil Donahue.

There are hundreds of reporters in Washington who don't hang around the White House briefing room all day. Perhaps it will be the Clinton administration that discovers them.

# XII

# War and the Military

In the clash between the press and the government, the coverage of a war raises some particularly vexing questions. First, governments need to control information more during wartime than at other times. Information about military strategies that gets into enemy hands will certainly damage a war effort. Second, governments usually need to make a special attempt to win support for a military action. War is always costly in lives and property. Why should people make such a sacrifice? Governments must win a war for the minds of their people before they can effectively fight a war against an enemy. Thus, they must promote the war to their citizens, primarily through mass media.

However, if there is significant opposition to a war, the American press feels obligated to tell the public about it. Most American journalists feel strongly that they should never lie or cover up what their government does. If the government makes a mistake, journalists regard it as their responsibility to reveal it to the people. They feel that citizens need to know everything the government does, even when such information might jeopardize that government.

Moreover, wars are fought by two sides, not one, and American journalists are trained to tell both sides of any story. The enemy version is sometimes given equal time and space with the American version. From time to time journalists have been regarded as traitors when they have not blindly supported a government action, but the journalists themselves regard such reporting as faithful to their journalistic traditions.

The problem was not so severe in World War II and the Korean War, the purpose of which was generally well accepted by the people. In addition, print media could be controlled to some extent to serve the government's purposes, perhaps because they were slower and thus easier to manipulate or censor.

The issue came to the fore primarily in Vietnam, the first "TV war." Television was harder to control; it was faster and more compelling. It could bring the war almost instantaneously into the living rooms of all Americans. When citizens for the first time saw on television some of the war's brutality and horror first-hand, many were repulsed and withdrew their support of the war. Some critics say that America lost the war in Vietnam because television damaged public support for it at home.

Since Vietnam, the military has made a greater effort to control the news media as a way of winning the war for people's minds. The military had long paid attention to its public relations as an aspect of a war effort. In the past two decades it has become much more sophisticated about limiting the role of mass media. In the 1970s, the British limited media access to the war in the Falklands, with considerable success. In the 1980s, Reagan was able to control media coverage of the skirmishes in Grenada and Libya, and in 1990 Bush was able to do so in Panama.

No American war was ever as thoroughly successful from a PR point of view as the war in the Persian Gulf in 1991. It was a short war, and the mass media would probably not have been so successfully managed by the military if it had gone on much longer. But it provided some classic examples of new issues about mass media and the military in a war.

In some respects, mass media themselves have become weapons of modern warfare, and they are being used by both sides.

# 51

# Mass Media as Weapons of Modern Warfare

## *by* Ray Eldon Hiebert

*Editor's Note:* Mass communication has become an essential part of modern warfare, and therefore the military has increasingly used public relations in fighting wars today. The war in the Persian Gulf in 1991 is an excellent example and demonstrates how the military's use of PR techniques successfully managed the news flow.

This article was first presented as the Robert Godlonton Commemorative Media Lecture in Pretoria, South Africa, on March 20, 1991, shortly after the war ended. Much additional information supporting this thesis has been made public since that time. Godlonton, a nineteenth-century South African editor, is regarded as the father of press freedom in that country.

Hiebert, the first American to deliver the Godlonton Lecture, is a professor at the University of Maryland and the editor of this book. This article was published in the *Public Relations Review*, Summer 1991.

We have witnessed, in the war in the Persian Gulf, either history's most impressive use of military weapons, or history's most thorough use of words and images as weapons of war, or both.

As a democratic society, Americans have always believed in the public's right to know, and the press's freedom to seek the truth. We have always felt that the people have a right to learn all the facts about government, to make sure government is serving the people's interests. And to that end we have not wanted government to play too big a role in telling us what is going on. We believe the facts should come from a free and independent press. We believe government should not operate any newspapers, magazines, radio or television stations or any other mass media, lest such ownership and control would allow government to hide or distort the facts in its favor. But that doesn't mean governments should not exercise leadership, because without leadership, including the leadership of public opinion, democracy becomes anarchy.

War provides a good case in point. Wars are waged today by governments, and in democratic societies governments must win public support from their own citizens before they can fight and win a war against the enemy. To win the minds at home in the recent war, the American government launched a public relations campaign on an unprecedented scale, and with unprecedented success. The smart bombs of the war succeeded in part because of smart words.

It is my thesis that mass communication is today an essential part of modern warfare, that public relations is a primary weapon of war—increasingly for all sides. In the Gulf War, both sides attempted to manage the words and images of battle. There is nothing new about that. Propaganda has always been a part of war. What was new about "Desert Storm" was the extent to which the American government and its military concerned itself with fighting the war for public support at home by using all the classic practices of public relations, including political strategies, media relations, community relations, employee relations, and crisis management. There were times, of course, when the practice was not perfect.

Today, even in democratic societies, governments under threat must exercise political leadership in order to survive. The problems for such leadership sometimes seem almost insurmountable. The French writer Alexis de Tocqueville, a shrewd observer, wrote the following about the new phenomenon of American democracy in his journal in 1831:

> In thus pressing democracy to the utmost limits, we have in actual fact handed over control of society to those who have no interest in stability since they possess and have but little understanding. Also, we have built our social order on ever moving ground. With us, every year, not only do public officials change, but principals, maxims of government and parties succeed to power at an incredible rate. Social standing and wealth are everlastingly caught up in this all-embracing change. There is no continuity in undertaking.[1]

In the war in Vietnam, Americans had relatively little understanding of the government's position, and little or no interest in the stability of the government's role or the continuity of its undertaking. Many blamed the press for this destabilization. Others blamed the government for not assuming better leadership, for not taking charge of the crisis, for not controlling the communication. Many in leadership roles have been saying since Vietnam, "never again."

When the British fought their war in the Falkland Islands, they did take charge. They put the war off limits to the press, moved in quickly and finished the job, before the public back home could destabilize the effort and destroy the continuity needed to get the task done. The British handling of the press in the Falklands war has become the model for all American military action since then.

I would suggest that to insure some continuity, which is essential for stable government, and especially for winning a war, public officials must exercise leadership in winning the collective mind of the people. And political leaders today use public communication and public relations to do just that—to inform, influence, change, or at least neutralize public opinion.[2]

## Media Relations for a Media Event

In many ways, the war in the Gulf was a media event. It was, without doubt, the most widely and certainly most instantaneously covered war in the history of mankind. In no other war had people been able to see the action in real time, at precisely the moment the battle was taking place. Sometimes, in fact, the military depended on mass media reporting to learn what was going on.

Nearly a thousand reporters thronged to Saudi Arabia, hundreds of times more than covered the Allied invasion of Normandy on D-Day during World War II. Newspapers and magazines were saturated with war news and comment. Radio and television made it the major story day after day. CNN provided nearly round-the-clock coverage throughout the war, and the coverage was seen world-wide. I was in a hotel room in Budapest, Hungary, when the war started, and I watched the same CNN coverage of the war that my wife was seeing in Silver Spring, Maryland, back in the United States. If Marshall McLuhan's global village was ever a reality, this was it.

But the news about the war was carefully managed by the government in a variety of ways. First of all, there were security guidelines about what kind of news was too sensitive to be covered, such as troop movements, future operations, and the like. No journalist objected to these kinds of guidelines. But military public relations sometimes went awry, especially when elements of news management seemed to have more to do with political policy than with the military security.

The military required the media to "pool" their reports, meaning that only a few reporters could ever visit a sensitive area, and their reporting was then shared with all the media. This certainly gave the government greater control over press access to information. Only a fraction of the journalists, and those mostly from the largest media organizations, were able to qualify for the pools. Unfortunately, reporters who broke the rules and went to forbidden zones on their own were sometimes taken into custody and shipped out of the area. (At least two dozen reporters suffered this fate.)[3]

Today it is standard operating procedure for a public relations person to accompany an official who is giving an interview to the press. The purpose is to help the official with facts and figures and make sure that the interview goes well. This PR policy was adopted by the military in the Gulf, requiring all reporters to be accompanied by an escort officer for all interviews. Sometimes this policy, too, went astray. One *New York Times* reporter had his press credentials taken away because he was conducting, without an escort, an "unauthorized" interview with Saudi shopkeepers 50 miles from the Kuwaiti border.[4]

At the same time, all reports had to be submitted to a "Joint Information Bureau (JIB)," which would review it for sensitive security information. Not a great deal was censored, because reporters were careful. But often copy was delayed, sometimes unconscionably. One reporter writing about an interview with a returning pilot used the word "giddy" to describe him. The escort officer objected, and the story was delayed two days while it was sent to the JIB for a ruling. An overzealous military sometimes found other delaying tactics. They used motorcycles—in an age of high-speed helicopters—to bring back pool reports from the reporters at the front line 600 miles from Riyadh. The long trip meant the news was old by the time the motorcycles arrived with the copy.[5]

Sometimes news subjects put off limits seemed to have little to do with military security. One regulation banned all photographs of coffins arriving at Dover Air Force Base in the States, presumably to reduce the coverage of U.S. casualties. Other facts were classified as top secret that seemed to have little to do with the war. For example, General Norman Schwarzkopf's body weight was a military secret. Photographs of the bombings in Iraq were not given to the press because "it would show the Iraqis how good we were."[6] Of course, the Iraqis had the photographs to begin with. They knew all about the precision of our smart bombs first-hand.

## War as Crisis Management

Crisis management has come to be a very important part of public relations. In the U.S. today, there are at least a dozen current books available on the subject, and everyone in PR is either taking or offering a crash course on dealing with emergencies. It is not surprising that the military, too, should have learned the lessons of crisis management.

The public relations rules for crisis management are relatively simple: tell as much as you can and tell it fast; centralize the source of information with an effective and well-informed spokesman, usually the chief executive; deal with rumors swiftly; make as much available to the press as possible; update information frequently; stay on the record; and never tell a lie.

The military in the Gulf War followed this prescription almost to the letter. They quickly organized regular briefings for the press. They had a bit of trouble at first finding the best spokesman, but they finally settled on General Neal, who played the role brilliantly. Ultimately they found that the commander himself, General Schwarzkopf, was the best briefer of the lot. He had all the information at his fingertips, had an authoritative presence, and was wonderfully articulate in explaining details. In Washington, General Kelly proved to be equally adept as the briefing officer. It is interesting to note that his formal training wasn't in military science; he has a degree in journalism.

In fact, one important element of this war was the high level of intelligence and education of the American military. *Time* magazine noted the "remarkable professionalism . . . exemplified most visibly by the smooth TV performances of top military officers. . . . Intelligent, frank, sometimes eloquent, these men seemed to personify a new class of American military leaders who not only have a thorough grasp of their trade but also demonstrate broad political and worldly sophistication—not to mention PR savvy."[7]

Many of the military officers today have advanced degrees, often doctorates, and that is true as well of the officers whose primary duty is public relations. In the Navy, for example, more than 80 percent of the public affairs officers have advanced degrees, most in the subject of public relations itself.[8] In fact, the Armed Forces have their own post-graduate course, the Defense Information School, where officers and enlisted men and women can get advanced training in public relations.

Thus the military was able to articulate its facts and its point of view in its dealings with the press. Said *Time:* "With little access to the battlefield, reporters had to depend on the daily briefings in Riyadh and Washington for news. Those were handled with extraordinary skill. The briefings were filled with facts and figures (number of missions flown, Scuds fired), and the men who conducted them were cooperative, usually candid and, when it came to estimates of enemy damage, very cautious. The goal was to avoid excessive optimism and reduce expectations."[9]

If anything, the military overwhelmed the press with information. Reporters could not keep up with or digest the enormous quantities of details from briefings and press releases. Of course, all the detail was only that which the military wanted to make public.

One of the cardinal sins of public relations is to tell a lie. In an open marketplace of news, we hold, the truth will always come out, and if you've told a lie, it will ultimately hurt more than help. Of course, there are slips, deliberate and accidental. But for the most part, the press in the Gulf War was never able to catch the military in an outright lie. The reporters had great faith in the veracity of what they were being told. They might have been often overwhelmed with facts about some things, and underwhelmed about others, but they were not the victims often of outright lies.[10]

Reporters looked for lies, suspecting them at every turn. At one point, word got out—it later proved to be from a Saudi official—that six Iraqi helicopters had defected to the Allies. When the helicopters were not immediately found, the press shouted that the government had deliberately lied in order to encourage Iraqi defections. Later, after it was no longer news, it turned out that six "Iraqi" helicopters had indeed flown into Saudi Arabia, but they were in fact American helicopters camouflaged to look like Iraqis, returning from a spy mission.[11]

## Sound Bites and Photo Ops

Gulf war public relations made use of the same techniques that had been so successful in the last presidential election campaign. In the 1988 campaign, the two major candidates, George Bush and Michael Dukakis, both followed a strategy of limiting access by the press to the candidates. Few spontaneous interviews of the candidates were granted to reporters. Tough questions about taxes, government spending, a declining economy, and other hard issues, were never dealt with.

Instead, reporters were allowed to cover carefully prepared and rehearsed speeches. The speeches were written so they would contain pithy statements of the kind that television uses for a "sound bite," a 20- and 30-second snippet of the candidate saying something that sounded important and meaningful for the evening TV news. And newspapers had to settle for these same concocted quotes.

In addition, the candidates would arrange for photo sessions with media photographers and cameramen, carefully staged to convey the proper image to deal with the current problem on the front page or the evening news. Thus, when Dukakis was attacked as a man who had little experience managing a major nation or knew nothing about defense and war, his handlers arranged a "photo op" showing the candidate riding in an army tank. This one backfired, but the sound bite and photo op campaign in general was a public relations success.

These same strategies were brought to the public relations of "Desert Storm." In many ways, this was the world's first war based on sound bites and photo opportunities. What we read were the carefully chosen words and what we saw were the carefully selected images, sanitized of blood and gore and death and destruction.

Almost every television news show every day carried pictures of the sleek instruments of war, silver jet fighters, bombers floating through the air like hawks playing a summer breeze, powerful tanks treading through the desert sands. One had to view all this with a mixture of pride and awe and admiration.

The fighting men who got on television were also orchestrated to present the best possible side of the war. When pilots returned from a bombing mission, we got thirty seconds of handsome young men standing in front of their airplanes, and the quotes we heard over and over again were sound bites of about how exhilarated they were, how easy it had been for them to score, how victory was in their grasp. The war was reported as if it were a sporting event and these key players were caught by TV for a few moments during a time-out in the game, a break in the action.

No hard questions were ever asked, or at least the answers were never shown on TV.

Television was allowed frequently to show us the video pictures taken by the cameras in noses of smart bombs. A whole nation watched mesmerized, looking at targets coming into view on the screen and then seeing the explosion. But, naturally, no more pictures followed; the camera was blown up together with the smart bomb and of course the target. The death and destruction that occurred were never shown. At least not until Saddam gave the world some other kinds of pictures. But we'll come back to that later.

## Community Relations and Employee Relations

The American military did not deal exclusively with the press in Riyadh and Washington in the conduct of its public relations campaign. They properly realized that there were many publics which had to be served. One of these publics was their own troops—soldiers, sailors, airmen and women, and marines who have opinions that need to be informed, influenced, changed, or at least neutralized.

The military has long provided its own employee media—newspapers, magazines, and broadcasts—for troops serving abroad. One of the first things the Americans did was to establish a radio station in Saudi Arabia for its troops, later TV and print media as well. Every navy ship had its own internal closed circuit TV system for information and entertainment.

All of the military people had families back home, and those families help to form opinions. So the military had elaborate home port and hometown news operations. Whenever anything happened to a member of the military—new assignment, special duty, commendation, battle action, or whatever—a news release was generated by computer and targeted at the home port or hometown media of the person involved. Although these releases were not apt to be used by large daily newspapers or major television stations, they were widely picked up by small town dailies and weeklies and local radio.[12]

Most of the personnel in the American military today are older than they were in World War II, Korea, or Vietnam. They are all volunteers, not draftees. They are in the military by their choice, are more professional, and most have families. The military has taken a strong stand on having an effective family relations program as one way to maintain loyalty and well-being of its employees.

## Public Relations and the Other Side

The Americans were not only concerned with communicating their message to the citizens and their soldiers. They also sent many messages, directly and indirectly, to the rest of the world and especially to the Iraqis. Sometimes those messages literally fell from the sky. We not only dropped bombs, but also hundreds of thousands of leaflets, in Arabic, urging the Iraqis to give up, to defect, to turn their backs on Saddam. Unfortunately, when an American reporter asked to see some of these leaflets, he was told that they were classified as secret. Just why wasn't he told? Certainly the enemy knew all about them.[13] Who was the potential enemy from whom these secrets must be kept? Could it have been the people back home, who might have destabilized the situation if they had known about these leaflets?

The Allies, of course, were not alone in using information and communication as a weapon in the war. Saddam Hussein thought of himself as a great communicator, too. He had the ability to have a commanding presence on television and often used it to his advantage. He liked to perform to the camera. And he understood the dynamics of using public relations on the American public.

After the August invasion, Iraq allowed more than 1,800 journalists from all over the world to work out of Baghdad.[14] Early in the crisis, Saddam got considerable sympathetic coverage. When he was holding hostages from Kuwait in

Baghdad, he frequently posed on television with small children of the hostage families. He appeared to be a benign grandfather, patting the children on the head, holding them on his knee. He conducted a well-orchestrated campaign to show himself to be a champion of the Arabs and a victim of unfair U.S. aggression. His army was presented as a formidable, perhaps unbeatable force.

A producer for a U.S. television network said, "It's obvious why they let [foreign reporters] in. It's like when ABC correspondent Sam Donaldson did a piece that really creamed former President Ronald Reagan, and the next day Reagan shook his hand. People don't listen to the words. They see the images, and these guys in Baghdad realize that."[15]

That statement was echoed by an Iraqi official, Sa'doun al Janabi. "We know the Western media, and we know something about what they want, so we try to give it to them. We decided to be open, to answer questions, to tell the truth." Janabi serves as public relations director for the Iraqi Ministry of Information. He speaks fluent English, and from August to February, he held court each day with the hordes of Western reporters who came to his ministry for information. He also carefully monitored the Western coverage coming out of Iraq. At one point, Saddam Hussein was quoted as saying, "We watch CNN, too."[16]

Saddam's biggest public relations coup came when the Allies dropped a smart bomb on a bunker near Baghdad, thinking it was a military operation. But in fact it had been a bomb shelter for families, resulting in the killing and maiming of dozens of women and children. The world's TV cameras were brought to the scene as the bodies were removed from the smoking wreckage, and this became world news.

## War as a Political Campaign

What is interesting about the recent war is the extent to which it was conducted as a political campaign. Five of eight of President Bush's closest advisors on the war had played major roles in Republican presidential campaigns over the past fifteen years. One of these senior officials told the *Washington Post* that, in the war, they used "the same basic tenets that would be used in managing the closing weeks of an intensely fought presidential campaign."[17] The President and his key advisors all used the language of politics in arguing how answers to Baghdad should be framed and timed. This is what they advised:

> You answer everything quickly and aggressively, put no trust in your opponent, and prevent him from ever gaining the initiative.[18]

They were not talking about the battlefield here; they were talking about the war of words, even though it might sound like military actions. In an age of almost instant communication, it is widely accepted in political campaign circles that charges by opponents must be answered within a few hours, or the charge becomes the dominant and unanswered news story for the better part of a day.

So for example, when the Soviets announced that Iraq had agreed to "unconditional" withdrawal, the White House quickly indicated Bush had serious reservations. Three hours later, officials concluded they needed a more definitive answer to the Soviet initiative and began planning for the next day's announcement of a deadline and demands, and they began putting out the word that the Soviet plan was "unacceptable," lest it remain unchallenged and would begin to gain momentum in Europe, where it was already daytime.

John Sununu, White House Chief of Staff, told the *Washington Post*, "There is an old political maxim that you can't beat somebody with nobody. In the same way, you can't beat a bad plan with no plan. And the President had a real sense—and others did—that we had to put out our plan, our requirements, quickly so the two could be compared. You could not allow the Soviet plan to be the only one in the public domain."[19]

On the last Monday night of the war, when Baghdad Radio reported that Saddam had finally ordered a withdrawal of his troops from Kuwait, the White House immediately put out a statement that "the war would go on." The officials needed to make that clear while the early evening television news programs were still on. An even harsher statement followed for the late evening TV news. As one official said, "We did not want the Baghdad Radio report to hang out [unanswered] for 10 or 12 hours."[20]

## The End Game

In the end, the Iraqis lost both the military war and the media war. From my point of view, they were not good enough at either. One of Saddam's biggest public relations gaffes of the war was his last minute threat that this would be "the mother of all wars," perhaps the hollowest and flakiest bit of hype since Adolph Hitler's boast of a super race, proving once again that words have to match reality to be effective as public relations weapons.

It must be said, although I haven't said it yet, that words alone will not win a war. All the best public relations in the world may not overcome smart bombs, sophisticated weaponry, and highly trained professional military. But, on the other hand, those weapons alone might no longer win it, either.

We live in a world today where people's opinions count, because they can get translated into action. We also live in a world where the means of communication have become as sophisticated as the means of war. We have "smart media" that can deliver messages to target audiences across local, regional, and national boundaries, across racial, ethnic, and cultural barriers. Unless governments take these developments into consideration, they will fail in exercising the leadership that de Tocqueville found missing in the democratic United States in the early nineteenth century.

The effective use of words and media today, in times of crisis, is just as important as the effective use of bullets and bombs. In the end, it is no longer enough just to be strong. Now it is necessary to communicate. To win a war today, government not only has to win on the battlefield; it must also win the minds of its publics. Or, put in another way, when the government has to win, it also has to explain *why* it has to win. Stability, continuity, and even victory in the long run will only come when both action and communication are effective. The war in the Gulf has just given us a case in point. It may well be a scenario for all future wars to come.

## NOTES

1. Alexis de Tocqueville, *Democracy in America,* Bradley ed. (Anchor Books, 1945), first published in 1835.
2. The best simple definition of public relations comes from two leading current practioners, Stan Sauerhaft and Chris Atkins, in their book *Image Wars: Protecting Your Company When There's No Place to Hide* (John Wiley & Sons, 1989, p. 13), i.e., "Public relations is the art and science of creating, altering, strengthening, or overcoming public opinion."
3. Sydney H. Schanberg, "Censoring for Political Security," *Washington Journalism Review,* March 1991, p. 24.
4. Ibid.
5. Interview with Juan Walte, Pentagon correspondent for *USA Today,* March 13, 1991.
6. Ibid.
7. *Time,* March 11, 1991, p. 58.
8. Interview with Gordon Peterson, Deputy Chief of Information, U.S. Navy, March 11, 1991.
9. *Time,* March 11, 1991, p. 56.
10. Interview with Juan Walte, op. cit.
11. Ibid.
12. Interview with Gordon Peterson, op. cit.
13. Interview with Juan Walte, op. cit.
14. *Virginia Pilot and Ledger Star,* December 30, 1990, p. A9.
15. Ibid.
16. Ibid.
17. *The Washington Post,* February 27, 1991, p. A27.
18. Ibid.
19. Ibid.
20. Ibid.

# 52

# The Pentagon Position on Mass Media

## *by* Pete Williams

---

*Editor's Note:* Whereas the previous article raises some of the issues that might concern a journalist, it is only fair and appropriate to give the government's point of view as well.

This article is the statement made by Pete Williams, the assistant secretary of defense for public affairs. It was given during hearings on the Persian Gulf war conducted by the Committee on Governmental Affairs in the U.S. Senate on February 20, 1991.

---

Some of the most enduring news reports during World War II came from Edward R. Murrow, who stood on a London rooftop and reported the German bombing raids. Fifty years later, Americans watched reporters on the rooftops of hotels in Riyadh and Dhahran—and their colleagues with gas masks on in Tel Aviv—describing incoming Scud missile attacks from Iraq.

It was the writer Henry Tomlinson who said, "The war the generals always get ready for is the previous one." The same might be said of journalists: the coverage arrangements for military operations in the Persian Gulf are frequently compared to what's remembered from Vietnam, Korea, or World War II.

But Edward R. Murrow's proposal to talk without a script so concerned the military that he had to record a series of trial runs on phonograph discs. He submitted them for approval, but they were lost. So he had to record six more before he persuaded the authorities that he could speak off the cuff without violating the censorship rules. Today, Arthur Kent, Sam Donaldson, Eric Engberg, and Charles Jaco can describe what they see—and show it on television—with no military censorship of any kind. And there are two other notable differences: they are live, and, at least in the case of CNN, their reports can be seen by the commanders of enemy forces just as easily as they can be seen by American viewers at home in their living rooms.

Operation Desert Storm isn't taking place in the jungles of Vietnam, or the hills of Korea, or across the continents and oceans of World War II. The campaign on the Arabian Peninsula has been designed to get a specific and unique job done. The press arrangements are also suited to the peculiar conditions there. But our goal is the same as those of our predecessors—to get as much information as possible to the American people about their military without jeopardizing the lives of the troops or the success of the operation.

## Origin of the Persian Gulf Press Arrangements

Saddam Hussein stunned the world when his troops rolled across the northern border of Kuwait last August 2nd. Within five hours, his army had taken Kuwait City. And from that day forward, the number of Iraqi troops in occupied Kuwait continued to grow and to move south, stopping only at Kuwait's southern border with Saudi Arabia.

That weekend, August 5th, President Bush sent [Defense] Secretary Cheney to Saudi Arabia for discussions with King Fahd on how best to defend Saudi Arabia and the stability of the Persian Gulf. As history now knows, the first US forces began to arrive a few days after their meeting, joining US Navy ships already in the region. On Wednesday, as the first US Air Force F-15's landed on sovereign Saudi territory, there were no western reporters in the Kingdom. We urged the Saudi government to begin granting visas to US news organizations, so that reporters could cover the arrival of the US military.

On Friday of that week, Secretary Cheney again called Prince Bandar, the Saudi Ambassador to the United States, to inquire about the progress for issuing visas. Prince Bandar said the Saudis were studying the question but agreed in the meantime to accept a pool of US reporters if the US military could get them in. So we activated the DOD National Media Pool, a structure that had been in use since 1985.

## The National Media Pool

The pool was set up after the 1983 US military operation in Grenada. While Grenada was a military success, it was a journalistic disaster, because reporters were kept off the island until the fighting was over. So a retired army major general, Winant Sidle, from whom this committee will hear later today, was asked to head up a panel of military officers and journalists to work out a plan for news coverage of future military operations. The result of their work was the Department of Defense National Media Pool, a rotating list of correspondents, photographers, and technicians who could be called up on short notice to cover the early stages of military missions.

It was this pool that covered the US Navy's escort of oil tankers in the Persian Gulf in 1987. Its first big test in ground combat came in December of 1989, during Operation Just Cause in Panama. Just Cause was a mixed success for the pool. It arrived within four hours of when the shooting started, but it took too long to get reporters to the scene of the action. I think we learned some important lessons from what happened in Panama, and we've applied them to what's going on in the Gulf.

The true purpose of the National Media Pool is to enable reporters to cover the earliest possible action of a US military operation in a remote area where there is no other presence of the American press, while still protecting the element of surprise—an essential part of what military people call operational security. Of course, Operation Desert Shield was no secret. The President made a public announcement that he was ordering US forces to the Gulf. But because there were no western reporters in Saudi Arabia, we flew in the DOD media pool.

## First Reporters Came on the DOD Pool

We moved quickly, once we received permission from the Saudi government on Friday, August 10th. We notified the news organizations in the pool rotation that Friday night. They brought in their passports Saturday morning, and I took them to the Saudi embassy myself that afternoon, where the appropriate staff has been brought in to issue the necessary visas. One reporter had run out of pages in his passport, so we carried it across town so that the State Department could add some more.

The pool left Andrews Air Force base early Sunday morning, August 12th, stopping off to see the US Central Command operation in Tampa, Florida. The reporters interviewed General Schwarzkopf, who had not yet moved his headquarters to Riyadh. So the press pool got to Saudi Arabia before the commander of the operation had even set up shop there. The reporters arrived Monday afternoon, August 13th, and continued to act as a pool until August 26th. After the pool began filing its reports, the Saudis started to issue visas to other reporters. But the news organizations in the Pentagon pool asked that we keep it going until the visa picture cleared up.

Jay Peterzell was Time Magazine's representative on the pool. Afterward, he wrote this: "The Pentagon people worked hard to keep the press in the country." And he offered this assessment:

> The pool did give US journalists a way of getting into Saudi Arabia and seeing at least part of what was going on at a time when there was no other way of doing either of those things. Also, in the first two weeks after the wave of TV, newspaper, and magazine correspondents flooded into the country, they did not produce any story that was essentially different from what we in the pool had filed.

Starting with those initial 17—representing AP, UPI, Reuters, CNN, National Public Radio, Time, Scripps-Howard, the Los Angeles Times, and the Milwaukee Journal—the number of reporters, editors, photographers, producers, and technicians grew to nearly 800 by December. Except during the first two weeks of the pool, those reporters all filed their stories independently, directly to their own news organizations. They visited ships at sea, air bases,

Marines up north, and soldiers training in the desert. They went aboard AWACS radar warning planes. They quoted generals who said their forces were ready and privates who said they were not. They wrote about helicopter pilots crashing into the sand, because they couldn't judge distances in the flat desert light. And reporters described the remarkable speed with which the US military moved so many men and women to the Gulf with so much of their equipment.

## Planning for Combat Coverage

The mission given US forces in Operation Desert Shield was to deter further aggression from Iraq and to defend Saudi Arabia if deterrence failed. After the President in mid November announced a further buildup in US forces, to give the coalition a true offensive option, my office began working on a plan that would allow reporters to cover combat while maintaining the operational security necessary to assure tactical surprise and save American lives.

One of the first concerns of news organizations in the Pentagon press corps was that they did not have enough staff in the Persian Gulf to cover hostilities. Since they did not know how the Saudi government would respond to their request for more visas, and since they couldn't predict what restrictions might be imposed on commercial air traffic in the event of a war, they asked us whether we'd be willing to use a military plane to take in a group of reporters to act as journalistic reinforcements. We agreed to do so.

A US Air Force C-141 cargo plane left Andrews Air Force base on January 17th, the morning after the bombing began, with 127 news media personnel on board. That plane left at the onset of hostilities, during the most intensive airlift since the Berlin blockade. The fact that senior military commanders dedicated one of their cargo airplanes to the job of transporting another 127 journalists to Saudi Arabia demonstrated the military's commitment to take reporters to the scene of the action so they could get the story out to the American people.

The plan for combat coverage was not drawn up in a vacuum. We worked closely with the military and with the news media to develop a plan that would meet the needs of both. We had several meetings at the Pentagon with the bureau chiefs of the Pentagon press corps. We talked with the reporters who cover the military regularly. And we consulted with some of the people you'll hear from later today—General Sidle and Mr. Hoffman—and several of my predecessors in the public affairs office at the Pentagon. Because an important part of our planning was working with the news media, our drafts and proposals frequently became public. We did our planning in Macy's window, which meant that our false starts and stumbles were in full view.

## Safeguarding Military Security

The main concern of the military is that information not be published which would jeopardize a military operation or endanger the lives of the troops who must carry it out. The preamble to the rules of reporters covering World War II summarized the issue by saying that editors, in wondering what can be published, should ask themselves, "Is this information I would like to have if I were the enemy?"

In formulating the ground rules and guidelines for covering Operation Desert Storm, we looked at the rules developed in 1942 for World War II, at those handed down by General Eisenhower's chief of staff for the reporters who covered the D-Day landings, and at the ground rules established by General MacArthur for covering the Korean war. We carefully studied the rules drawn up for covering the war in Vietnam.

The rules are not intended to prevent journalists from reporting on incidents that might embarrass the military or to make military operations look sanitized. Instead, they are intended to prevent publication of details that could jeopardize a military operation or endanger the lives of US troops.

Some of the things that must not be reported are:

- Details of future operations,
- Specific information about troop strengths or locations,
- While a specific operation is underway, the details of troop movements or tactics,
- Specific information on missing or downed airplanes or ships while search and rescue operations are underway, and
- Information on operational weaknesses that could be used against US forces.

American reporters understand the reasoning behind these ground rules. They are patriotic citizens, and they don't want anything they write to endanger lives. The ground rules are the least controversial aspect of the coverage plan for the war in the Persian Gulf. Mr. Chairman, I'd like to ask that a copy of the ground rules and the guidelines be inserted at this point in the record.

## The Ground Rule Appeal Process

The reporters covering World War II wrote their stories and submitted them to a military censor. The censors cut out anything they felt broke the rules and sent the stories on. The decisions of the censors were final. There is no such system of censorship in Operation Desert Storm. There is, instead, a procedure that allows us to appeal to news organizations—before the harm is done—when we think material in their stories would violate the ground rules. And the final decisions belong to journalists.

Stories written by reporters who are out with troops in the field are reviewed by military public affairs officers to ensure troop safety and operational security, then sent on to the press center in Dhahran, Saudi Arabia for release. If, after talking things over with the reporter, the field public affairs officer believes information in a story violates the ground rules, public affairs officers at the press center review it before release. If they, too, believe the story would break the ground rules, they appeal it to us at the Pentagon for our opinion.

If we, too, think there's a problem, we call bureau chiefs or editors stateside and discuss the story with them. We understand that news must move quickly, and we act as fast as we can. Our appeal process is intended only to allow us to discuss potential ground rule violations with editors and bureau chiefs and to remind them of the need to protect sensitive information. But unlike a system of censorship, the system now in place leaves the final decision to publish or broadcast in the hands of journalists, not the military.

Since Operation Desert Storm began on January 16th, over 820 print pool reports have been written. Of those, only five have been submitted for our review in Washington. We quickly cleared four of them. The fifth appeal came to us over the weekend, involving a story that dealt in considerable detail with the methods of intelligence operations in the field. We called the reporter's editor-in-chief, and he agreed that the story should be changed to protect sensitive intelligence procedures. This aspect of the coverage plan is also working well.

Only the pool stories, from reporters in the field, are subject to this review, not live television and radio reports or the thousands of other stories written in Dhahran and Riyadh, based on pool reports, original reporting, and the military briefings.

## Getting Access to the Troops

As the number of troops in the desert grew, so did the number of reporters to cover them. The US and international press corps went from zero on August 2nd, to 17 on the first pool, rising to 800 by December. Most of those reporters, the good ones anyway, want to be out where the action is, just as they've done in previous conflicts. But with hundreds of fiercely independent reporters seeking to join up with combat units, we concluded that when the combat started, we'd have to rely on pools.

Before the air phase of the operation began a month ago, news organizations were afraid that we wouldn't get the job done. They reminded us of their experience in Panama. But as viewers, readers, and listeners know, we had the pools in place before the operation started. Reporters were on an aircraft carrier in the Red Sea to witness the launching of air strikes, onboard a battleship in the Persian Gulf that fired the first cruise missiles ever used in combat, on the air force bases where the fighter planes and bombers were taking off around the clock, and with several ground units in the desert.

Carl Rochelle of CNN was asked on the air if he felt he had been allowed access to everything he wanted onboard the ships, and he said, "I must tell you I am more satisfied with the pool shoot I just came off than any of the others I've been on." Four days into the air campaign, Molly Moore of the Washington Post said, "It's gone a lot smoother than any of us thought."

Those first days were not without problems. We know of cases where stories were approved in the field only to be delayed for over a day on their trip back to the press center in Dhahran. The first stories written about the stealth fighters were, for some reason, sent all the way back to the F-117's home base in Nevada to be cleared. I'm sure some of the reporters you'll hear from later today will have examples of their own.

The biggest complaint from journalists right now is that more of them want to get out into the field. They are worried about how much access they'll have to the Army and the Marines in the event the President decides to proceed with the next phase of the campaign, intensifying action on the ground. And here's where the contrasts with World War II and Vietnam are especially strong.

## Access to the Ground Troops

Unlike World War II, this will not be an operation in which reporters can ride around in jeeps going from one part of the front to another, or like Vietnam where reporters could hop a helicopter to specific points of action. If a ground war begins on the Arabian Peninsula, the battlefield will be chaotic and the action will be violent. This will be modern, intense warfare. Reporters at the front will have to be in armored vehicles or on helicopters. They'll have to carry their own gas masks and chemical protective suits along with all their other gear. Those with front line troops will be part of a highly mobile operation. It will be deadly serious business, and our front line units simply will not have the capacity to accommodate large numbers of reporters.

To cover the conflict, reporters will have to be part of a unit, able to move with it. Each commander has an assigned number of vehicles with only so many seats. While he can take care of the reporters he knows are coming, he cannot keep absorbing those who arrive on their own, unexpectedly, in their own rented four wheel drives. The pool system allows us to tell the divisional commanders how many reporters they'll be responsible for. And the reporters in these pools are allowed to stay with the military units they're covering, learning as much as they can about the unit's plans and tactics.

Our latest count shows that over 1400 reporters, editors, producers, photographers, and technicians are now registered with the joint information bureaus in Dhahran and Riyadh, representing the US and the international press. Not all of them want to go to the front. But more want to go than we can possibly accommodate. That's why we've had to rely on pools of reporters—rotating groups whose stories and pictures are available to all.

Of course, the ground war hasn't started yet. US military units are repositioning, some of them moving nearly every day. And if the ground war does start, it won't be like Vietnam, with minor skirmishes here and there and a major offensive every now and then. It will be a set piece operation, as carefully orchestrated as possible. In this sense, it will be like D-Day. It's useful to remember that 461 reporters were signed up at the Supreme Headquarters, Allied Expeditionary Force to cover D-Day. Of that number, only 27 US reporters actually went ashore with the first wave of forces.

So the situation on the ground in the Arabian Peninsula is a little like the picture before D-Day, with reporters waiting for the action to start. Even so, when Desert Storm began, 43 reporters were already out with ground units, and the number has been growing. By the end of this week, 100 reporters will be with Army units, 33 with the Marines on land, and 18 more will be out with the Marines on amphibious ships. That's in addition to the 19 covering the Navy on ships at sea, the 14 who have been roving around to air bases, covering the Air Force part of the campaign, and eight more covering the medical part of the story. So that's a total of 192 reporters who will be out with combat forces by the end of the week.

## Pools Are a Compromise

The news business is an intensely competitive one. Journalists are accustomed to working on their own. The best are especially independent. In the setup imposed now in the Persian Gulf, each correspondent files a story that becomes available to everyone else. Pools rub reporters the wrong way, but there is simply no way for us to open up a rapidly moving front to reporters who roam the battlefield. We believe the pool system does three things: it gets reporters out to see the action, it guarantees that Americans at home get reports from the scene of the action, and it allows the military to accommodate a reasonable number of journalists without overwhelming the units that are fighting the enemy.

The system we have now in Operation Desert Storm—with two briefings a day in Riyadh and one in the Pentagon, pools of reporters out with the troops, a set of clear ground rules, and a procedure of ground rule appeal—is intended to permit the most open possible coverage of a new kind of warfare. When it's all over, we very much want to sit down with representatives of the military and the news media to see how well it worked and how it might be improved.

I cannot deny that there have been problems. I know reporters are frustrated that they can't all get out to see the troops. But I believe the system we have now is fair, that it gets a reasonable number of journalists out to see the action, and that the American people will get the accounting they deserve of what their husbands and wives, and sons and daughters, are doing under arms half a world away.

When reporters arrived at General Eisenhower's headquarters in 1944, they were handed a book called *Regulations for War Correspondents*. In the foreword, he spelled out in three sentences the logic for the kind of system I've described to you today. Here's what he said to those journalists: "The first essential in military operations is that no information of value should be given to the enemy. The first essential in newspaper work and broadcasting is wide-open publicity. It is your job and mine to try to reconcile these sometimes diverse considerations."

# 53

# TV and Ankara's War for Central Asia

## *by* Blaine Harden

*Editor's Note:* Whereas all mass media have become weapons of war, the biggest weapon of all is television. "Without television you cannot have a war," wrote an Israeli minister of information in an earlier edition of this book. Since Vietnam, every country has realized the importance of having television on its side in any conflict, at any cost.

Here is yet another example of how this principle is working in international politics, in this case in Turkey and Central Asia. Blaine Harden is a reporter for the Washington Post Service. This story was published in the *International Herald Tribune,* March 24, 1992.

Turkey will play its trump card next week in a 1990s version of what British secret agents once termed the Great Game—the contest for hearts and minds, as well as political influence and market share, in Central Asia.

The Turkish card is satellite television. On April 1, according to Turkish state television officials, switches will be thrown in the six Muslim republics of the former Soviet Union. A Moscow TV channel that for decades has broadcast a Russian-language, Soviet-slanted view of the world will go off the air.

In its place, via the Intelsat VI satellite orbiting above the Indian Ocean, Turkish television plans to begin testing a signal that has the potential to mesmerize an expanse of the former Soviet empire that is isolated but rich in resources.

Suddenly, there will be 83 hours a week of Turkish-language news, entertainment and cultural programs. When the bugs are worked out, probably by mid-April, Turkish television expects to have about 57 million new viewers stretching from the ethnic battlefields of Azerbaijan to the oil-rich steppes of Kazakhstan.

As many as one-third of the programs will be in simplified Turkish, assessed to be comprehensible to an audience that speaks a variety of Turkic dialects. It is an audience that for more than 70 years was prevented from traveling to Turkey and was sealed off from the capitalist ways of its Western kin.

"The peoples of this region have been slaves for more than 70 years," Prime Minister Suleyman Demirel of Turkey said. "But in a couple of weeks, we will be there."

"We know the value of communication," he added.

The first programs will introduce Central Asian viewers to what they have been missing and what they might want to emulate—the Turkish model of Muslims looking to the West.

Turkey's 57 million people, whose ancestors migrated from Central Asia more than 700 years ago, would like nothing better than to lead their Turkic cousins to the capitalist promised land—while skimming off a percentage for themselves.

Mr. Demirel's government wasted no time after the collapse of the Soviet Union in December. It has signed economic protocols and opened embassies in every republic. President Turgut Ozal is the only foreign head of state to have toured the region.

Turkey is not the only major competitor in the Great Game. Iran has been busy dispatching mullahs, mosque-builders, diplomats and traders across Central Asia. Tehran is sweetening business deals with grants for schools and mixing it all with heavy doses of Islamic fundamentalism.

Saudi Arabia, too, is a player. It is estimated to have invested more than $1 billion in the region, much of it on Islamic-studies centers and efforts to promulgate Arabic.

The knockout punch in the contest for influence could prove to be which alphabet, Latin or Arabic, finds its way into everyday usage. An alphabet secures the moorings of intellectual, economic and cultural life, and for most of this century the region has been forcibly tied to Russian Cyrillic. But like communism itself, Cyrillic no longer makes sense in Central Asia.

Thanks to the satellite feed and agreements that Ankara has secured with all the Muslim republics for local broadcast, Turkey has the edge in the alphabet war. For three hours each weekday and nine hours on Saturday and Sunday, Turkish television plans to run Latin-alphabet subtitles with its programs.

"We will use subtitles for one year or maybe more, until they purify their language of Russian and Farsi words," said Sedat Orsel, deputy director-general of Turkish television.

One of the first hurdles in setting up the satellite system was securing broadcast agreements from government officials in the six Muslim republics. To make these arrangements, the Turks moved quietly.

"We did not want the Iranians to know what we are doing," said Muzaffer Baca, a producer for television news in Ankara. "They also are trying to get satellite TV. If this would have been widely known, then I think the Iranians would have offered large bribes to ministers in the republics to keep us out. They know that Turkish and Western television programs will hurt their religion."

While Turkish leaders are eager to boast about the new reach of state television, they vehemently insist that it is not part of a plan to carve a new zone of influence out of Central Asia.

"We are not Pan-Turkist," Mr. Demurel said in an interview last week. "All we want is that these countries should be standing on their own feet.

"In the last 1,000 years, the people of Central Asia have never gathered under one government. Let us have several governments, and having the same culture, the same language, then all of us are happy."

At Turkish television, there is less reticence about explaining the possible implications of the satellite connection.

"This television will be a terrible and extraordinary event," said Mr. Baca. "Those people are so hungry for information, for anything Turkish or from the West."

"Television is the most important victory Turkey could have," he added. "It could be said that it is the foundation for a Turkish commonwealth."

# 54

## Somalia's Invasion by the Media

### *by* Storer H. Rowley

*Editor's Note:* When American military forces moved into Somalia as part of a humanitarian campaign to get food to starving people, the invasion by the news media was almost as big as the invasion by the marines.

War has become a media circus, partly because violent action, especially in a far-off exotic setting, makes compelling television. And where television goes, the other media are sure to follow.

Storer H. Rowley is a reporter for the *Chicago Tribune,* where this article was published on February 7, 1993.

On marine patrol in the streets of Mogadishu, the radio crackled to life inside the column's command vehicle: "Downtown Six! Downtown Six!"

Capt. Bob Castellvi diverted his Humvees (the military's new Jeep) and armored vehicles to a private house where an American had just received death threats and needed protection.

"It's probably some [spy] or a State Department type," mused Castellvi, 30, of Bolingbrook, as he wheeled his light armored vehicle into action near the U.S. Embassy.

The mystery house turned out to be a compound rented by ABC-TV. The complaint was made by "Nightline" host Ted Koppel. The man in danger was Said Samatar, a Somali-born professor of African history from Rutgers University whom ABC had hired as a consultant.

Samatar, Koppel and a camera crew piled into Castellvi's armored vehicle, which was getting crowded. It might have been a metaphor for the media offensive in Somalia.

"Who are you?" demanded Koppel, when he saw another passenger taking notes, wedged in among the Marines in the crew.

"I'm from the Chicago Tribune. I'm spending the day with these Marines. Some of them are from Chicago. I can't believe this. Media people are falling all over each other on this story. You can't even go on a secret rescue mission without stumbling into other reporters."

Koppel smiled in agreement. Then he interviewed the Chicago reporter to that effect on camera. Then the reporter interviewed Koppel about his endangered consultant, who sat sheepishly on an ammunition crate as the windowless vehicle rumbled along.

"A high-level source in Somalia, someone whose word we trust, told us this man's life had been threatened, and we are taking it seriously," Koppel said. So ABC had called the Marines.

"I'm not surprised by this," Samatar said when he, in turn, was interviewed. "I've been threatened in the past.

"When I was in the States and so distant from this civil war, I could pretty much say and write what I wanted. But not here," Samatar said, fingering his suitcase nervously en route to Mogadishu International Airport and a secure flight home to the Rutgers campus in Newark, N.J.

In this civil war-ravaged country where more than 300,000 people have starved to death, hundreds of reporters were on hand to cover the mercy mission of thousands of foreign soldiers trying to provide security and food relief in Operation Restore Hope.

## A Study in Excess

After the first month, the bulk of them gave up on the story and moved on. Most pulled out after President George Bush's New Year's visit, but only after astonishing a starved and strapped Somalia with excess.

They shone TV lights in the camouflage-streaked faces of Marines hitting the beaches. They brought noisy electrical generators and erected a forest of satellite dishes on the roof of a makeshift hotel. They rented houses, chartered airplanes, sent in their most senior anchors and spent millions of dollars on coverage as sporadic clan gunfire rattled the nation.

"The first casualty was [journalists'] pride," opined an American network correspondent after throngs of unruly reporters and camera crews practically prompted Marine fire during the U.S. landings Dec. 9.

Koppel, Dan Rather of CBS and Christiane Amanpour of CNN were among those doing standups from the roof of the Mogadishu airport terminal as Marines splashed ashore in the background.

Tom Brokaw and NBC had taken over much of the space at the only functioning hotel in Mogadishu, a three-story building with 58 rooms dubbed the Sahafi ("journalist" in Arabic) Hotel by its enterprising Somali owner, Mohamed Jirdeh Hussein.

From its rooftop, wide microwave dishes yawned skyward toward satellites over the Indian Ocean. Primitive refugee huts covered with green plastic climbed a nearby hillside, forming a poignant backdrop for TV reports, along with the gunfire.

The distinctive stench of the dead, buried in shallow graves that marched sadly down the slope, wafted daily over the dusty road toward the hotel, suspended in the searing equatorial air.

## The Media Settle in

Each night, Brokaw and NBC staff members would march busily back and forth along a hotel corridor where Liz Sly, the Tribune's Africa correspondent, sat cross-legged on the floor typing her dispatches. A veteran of the foreign press corps in Somalia, Sly was forced out of her room by persistent power surges that tended to blow up anything plugged into the outlets.

In addition to Sly, the Tribune dispatched a succession of reporters to cover Somalia, including military affairs correspondent David Evans, Latin America correspondent Gary Marx and senior Moscow correspondent Howard Witt, an old Africa hand. Each took his turn venturing into Mogadishu's anarchy and Somalia's famine-stricken interior from their base at the Sahafi.

Up the street, inside a walled compound, CBS had the rarest of things in Somalia: an air-conditioned suite of offices. It was converted to a bureau and packed with food, fruit, supplies and equipment. CBS reportedly put down a $17,000 deposit for the house. The New York Times paid $12,000 for one month's rent for another house.

Farther on was the spacious ABC operation, another group of buildings in a compound guarded by a retinue of local Somali employees, not far from the U.S. Embassy. CNN also set up a private, well-stocked, impromptu bureau.

## What Famine?

This media assault on Somalia was among the most bizarre spectacles of the television age, but covering Somalia has generally been an odd experience for journalists for a host of reasons, ranging from the availability of food and supples in a country with seemingly little of both, to the red-carpet treatment given the press by the U.S. military, to the constant dangers of clan looting and robbery, leading journalists to hire armed bodyguards to protect them.

Despite widespread famine, the Sahafi provided meals of all kinds for paying guests, ranging from pasta and salad to rice and meat dishes for lunch or dinner. There were eggs, bread with butter and jam, or rolls with mangoes and coffee at breakfast.

Because the famine was created by warlords hoarding food and controlling its flow to Mogadishu's markets, there was plenty of food for those few who had money.

Most correspondents drank the juices and lemonade put out in pitchers before each meal, risking stomach ailments or worse. Others shared a Katadyn filter pump to purify their tap water, a ritual reserved for rare days when there was water in the pipes.

But the beverage of choice was Scotch whiskey, because it was potent, compact and lighter to carry in by suitcase than wine or beer. By the time midnight rolled around and everyone had filed their stories for the day, Scotch bottles would materialize in some of the rooms, flouting the unenforced Muslim taboo against drinking.

The media grew to depend on resourceful people like hotelier Hussein, who charged by the bed ($85 a night). He could always change dollars quickly into Somali shillings and tell guests where to buy things or get their laundry done in a day—even in chaotic, war-blasted Mogadishu, where there are no banks or cleaners.

In this powerless capital he kept gasoline-powered electrical generators running around the clock to light the hotel. This kept journalists, their laptop computers and their satellite telephones in business when darkness fell everywhere else.

## Military, Media Team Up

Help came from another unusual source for journalists in Somalia: the military.

The media and the military have enjoyed unusually good relations during Operation Restore Hope, especially compared with relations during other recent U.S. combat, from Grenada to Panama to the Persian Gulf.

The military in Somalia was so helpful, harried journalists grew to depend on U.S. troops for occasional rides, rations and refills of canteens and water bottles. Navy medics advised news gatherers on everything from sun block and heat exhaustion to diarrhea and drug-resistant forms of malaria in East Africa. And members of the U.S.-led military contingent occasionally came to the aid of journalists when gangs tried to rob them or, in one instance in Bardera, surrounded their compound.

American forces even allowed journalists to check their guards' guns at the gates when entering a secured base or airport.

Upon leaving, exchanges like this were common:

"Hello, staff sergeant, could I please have the Chicago Tribune's gun? It's a Soviet 7.62 mm pistol with 'CCCP' on the handle. Here's my card."

"Here you go, sir," a Marine would respond, emerging from a guard house with the weapon and the removed ammunition clip. "Please wait until you're outside the perimeter before putting the clip back in."

Normally, any media use of guards with guns would be a topic of hot debate and ethical soul-searching. Most professional foreign correspondents are adamant about never taking sides or carrying weapons. Packing a pistol can give the wrong appearance, as if one has become a combatant.

But such discussions were short-lived in Somalia, where private relief agencies, and even the United Nations, have been operating for months by hiring armed Somali guards.

In unwelcome redistributions of wealth, Western journalists were often forced to donate their gear, cash and personal belongings to gunmen and looters.

And, in at least one case, their own hired hands turned on them.

## Looters' Logic

American Deborah Amos, the London bureau chief for National Public Radio, said that in Baidoa, her bodyguards and drivers turned on her group, seized all of NPR's equipment and extorted $3,500 from NPR and two U.S. newspaper reporters, Amos and Carol Rosenberg of The Miami Herald.

"What happens in Somalia is looters' logic, and it hits them all that sooner or later, they can make more money this way," joked Amos, looking back on her ordeal.

Such incidents convinced journalists of the importance of finding honest bodyguards and other local helpers.

Tribune photographer Chris Walker realized that need when he was accosted one day by two men brandishing AK-47 assault rifles and motioning for him to turn over his cameras. The Tribune's interpreter, Abdul Rahman Abukar, 27, leapt from the paper's car, pulled out his small pistol and made the would-be robbers back down.

But even as Abukar covered the two men with his pistol, another man reached into the car and stole Walker's camera bag. Out sprang the Tribune's driver, Aden Hassan Ali, 20, another honest Somali tired of the looters ruling his country, who struggled with the thief, retrieved the bag and returned it to Walker.

Not everyone survived such acts of bravery. Ali Ibrahim Mursal, 37, chief driver for The Associated Press, was killed Jan. 5 defending three AP staff members in Mogadishu's main market.

When a robber tried to rip a gold chain off the neck of one of the three AP staff members, Mursal jumped on the thief's back. But another thug put the muzzle of an AK-47 in his back and pulled the trigger. Mursal died in surgery hours later at Digfer Hospital, a humid, blood-soaked, foul-smelling place.

Writing in the Jan. 11 APlog, the wire service's in-house publication, veteran war correspondent and East Africa bureau chief Reid Miller sketched out Mursal's life, death and devotion to his beloved, tormented Somalia.

Miller remembered Mursal's remark to AP special correspondent Mort Rosenblum, who had hired him in August, "I told him I was willing to do anything for the AP," Mursal had said.

He did.

# 55

# The Video Vise
# in the Bosnia War

## by Michael Beschloss

*Editor's Note:* As we have seen, to fight a war it is necessary for a democratic government to use the mass media to win public support. But it is
also possible for the mass media to foment public sympathy for a war
and force the government to fight it.

That is the scenario in Bosnia, as described in this article, in the war
among various geographic and ethnic divisions in the former Yugoslavia.
Michael Beschloss is a historian and author, most recently of *At the
Highest Levels* (with Strobe Talbott). This article was adapted from a
report for the Annenberg Washington Program called "Presidents,
Television and Foreign Crises" and published in the *Washington Post,*
May 2, 1993.

Recent experience suggests that the genocidal war in Bosnia will be the latest
example of an overseas crisis in which haunting television pictures arouse the
American people to demand that their government do something. If television
did not exist, such public pressure on President Clinton might not be growing;
Secretary of State Warren Christopher might not be leaving, as he announced
yesterday, to consult with allies on military and other options.

By the same token, one must suspect, in the week after the president dedicated the United States Holocaust Museum, that satellite and video pictures
of Auschwitz and Bergen-Belsen in 1943 and 1944 would have moved Franklin
Roosevelt, with his preternatural sensitivity to mass opinion, toward expanding
U.S. war aims to include the destruction of Nazi concentration camps and the
transport lanes that served them.

The new images from Bosnia demonstrate how television rewards crisis
management over crisis prevention. Had George Bush used U.S. political
and military power to avert the tragedy in Central Europe, he would have
had a difficult time overcoming American resistance to the notion of using
force for abstract aims in a land few people knew. Prompted and abetted
by the television pictures, Bill Clinton will have an easier time explaining why
he is acting, if he does, but will suffer the problems attached to making up for
lost time.

In the world of 1993, it is difficult to imagine the age when television did not occupy so central a place in the U.S. foreign policy process. As recently as 1962, European genocide would not have been so easily graven on the American mind. Pictures of overseas events were aired at least one day after they had occurred. Telstar, the primitive first communications satellite, had only just been launched. Sixteen-millimeter black-and-white film had to be developed, edited and flown to the United States, where it was hastily cut to fit into 11½ minutes of black-and-white evening news. The process was so rushed that viewers sometimes saw water marks and strands of human hair on the film.

In that era, a president of the United States enjoyed far greater influence over public information about foreign events. Consider the effect of television on the Cuban Missile Crisis of October 1962. Of that episode, John F. Kennedy's secretary of defense, Robert S. McNamara, could say, "I don't think I turned on a television set during the whole two weeks of that crisis." It is doubtful that his Bush administration counterpart, Dick Cheney, would say the same thing of the Persian Gulf War.

Throughout the Missile Crisis, Kennedy repeatedly benefited from a cocoon of time and privacy afforded by the absence of intense television scrutiny. When the CIA informed the president of Soviet offensive missiles in Cuba, he knew that he had an enormous political problem: He had just assured the public that there were no such missiles there and that if they appeared, it would cause a confrontation of the first magnitude with the Soviet Union.

As the veteran television newsman Sander Vanocur has said, "Now, in the present atmosphere, you have round-the-clock news. You have the beginning of the week with the Sunday morning shows. Then you have the weekdays that begin with the morning shows on the three networks and on local stations across the country. You end it with local television and 'Nightline.' "

Had the Missile Crisis occurred in the environment of the 1990s, a commercial satellite might have discovered the missiles at roughly the same time the CIA did. The news might have been revealed in a CNN special report, including tape of Kennedy's assurances and pictures of the missiles. On that report and on "Nightline" that evening, angry senators and congressmen would have demanded to know why Kennedy had kept the Soviet outrage a secret from Americans, and called on him to fulfill his pledge by bombing the missile sites immediately.

We now know that had he done so, the act could have quickly led to nuclear war. Instead, benefiting from life in 1962, Kennedy enjoyed six days during which the public was ignorant of the missiles to secretly convene his advisers, deliberate about the matter in quiet and then reveal the problem himself, in his own words, in a way designed to quash hysteria and gain support for his plan of action.

President Johnson presumed that color film of the carnage of Vietnam, aired night after night on newly 30-minute, newly all-color evening news broadcasts, which were gaining more and more millions of viewers, caused Americans to lose their stomach for the war. In 1968, he told the National Association of Broadcasters, "Historians must only guess at the effect that television would have had during earlier conflicts over the future of the nation: during the Korean War, for example, at the time when our forces were pushed back there to Pusan—or when our men were slugging it out in Europe, or when most of our Air Force was shot down on that day in June 1942 off Australia."

Johnson's "lesson" was later cited by President Reagan and his advisers while seeking to ensure that military action in Grenada and Libya was as brief and bloodless (at least on the American side) as possible, and by George Bush and his aides when they did the same thing in Panama, the Persian Gulf and Somalia. Yet, as the scholar Michael Mandelbaum has argued, it is equally plausible that pictures of Americans fighting and dying in Vietnam promoted support for the war by inspiring "the determination to see the way through to a successful conclusion, in order to give meaning to those sacrifices."

In fact, as early as 1969, the networks may have grown slightly bored with Indochina. The percentage of CBS and NBC evening news programs including stories on the war dropped from 85 to 90 percent during 1965–1968 to about 70 percent during the next two years. Determined not to "bug out" of Vietnam, President Nixon was probably aided by his shift in emphasis from the bloody (and photogenic) ground war in Indochina to the more abstract-looking air war, pictures of which were less emotionally provocative. The effect of the distinction between the two sets of images was not lost on military planners under Bush.

Saddam Hussein's invasion of Kuwait in August 1990 showed how far television had come from the epoch of 1962. Had Bush wished to follow Kennedy's example of secret deliberations in quiet, he would have been badly frustrated. Even at a time when the Cold War was ending, the gulf crisis was the story of the year and it monopolized the airwaves. As Richard N. Haass of the Bush National Security Council staff recalled, "We didn't have six minutes in some ways to contemplate [the invasion of Kuwait], and certainly not six hours or six days, if you'll look at the night when we first found out about it and then at every breaking point since then." Paul Wolfowitz, undersecretary of defense in the Bush administration, noted that Saddam's assault was "the first time in history that we had live coverage of a surprise attack."

While planning the Gulf War, Wolfowitz found his colleagues concerned that "you really have to get something like this over with quickly. . . . Perhaps the people thinking this were thinking, and sometimes they would say it, of what the effect of weeks and weeks of television coverage of bombing would do to support for the [anti-Saddam] coalition." Michael Janeway, dean of the Medill School of Journalism, felt that in the Gulf War, the Bush administration was singularly blessed by dealing with a media that was "very conscious of the Vietnam experience. It was conscious of having been the unwelcome messenger. . . . We must question what would have happened if the war had gone on longer, had casualties come more into play . . . if there had come to be many more questions about whether this was a just war or not."

In 1982, during the Israeli invasion of Lebanon, Ronald Reagan had been so disturbed by television pictures of the destruction that he telephoned the Israeli prime minister, Menachem Begin, to demand a halt to the bombing. (As it happened, Begin had already ordered the bombing stopped several hours earlier.) Bush would have scoffed at such "emotionalism." It is unlikely that at the start of the gulf conflict, he imagined that the war's endgame would be influenced by television pictures of the "highway of death" and other suffering by Kurds in northern Iraq, and Shiites in southern Iraq, of hundreds of thousands of people who were likely to start dying if nothing were done.

Bush's efforts to relieve that suffering foreshadowed his final foreign policy exercise—after the 1992 election, when he responded to the outrage of the American public over television pictures of the Somalian famine by sending U.S. troops to ensure that domestic turmoil would not prevent food and other supplies from going where they were needed. Bush declined to do the same thing in Bosnia. For this he was badly criticized by candidate Bill Clinton, who found the crisis waiting for him when he entered the Oval Office.

In the modern age, television can not only generate pressures on presidents for foreign intervention or for staying out of a crisis; it offers those presidents a superior weapon for framing issues and selling White House policy. It also amplifies public opposition, which, although most presidents forget it, can improve and strengthen their approach to foreign affairs. As demonstrated by the Iraqi invasion of Kuwait and the initial bombing of Baghdad, TV prevents presidents from presuming that they can maintain a monopoly on information for long. One may question LBJ's notion that the Vietnam war was lost on television, but experience suggests that it is in a president's general interest to design U.S. military adventures to be as brief and telegenic as possible.

When Saddam took American hostages in Iraq, Bush heeded the negative lessons established by President Carter over hostages in Iran a decade earlier: Discouraging television attention to such captives and presidential actions to free them lowers their value to their jailer; it also prevents Americans from rating the president on the basis of how quickly he is able to end the crisis. Presidents must always remember that other unexpected events shown on television can have inordinate influence on the American public's perception of a foreign crisis, encouraging, for instance, U.S. military planners during wartime to avoid bombing churches, hospitals and other civilian sites. Had the CNN "boys in Baghdad" been badly injured by American bombs, American public support for the Gulf War would likely have been eroded.

For Clinton, the crisis in Bosnia could prove to be many of these problems rolled into one. Clinton's advantage is that he comes to the problem as the first U.S. president who has lived more than half of his life in the television age. Unlike a Richard Nixon, he does not long for the time before intensive coverage of foreign events. He presumes it. For all of his adulthood, television has been a staple of American foreign policymaking, since the escalation of the Vietnam conflict against which he now-famously demonstrated.

If Clinton does not act in central Europe, he will have to struggle against those television pictures. If he intervenes, it would be one of the cardinal ironies of this moment if the resulting scene shows the 42nd president brooding in the White House, LBJ-style, about strategies to ensure that television does not draw thousands of college students to the Mall, the Ellipse and the Pentagon to fan opposition to his policies or demand premature extrication from the conflict.

# ——————— XIII ———————

# Minorities

Although some progress has been made since the first edition of this book was published in 1985, mass media in America are still produced mostly by white males and their content is still culturally biased from a white male perspective.

William Raspberry of the *Washington Post* relates the following story about an eleven-year-old boy who asked his father, "Daddy, do white people take drugs?" "Of course," the father answered. "Well," said the boy, "I never hear anything about it." That brief conversation, writes Raspberry, stands as an indictment of journalism. He points out that 70 to 80 percent of the consumption of illicit drugs occurs outside of the black ghettos. "But that knowledge rarely informs our stories and commentaries," writes Raspberry.[1]

A year later a deeply offended man called the *Washington Post* because a TV special on urban crime emphasized black criminals. The caller implied that mass media—especially television—are going out of their way to perpetuate a negative image of young black men, and the result is that these men have come to see themselves only in negative terms. Raspberry, however, points out that although a disproportionate amount of street crime *is* black, often black-on-black crime,

> The media could do a lot more than they are doing to show that people from unlikely backgrounds—from tough neighborhoods, fatherless households and underfunded inner-city schools—are succeeding in any number of fields. . . . The media can help drive home the fact that failure isn't inevitable for youngsters born to unfortunate circumstances—not by refusing to report the truth about criminals, not even by showing that poor kids are sometimes extraordinarily gifted, but by helping to teach our children that commitment and hard work pay off, even for people of ordinary gifts.[2]

One of the problems is that mass media personnel do not represent minority cultures. For example, in Chicago the population is 36.5 percent white, 41.1 percent black, 17.9 percent Hispanic, and 4.5 percent other minorities. The *Chicago Tribune* has 594 newsroom employees, of whom only 10 percent are minorities. At the *Chicago Sun-Times*, 10.3 percent are minorities, 7.4 percent black. Only 1 of 37 editorial employees in management positions at the *Sun-Times* is black, and only 2 of the paper's 52 copy-desk employees are black.[3]

In fact, says David Jackson of *Chicago Magazine,* "Newspapers across the country are trying to bring minorities on board." One-fifth of all new reporters hired in 1985 were nonwhite, according to the Institute for Journalism Education. But 40 percent of all minority newsroom employees told the institute they intend to leave the profession soon. "Most said they were discouraged about the prospects for advancement."[4]

Minorities, of course, have long had their own media, and the black press in the past has been particularly strong. As mainstream media have tried to hire more minorities, for a time the black press was weakened, but there are signs of a turn-around in the 1990s. In addition, the ethnic press is growing rapidly.

To be sure, black, Hispanic, and other ethnic media are not going to perceive news in exactly the same way as the so-called white press—which only reinforces the knowledge that the white press is biased in its own cultural perspectives, just as is the minority press.

Coverage of the warfare between media and minorities probably reached a new level of intensity in July 1994 when "Unity," an international conference on media and minority issues, was held in Atlanta, attracting thousands of journalists and media critics. *USA Today*, CNN, and Gallup conducted separate polls on minority attitudes toward the media in June 1994 and released the data at the conference. Some of the poll results:

Blacks were far more dissatisfied with and angry at media coverage of minority issues than Hispanics or Asians. A majority of blacks thought local and national TV news coverage of crime treated blacks unfairly, while slightly less thought the same about newspaper coverage. In contrast, strong majorities of Asians and Hispanics thought coverage of crime by all three media was fair to their group. More than two-thirds of Hispanics were satisfied with media coverage related to their group, while slightly less than two-thirds of Asians were satisfied.

**Notes**

1. William Raspberry, "The Drug Problem Isn't Black and White," *Washington Post,* 1 June 1990, p. A-21.
2. William Raspberry, "Minorities, Media, Success," *Washington Post*, 25 February 1991, p. A-9.
3. David Jackson, "Black, White, and Read All Over," *Chicago Magazine,* April 1987, pp. 13–16.
4. Ibid.

# 56

# Today's Press Ignores the Real Problems

## *by* William J. Raspberry

*Editor's Note:* Perhaps no one in the United States has dealt with the problem of minorities and mass media as even-handedly and rationally as Bill Raspberry. He is an urban affairs columnist for the *Washington Post,* and his column is published in many other newspapers around the country.

The following excerpts are from his keynote address at a conference on "Civil Rights and Journalism, Then and Now," commemorating the twenty-fifth anniversary of the 1964 murders of civil rights activists James Chaney, Andrew Goodman, and Michael Schwerner in Mississippi. The conference was held at Queens College of the City University of New York. The excerpts presented here were published in the *ASNE Bulletin,* July/August 1989.

If the media of the 1950s and certainly of the 1960s are justifiably proud (of coverage of the civil rights struggles), can we say as much for the media of the late 1980s? Have we continued that proud tradition? As Mayor Koch might put it, if he were a member of this profession, "How're we doing today?" The answer, I am afraid, is, "Not all that good."

Maybe we can't do as well now as we did then. As John Seigenthaler pointed out, "it was a lot easier to cover the black struggle when it was literally and figuratively a story that could be told in black and white. . . . When Jim Crow was the enemy, the white press found it easy enough to be horrified and outraged. . . ."

But now, in the story about D.C. Mayor Marion Barry, or gang warfare in Los Angeles, or dead drug dealers in Washington, D.C., who is the underdog? Who is there to direct the sympathy of the press? And toward whom? The story of racial progress in the 1980s and 1990s is enormously more complicated than it was in the 1960s, which is one of the reasons the media aren't covering it very well.

Here's another reason. Journalism, to a dismaying degree, has lost interest in the story. We are far more interested in nailing individual miscreants, black or white—although we seem to feel there is too much focus on the black—than in pursuing the story of racial progress, or in being a part of the story of racial progress.

*After recounting the influx of blacks into the media in the 1960s, and statistics on the persistent lack of blacks in all mass media today:*

Dismaying as these figures are, honesty compels me to say that the loss of interest in nurturing young black journalists is not the only reason the press is doing poorly in its coverage of the latter-day civil rights movement.

One reason, to which I have already referred, is the difficulty of the story. Blacks themselves are less clear as to what the story is. Is it the plight of the black underclass? Is it income gaps? Infant mortality gaps? Life expectancy gaps? Educational gaps? Is it the artificial ceiling on the aspirations of black professionals?

Some black leaders, I am afraid, behave as though their primary goal these days is to get white people to admit that they are racists. . . . I keep wondering, if you get the admission—they say, "OK, you convinced me, you're right"—then what do we do with it?

That makes it more difficult for journalism. Journalists who only had to be there when the story was Jim Crow now have to find and develop the story of racial progress, or its absence. It takes more insight than most of us possess to uncover the impediments to black progress in the absence of such obvious villains as Bull Connor, Orval Faubus and Lester Maddox.

We're not even sure as journalists whether our role should be as active advocates for justice or merely mirrors of the obvious. Our forays, when we make them, into the depressed black communities are likely these days to be seen by the residents there not as attempts to correct injustice but a cold-hearted attempt to humiliate an already battered community.

And even when some of us find a way to tell part of that story, we may find ourselves dealing with editors who keep asking us, "Well, what's the angle? What's the hook?" You are not likely to get it in the paper.

The Mississippi of Goodman, Schwerner and Chaney was awful, clear-cut and distant. The racial evils of today are less likely to have clear-cut villains or sympathetic victims.

In what DeWayne Wickham has called the "Sri Lanka syndrome," the closer the problem comes to a newspaper's home turf, the less the editors feel an urgency for justice. We can see so clearly a thousand miles away, and become so myopic when we look at our own backyard. It is hard to lead that way.

Maybe the press never did lead the fight for justice. It certainly doesn't now. The press seems to have bought the notion that has engulfed much of white America: that blacks are tiresome crybabies who don't seem to know what they want, and, in any case, white America has done enough for them.

Not all of that is white America's fault. The truth is, the black leadership has done a couple of things that make it harder for white people, including the white-run media, to sympathize with its goals.

The first thing it has done is to refuse to set priorities. There were all sorts of problems facing blacks in the South in the '60s. These were the problems of blacks as small farmers or sharecroppers; of blacks as economic outsiders; of blacks as under-educated peasants; of blacks denied jobs and promotions commensurate with their skills; of blacks as consumers rather than producers.

But the movement's focus was on blacks as disenfranchised Americans. And because that is where the movement focused, that is where the press focused. Today's black leadership too often attempts to focus on everything, which is the same as focusing on nothing. And the press, left to its own notions, has focused on violence and incivility; not on poor blacks as victims, but on blacks as threats to white tranquility.

The second thing the leadership has done is to change its goals without telling anybody. The driving force behind the activism of the '50s and '60s was the quest for equality of opportunity and an end to race-based restrictions. But as the quest for increased opportunity and desegregation began to show signs of success, the goal was switched, not to desegregation but to integration, which in some cases amounted to black submersion.

The predictable result was the devastation of black businesses and institutions, from restaurants and hotels and retail stores to schools and professional organizations. And when the leadership saw that devastation, both in lost economic power and in lost influence, to help in those hard-hit black communities, they charged whites with abandonment.

One result is a loss of patience for and even interest in many of the problems that confront black America today. The white-run media, like the rest of white America seem, if not heartless, at least frustrated into inaction. Its underlying theme seems to be, "It's not my fault, and, in any case, I don't know what to do."

Meanwhile, much of the black leadership seems to have no more of an agenda than to say, "Yes it is your fault—though we don't know what to do, either."

So what should the media be doing about the black plight today? . . . We should do what we do with any other complex story, whether it is the budgetary shell game of the White House and the Congress, the Alaska oil spill or the controversy over fusion versus fission.

First, try to understand it, in all its complexity. Then, undertake to explain it to our audience. The black leadership, for its part, will have to learn to set priorities and assume responsibility, which is what happened during the civil rights movement.

I am confident that, now as then, if blacks can set priorities and undertake the leadership in fashioning solutions, we will find white America ready to lend a hand. . . .

As blacks, as whites, and as members of the media, we have lost our passion for justice. And, saddest of all, nobody seems to be looking to recover it.

# 57

# Black on Black

## *by* Jim Strader

*Editor's Note:* Once influential and essential, black newspapers have lost many of their readers, as well as their political role and impact. Now they seem to be coming back, largely because they can provide significant local coverage that major newspapers are often ignoring.

Jim Strader is a wire service reporter in Pittsburgh. This article was originally published in the *Washington Journalism Review*, March 1992.

Forty years ago in Pittsburgh, people couldn't wait to read the Courier. Thursday afternoons, "everybody went to the drugstores to buy the Courier," says Ruth White, a reader for more than 50 years. "That's how we got news from across the country." Mayor David Lawrence would send a cab each week to pick up a copy before the ink had even dried. "I can see that cab driver now, wiping the ink off his hands and cussing at Lawrence," recalls former Courier Editor Frank Bolden.

In the late 1940s and early 1950s, the Courier and other leading black newspapers boasted circulations of a quarter-million or more. Editors whose publications reached far beyond their own cities wielded considerable influence and helped shape the political consciousness of America's blacks.

Now, the readership of those papers has dwindled and competition from the mainstream press and black magazines for both readers and writers has intensified. Papers that once had tremendous presence are shells of what they used to be. Publications familiar to and eagerly awaited by black communities across the country—the New York Amsterdam News, the Chicago Defender, the Pittsburgh Courier—no longer inspire the same anticipation they once did.

"It was the old Pittsburgh Courier that was the great paper," says Phyl Garland, a professor of journalism at Columbia University who read the Courier while growing up and worked there as a reporter from 1959 to 1965. "Now, it's not at all what it was then.

"It gave me my sense of identity and also gave me an opportunity to see and understand what black people had done in the past and see what they were achieving in the present," says Garland. "It was a fine newspaper and my inspiration."

Veteran journalist Chuck Stone also has fond memories of that paper. "I had my consciousness awakened by the Pittsburgh Courier," he remembers. "It was like an umbilical cord that tied us all together. It was powerful as hell and could really affect political decisions in the early days of the civil rights period."

But the black press has changed, says Stone, who was an editor at three black papers and spent 19 years at the Philadelphia Daily News before leaving to teach at the University of North Carolina's School of Journalism and Mass Communication. "[The black press] can't represent all African-Americans. It is not as dominant a force as it was 20 years ago."

## Roots

The first black papers of any size were published in the 1890s, mostly in the Northeast and Midwest. The Baltimore Afro-American first appeared in 1892, the Indiana Recorder in 1895, the New York Amsterdam News in 1909 and the Pittsburgh Courier a year after that. The St. Louis Argus debuted in 1912. Roland Wolseley in "The Black Press, U.S.A." estimates that some 3,500 black newspapers have been published since the first, the Freedom's Journal, in New York City in 1827.

The advent of most of these papers corresponded roughly with the founding of organizations advocating equal rights for blacks. The National Association for the Advancement of Colored People was established in 1909 and the National Urban League in 1910.

Many black newspapers crusaded for black causes, campaigning first for black freedom and then, after the Civil War, for equality. The Chicago Defender's best-known crusade resulted in the migration of 110,000 Southern blacks to the city, Wolseley writes; in 1917 the paper urged blacks to leave the stronghold of the Ku Klux Klan and helped organize clubs that could get group rates on train fares. The Pittsburgh Courier's advocacy helped Jackie Robinson become the first black player in major league baseball in 1947. Wolseley notes that Time reported in 1949 that the Norfolk Journal and Guide "was responsible for the county floating a $750,000 bond issue to improve black schools and for changes in pay scales so black and white teachers were treated equally."

Black papers "gave the Negroes hope and did the fighting for them, because they were too weak to fight for themselves," says Bolden.

Black papers of the 1920s also carried news of church, society and sports activities in the black community, items that didn't appear in white-owned publications, as well as occasional reports of national and international events. Garland says they were needed because "black people were invisible as far as the mainstream media were concerned. Maybe there would be a two-inch column in a corner on the back page: 'Afro-Americans in the News.' " Like the white-owned tabloids of the era, many ran sensationalized articles on crimes and scandals.

Over the years, several black papers grew dramatically and became a link for blacks nationally. In the 1930s the Chicago Defender distributed 300,000 copies. At its height in the late 1940s, the Pittsburgh Courier's circulation was over 400,000, while the New York Amsterdam News distributed 200,000. In 1945 the Afro-American's national circulation was 137,000.

The papers' readership was by no means limited to the cities in which they published. From Pittsburgh, for example, more than a dozen regional editions of the Courier were shipped across the country. The Defender and the Baltimore-based Afro-American also distributed nationwide.

## Spreading the News

Distribution was difficult, especially in the South. Bolden says bundles of papers often were burned as soon as they were unloaded from rail cars at Southern depots. In his 1922 book "The Negro Press in the United States," Frederick Detweiler describes a 1920 Mississippi law that forbade publications advocating equality for blacks.

To circumvent such problems, the Courier depended on black railroad porters to safeguard shipments, says Rod Doss, current general manager of the paper, now called the New Pittsburgh Courier. Black ministers also agreed to receive the papers and encouraged parishioners to subscribe.

There were other difficulties with putting out newspapers that weren't for the larger, more affluent white population, and high on the list was money. Advertising dollars were scarce for some papers. "Our budget was tight. We didn't begin to make money 'til late," Bolden says. "White businesses don't give you a lot of advertisements when you're criticizing white people."

Photographer Teenie "One-Shot" Harris found a way to live with the Courier's tight budget. When he photographed Lawrence, "there were 12 photographers in the building, all shooting pictures," Harris says. "I'd just come in and take one. So he called me 'One-shot.'

"They only paid me for one picture, so why take two?"

## Losing Readers

A number of these papers no longer have their former reach. The New Pittsburgh Courier still publishes a national edition with a circulation of 50,000, Doss says. And the local edition, which now comes out biweekly, has a circulation of just 28,500. The Chicago Defender, one of only three black dailies—the Atlanta Daily World and the New York Daily Challenge are the others—has seen its circulation drop tenfold, to 30,000. The Amsterdam News now publishes only about 60,000 copies per week.

Some claim the papers' contents have contributed to the circulation decline. "Today's black press does not have the political leadership that the old black press had," says Columbia professor Garland. "A lot of people I know who used to read the Courier no longer read it because it's not as tough-minded and it's not as plugged in to the community as it was."

"Today's black newspaper is not the same paper it was 30 years ago at the height of the civil rights period," says Steve Davis, executive director of the National Newspaper Publishers Association (NNPA), a black newspaper organization based in Washington, D.C. "We were the source of telling the story to the public. Now, we've gotten complacent and lost that urgency."

Observers also trace the decline to the emergence of national magazines aimed at blacks. "We now have Ebony and Jet and you can get the news from around the country," says Garland, a former Ebony editor. Publisher James E. Lewis, whose Birmingham Times has distributed about 10,000 copies weekly since it was founded 28 years ago, concedes that some functions of the black press a half-century ago have been usurped by the white-oriented media. News about black issues, celebrities and especially athletes now is found in white-owned daily newspapers and on television, Lewis says. In decades past, that kind of coverage was relegated to black papers.

"Those papers used to be the only place blacks could read about blacks," says Frederick Benjamin, editor of the Augusta, Georgia, Focus. "Now there's competition everywhere."

But Garland says black national magazines, and black television, often devote too much space to entertainment "glitz and gloss." "That presents a distorted view of what is important to us, but it sells magazines."

By emphasizing gossip about black celebrities and the achievements of black athletes, the magazines also neglect the more serious role black newspapers used to play, particularly on political matters, Garland says. "Nothing does that today. It's just unfortunate."

Another drain on black papers is the increased presence of black journalists in the mainstream media. Some, such as Bernard Shaw of CNN, Carole Simpson of ABC News and Ed Bradley of CBS' "60 Minutes," are in highly visible positions. The result, Stone says, is that the mainstream media now address black issues more frequently.

In addition, minority internships and scholarships offered by media companies steer young black journalists away from the black press. These programs also force black publishers and broadcasters to compete against more established and better-funded rivals for qualified reporters and editors.

"Most of these kids that get these scholarships go into the mainstream media. Very few go into the black press," Stone says. "The increase of black journalists . . . helps the white media."

Black columnists as well are no longer limited to writing strictly for black publications, says Stone, who wrote a column for the Philadelphia Daily News before accepting the faculty position at the University of North Carolina. He points to colleagues such as William Raspberry and Clarence Page, who are syndicated nationally, and Vernon Jarrett of the Chicago Sun-Times. "We exert as much influence on some issues as the African-American press," Stone says.

But black opinion-writers in the mainstream press have to be careful not to let themselves get pigeon-holed on the basis of race or they run the risk of losing their influence, Stone says. "We can't always write about African-American issues, because people get bored as hell."

Finances were another factor in the decline of the big newspapers. "These newspapers that had vast national circulations—there's just no way to sustain them. It costs too much," says Benjamin.

Readership has also changed, shifting from "practically all of black society" to a segment of the population, says Wolseley. Now, most readers are urban blacks who want news about their own community and "crusaders" of the civil rights movement, he says. "There is a portion of the black community that is indifferent to the black press. Editors don't like to be told this. They have a tough job holding the interest of middle-class blacks."

But G. M. Doss says the Courier made changes to keep its main audience, the middle class. "We realigned the product so it gave a more positive reflection of the core readership, which is mostly upscale, better educated, employed, socially and politically active and aware," he says. However, he says the paper remains relevant to its traditional readership—lower-income, inner-city blacks.

Benjamin of the Augusta Focus characterizes the future of black newspapers as "pretty bright" but says they can't expect to survive by continuing to conduct business as usual. "Traditionally, black newspapers have taken the audience for granted—they've felt that they had a captive audience. At times, they felt it was enough to keep publishing to keep going."

## Alive and Kicking

Media observers and several editors of black papers say that although the black press may have lost its sweeping influence, black newspapers remain vital. They say black communities still need a black perspective on the news and advocacy on black issues.

"The black press finds it necessary to take up a leadership role, because it's not being taken up by anybody else," says the NNPA's Steve Davis.

Many more blacks now trust the non-black media, Lewis says, since the mainstream press has discovered that blacks make news. But that faith is not total.

"Blacks trust CNN. They trust USA Today," Lewis says. "But on the local level, black people do not trust the information that's in the local newspaper as it applies to them."

Hit by the same problems as white-owned papers—decreasing readership and ad revenues—black papers are taking steps to solve the problems. In Augusta, Benjamin says he revamped the design of the Focus with a new layout, color photos and graphics, and added special editions on business, culture and social activities.

In 1988 the Afro-American chain dropped its national edition. "We looked at our national edition and said, 'That's not our market,'" says Frances Murphy

Draper, president of the company that publishes the Baltimore Afro-American and papers in Washington, D.C., and Richmond, Virginia. "We said, 'We're a community newspaper.' "

Draper says circulation of the three local papers has climbed steadily in the past five years. The Baltimore paper publishes about 15,000 copies now, up from 8,000 in 1986; Washington circulation has increased to 10,000 from 4,000; and the Richmond paper now publishes 4,000 copies, up from its circulation of 2,500 five years ago.

In August 1990 the NAACP launched an effort to revitalize black-owned newspapers and television and radio stations. Executive Director Benjamin Hooks, saying black media outlets are "locked in a struggle for survival," called on the nation's 500 largest corporations to devote more ad dollars to the black media, directed the NAACP's 1,500 branches to give more support to black papers and broadcast stations and assigned organization staffers to assist black media owners.

Now more than a year and a half old, the effort has made progress, says NAACP spokesman Jim Williams. He says 250 of the Fortune 500 companies have responded to a letter Hooks sent their CEOs. Half replied that they already were advertising in the black media, and about 10 percent said they would consider doing so. The rest responded that they weren't doing any consumer advertising. Linking those companies with newspapers and stations in their areas is a joint project of the NAACP and the NNPA.

Davis contends that the black press as a whole is healthy, noting that no member of the NNPA has gone out of business in the past four years. But he thinks it should do more.

"People say, 'Where's the black press? They're not out in the streets marching.' Well, maybe we should be."

# 58

# Its Own View of New York

## *by* Michael Specter

*Editor's Note:* Journalists who come from different cultures, races, or ethnic groups are going to have different versions of reality. We all have been molded by our own backgrounds, which shape the way we see the world. One problem with mainstream gatekeepers of mass media is that they often think they have a franchise on objective observation and the presentation of truth. But people who don't share their mainstream culture often do not share their view of the world either.

To confirm this statement, simply read, watch, or listen to a news story presented by mainstream mass media and the same story presented by alternative media. The 1990 trial in New York City of a black man charged with raping a white woman jogger is a good case in point.

In this article, *Washington Post* staff writer Michael Specter looks at the main black newspaper in New York City, the *Amsterdam News*, and compares its coverage of the trial with white media. This article appeared in the *Washington Post*, August 21, 1990.

While many New Yorkers waited in uneasy silence last week for a verdict in the racially charged Central Park jogger rape case, Bill Tatum wondered aloud why anyone thought there had been a rape at all.

"There is just no evidence of a rape, none," said Tatum, 56, the portly, stylish editor and publisher of the Amsterdam News, the city's oldest and most influential black newspaper. "Something bad happened that night, but they certainly can't say it's rape."

After 10 days of often bitter deliberations, a Manhattan Supreme Court jury disagreed, convicting all three teenagers of rape, robbery, assault and riot. But none of that has muddied Tatum's view of this case as the work of racially motivated prosecuters with the mentality of a lynch mob.

His assertions, repeated often and published in his weekly paper, have left many readers here, black and white, stunned and angry. But the Amsterdam News, which sees itself as one of the few voices willing to carry the truth to black New Yorkers in troubled times, has no fear of causing outrage. And although city leaders are quick to condemn the paper for its breezy publication of the slightest innuendo, almost none is willing to take it on in public.

"Other newspapers report on our community," Mayor David N. Dinkins (D) said. "The Amsterdam News is based in it. Therefore, in many instances, it is able to provide its readers with a more accurate view of the African-American experience."

The Amsterdam, as it is frequently called, carries weight not just as a newspaper but also as one of the city's most prominent black-run enterprises. But some of its former supporters say the paper has drifted from its stated goal of informing blacks and promoting their achievements.

They cite its inflammatory reporting on the jogger trial, its allegiance to such incendiary public figures as the Rev. Al Sharpton and insistence that Dutchess County teenager Tawana Brawley was raped by white police officers although virtually all other media outlets and a New York grand jury have concluded that her celebrated case was a hoax.

The paper's coverage of the jogger trial repeatedly startled its readers with its openly antagonistic reporting, never as strikingly as at the close of testimony in the seven-week trial.

In its Aug. 11 issue, the paper reported that much of what its reporter referred to as "evidence"—including a full moon, unconfirmed reports of a ring of fire in the park and the fact that the victim lost three-fourths of her blood—suggested that, instead of a brutal assault and gang rape, a Satanic ritual occurred in Central Park on the night of April 19, 1989.

"The media called the attack 'wilding by a group of wolf packs,'" reporter Vinette K. Pryce wrote in her front-page article on the closing of testimony. "They did not manage to report on the 'ring of fire,' which was said to be soaring 100 feet into the air near the area where the jogger was found." Police said they had no such reports.

"It's humiliating to all of us," said one of the city's top black officials, who, like other elected and appointed leaders, would speak only if his name were withheld. "We deserve much better from our most important paper."

Many blacks, who grew up relying on The Amsterdam for information that the major, white-run papers rarely cover, have given up on the publication, which reports a circulation of slightly more than 40,000, less than half of the total in its glory days during the early 1960s.

At that time, the Harlem-based publication often filled a role similar to that of the 19th century political press, as a major advocate in the jarring battles for civil rights.

Although it no longer is considered essential reading for informed New Yorkers, politicians still court its approval. And while many people in this media-hungry town have said they loathe Tatum's rambling and provocative editorials, he is difficult to ignore. Many of those who watch The Amsterdam express remorse about lost opportunity.

"It had a chance to be a powerful and important paper," said a black reporter for one of city's major dailies. He, like other blacks critical of the paper, asked not to be named. "But it walked away. Bill Tatum is not really a serious man."

Tatum's editorial Aug. 11 was titled, "Jogger Trial: The Lynching Attempt That Must Not Succeed."

"The truth of the matter," he wrote, "is there is no evidence that connects these boys to the crime. The 'confessions'-[videotaped and graphic descriptions of the crime provided to detectives by two of the three defendants] clearly tainted and illegally obtained, should not have been allowed into evidence."

Tatum, like defense attorneys for the three youths accused of raping and assaulting the jogger, contended throughout that police officers rounded up the trio in a dragnet because they were in the park after dark on a night when violence occurred. Further, he discounted the only hard evidence presented by the prosecution, the videotaped confessions, saying that the youths were scared and, in order to be allowed to go home, would have done whatever they were told.

"This whole trial has gotten so much publicity that it does not deserve," Tatum said during a recent interview that began in his downtown office and continued in his chauffeur-driven car where it was punctuated by calls on his car phone.

"Twenty-eight other women were raped in this town that week," he said. "A black woman in Fort Tryon Park was almost beheaded after she was raped. But she was a prostitute, so who cares? Another black woman was raped and thrown from the roof. It was a two-day story.

"But the jogger was the American Dream of what America never was and never will be: blond, blue-eyed and perfect. She was what America wants to believe it is and, whoever assaulted the jogger, assaulted the American Dream."

Tatum has become a noted and besieged figure in the city. He received death threats after publishing the jogger's name in his editorials. "I don't have a policy against printing the name," he said. "The white press certainly never minded printing Tawana Brawley's name."

Even his most bitter opponents admit that he is charming and witty, an easy man to talk to and fast to laugh at himself.

"He's suave," said former mayor Edward I. Koch (D), who denounced Tatum each time he had the opportunity and whose reelection bid, according to Tatum, was overcome by Dinkins last year in part because of the tireless efforts of the Amsterdam News.

"He's silky, but if you listen to him, he makes no sense," Koch said. "People are afraid of Bill Tatum because they know that, if you take on any cause he doesn't like, he will brand you as a racist."

None of that bothers Wilbert A. Tatum.

"You can call me anything you want, but I own my paper, lock, stock and barrel, and there is not a living person who can tell me how to run it," said Tatum, chewing on antacid tablets he keeps in a big jar on his desk.

"I know what the whites say, and they are right. I got an attitude. But we wouldn't be doing our job, we wouldn't be a newspaper if we were feeding people what they want to read."

# 59

# Bad News for Hispanics

## *by* Michele A. Heller

*Editor's Note:* To find out how some of the most prestigious and influential papers in the United States cover the booming Hispanic communities in their respective cities, an analysis was conducted of the *Chicago Tribune, Los Angeles Times, New York Times, San Antonio Light*, and *Washington Post* during the week of August 24–30, 1992.

All stories in all sections of the papers were reviewed, except for obituaries, letters to the editor, play-by-play coverage of athletic games, and special "zoned" sections like the *Los Angeles Times*'s *Nuestro Tiempo*. Any story in which the main subject was Hispanic was put into one of five categories and graded as positive or negative. The author concludes that Hispanics are still almost invisible in America's main newspapers.

Michele A. Heller is an editorial assistant at *Hispanic* magazine, which published this article in November 1992.

How does your newspaper cover the Hispanic community? "I find it a ridiculous question!" declared the metro editor of the long-time standard bearer of the American press, the *New York Times*, when he was asked to rate his paper's coverage of Hispanics.

Until recently, the only Hispanics who made it onto the newsstands were criminals, drug dealers, gang members, or their victims. But with demographic change breathing down their necks, newspapers are slowly opening their eyes to the diversity of the Hispanic community. But regrettably, this revelation doesn't translate into more coverage, as evidenced by this editor's comment.

To find out how newspapers view the Hispanic community, HISPANIC analyzed the coverage of Hispanics in the *Chicago Tribune, Los Angeles Times, New York Times, San Antonio Light,* and *Washington Post* during the week of August 24 through August 30. We counted the number of stories about Hispanics and classified them into five categories—crime, culture, business, people, and issues—and then graded them as either positive or negative.

We had to look carefully in each paper to find any story—positive or negative—about or including Hispanics. And, when we did stumble across a Hispanic, he or she had a strong chance of appearing in a crime story, as the perpetrator, victim, police officer—or all three. It can be argued that since blood and guts are what keep newspapers in business, the negative stories will always out-number the positive. But, as Melita Marie Garza, ethnic affairs writer for the *Chicago Tribune* and Vice President, Print for the National Association of Hispanic Journalists, explains: "The prime component of news itself tends to be crime and conflict, so when Hispanics commit a crime, that is news. The problem comes when the only coverage of Hispanics is of Hispanic criminals. That needs to be written, but papers also need to expose the other side. Half of the truth results in a distortion, basically an un-truth. If Hispanics do not appear [in the papers] as experts, as people in the mainstream, as leaders, then the image of Hispanics that rests in the minds of society is in fact negative."

If a foreign visitor spent the week of August 24 in the United States and never came into contact with a Hispanic, save for what he read in the newspaper, here's what he would learn:

The *Chicago Tribune*, serving a metropolitan area that is at least 20 percent Hispanic (all population figures are quoted from the 1990 Census), had only fifteen Hispanic stories, but of those, nine were positive. Even the stories that included a negative stereotype quickly balanced themselves. For example, in an August 24 story about a small town and its booming economy, the first Hispanic we meet is Noe Martinez who is "interviewed as he picked fruit for [greenhouse manager Carl] Ford last week. Martinez, an immigrant from Chihuahua, Mexico, estimated his pay at $200 a week and noted that most places to rent cost more than $300 a month." In just a paragraph the *Tribune* managed to hit at least two stereotypes: Hispanics are manual laborers and they don't make enough money to make ends meet. But a few paragraphs later, Joe Medina, "a local businessman and former Chamber of Commerce president," goes to a city council meeting and relays his opinion on an economic issue important to his community. The story leaves us with the impression that Hispanics aren't invisible in this tiny town, and that they can't be lumped together by profession or any other arbitrary category.

The problem, though, is not so much with quality as with quantity. "The *Tribune* covers good and bad stories about equally. It's just that there's not sufficient coverage at all," says Mayra Martinez, Director of Communications for the non-profit Latino Institute in Chicago. "Once a year the *Tribune* puts out a 36-page insert called 'Hispanic Heritage Month,' and that's really the extent of its extensive coverage of the huge Chicago Hispanic community. And, of course, they need more than one reporter to cover us."

That one reporter is Garza. Earlier this year she proposed establishing an ethnic affairs beat, and she was subsequently made ethnic affairs writer. Now she not only covers all of Chicago's ethnic and racial minorities, but also serves as a liaison to other reporters in the newsroom who have questions about ethnic issues on their beats.

Martinez describes repeated errors that show the *Tribune's* ignorance of issues important to Hispanics, who number 545,852 in Chicago. For example, the Northwest side of Chicago was mainly populated by Puerto Ricans ten years ago, but now there are an many people of Mexican heritage living there. Yet she finds the *Tribune* continuing to refer to the area and people there as Puerto Rican. In another example, last year most of the stories in the annual Hispanic Heritage insert were about Mexican traditions, leaving the reader to believe that Hispanic Heritage Month was strictly for those of Mexican heritage. She saw some improvement in this year's Hispanic Heritage insert, though.

The *Tribune* is aware of its shortfalls when it comes to covering the many groups that make up Chicago's Hispanic community. "I haven't seen any major metropolitan newspaper doing a very good job covering the Hispanic community. Papers tend to do stories that give the impression that we've just discovered something a community has known all along," says Reginald F. Davis, a *Tribune* deputy metro editor. "We have improved, but we have a long way to go."

On the other hand, stories about Hispanics are much easier to find in the *Los Angeles Times (LA Times)*. The problem is that they are much more negative. Of the 56 Hispanic stories we counted, 25 were negative. Though the *LA Times* gave extensive coverage to the North American Free Trade Agreement (NAFTA) and other business subjects important to Hispanics, stories specifically referring to Hispanics in L.A. were for the most part about gangs and the after-effects of the L.A. riots. In a city that is at least 40 percent Hispanic, one would think the *LA Times* could have found more Hispanics who were doing positive things.

Even reports of Hispanics taking positive steps in their communities are filled with cliches, leading the reader to believe that most of L.A.'s more than 1 million newsworthy Hispanics live in gang-infested neighborhoods, if they are not gang members themselves. The front page of the August 27 metro section sported a story titled "Making a Bid to End a Bloody Cycle." The sub-headline read: "Violence: Latino gang members meet at USC to talk of Brown Pride and to seek ways to stop the murderous rivalries." After quoting some of the "battle-scarred" members in attendance, the story portrayed the Latino community activists, who helped organize the meeting, as anomalies in a violent Hispanic world. The successful Latinos talked of the dangerous communities and dysfunctional families they overcame, giving the reader the impression that most Hispanics come from such backgrounds.

"The *LA Times* had the opportunity to do a solid, positive story. Unfortunately, the story was not representative of what took place," says Gus Frías, one of the meeting organizers and a criminal justice and education specialist for the Los Angeles County Office of Education. "The story had no positive sentence about uniting and doing good for the community." A regular *LA Times* reader, Frías believes the paper's coverage of Hispanics is "degrading, unfair, and racist. They think they are the judges of our community and will decide who our leaders are. They are wrong."

Esther Renteria, National Chair of the National Hispanic Media Coalition, says: "The *LA Times* needs to start covering the Hispanic community, talking with Hispanic organizations, and sending reporters to news conferences called by Hispanic leaders. They totally ignore the growth and importance of the Hispanic community." She cites an example of a news conference that California Hispanic elected leaders called during the L.A. riots. The *LA Times* did not send a reporter. In another example, the sale of Univision was covered extensively by the *Wall Street Journal* and the *Miami Herald,* but the *LA Times* provided very little coverage.

In stories that attempt to include minorities, "Quite often racial and ethnic issues are framed in black and white, and you find Latinos don't exist," observes Cheryl Brownstein-Santiago, an *LA Times* news editor and associate editor of *Nuestro Tiempo,* the *LA Times* bilingual supplement. For example, in *LA Times* stories about rebuilding after the May riots and about minority contract programs, one wouldn't know that Hispanics outnumber blacks almost four to one in the Los Angeles metropolitan area. Often, Hispanic business owners weren't even mentioned in a story filled with black and Asian merchants.

However, the *LA Times* recently launched two new editorial features—the *City Times* and *Voices*—aimed at expanding its coverage of multi-cultural communities in Southern California.

Hispanics were also hard to find in the *New York Times (NY Times).* Of the week's nineteen stories on Hispanics, only eight were positive. Hispanics in New York—where one in four residents is Hispanic—were overwhelmingly portrayed as swindlers, murderers, sex maniacs, and residents of crime-infested neighborhoods. Stories about the decline of Hispanic barrios and increasing crime received front-page coverage on August 28 and 30 and page-23 status on August 29.

The August 28 front-page story headlined "Gunfight Steals Dreams for Rebirth in Bronx" gets mixed reviews. The article begins with a Puerto Rican immigrant who, the reader is led to believe, does not speak English and is the helpless victim of increasing violence that recently climaxed with a shooting spree that wounded twelve bystanders. But the story then moves beyond the sensational shooting and "typical" Hispanic victim to the reasons why this once-hopeful neighborhood is retreating into its undesirable past. The reader is introduced to Hispanic small business owners who have been victimized by the rapid decline of their neighborhoods and Hispanic police officers who knew the area in its heyday. The story quotes Luis L. Suarez, a police detective in the area: "The shooting [Suarez said,] doesn't reflect what's going on in this neighborhood, where most people are not dealers and criminals, but law-abiding, working-class people struggling to rebuild a community." Unfortunately, the reader had to jump from the A section—where the story began with the poor Spanish-speaking Latina—to the B section and then read through 21 inches of text before meeting Suarez and hearing the positive way he portrays the people in his neighborhood.

Suarez was satisfied with the story after it was published, however. "I was surprised the *NY Times* gave a fair overview of the area. We got calls from community groups, and they said they were pleased with the article," says Suarez, whose Hispanic first name, Luis, was incorrectly anglicized to "Louis" by *NY Times* reporter Steven Lee Myers.

But a shopkeeper also interviewed wasn't so pleased. "The *NY Times* wasn't dealing in substance. It could have been a far better story," says the man who immigrated to the neighborhood from Puerto Rico thirty years ago and who didn't want to be identified. "They didn't explain the events that led up to the shooting. They shouldn't just scratch the surface just to get headlines."

*NY Times* metro editor Gerald Boyd, who thinks it's "ridiculous" to generally rate coverage of Hispanics, believes that his paper's "record speaks for itself."

"I think we have made enormous strides, not just covering Hispanics but all stories relevant to the people in the city," he says.

Smaller and less worldly than the country's leading papers, the *San Antonio Light* has what the others lack: fair and balanced coverage of its population, which is 56 percent Hispanic. With only about half the pages of the giant *LA Times*, *NY Times*, and *Washington Post*, the *Light* managed to squeeze 49 Hispanic stories into its daily editions. Of those 49, a whopping 37 were positive and only twelve were negative. These numbers indicate that the *Light* knows something the other papers do not: There is more to covering Hispanics than the crime beat. Sure, there are stories about Hispanic crime in San Antonio—it wouldn't be a normal city if there were not. But, as with any population, the number of Hispanic criminals is small compared to the number of Hispanic leaders and cultural events and their positive influence on their community.

For example, a front-page profile on a Hispanic nurse, Paul Rivera, showed the man as professional, intelligent, and active in his community. Save for his name, the fact that he is Hispanic isn't even mentioned in the story, therefore allowing his accomplishments, rather than his ethnicity, become the focal point of the story. Interviewed after his profile was published, Rivera said the fact that the *Light* interviewed a public employee, especially a nurse, was more surprising than the fact that a Hispanic was profiled. "The majority of people in San Antonio are Hispanic, so we get a lot of news coverage," he says. "I would say the *Light* does a good job. They don't just skip over things. They give in-depth coverage to [Hispanic] issues and people."

*Light* Managing Editor Jeff Cohen explains his paper's mission: "We're constantly trying to innovate and reach out to the various cultural communities in the city. We talk each day about making sure our coverage of people of color, women, special interest groups, and the Hispanic community is complete and representative. I feel we're doing a pretty good job serving our readership."

In contrast to the *San Antonio Light*, the *Washington Post* seems to have forgotten the statistics recently printed in its own pages: The Hispanic population in the Washington area alone doubled from 1985 to 1990. A very conservative estimate counts nearly a quarter of a million Hispanics, about 5.7 percent of the area's population. Only fifteen of the hundreds of stories the *Post* ran in a week were about Hispanics or Hispanic issues. But the *Post* seems to adhere to the argument that quality is better than quantity. The ten of the fifteen stories that can be considered positive show insight and sensitivity to issues affecting the Hispanic community, both in Washington and other areas of the country. Hurricane Andrew coverage dominated the pages of all the papers reviewed, but the *Post* was the only paper to run two stories specifically on the storm's effect on Hispanics in South Florida. An August 26 story reported the particular impact of the hurricane on Mexican migrant workers. The August 29 story on hurricane news being beamed by radio to Cuba to ease the minds of concerned relatives of Cubans in Florida showed sensitivity and familiarity with Cuban-American relations.

But alongside this coverage, the *Post* managed to sneak in a story titled "Immigrant Anglers Line Potomac [River] Banks" on August 25. Hispanics were portrayed as new immigrants, poor, unemployed, non-English speaking, and even ignorant of the law: "For many of the low-income newcomers, some of whom speak little English, the river is an important source of food. . . . " A few paragraphs later: "Police and park officials say it's difficult to determine how many immigrants fish the Potomac each day, in part because most do not buy fishing licenses."

The *Post* acknowledges that it has some way to go in better serving its Hispanic readers. "I think we have improved our coverage [of Hispanics] considerably in the past several years, but I don't think we are anywhere near doing as much as we should be doing," says Milton Coleman, Assistant Managing Editor of the metro section.

Comparing the papers across the country from a Hispanic business perspective, Patricia Rivera, the Washington, D.C.-based public relations coordinator of the U.S. Hispanic Chamber of Commerce, ranks the *NY Times* at the top. "If I was a Hispanic businessperson in Washington, I would not read the *Washington Post* alone. I would definitely get the *NY Times* and the *Financial Times*," says Rivera. "If I had to compare the *Post* to the *NY Times*, the *Times* definitely covers [NAFTA] a lot better." Rivera, who works with media around the country, also has praise for the *Chicago Tribune's* extensive coverage of the Chamber's convention last year, which was held in the Windy City.

Cynthia Muñoz, a partner in San Antonio-based Muñoz y Marín Public Relations, isn't so pleased with the papers that she tries to pitch Hispanic stories to. She explains that when she sends Hispanic-oriented stories to the *LA Times*, the idea is typically not considered for the regular paper but is instead referred to the bilingual supplement *Nuestro Tiempo*, thus effectively segregating the news. "This is important news the general market needs to be educated on. They are withholding news," she says. "But I do praise the *LA Times* for very positive coverage of the Hispanic arts. The *NY Times* is weak all around, the *Chicago Tribune* is pretty good at covering a variety of Hispanic issues, and the *San Antonio Light* is doing the best job of all."

It can be argued that while newspapers have a journalistic obligation to fairly cover Hispanics, this ideal really translates into dollar signs. As newspapers are going out of business left and right, old-time editors blame the 30-second sound bites of TV and the "McNews" of *USA Today*. But they don't blame their own troops for failing to adapt coverage to their changing readership.

"Who a newspaper's public is and who its advertisers need to cater to has changed over the years," says Brownstein-Santiago of the *LA Times*. "The mainstream is no longer what it used to be. It's becoming multicolored. Newspapers have been trying to adapt to this new reality, but not as quickly as some of us would like."

One reason for the slow pace is the low number of Hispanics in the newsroom. The *Chicago Tribune* newsroom is 3 percent Hispanic, *LA Times* is 7 percent, *NY Times* is 3 percent, *San Antonio Light* is 17 percent, and *Washington Post* is 1.4 percent, according to a recent study. Once Hispanics start appearing in the newsroom, perhaps the Hispanic community will start appearing in the paper.

But papers can't rely on Hispanic reporters to act as watchdogs against the negative cliches writers love using. Many reporters and editors need a crash course in cultural awareness, to learn that just because someone only speaks Spanish doesn't mean he is a new immigrant; that gang members aren't all "battle-scarred;" that our countries of origin aren't all "banana republics" ruled by "drug kingpins" who do away with their enemies "execution-style."

Ironically, there seems to be an inverse relationship between the historical prestige of the paper and the quality of its coverage of Hispanics. The more clout a paper has, the less coverage Hispanics get. Perhaps the reason is that papers like the *NY Times*, *Washington Post*, and *LA Times* are famed and respected around the world for their coverage of national and international issues. Unfortunately, coverage of their own back yard is put on the back burner and the back pages. It takes a quality paper that does not have world recognition, like the *San Antonio Light*, to provide fair, balanced, and quality coverage for and about its readers.

"There's a wide disparity in covering the Hispanic community," says Garza of the *Chicago Tribune*. "Some papers have improved greatly, but others still lag behind with their stone-age perception of Hispanics. The fastest growing segment of the population doesn't see itself reflected in the media."

Hispanics have been invisible in the eyes of newspaper publishers, and therefore readers, for years. Unless this changes, newspapers are in for some bad news themselves. As Garza sums up: "How can the media expect people to read the paper when their community is not covered, or is only covered in a negative light?"

# 60

# Comics and the Color Barrier

## *by* Anna America

*Editor's Note:* This examination of the comic strips and "funny pages" on America's newspapers finds one not-so-funny fact: They still portray a very white world, although there is some hope for change in the near future.

Anna America is a former staff writer on *Presstime*, the monthly magazine of the Newspaper Association of America, where this article was published in November 1992.

Cartoonists swear by the motto, "Draw what you know," and it's clear looking at newspaper comic pages that what most of them know is a white, middle-class world.

A few strips created by minority artists are flourishing, and more minority characters are popping up in other established comics. But despite the perennial calls for more diversity voiced by many in the field, the faces in the funny pages, and of those who create them, are still overwhelmingly white.

"I'm surprised that we haven't gotten further," laments Lee Salem, vice president, editorial director for Universal Press Syndicate. "When you look at other creative areas—music, fiction-writing, movies—you find much stronger minority representation."

A big part of the problem, he and other syndicate representatives say, is that few submissions come from minority artists.

"I'm just not getting anything over the transom," says Sarah A. Gillespie, vice president-director of comic art for United Media.

Mell Lazarus, president of the National Cartoonists Society and creator of "Momma" and "Miss Peach," adds that minority artists are the only ones who can give true voice to the minority experience.

"I can't sit down and do a comic strip about the Asian experience," he says. "I don't know anything about it. It has to come from the people who are living it."

Out of the hundreds of U.S. comics features offered by the major syndicates, only five are penned by minority artists, all of them African Americans.

Of those—King Features Syndicate's "Curtis," United Media's "Jump Start," Universal Press Syndicate's "Where I'm Coming From," Tribune Media Services' "Herb and Jamaal," and Creators Syndicates, "Wee Pals"—the 4-year-old "Curtis" is the undisputed leader, appearing in more than 250 newspapers and appealing to a broad audience of all races.

"When I read ('Curtis'), I enjoy it because it has a funny little guy, and the things that happen to him are pretty typical no matter what color you are," notes Mort Walker, who draws the popular comics, "Beetle Bailey" and "Hi and Lois."

"Curtis" artist Ray Billingsley is used to being billed as the pioneer who was supposed to blaze the way for other minority artists [presstime, May 1989, p. 78]. But he admits being a little frustrated that more success stories haven't followed in his wake.

"I thought 'Curtis' would break the doors down, that there would be a flood of minority artists," he says. "I thought there would be a Hispanic, maybe an Asian strip by now. It's not happening."

Although he speaks to young people and tries to spawn more interest in cartooning, like syndicate executives, he doesn't find many aspiring cartoonists.

Continued encouragement of young artists will help, but progress cannot be forced, he insists. "All we can do is give the inspiration and incentive. It's up to the artists to take it from there. Their own imagination has to be what pushes them," he says.

## Slow Acceptance

Gillespie says one major obstacle to diversifying comics is that it is an exceptionally difficult field to break into. With the passionately loyal followings of most well-established features, editors are leery of tampering with their comics page to give new artists a shot.

"In the old days, comics had time to grow over a few years. That's becoming rarer and rarer," she asserts.

Another problem is that some newspapers feel they need to have only one "black strip." United Media has run into that with "Jump Start" by Robb Armstrong, which some editors say they don't need because they already run "Curtis" or another minority-drawn strip.

"There's a concern that it becomes 'ghettoized,' that newspapers feel they already have their 'black strip' and don't look at others," Gillespie says.

Universal Press' Salem says he faces the same reaction with "Where I'm Coming From," or editors tell him they don't need such a strip because few minorities live in their circulation areas. In response, he points to the tremendous success of television's "The Cosby Show," which scored well in all demographic groups.

For several years, Marty Claus, managing editor/features and business for the Detroit Free Press and first vice president of the Newspaper Features Council, has prodded the syndicates to diversify all their offerings, including comics. "Detroit has a relatively high black population that I want to serve and reflect," she says.

The lack of minority role models in comics was one of the problems cited by local focus groups of young people in the late 1980s. In one month in 1987, the Free Press found that 0.6 percent of the characters in the 5,000 strips published were minorities. In 1988, it rose only to 2.4 percent. So Claus launched her own search for minority cartoonists and in 1989 discovered Barbara Brandon, creator of "Where I'm Coming From," which the Free Press ran for several years before Universal Press picked it up.

Claus says the industry's early response to the diversity efforts was "fairly rewarding. . . . Three syndicates started offering minority cartoonists ('Jump Start,' 'Curtis,' and 'Herb and Jamaal'), and we discovered ('Where I'm Coming From') for the Free Press."

The Free Press now runs all four of those strips and has gotten good response from the community.

## White Efforts

In the past few years, progress seems to have slowed, Claus says, although one good sign is that white artists are including more minority characters in their strips.

Garry Trudeau's "Doonesbury," distributed by Universal Press Syndicate, has long led the way, featuring a diverse set of characters from a variety of backgrounds.

Other strips cited include, "The Middletons," created by Ralph Dunagin and Dana Summers, and "Luann," created by Greg Evans, both distributed by King Features Syndicate; "Tank McNamara," crated by Jeff Miller and Bill Hinds and syndicated by Universal Press; "Outland," created by Berke Breathed, and "Safe Havens," created by Bill Holbrook, both distributed by The Washington Post Writers Group; "On the Fastrack," also by Holbrook and syndicated by King Features; and "Peanuts," by Charles Schultz, syndicated by United Media.

"Big Nate," a United Media strip focusing on the misadventures of a recalcitrant sixth-grader created by Lincoln Peirce, recently added an African American woman as one of Nate's teachers.

Peirce says he put a lot of thought into making a strong and sympathetic female character. "Minorities and women and characters with alternative lifestyles are under-represented in comics. Because my strip focuses on a child's school experience, it was only responsible on my part to introduce minority characters, who are a part of that environment."

Peirce plans to add another African American character in February, a female student who will be the romantic interest of Nate's best friend, Francis, who is white.

Although most cartoonists endorse diversity in concept, many also contend minority characters should be thoughtfully portrayed.

"I don't think artists should be forced to do it," Billingsley says. "If a well-developed black character can add to the strip, great. But it shouldn't be just to add a black character.

"Cartoonists should draw what they know. Some of these older cartoonists maybe didn't know blacks that well, and if they tried to draw a black (character), it would end up a shallow stereotype."

Any cartoonist can have token minorities walking through his or her strip, says Lazarus. "That's not what we're looking for. We want strips about the Latino experience, the black experience, and that has to come from the Latino and black backgrounds."

Some white artists have found that even when they add minority characters with the best of intentions, their efforts can seem offensive or patronizing.

Walker had that problem with "Beetle Bailey," one of the longest-running and most popular strips around. Distributed by King Features, it has featured an African American character, Lt. Flap, for a decade or so, and Walker added an Asian American soldier last year. The new character, Cpl. Yo, irked readers who complained that the slanted eyes and other characteristics amounted to a caricature. Walker tried larger, round eyes that also were criticized before returning to the original version. The character also has been termed a stereotypical Asian because he is particularly smart, hardworking and a perfectionist.

Walker says he understands those who would prefer a more fully developed character, but he points out that in a strip such as his, *all* the characters are caricatures. Beetle is the lazy one, Zero is the dumb one, etc.

Reaction has subsided, and now occasional letters even praise his inclusion, Walker says. "They got used to him. He's just another funny guy like everybody else."

## Avoiding Offense

The fear of stepping into controversy looms for many artists, Lazarus says. "You wonder how that character is going to be received by the people he or she is supposed to represent," he says. "I don't think the black cartoonists have that problem."

Actually, they do. "Curtis'" Billingsley says when he decided to add a regular white character to the strip, he realized he didn't know anything about the experiences of white teen-agers. So rather than misrepresent them, he made Gunk come from the mythical Flyspeck Island, with a strange and wonderful background created entirely from the imagination.

Another problem for some artists is that drawing minority characters can be more time-consuming and technically difficult than white ones, Gillespie says. And many artists don't feel comfortable drawing characteristics that are intended to depict minorities.

But the Free Press' Claus doesn't buy that. "If I had an artist who said he couldn't draw black features, I'd arrange for some training," she notes dryly. She agrees, however, that even the most well-intentioned efforts can cause unintended reaction. "Humor is kind of a dangerous thing."

Gillespie says she thinks real progress will have been made when syndicates start offering "the black Gary Larson or the female Gary Larson"—comics that aren't identified as "black humor" or "female humor" just *good* humor. "I'm not asking black cartoonists to deny their blackness, but I guess I'm just old-fashioned, and I still am waiting for the color-blind days to come."

Most agree that progress will come only with time, as syndicates and newspapers continue to spread the word that they want more diversity and as more minority youngsters see faces like their own in the comics pages.

Billingsley says in the next five to 10 years, he expects to see several new comics by black artists and maybe some about Hispanic, Asian or Jewish characters. "I really think it will happen. A lot of newspaper editors and cartoonists are getting older and retiring, and ideas will start to change as more new people come in."

# XIV

# Women, Men, and Children

One of the reasons media aren't quite so "mass" any longer is that audiences have made it clear that the same formula doesn't work for everyone. Audience appetites are always evolving, and different segments want different media content. Also, within media—among those who write, edit, and produce materials for print and broadcast—different points of view brought to the process by employees of different genders, ages, and racial and ethnic backgrounds, have transformed a mass formula into many different equations.

Two main obstacles must be resolved before media can accurately reflect the world and the people in it. First, stereotypical characters in entertainment programming and stereotypical treatments in news reporting must be eliminated. Second, employment pathways in news and entertainment media must be opened to groups besides white males, who have dominated mass media decisionmaking.

Progress on these two main issues has occurred, most of it apparent only in the 1990s after two decades of activism and challenges to business as usual. Many more women are now employed at levels of influence and compensated at levels comparable to those of their male colleagues. Many more men are now convinced that this development is right. But it didn't happen because male bosses woke up one morning and decided things should change. It happened because of a series of lawsuits and complaints to the Equal Employment Opportunity Commission in the late 1970s and 1980s, forcing employers to recognize the rights of all their employees, especially those of women. Very few major media institutions escaped legal challenges. Among those who did not were the *New York Times,* the *Washington Post, Newsweek, Time, Newsday, Reader's Digest,* the Associated Press, and NBC.

Although equity in employment has improved as a result of these initiatives, debate about sex stereotyping in news coverage and advertising rages on. So does discussion about the disproportionately small amount of space devoted to news coverage of the activities and issues of concern to women and children. The term coined to describe media treatment that favors stereotypes and omits realistic portrayals of a population subgroup is *symbolic annihilation.* The most frequent victims have been women, minorities, and children.

None of this is to say that men, particularly white men, have not been affected by stereotyping in news coverage, advertising, and entertainment programming. They have. They also have had to contend with competition in the work force from groups that formerly hadn't posed much of a threat. This development has antagonized some men and presents yet another point of conflict that needs to be resolved.

Children, of course, don't make demands in the workplace. But they are an important audience segment with influence over a tremendous amount of spending power—their parents' and, as they mature, their own. Adults in media organizations spend a great deal of time researching and testing ways to reach children and inculcate in them the habit of media use—newspaper and magazine reading; television viewing; and enjoyment of videos, films, and sound recordings. Because children have no organized voice of their own, some adults have become active in urging intelligence in programming directed at children and limiting the advertising such programming can contain. The goal of groups such as Action for Children's Television (ACT), which disbanded in 1992 after two decades of activism on behalf of child viewers, was to raise the quality of children's programming and somewhat restrain the advertisers' bombardment of a young audience. ACT also pushed hard, and successfully, for nonstereotypical treatment of girls and boys in programs and ads.

Media of all types have been enriched by the recognition that there is no such thing as a "mass audience," to be served by only one type of media employee. There are now many more choices for all of us and many more kinds of faces in our newsrooms, production studios, and advertising agencies. These changes have been important, and we can be certain that there will be more.

# 61

# We've Come a Long Way, Maybe

## *by* Kay Mills

*Editor's Note:* Women have made a good deal of progress in mass media over the past thirty years, both in the way they are portrayed and in the roles they are playing as gatekeepers. Much still needs to be done, especially in getting into high-level, decision-making positions in mass communication.

As an activist woman journalist, Kay Mills has been very much a part of the progress that has been made. She hopes that a new generation will be able to take up where hers is leaving off and complete the work that still needs to be done.

Mills has been an editorial writer at the *Los Angeles Times* and is the author of a book about women in journalism, *A Place in the News* (New York: Columbia University Press, 1990). This article was published in *The Quill*, February 1990.

Some 30 years ago, I walked into the clatter of the Washington bureau of United Press International, an awestruck college freshman thrilled to begin a summer job typing news stories dictated by the reporters from the White House, the Justice Department, the State Department.

I've been in the newspaper business ever since. And over the years, I encountered a host of problems rooted in male resistance to the presence of women in the newsroom, problems I never anticipated and that I never want to deal with again.

I was not alone. No woman who entered the newspaper business in those days of manual typewriters, smudgy carbon-copy "books," paste pots, and cigar smoke could have imagined the changes that were to occur in their professional lives.

Fortunately, changes did occur regarding the acceptance of women in the newsrooms. Women now have a place in the news. Young women entering the field of journalism today often think we who have been around for a while are talking paleolithic history when we bring up our battles against discrimination. They are wrong.

There still are problems for women in the newspaper business, problems far more subtle and intractable than the blatant discrimination we faced years ago. These problems, too, should be history, like my hoary war stories of taking dictation from Merriman Smith.

But they aren't history, and they won't become history until the leaders of our profession finally wake up to the fact that they are failing to cover a substantial part of their community and that the only way they can perform that mission is by opening the editorial decision-making process to more than white males.

Some of my best friends are white males, but they do not have an exclusive franchise on news judgment. They covered the savings-and-loan bailout with stories and charts and open pages, but they didn't provide the same depth in covering major congressional debates on child-care legislation.

They rarely cover their areas' black communities systematically. They rely on Asian-American and Latino journalists to understand the distinctions among the various ethnic groups in their communities rather than getting out and learning about them themselves. Or worse, they don't have any Asian-American or Latino journalists on their staffs, which means they provide even poorer coverage.

If a paper is dominated by white males, the newspaper has little diversity of coverage, and it won't get it until it has a better mix of people throughout the newsroom and—especially—at the daily page-one meetings of top editors. Women and people of color are not at those meetings in any numbers yet.

But I have gotten ahead of myself. You see where I am going. Now you have to see how we got where we are.

The day that I introduced myself as the new UPI dictationist, I knew precious little about the history of women in my new profession.

I had watched May Craig of the *Portland Press Herald* on *Meet the Press*. But I didn't know that she had had to crusade to get a women's restroom in the press gallery at the Capitol. I soon took dictation from Helen Thomas, who in my two summers at UPI was the new third person on the White House beat. But I didn't know how many years she had waited to get that job. For that matter, I didn't know that for many years when she covered speeches at the National Press Club, she could not sit on the main floor with the male reporters but had to sit in the balcony.

Indignities such as having to sit in the Press Club balcony seem small today, but they were indicators of the second-class citizenship women had long held in the newspaper business. There had always been a few women in the American newsrooms, but they were so rare that their names come readily to mind.

A dozen or so women published newspapers in colonial times. Anne Royall was the first Washington gossip columnist in the early 19th century. Margaret Fuller, best known as a member of the Transcendentalist literary set, became the first female foreign correspondent when she traveled to Europe and covered the Italian version of the upheavals of 1848 for Horace Greeley's *New York Tribune.*

Starting in late 1889, Nellie Bly traveled around the world for the *New York World,* beating Phileas Fogg's fictional record of 80 days and sending back stories of her adventures.

In this century, Dorothy Thompson was pre-eminent in the 1930s. She was the first American journalist thrown out of Nazi Germany, and she later wrote an influential political column.

Marguerite Higgins talked her way into an overseas assignment late in World War II, walked in at the head of the column liberating Dachau, served as *The New York Herald Tribune*'s Berlin correspondent, and later shared the Pulitzer Prize for coverage of the Korean War.

But most women in journalism in the 19th and well into the 20th century were either "sob sisters," covering trials and bleeding-heart human interest stories, or they were hired for the women's pages.

In general, male editors seldom let any real news appear on the women's pages, and the staffs of many women's pages were physically segregated from the rest of the newsroom. The newsroom was "no place for a lady."

Indeed, when Kay Harris was hired in the Associated Press bureau in San Francisco in the 1930s, she was mainly assigned to stories outside the office. Today, she suggests that the attempt to protect her sensitivities (or the men's turf, perhaps) worked to her advantage. Being on the street, she had an opportunity to cover a wide array of stories, from union organizing to the treason trial of "Tokyo Rose" to meetings at which the United Nations was chartered.

These women were the exceptions in the newspaper field. The rule was that women were not hired for the newsroom. But that barrier broke down during three major periods of change for women in the newsroom.

• Eleanor Roosevelt decided that only women could cover her news conferences as First Lady. Since Eleanor Roosevelt made news quite independently of her husband, her decision meant that each wire service, Washington newspaper, and Washington newspaper bureau had to have at least one female reporter.

In many cases, that was *all* they had. But it meant that a succession of talented women got jobs in Washington or held onto them during the Depression, women like Bess Furman, Beth Campbell Short, and Ruth Cowan Nash, who followed one another at the Associated Press.

(Furman and Short eventually left AP because women were expected to leave their jobs when they became pregnant. Some women were fired if they didn't get the message.)

• Just as Rosie the Riveter filled in for men in the shipyards and airplane factories during World War II, so Rosie the Reporter finally got her break in American newsrooms. Helen Thomas got her start at what was then the United

Press during the war, as did Eileen Shanahan, later a distinguished economics reporter for *The New York Times.*

Once in the nation's newsrooms, women found there was no special mystique to writing a headline or editing copy or covering a basketball game. Mary Garber of the *Winston-Salem Journal Sentinel* started covering sports then. Flora Lewis of *The New York Times* got overseas in time for VJ Day.

But many women lost their jobs when the war ended, even when servicemen did not return to reclaim their positions. The late 1940s, the 1950s, and well into the 1960s were dreary times for women who wanted to be journalists. As recently as the mid-1960s, after I had worked for UPI two summers in Washington and three years in its Chicago bureau, I tried to get a newspaper or news magazine job. The excuses delight me today but sent me into a tailspin then.

The *Chicago Daily News* already had four women so it couldn't possibly hire another. *Newsweek* had a small bureau and needed someone who could go anywhere. Presumably, I couldn't. Besides, what would I do if someone I was covering ducked into the men's room? Of course no one covered by men would duck into the women's room, because few women were perceived as making news.

• In the '60s and '70s, women on some women's sections began covering the real news of their world—women seeking better educations, women organizing for political influence, women seeking economic parity, women demanding better health care.

Others were campaigning to open the National Press Club to membership and full privileges for women. Others sued their employers, most notably *The New York Times* and the Associated Press.

While these women won only limited gains—and often extra trouble—for themselves (the pioneers-take-the-arrows syndrome), they put their organizations and others on notice that they must hire more women, promote them, and give them better assignments.

Equal opportunity at the Associated Press was especially important beyond the obvious fact that more women got jobs. More women's bylines appeared on the wire and therefore in newspapers around the country; women sometimes did their enterprise stories on issues that affected women; and women were getting the valuable wire-service training that often leads to good jobs at other news organizations.

By the early '70s, more and more women were coming out of college journalism programs, and they simply assumed they could get jobs in newsrooms. Some did.

It took longer for women to be hired in any numbers as photographers, sportswriters, and foreign correspondents, but that has happened, too. However, men still seem to get the benefit of the doubt when these assignments are made; women don't.

So where are we today and where do we still have to go? Huntly Collins of *The Philadelphia Inquirer* remembers that when she joined that paper only a few years ago, there were few women on the business staff. Now the business page is dotted with women's bylines. When I started out, the only women who covered politics were columnists like Mary McGrory. Today Timothy Crouse could no longer title his book *The Boys on the Bus*.

Marguerite Higgins was a rarity as a war correspondent in Korea. By the 1980s, women often were *the* experts on the guerrilla warfare in El Salvador and Nicaragua.

Solveig Torvik says that when she started at the *Seattle Post-Intelligencer* in the early 1970s, attitudes were such that editors hesitated to send a woman on an overnight assignment or out of town with a male photographer. That has changed, in part because there are now often more women on the city desk than men.

The number of women in middle management constitutes "a dramatic change," Torvik adds, "but that last leap into being final decision-makers is not being made. I'd like to see a woman's name on every masthead of every newspaper worth calling itself that."

Indeed, the lack of room at the top is a major problem. A recent survey conducted by Jean Gaddy Wilson, executive director of New Directions for News at the University of Missouri, showed that women now have only 14 percent of the top decision-making editing jobs at American newspapers. They are 18 percent of the directing editors at the smallest papers (under 10,000 circulation); 10 percent at papers of 25,000 to 50,000; 13 percent at papers of 100,000 to 125,000 circulation; and 16 percent at the nation's largest papers (more than 250,000 circulation). They fare less well as publishers, averaging 6 percent of the total.

The higher you look in a newspaper hierarchy, the fewer women you will see. That is partly because women have not been part of the pool of candidates as long as men, partly because some women take themselves out of the running (or are taken out of the running) as they raise their children, and partly because too many newspaper managements still have not done all they can do to recognize female talent the way they are somehow able to spot the bright young man who walks in the door. It may be because he looks like the bosses; we still don't.

"There have to be more voices," says Torvik, now an editorial writer and columnist at the *Post-Intelligencer*. "The task in the 1990s is to broaden newspaper appeal to a vast number of people out there who may not find us very interesting. It's in our own interests of self-preservation to do so."

The question remains: How can the men who run American newspapers be convinced that it is in their long-range self-interest to promote women and thus share power? It's like reinventing the wheel. The men at the top must be constantly convinced that readership exists for broader coverage of issues like child care or women's economic aspirations.

We've told them and shown them and told them again, but that coverage still isn't second nature to them in the way that coverage of political party conventions and plane crashes is.

We simply must keep covering the stories that we know are there. Women must not be afraid to show how women could survive in Central America or cover dramatic political change in the Soviet Union. Only if newspapers cover a wider range of subject matter will they attract a wider range of readers and thus advertisers. The link between the breadth of coverage to the health of the bottom line seems obvious.

Just as women must do more of the same in terms of coverage, so must we keep up our friendly persuasion on the personnel front. Editors and publishers need to be shown again and again, evidently, the common sense behind promoting women. For their part, women must constantly push their bosses to make changes in what's covered—and who covers what.

Lawsuits, the tool of the 1970s in the effort to end discrimination, will be harder to win in the future. The Supreme Court has chilled that form of attack, but employers who blatantly pass over women for top jobs shouldn't be allowed to feel immune from such threats.

Betsy Wade, one of the women who sued *The New York Times* (and who still works there), says the next fight will have to be waged by the young women, however. It won't be fought by the people who fought it before.

"Everything needs to be done. I don't think we have enough accomplishments to say anything has been done. You look at the hiring lists. You are not seeing what you were seeing when there was legal pressure. It is going to take action of an unrealized sort to make the situation move to benefit women and minorities again.

"We cannot take our daughters and our granddaughters over the waters, much as we would dearly love to do so. They are going to have to muddy themselves."

But first young women have to realize that changes still must be made. I am betting they will wise up when they talk to their friends in other fields about the child-care perks their companies offer and they look at what newspapers don't do for them. And now that women make up one-third of the newspaper work force (and two-thirds of the journalism school graduates), newspapers act at their own risk if they ignore the need.

While child care is, of course, only one issue, employers who do a better job of providing such care would free many women to concentrate more on their work while they are on the job. More important, it would symbolize a real commitment by newspapers to clearing away obstacles to women's progress.

One of these days, younger women are also going to look at their newsrooms and then at their mastheads, and they will want to know why women aren't making it to the top as readily as they have in many other businesses. If newspapers don't change, these young women will vote with their feet, and the profession will lose talent.

These younger women also are going to check out the subtle bias in assigning stories and perhaps get to work on that. Or they may concentrate on the nature of the stories that are and are not covered. Or they may more closely examine the language that is still used to describe women as opposed to that used to describe men. Or they may assess the way a paper's resources are allocated to sports as opposed to social problems, and to men's professional sports teams instead of to women's—and men's—recreational sports activities.

They could well raise questions, too, about why black, Latina, and Asian-American women remain even more underrepresented in top jobs on newspapers and about why white women so often forget to include the concerns of women of color on their agendas.

There are individual successes, to be sure, such as Pam Johnson, a black woman who is publisher of *The Ithaca Journal* in New York State. And there is a growing number of black women who write editorials. But as one of their number said, an editorial writer affects only one editorial on one day, while a black woman at the page-one conference or drawing up a news staff budget can have far more impact on the operation of the paper. It's time for more black journalists to have a shot at running a department or the entire newspaper, but too few organizations seem comfortable with that notion.

We've come a long way from the days of not being allowed to sit on the main floor of National Press Club, but we're not there yet. And we won't be until young women and older women, white women and women of color, stop thinking only of their own careers and form alliances for change at every newspaper in the United States.

# 62

# No News Is Women's News

## by Junior Bridge

*Editor's Note:* In spite of progress, women's emerging role in society is not reflected in the nation's news media, as this article demonstrates. The United States is not alone; many other countries deal with women in the same or even in a more negative way. In the Philippines, for example, according to one study, only women in the upper 5 percent, those who belong to the cultured elite or to the monied politician class, can be newsmakers. Failing that, women either have to be victims (mainly of sex crimes) or criminals to merit mention and to land in the headlines.

Junior Bridge is president of Unabridged Communications in Alexandria, Virginia. This article was published in *Media & Values*, Winter 1989.

In bold, large letters, the August 7, 1989 issue of *Time* magazine asked: "Is She Worth It?" The "she" was Diane Sawyer, prime-time newscaster, who had just landed a plum of a job with ABC.

Can you remember any instance where the headlines read: "Is *He* Worth It?"

In a field overwhelmingly dominated by men, many of whom are making enormous salaries, it took the rise of this one woman for a corporate media giant like *Time* magazine to question high media salaries. Why?

Consider, too, how *Time* described Sawyer. First, she "has it all" because of her "blond-haired good looks." Second, *Time* lists her charming personality. Last on the list, Sawyer's journalistic skills are noted. How often are men defined primarily by their looks and personalities, and lastly by their capabilities?

The continued low economic and social status of women in this country prompts, among other activities, an examination of media coverage of and by women. Focus on the media produces a widely accessible and understandable indicator of women's societal status and their value.

In March 1989, I directed a study of women's roles as newsmakers and creators, one of several related studies released at the second annual Women, Men and Media Conference held in Washington, D.C. in April, 1989. During our monitoring period, the front pages and the first pages of the local section of 10 major general-interest newspapers were examined daily. Counts of bylines by gender, photographs of men and women, and references to men and women were noted.

The newspapers included: the *Atlanta Constitution, Chicago Tribune, Houston Chronicle, Los Angeles Times, Miami Herald,* the *New York Times, St. Louis Post Dispatch, Seattle Times, USA Today,* and the *Washington Post.* Consideration in the selection of papers was given primarily to geographic location. Also, an effort was made to include papers from states considered to be bellwether areas for social change.

The pages examined were also chosen to see if there was any difference in news coverage of and by women at the international/national level (usually found on front pages) and the local level.

The findings were discouraging.

• *Bylines.*    Female bylines on the front pages averaged 27 percent for the month. They were a little higher on the local front pages, registering 33 percent on average.

• *Photographs.*    Females were represented in only 24 percent of the front-page pictures and appeared in only 28 percent of local-page photos. Unlike men, females appeared primarily in group shots and were most often seen with their spouses and children.

• *References.*    The average percentage of references to women was abysmally low: 11 percent. They appeared only slightly more frequently (20 percent) on local pages.

The conclusion is obvious. Many women may have positions of power and influence and their own unique perspective of society's workings. But their special knowledge is not reflected in the nation's newspapers.

Their relative invisibility occurs despite the fact that females comprise over half of the U.S. population, about half of newspaper readership, 45 percent of the total labor force, 60 percent of new investors in the New York Stock Exchange companies and more than half of all college students. During the month of the survey, there were days when there were no female bylines, photographs or references to women at all on the front pages. Imagine a front page without a male byline, photo, or reference!

An unexpected finding was the paucity of female sources in stories written by women writers. Female reporters don't appear to seek out female sources any more often than do male writers. Even stories on topics of specific and great concern to women, such as abortion, often contained more quotes from men, and few or no quotes from women.

## Subordinate References

Most often, females were portrayed as victims of brutal acts, or in terms of their familial relationships, as "Mary, the daughter of"; "his wife, Barbara"; or, "Joyce, mother of four." It was noted, too, that women were referred to more frequently by their first names than men.

*USA Today* averaged higher percentages of female bylines (41 percent), photos (41 percent), and female references (21 percent) than the other papers examined. *The New York Times* averaged the lowest percentages of female bylines (16 percent), photos (16 percent), and references (5 percent).

The results from two other media monitoring studies were released at the same time as the aforementioned print study. Also made public during the conference, held in Washington, D.C., on April 10, 1989, the findings from the three studies stunned the audience.

## TV Tokens

A month-long (February 1989) television news-monitoring effort by the Communications Consortium, a Washington, D.C., public-interest organization, found no women as regular anchors at any of the three networks during weekday evening news programs. Most startling was the finding that since similar studies were conducted in 1974 by the U.S. Commission on Civil Rights, and again in 1984 by the Women's Media Project (NOW Legal Defense and Education Fund), the total percentage of women correspondents reporting the news increased by only six percent over the past 15 years.

CBS topped the list (as it did in 1984) with just over 22 percent of news stories reported by women, and ABC again was at the bottom with 10 percent of female reporters for network stories. At two of the networks, at least one-fourth of the broadcasts had no women correspondents.

As newsmakers, women fared worse than as news reporters. Overall, women were one in 10 of those interviewed or featured on network nightly news.

On the employment side, a five-year study of hiring trends and pay scales by researchers at the University of Missouri shows that female media employees earn only 64 cents for every dollar that males are paid. The national average for all industries is 70 cents for every dollar paid to a man. The study shows that the media fail to promote women as often as their male counterparts, and that women are segregated into the least powerful support staff jobs.

Is the media creating a false reality, or reflecting an actual one? Is the low coverage by and about women due to sexist attitudes? The studies do not address these questions. The numbers these studies did produce, though, make one point abundantly clear: women are still not considered "worth it."

# 63

# Media Myths and Men's Work

## *by* Ian Harris

*Editor's Note:* Although men are much more widely represented in mass media, they too are sometimes victims of stereotypical coverage. This article points out that the picture of most men "enjoying the material benefits of the successful white-collar professional is a media hoax."

As today's economic shakeups threaten their jobs, many men feel inadequate in the face of a media culture that venerates executives in three-piece suits, says Ian Harris, chair of the department of educational policy and community studies at the University of Wisconsin, Milwaukee. This article was published in *Media & Values,* Fall 1989.

The dominant image of the American male portrayed on television, in film and in magazines depicts a white-collar gentleman living in the suburbs in affluent circumstances. These individuals own American Express credit cards and buy the latest model cars. From Ozzie and Harriet to Bill Cosby, these images occupy a powerful place in the American psyche and set standards for male behaviors. They run the media and the large corporations. They speak to us through radios and television. They teach our children. They are not only standard bearers but also the image makers who provide a model for male expectations.

While entertainment programs often create the stereotype of the violent adventurer, advertising campaigns used to promote American products create the deceptive view that the majority of men enjoy the privileges of white-collar professional status. But these images are a myth. In reality . . . few achieve the success portrayed by media images.

Of those men fortunate enough to be employed at all, most work in jobs where they cannot live out the media's version of "the American dream." According to 1981 U.S. government statistics, individuals who fit the category "Males in Professional White Collar Occupations" account for only 15 percent of all employed men, or eight percent of the total male population. Yet certainly they are not the only men satisfied with their professional lives. The nonprofessional technical occupations, representing an additional 27 percent of employed men, include engineers, skilled craftsmen and other technicians who experience relatively high status and success. Some males in blue-collar jobs and service and farm occupations also earn good salaries and, by their own accounts, feel successful in their work and in their lives. Yet men in all classes are affected by white-collar professional images broadcast through the media and rarely supplemented by images of men in other job categories and occupations. The restriction of work images to wealthy white-collar professional has severe consequences. Raised in a society that honors the Horatio Alger myth, most men believe that a man who works hard will get ahead. Male sex role standards describe a life where American men are supposed to be good fathers, contribute to their communities and occupy positions of power and wealth. The reality of most men's lives, however, is very different from those media-promoted financial and professional success images.

## Most Men's Lives

With 71 percent of U.S. men making less than $25,000 annually in 1984, relatively few male workers and their families can approach the standards of consumerism portrayed by television and advertising. The media myth that most men enjoy or have access to the material benefits of the successful white-collar professional is a hoax. Most men will never get status jobs. The vast majority of men either work in occupations other than white collar, are institutionalized, unemployed or have dropped out of the active work force. However, their stories are not told in the media and their plight is ignored.

The 45 percent of working men in blue-collar jobs "man" the factories and other skilled or unskilled trades. Although often taking great pride in their work, many of them labor in positions that offer little or no opportunities for advancement and that may be dull, repetitive and dangerous. Their lives are marked by economic stress, they usually have little or no control over their working conditions and are increasingly threatened by company shifts to cheaper overseas labor and other contractions of the global work force.

Although always the unsung heroes of the U.S. economy, their current media invisibility is something of a change. From 1950 to 1978, this group of men enjoyed some economic security, and media images of the happy, beer-drinking, blue-collar worker abounded in the broad range of ads and commercials and such TV programs as *The Life of Riley*.

Although these men are excluded from the mediated version of the American dream, it is incorrect to assume that men who do achieve some measure of white-collar success necessarily lead more fulfilling lives. The majority of white-collar men spend their lives battling within highly competitive organizations that are so stressful that working within them predisposes them to cancer, heart attack and other stress-related diseases.

Displaced from the labor statistics as they are from society, underclass men lead desperate lives. Seventy percent of these hard-pressed males belong to minority groups. As the migrant workers, prisoners, welfare recipients, homeless street people and patients in mental hospitals, the underclass appears in entertainment programming mainly as criminals. They are seen as a threat to society, but the portraits drawn of them seldom prove the violent worlds that shaped them and their constant fights—often unsuccessful—to survive.

Underclass men do not have regular work. Their hustles for survival include part-time work at low wages, robbery, pimping, drug pushing and other illegal activities. Many end up in prison when they break the law to earn their livelihoods. In fact, prison becomes a sort of brutal haven to escape the viciousness of the street. For the thousands of men of this class, life has no future, few possessions and little purpose. Many are filled with anger at a system that denies them access to the cultural norms of success.

Whether employed or unemployed, whether blue or white collar, men in the United States share a common alienation regarding the conditions of their employment. This alienation is rooted in the realization that a man's work (or lack of work) is at odds with his personal goals.

Unfortunately, male socialization does not help men cope with the realities of the modern workplace. Indeed, male training is designed to create good workers, not full human beings. To cope with deep-felt insecurities, men learn to put up a facade that they are competent and in charge of their destiny. The intense competitiveness of the workplace causes men to be distrustful of their peers, preventing real communication and empathy with others.

These problems in men's lives have become issues for the men's movement. They are also media issues to the degree that the movement seeks to shatter media myths that set sex-role expectations. The mostly white, middle-class leaders of the movement are shaped by the media they see and hear. They are largely ignorant of the problems of most men in the United States, in part because the media seldom, if ever, realistically present underclass and working-class existence.

The media and society as a whole need to bury the popular myth that male success consists of making money. Instead of glorifying male violence, they should portray the pain that causes it. Let's create a new American myth where men are concerned human beings promoting a better life for all creatures on this planet. Liberation is a long and difficult struggle that requires the economic transformation of society as well as the alteration of personal relationships. The media has played its role in creating the problem. It must also be a part of the solution.

# 64

# Male Bashing on the Rise

## *by* Frederic Hayward

*Editor's Note:* It is inevitable, of course, that women's efforts to achieve equality in mass media would have an impact on men. To many men, it seems that entertainment media in particular have increasingly denigrated males in an effort to appease females. The backlash has been the rise of men's organizations fighting for male rights.

The author of this article, Frederic Hayward, is a lecturer and writer on men's issues; he creates multimedia presentations on "Men's Images in Media." He is executive director of Men's Rights, Inc., an antisexist, nonprofit corporation in Sacramento, California. This article was published in *Media & Values*, Fall 1989.

By far, "male bashing" is the most popular topic in my current talk shows and interviews. Reporters and television crews have come to me from as far away as Denmark, Australia and Germany to investigate this American phenomenon. What is going on, they ask? Why do women want it? Why do men allow it?

The trend is particularly rampant in advertising. In a survey of a thousand random advertisements, 100 percent of the jerks singled out in male-female relationships were male. There were no exceptions. That is, whenever there was a husband-wife or boyfriend-girlfriend interaction, the one who was dumped on was the male.

One hundred percent of the ignorant ones were male; 100 percent of the ones who lost a contest were male. One hundred percent of the ones who smelled bad (mouthwash and detergent commercials) were male; 100 percent of the ones who were put down without retribution were male. (Sometimes the male would insult the female, but she was always sure to get him back in spades before the commercial ended.) One hundred percent of the objects of anger were male; 100 percent of the objects of violence were male.

In entertainment, the trend is similarly discouraging. Some television shows are little more than a bunch of anti-male jokes strung together. Deciding to count the phenomenon during an episode of *The Golden Girls*, I found 31 women's insults of men compared to two men's insults of women. Family sitcoms like *The Cosby Show* or *Family Ties* have an unwritten rule that mothers are *never* to be the butt of jokes or made to look foolish.

As to literature, just glance through the recent best-seller lists. There is no anti-female literature that matches the anti-male tone of *Smart Women, Foolish Choices, Men Who Can't Love* or *Men Who Hate Women and the Women Who Love Them.* Two authors told me about pressure from their editors to create anti-male titles as a way of increasing sales.

Products also reflect the popularity of hating men. One owner of a greeting card store reports that male-bashing cards are her biggest-selling line. A variety of post-its from 3M such as "The more I know about men, the more I like my dog" are big sellers. A 3M spokesperson added that they have no intention of selling similarly anti-female products. Walk through any T-shirt store and compare the number of anti-female slogans to anti-male slogans. Women might take offense at sexual innuendos, but there is a qualitative difference between something that is interpreted as insulting and something that is intended as insulting.

The current male-bashing trend appeals to the female consumer, upon whose whims our economy depends. It is comforting for women to think that men are always at fault, while women are always innocent. Interestingly, male-bashing even appeals to the male mentality. Forced to compete with each other, in contrast to the way women are allowed to empathize with each other, men enjoy male-bashing (as long as the bashee is another male). Males have long had negative self-images, and every man has a deep fantasy that he can be better than all other men . . . the hero who will earn women's love by rescuing her from all the other rotten men.

For society's sake, however, and for the health of future male-female relationships, we had better start to curb the excesses of male-bashing. The alternative can only lead to a men's movement as angry with women, and far more violent, than the women's movement has been toward men.

# 65

# Boob Tube and Children's Brain Drain

## *by* Don Oldenburg

---

*Editor's Note:* As we have shown earlier in this book, television takes up an enormous amount of American children's time. And to what effect? We have looked at the impact of TV violence and sex on aggressive and sexual behavior. But there may be an even more sinister problem. Some scientific studies are showing that TV viewing may have serious negative effects on the way a child's brain works.

In this article, Don Oldenburg summarizes some of the scientific findings that have led to such a conclusion. He is a staff writer for the *Washington Post*, where this article was published on October 12, 1992.

---

Are children experiencing technical difficulties due to television?

Perhaps it should be no surprise that when leading psychologists and scientists who study the developing brain met at a conference in Washington just over a week ago to consider that prime-time question, America's top entertainer and babysitter got another bad reception.

Tormenting concerns over what too much TV watching may be doing to our children of course were reiterated. Who can ignore current estimates that the average child watches 22,000 hours of television before graduating from high school—twice the amount of time spent in a classroom? Who isn't troubled by the evidence "from the trenches," as one participant termed the schools, where today's students seem to suffer from an epidemic of attention-deficit disorders, diminished language skills and poor reading comprehension, where teachers report that more than ever children lack analytic powers, creativity and persistence? For that matter, who can organize a conference on television's effects on learning ability without repeating the symptoms?

But if that sounds like a rerun of all the usual suspicions about TV's negative effects, don't touch that dial. Because this daylong highbrow talk show dramatically raised the level of debate over television's undeniable influence—positive and negative—on young minds.

It also raised the ante in what people's worst fears suggest is a potentially devastating game of high-tech Russian roulette: Television's electronic transmissions and programming are blowing out the brains of the remote-control generation.

At the invitation of the U.S. Department of Health and Human Services' Administration on Children, Youth and Families, these researchers, policy makers, educators and clinical psychologists broadened the long-standing question of whether television influences how children use their minds to whether television affects the physiological growth and neural functioning of the brain.

In other words, is television biologically altering—or stunting—the brain power of TV-programmed kids?

## We Interrupt This Program

Jane M. Healy refers to the context of such concerns as "our uneasy relationship with a medium that we suspect of rotting our children's brains."

It should be noted that Healy, the conference's moderator, seldom pulls punches when the target is TV's enslavement of children; she prefers to pull the plug instead. One of the nation's most outspoken critics of television's impact on cognitive development, in her 1990 book "Endangered Minds: Why Our Children Don't Think," she blamed the usually acclaimed PBS program "Sesame Street" for contributing to the death of reading and for misinforming children about the nature of learning.

Generally Healy says she believes television viewing leaves children's growing and pliable brains "disadvantaged" for the learning tasks ahead. She is outraged that any medium possibly that harmful to our progeny has barely been investigated—and is taken so lightly by so many parents.

"Any significant amount of time devoted to an activity has the potential to change the growing brain, [so] what is television doing to or for our children?" asks Healy.

Conceding the TV habit is but one of many influential changes in the lives of children during the past 20 years, she doesn't discount the faster pace of life kids must endure, the fewer models and moments of reflective thinking, the diminishing opportunities to converse with parents and adults. Too often, she believes, teachers and school are unfairly blamed for low achievement scores and learning problems.

"All of this is not attributable to the schools," says Healy, whose work often applies brain research in practical classroom situations. "Teachers are not doing that bad a job, nor are they doing that different a job than they did 10 and 20 years ago. Something is different. The kids appear to be different."

## Pumping Brain Cells

Citing a "Calvin and Hobbes" cartoon showing a slack-jawed, heavy-eyed and drooling Calvin mesmerized by a TV screen, the educational psychologist based in Vail, Colo., laments, "It is surprising, even shocking, that we can laugh at this situation and draw cartoons about it without demanding the facts. There is virtually no research on the effects of TV viewing on neural development."

Some physiological research does exist, however, that hints of a connection between the kind of experience television provides and a decrease in nerve-cell growth and functioning in the brain. Unfortunately, while that basic research has proven to be significant in demonstrating the incredible changeability of the brain's structure, it only can be speculative about TV's physiological effects. Also, the subjects were laboratory rats, not children.

"Before we did this work, nobody thought the brain could change," says Marian Cleeves Diamond. "It was essentially regarded to be a stable structure except when it deteriorates with aging."

A professor of anatomy at the University of California at Berkeley, Diamond has conducted experiments that compare brain-cell growth in rat pups that are provided with opposite extremes in mental stimulation. While some young rats (equivalent to the age when human children show the most rapid neural development) lived in large cages with playmates and three mother rats, with access to a changing supply of toys, the other rat pups were isolated in small cages without toys or playmates.

Brain samples from the young rats showed increases in every part of the nerve cells measured (dimension of the cerebral cortex, blood vessels, the cell body, nerve branching, synaptic junctions, etcetera) in the enriched subjects and a decrease from the standard measurements in the impoverished subjects.

"This is very simple work to show that with enrichment you can grow not new nerve cells but bigger and better nerve cells," reports Diamond. "And with impoverishment you get less."

How do these findings relate to the influence of television? Many critics charge that television viewing is a largely passive experience that steals from children hours of otherwise active and creative play, of reading and other exercises for the mind, of interacting with other children and parents. It could be argued, in other words, that in terms of the learning development of the human brain, television represents an impoverished environment.

"Investigators have shown that if rats sit alone in cages, watching those rats in the enriched environments, their brains do not demonstrate measurable changes," says Diamond. "It is important to interact with the objects, to explore, to investigate both physically and mentally. Mere observation is not enough to bring about changes. A passive existence is not enough."

While psychologist Jane Holmes Bernstein isn't prepared to label television the sole culprit in disadvantaging young brains, she has come to believe that learning disorders rightly or wrongly used as the label for a host of symptoms that plague up to 20 percent of the school-age population—can sometimes result from environmental impact.

"We create them by asking small brains to do things they are not yet ready to do," says the director of the neuropsychology program at Children's Hospital in Boston and assistant clinical professor of psychology at the Harvard Medical School. "And by not facilitating a typical growth or development in the brain."

Although the critical principle "is that of the interaction of brain development and experience," she cautions against rushing to any easy conclusions about television viewing during sensitive periods of brain-cell growth.

"The answer is not going to be simple," she predicts. "Brains are differently influenceable at different times by different events or inputs. So television as a medium, like any other type of input, could be very benign or even positive at one age, and quite deleterious at [another] in the same animal."

But Bernstein worries that high levels of TV exposure in children at the most susceptible ages might be limiting opportunities for the kind of interactive conversation and experiences that promote strong language skills. "The reason why this is important," she says, "is that the active engagement in the processing of language use is crucial to being able to take part in the educational system in the early and later grades."

## Home Alone (with TV)

When examining TV's impact on children, Jerome L. Singer is convinced the greatest influence is if and how parents "mediate" that experience—perhaps supporting the idea that the absence of such interaction is what contributes to the impoverishing effect of television.

"We are seeing some hazards of heavy television viewing. We're talking here of the kind of programs on commercial television . . . particularly the more rapidly paced violent action programs," says Singer, a professor of psychology at Yale University and co-director of the Yale Family Television Research and Consultation Center.

"Most [heavy-viewing] kids show lower information, lower reading recognition or readiness to reading, lower reading levels," says Singer. "They tend to show lower imaginativeness, and less complex language use. We consistently find heavy viewing . . . is associated with more aggressive behavior."

But a most important variable in mitigating those results, says Singer, was parents who were involved in the child's viewing habits. "When parents control television and explain things to the children, we find somewhat dramatic results over years of time," says the coauthor of "Television, Imagination and Aggression" and "The Parent's Guide: Use TV to Your Child's Advantage." Children in families with high levels of parental mediation and low levels of TV viewing scored the highest on reading recognition tests, he reports. High mediating families with high television viewing still had "pretty good scores," followed in order by low mediating families and low TV, and at the bottom low mediating families and high TV viewing.

"The situation is a clear hazard for the child who is watching four or five hours or more a day," says Singer. "We have reason to be seriously concerned about those effects. But [with] the kinds of parents who talk to the children, respond to the TV with explanations, you get interesting changes in the overall pattern. The parents who take the trouble . . . are also going to be discriminating viewers of the television and point the kids to child-oriented programming.

"What I think we have to look forward is to a more careful and thoughtful role by adults in helping [the child] deal with the potentially hazardous but also potentially useful medium."

## New and Improved

If his colleagues at the conference are pioneers in exploring the impact of television on our brains, Byron B. Reeves has advanced to the next technological frontier.

While they examine the influence of images flickering from standard 19-inch-diagonal screens, the professor of communications at Stanford University who specializes in the psychological processing of television is projecting the effects of state-of-the-art TVs with screens whose diagonals measure 27 inches and may soon stretch to 6 feet. He's concerned about sets with resolution and color nearly the quality of film, with a panoramic-aspect ratio that provides a movie-like horizontal effect, with high-quality sound that surrounds the viewer.

"New changes in television sets . . . may dramatically alter what can be said about how television educates and influences children," says Reeves, who notes with both enthusiasm and caution the significant changes in the size, shape, resolution and sound of TVs in the past decade—with more to come in the next five years. The median diagonal length of TV sets in 1990, for instance, was 22 inches—a 33 percent increase in picture screen area over the standard 19-inch sets of yesteryear. The now-popular 27-inch screen is about a 100 percent increase in picture area over the 19-inch set: One-third of the sets sold in 1990 were larger than 27 inches.

The difference in what happens inside a viewer's head? "It is more likely to be surprising and arousing," says Reeves. "It can be processed without conscious awareness. And it creates a more literal sense of motion—enough to make it more likely to get seasick watching a boat on a big-screen TV. Big screens are also accompanied by big sounds.

"All of these developments," he continues, "make television viewing increasingly lifelike. . . . Our bodies cannot afford to mistakenly dismiss a picture as being inconsequential, even if nothing can actually jump from the screen. The many psychological responses to the illusion of reality can be as powerful as reality itself."

In pilot studies he completed last year on this advanced technology, Reeves found that for adults larger images and higher fidelity increased viewer attention and feelings of excitement, amplified perceptions of people on TV as both more positive and more negative, and inhibited thoughtful processing and produced poorer memory.

"In short," he says, the subjects "liked the experience but they couldn't remember much about it. In children, viewers that we know are even more prone to the influence of visual and auditory form, new televisions could reshape the viewing environment even more radically. . . . Despite the excitement for these new products, they may be introduced without consideration for viewers who will spend the most time using them—children."

## Public Broadcast

Wade F. Horn considers the impact of television on children's brains an "extraordinarily serious and important" topic. As commissioner of HHS Administration on Children, Youth and Families, and a child psychologist with kids of his own, he's concerned that too many of America's children are arriving at the beginning of their schooling mentally unprepared to succeed—psychologically not equipped with the basic cognitive skills required for learning.

"For good or bad, each of these skills can be influenced by time spent watching television," he says. Horn says he knows there are many contributing factors. But excessive TV viewing is one that parents—with the help of the federal government—can do something about.

"We can begin to focus the attention of the nation on such critically important issues of how television affects the developing mind," Horn says. "And the federal government can disseminate this information to the most important people in children's lives—their parents—so that they can make more informed judgments as to how and what type of television viewing children engage in."

# 66

# The Right Place to Find Children

## *by* S. K. List

*Editor's Note:* Children of course have become an enormous mass media audience, much sought after by advertisers and marketers. Children watch a great deal of television, from preschool years right through high school, and television has exploited that market thoroughly.

Now print media are getting into the act as well. Magazines and newspapers for children offer a smaller and more select audience than children's television. Many of the magazines do not take advertising, but corporate sponsorship is often allowed. Children are an elusive audience, and some experts feel that the new wave of print media is the most efficient way to reach them.

S. K. List is a freelance writer living in Trumansburg, New York. This article appeared in *American Demographics*, February 1992.

Saturday morning has been the home base of children's television for decades. That may soon change. NBC's Saturday morning programs have been suffering from low ratings, and so the network has decided to get out. "We're going to abandon Saturday morning cartoons," says Horst Stipp, NBC's director of social and developmental research.

Today's parents prefer to plop their children in front of a television during the hours after school, from 4 to 6 p.m. Twenty-nine percent of children aged 2 to 11 watch TV before dinner, compared with 24 percent who give their parents an extra hour of sleep on Saturday morning, according to Simmons Market Research Bureau. Like everyone else, children spend the most time watching prime-time TV.

Children are an audience worth targeting in hundreds of consumer markets. But reaching them with television commercials is rapidly growing more expensive and less efficient. Advertisers are looking for better ways to deliver messages to American youth. Increasingly, they are turning to magazines, newspapers, and radio.

Children's versions of *Sports Illustrated, National Geographic, Field and Stream,* and *Consumer Reports* are already being thumbed by little hands. The number of periodicals for youngsters almost doubled between 1986 and

1991, with 81 new titles, according to professor Samir Husni at the University of Mississippi.

## Smaller and More Select

Fifty-seven percent of children read magazines, according to Pamela Baxter, executive vice president at Simmons Market Research Bureau. That is more than the share of children who read comic books. Children who read magazines are slightly more likely to be boys than girls, and they are also more likely than nonreaders to live in high-income households. Compared with the audience for children's TV, they are a smaller and more select group.

The demographics are convincing enough that many established children's TV shows are now crossing over to print. The list of crossovers includes *Sesame Street Magazine,* the monthly *Nickelodeon,* Fox's *Kids' Club* magazine, and Disney's *Duck Tales. Sesame Street Magazine,* like its parent television show, has a strong educational emphasis. But the magazine's parents' guide carried almost 200 pages of advertising in 1990.

A brand new magazine called *Spark* targets the creative side of children aged 6 to 11. It's filled with art and writing projects, plus ads for Crayola crayons, Pentel pens, and Fruit Stripe gum. The projects "are things kids can do on their own with minimal assistance from parents," says managing editor Beth Struck. But the marketing plan is aimed squarely at mom and dad. *Spark for Parents,* a 16-page insert in the November issue, includes a creative guide and tips on exposing children to art museums in a positive way.

Some magazines for children try to establish brand loyalty at an early age. *Sports Illustrated for Kids* made a big splash when it was launched by Time Inc. in 1989. Following the debut, then-publisher Ann Moore said, "We believe children make brand decisions very early that they will carry into their adult lives."

Current publisher Susan Sachs defines "brand loyalty" broadly. One of the magazine's primary purposes, she says, is "fighting illiteracy and creating long-term readers. Another is getting the magazine into the hands of those who couldn't otherwise afford it." About 250,000 free copies of *SI for Kids* are distributed nationwide to classrooms in low-income schools, along with a monthly teacher's guide. The program is co-sponsored by the advertisers.

*Sports Illustrated for Kids* is a success because it offers advertisers a mix of flexibility and precision in reaching children. One advertiser, Wheaties, offered a free subscription on cereal boxes; another, McDonald's, co-produced a nutrition and fitness guide for teachers' use.

"We help advertisers see what kids like," says Sachs. "A lot of our creative [material] is busy, colorful, fun, and interactive. It's a new field."

The owners of *SI for Kids* also collect mountains of information about their readers. Paid subscribers draw an average of about $4 a week in allowance. That amounts to $125 million in spending money each year. The copy is geared to a fifth-grade reader, but the average reader is slightly younger—about 9 or 10. About half of the subscribers live in two regions: the Middle Atlantic states of New York, Pennsylvania, and New Jersey, and the East North Central states of Ohio, Indiana, Illinois, Michigan, and Wisconsin. Boys outnumber girls two to one on the readership.

If boys outnumber girls, why does *SI for Kids* give equal attention to women's sports? Perhaps it's because the magazine's real customers are affluent working couples. More than 70 percent of the parents of paid subscribers fall between the ages of 35 and 44, and more than three-quarters of the parents have attended college. The parents' median household income is $54,700.

## No Advertising, But . . .

Many children's magazines do not accept advertising, but some of the ad-free magazines still seek relationships with businesses. *P3* (or *Planet Three*) is an environmental magazine for readers aged 6 to 12, printed in color on recycled paper and published by the Vermont-based P3 Foundation. The magazine does not carry advertising, but the foundation does encourage "corporate sponsorship." One such contribution resulted in a full-page message from the Patagonia clothing company in the spring 1991 issue, describing the company's commitment to preserving nature.

One of the largest-circulation children's magazines is *National Geographic World,* with 1.2 million paying readers. The magazine carries no ads, just as the grown-up version of *National Geographic* refused advertising for many years. But "the possibility of ads has been discussed," says *World* editor Pat Robbins. "It is our board's policy not to carry them, but that's not to say that the policy won't change."

It's fair to assume that *Zillions* will never carry advertising. The child of *Consumer Reports, Zillions* is an advocate for a "kids' market" it says has $8 billion a year to spend. The bimonthly magazine's mission is to help children get the most for their money. Toys, peanut butter, jeans, mail-in clubs, and TV shows have all been scrutinized. One regular feature is "The Sneaky Sell," which encourages kids to read fine print and spot ad double-talk.

The 250,000 subscribers to *Zillions* are highly involved with the magazine. "We do reader surveys after every issue," says editor Charlotte Baecher. A hundred children from across the country make up the Product Test Team, and a larger panel of subscribers regularly advises staff on products the magazine evaluates.

Some children's magazines have been around for generations, such as *Ranger Rick, Cricket,* and *Highlights for Children.* But even these are reaching out. *Cricket's* Illinois publishers, Carus Corporation, introduced the monthly *Ladybug* for younger readers in 1990. The *Ranger Rick* staff also produces *Your Big Backyard,* an environmental magazine for children aged 3 to 5. It's an improbable idea—print media for people who haven't learned to read. But the niche is growing because the real customers are grownups.

The main reason for the explosive growth in children's magazines is not advertiser interest. It's the growing number of well-educated parents and grandparents who want to give every advantage to their progeny. For example, *National Geographic World* began 16 years ago when Gilbert M. Grosvenor, president and chairman of the board at the National Geographic Society, became concerned that his children were watching too much TV. "He wanted to launch a magazine that would offer good competition for television and offer the same types of quality material as other Geographic products," says Pat Robbins. "Essentially, that's been our mission since then."

The mission may remain unchanged, but Robbins says the magazine's design and features are always evolving "because kids are not a static population." The *World* staff monitors changes in that population with children's focus groups, post-publication surveys, and analysis of their "enormous amount of mail—hundreds of pieces every month."

## Elusive Audience

Newspapers are not overlooking children, either. More than two-thirds (68 percent) of teenagers read at least one daily newspaper a week, according to Simmons Market Research Bureau. Not surprisingly, readership increases with age: half of teenagers (aged 12 to 17) read both daily and Sunday editions of a newspaper. The demographics of teenaged newspaper readers are similar to those of adults. White teenagers are more likely to read than blacks, for example, and Sunday readership is higher than weekday readership. Teens who live in the Northeast are most likely to read a newspaper, while those in the South and rural areas are least likely.

Dozens of newspapers now print special sections for children. The national leader may be a weekly children's section in the *Fort Worth Star-Telegram* called "Class Acts." The material in the 12-page supplement is syndicated to about 20 other papers. Article topics range from what it means to be adopted to getting a fair shake at allowance time. The target is a reader aged 8 to 14, but editor Sharon Cox says her 300 to 500 pieces of weekly mail also come from kindergartners and high school students.

Several weekly pages and sections in the *Chicago Tribune* are aimed at children, including "Spots," in the Sunday funnies; "In-Style," a fashion spotlight; "Preps Plus," on school sports; and "Take 2," which includes a panel of high school movie reviewers. "Newspapers have an aging audience," says *Tribune* comics editor John Lux, so they must try to develop the daily habit among younger groups.

There are even signs of an emerging children's radio network. Hundreds of stations already feed the voracious appetite teenagers have for pop music. But in Minneapolis, WWTC-AM offers news, theater, and music for younger children in a format called "Radio Aahs." Owner Chris Dahl says his station reaches 50 to 60 percent of children under age 12 in St. Paul and Minneapolis. He hopes to project the station via satellite to other markets, and he's looking for backers.

He isn't alone. Philadelphia-based Kidwaves is also trying to gather affiliates and support. In Cleveland, the Kids' Choice Broadcasting Network shut down a year ago.

Children's radio is an idea ahead of its time. Part of the problem is an almost total lack of information on how young children use radio. The Arbitron Company gathers information on radio use from diaries kept by 12-to-17 year-olds, for example. It would be possible to do a study of younger children, using adult assistance, says vice president Tom McCarskey. But so far, few advertisers have expressed any interest in knowing the answers.

Measuring the audience for any kind of media is a tricky business. When the audience is children, the task gets even trickier. Advertisers who sponsor children's television programs can get estimates of the number of 2-to-5-year-old and 6-to-11-year-old viewers, but it's almost impossible to gauge the accuracy of those estimates.

Arbitron's ScanAmerica system measures television audiences using a "people meter," which combines a remote-control wand and a measuring device wired to the set. Each member of a participating household is assigned a code to enter when they start and stop watching TV. Very young children are represented by older household members, says McCarskey. Older children get special coloring-book training manuals and jingles to help them remember which buttons to push. But when you come right down to it, no one knows how often children forget to use the wand.

If the people meter system is accurate, Saturday morning cartoons are in serious trouble. Between 1990 and 1991, the A.C. Nielsen Company's people meters recorded a 13 percent decline in Saturday morning TV-watching among children aged 2 to 11. Saturday morning cartoons produce an estimated $200 million a year in ad revenue to the networks, according to *Mediaweek* magazine, so a 13 percent drop in viewers could cost the networks $25 million. Network executives say that for some reason, children simply didn't push the buttons this fall. But Arbitron has been using people meters since 1986, and their data show a 15 percent decline in Saturday morning viewing over five years.

It's easier to gauge children's use of print media. And fortunately for the producers of those media, it's easy to prove that children influence billions of dollars a year in consumer spending. As long as children remain a choice market segment, media options for them should grow more plentiful, more sophisticated, and more focused.

# XV

# Mass Culture

Culture has two different meanings in this section: one is the quality of a society that arises from its arts and literature; the other is the particular form or stage of civilization that characterizes a society. Here we look at both aspects.

America is, without doubt, the home of one of the greatest mass cultures or popular cultures in history. Americans are known most throughout the world for their movies, music, pop songs, and television serials, not for their poetry, symphonies, or sculpture. Much more of the world enjoys our popular mass media products than our works of noble art.

Some critical observers have divided societies and their arts and literature into high, middle, or low cultures, or into elite and mass. American mass media fall easily and quickly into the middle or low or mass categories in the eyes of most critics. And yet occasionally some (but not much) of the popular arts and literature of American mass media have achieved a surprisingly high regard among thoughtful critics.

The quality of American journalism is highly regarded by most thoughtful critics in the world, as is the role of journalism in keeping America free. The technological developments that have made the journalistic media strong in America are a source of envy in much of the world. This, too, is part of our culture. But journalism is changing, as we've seen earlier in this book and as we will see now from a different perspective.

To some extent our culture is the product of our media, and as the media change our culture changes. We started as a print media society and have become an electronic media society, a change that is revolutionizing almost everything about our civilization.

Now, to some extent, we are moving from mass media to specialized media, as we will see further in the last section of this book; and that development, too, is changing our civilization in deep and significant ways. In fact, this may be the most important issue concerning mass media in the 1990s.

---

# 67

# "New News" and a War of Cultures

## *by* Bill Moyers

*Editor's Note:* There is a "new news" today that is replacing the "old news," and it is creating a whole new culture. The "new news" may not be in the newspapers or the other news media, which many Americans increasingly ignore because they feel they are no longer relevant.

Bill Moyers sees this development as foreshadowing catastrophe in our civilization. He is one of the most thoughtful media and culture critics in America today. Former press secretary to President Lyndon Johnson, former newspaper editor and publisher, television journalist and documentary producer, his article here is excerpted from a speech he delivered to the Center for Communication. This excerpt appeared in the *New York Times,* March 22, 1992.

Where is America's mind today? It's in the organs, for one thing. Remember that country song that goes "No one knows what goes on behind closed doors." Now we do.

Americans can turn on a series called "Real Sex" and watch a home striptease class; its premiere was HBO's highest-rated documentary for the year. Or they can flip to NBC News and get "I Witness Video." There they can see a policeman's murder recorded in his cruiser's camcorder, watch it replayed and relived in interviews, complete with ominous music. Or they can see the video of a pregnant woman plunging from a blazing building's window, can see it several times, at least once in slow motion.

Yeats was right: "We had fed the heart on fantasies, the heart's grown brutal from the fare." I wonder if "Real Sex" and "I Witness Video" take us deeper into reality or insanity? How does a reporter tell the difference anymore in a world where Oliver Stone can be praised for his "journalistic instincts" when he has Lyndon Johnson tell a cabal of generals and admirals, "Get me elected and I'll get you your war."

Rolling Stone dubs all this the New News. Straight news—the Old News by Rolling Stone's definition—is "pooped, confused and broke." In its place, a new culture of information is evolving—"a heady concoction, part Hollywood

**415**

film and TV, part pop music and pop art, mixed with popular culture and celebrity magazines, tabloid telecasts, cable and home video."

Increasingly, says the magazine, the New News is seizing the function of mainstream journalism, sparking conversation and setting the country's social and political agenda.

So it is that we learn first from Bruce Springsteen that jobs aren't coming back. So it is that inner-city parents who don't subscribe to daily newspapers are taking their children to see "Juice" to educate them about the consequences of street violence; that young people think Bart Simpson's analysis of America more trenchant than that of many newspaper columnists; that we learn just how violent, brutal and desperate society is, not from the establishment press but from Spike Lee, Public Enemy, the Geto Boys and Guns 'n' Roses. Now even MTV is doing original reporting on this year's political campaign. We are having to absorb, and come to grips with, the news wherever and however we find it.

Once, newspapers drew people to the public square. They provided a culture of community conversation by activating inquiry on serious public issues. When the press abandons that function, it no longer stimulates what John Dewey termed "the vital habits" of democracy—"the ability to follow an argument, grasp the point of view of another, expand the boundaries of understanding, debate the alternative purposes that might be pursued."

But I also know that what Dean Joan Konner said recently at the Columbia School of Journalism is true: "There is a civil war in our society today, a conflict between two American cultures, each holding very different values. The adversaries are private profits versus public responsibility; personal ambition versus the community good; quantitative measures versus qualitative concerns."

And I sense we're approaching Gettysburg, the moment of truth, the decisive ground for this cultural war—for newspaper publishers especially. Americans say they no longer trust journalists to tell them the truth about their world. Young people have difficulty finding anything of relevance to their lives in the daily newspaper.

Non-tabloid newspapers are viewed as increasingly elitist, self-important and corrupt on the one hand; on the other, they are increasingly lumped with the tabloids as readers perceive the increasing desperation with which papers are now trying to reach "down market" in order to replace the young readers who are not replacing their elders.

Meanwhile, a study by the Kettering Foundation confirms that our political institutions are fast losing their legitimacy, that increasing numbers of Americans believe they are being dislodged from their rightful place in democracy by politicians, powerful lobbyists *and* the media—three groups they see as an autonomous political class impervious to the long-term interests of the country and manipulating the democratic discourse so that people are treated only as consumers to be entertained rather than citizens to be engaged.

That our political system is failing to solve the bedrock problems we face is beyond dispute. One reason is that our public discourse has become the verbal equivalent of mud wrestling.

The anthropologist Marvin Harris says the attack against reason and objectivity in America "is fast reaching the proportion of a crusade." America, he says, "urgently needs to reaffirm the principle that it is possible to carry out an analysis of social life which rational human beings will recognize as being true, regardless of whether they happen to be women or men, whites or blacks, straights or gays, Jews or born-again Christians." Lacking such an understanding of social life "we will tear the United States apart in the name of our separate realities."

Taken together, these assumptions and developments foreshadow the catastrophe of social and political paralysis: a society that continues to be governed by the same two parties that are driving it into the pits; a society that doesn't understand the link between two students killed in the hallways of a Brooklyn high school and the plea bargain that assures Michael Milken of being able to scrape by on $125 million; a society that every day breaks open its children's piggy banks and steals $1 billion just to pay the daily bills; a society that responds with anger at check-kiting in Congress but doesn't even know that the executive branch has lost track of tens of billions of dollars appropriated for the savings and loan bailout; a society where democracy is constantly thwarted by unaccountable money; a society where more people know George Bush hates broccoli than know that he ordered the invasion of Panama, and more know Marla Maples than Vaclav Havel, and where, by a margin of two to one, people say the Government's ability to censor the news during the Persian Gulf war was more important than the media's ability to report it.

What's astonishing about this civic illiteracy—some call it a disease—is that it exists in America just as a series of powerful democratic movements have been toppling autocratic regimes elsewhere in the world. While people around the globe are clamoring for self-government, survey after survey reports that millions of Americans feels as if they have been locked out of their homes and are unable to regain their rightful place in the operation of democracy. On the other hand, those same millions want to believe that it is still in their power to change America.

Conventional wisdom says people don't want the kind of news that will bring them back to the public square. Well, conventional wisdom is wrong. Just ask The Philadelphia Inquirer. Last fall, The Inquirer ran a nine-part series that attempted to find a pattern in the economic chaos of the 1980's. Donald Barlett and James Steele, twice winners of the Pulitzer Prize, spent two years traveling to 50 cities in 16 states and Mexico. They talked to government officials, corporate managers and workers in lumber mills, factories and department stores. And they amassed a hundred thousand documents.

When they were done, they had exposed a money trail that helped readers to understand how rule makers in Washington and deal makers on Wall

Street connived to create much of the pain inflected on American workers and the middle class.

The series was about tax policy, health care, pension rules, corporate debt and the bankruptcy code—all that "stuff" we usually think no one wants to read about. But it was written crisply and laid out vividly, and when the series appeared so many people thronged the paper's lobby wanting reprints that security guards had to be summoned for crowd control. At last count, the number of reprints had reached 400,000.

People want to know what is happening to them, and what they can do about it. Listening to America, you realize that millions of people are not apathetic. They will respond to a press that stimulates the community without pandering to it, that inspires people to embrace their responsibilities without lecturing or hectoring them, that engages their better natures without sugarcoating ugly realities or patronizing their foibles.

Those of us who are reporters can only hope this generation of publishers understands that what keeps journalism different is something intangible. For all the talk of price-earnings ratio, bottom line, readouts and restricted stock, what ultimately counts is the soul of the owner. The test today for capitalism is whether shareholders have souls, too.

# 68

# The Cultural Elite

## by Jonathan Alter

*Editor's Note:* America's pop culture, aimed for the most part at the lowest common denominator, has ironically created a cultural elite. Half a century ago, sociologists began to identify an effect of the mass media that they called "status conferral." People who were mentioned in the media acquired status. Ordinary people could become stars (Marilyn Monroe), heroes (Charles Lindbergh), and statesmen (Dwight Eisenhower) if their names got into enough headlines.

The media people who make the stars, heroes, and statesmen have themselves become a new cultural elite. Jonathan Alter examines this phenomenon in this article, published in *Newsweek*, October 5, 1992. Aiding in the research were Donna Foote and Linda Wright in Los Angeles.

Kenny Rogers is not in the "cultural elite." While he still knows when to hold 'em and when to fold 'em, none of his songs are currently shaping American culture. But Madonna certainly meets the entrance requirements. Ted Kennedy has been expelled. But Dan Quayle is a member.

*Dan Quayle?* Obviously Quayle would not identify himself as a part of the cultural elite he so actively denounces. He spits the words out, trying to win votes for the Republican ticket by creating a social chasm: *Us* versus *Them*, with the *Them* being dangerous Hollywood and media types inflicting their sinful values on the rest of *Us* regular folks. It's a time-honored, divide-and-conquer approach, and one that's had surprisingly little political bite this year. "We in Hollywood did not audition for the role of Willie Horton, and we're not going to play it," says Gary David Goldberg, creator of shows like "Family Ties" and "Brooklyn Bridge." Polls show the voters overwhelmingly think the whole fuss is a distraction from their real concern—the economy.

But whatever his motives, the vice president is on to something. If the cultural elite isn't a proper political issue, it's at least a compelling sociological one. While the United States has never featured the rigid social and cultural hierarchies of Europe, some kind of elite class has always existed here. It has often produced this country's most brilliant inspirations, from the Constitution to Huckleberry Finn. It continues to ensure that museums and orchestras and other remnants of old culture survive. What's changed in recent years is that

**419**

the cultural elite has become much less intellectually elite—and much more connected to commerce. With the help of television, that elite has expanded to produce all of America's powerful and highly exportable mass culture—including our worst trash.

Without question, Americans are dissatisfied with the tone of their popular culture. As the wild-and-crazy baby boomers become parents, they are trying to protect their children from being kidnapped by celluloid fiends like Freddy Krueger. According to a *Newsweek* Poll, only 26 percent think parents have the most influence on their kids, a poor second to television's 49 percent. Fully 80 percent believe that movies contain too much violence and sex. But poll respondents conclude that what matters most to the creators of this culture is money, not politics. Only 33 percent agree with Quayle's idea that a cultural elite in the news and entertainment business was trying to push its own values on the public. Nearly 60 percent thought the real motive was just to appeal to the biggest possible audience.

Who are the people who comprise the CE? What are their values? How influential are those values, especially on children? Can Hollywood be persuaded, finally, to take responsibility for the gratuitous sex and violence it produces? Just by generating agitated discussion, Quayle is helping to shape the debate, which is the only real requirement for membership in the cultural elite. You're in, Dan, whether you like it or not.

## Who's in It?

If it's any consolation, *Newsweek* and other major news organizations are also part of the cultural elite, as are academics and government officials who affect the national dialogue. So are smaller publications and cultural hunter-gatherers who move stories up the great media food chain. So are the people who write or publish important books, who produce, direct or "greenlight" movies, who sketch our visual landscape. And prime-time television—where even a flop reaches more people than most movie hits—is at the white-hot center of this universe.

At a recent Hollywood fund-raiser, Bill Clinton said that he had "always aspired to be [in] the 'cultural elite' that others condemn." (That was another sign that Quayle's political punch was not hitting home; if it had, Clinton would never have admitted membership.) Lynne Cheney, conservative director of the National Endowment for the Humanities, acknowledged last week that while the term is so broad as to be almost meaningless, "I suspect that it includes me." Most de facto members are less honest. The usual reaction is, *no, not me, but that person over there is*—just as many Yuppies denied being "Yuppies" in the 1980s. They want the rewards of elitism but not the stigma that comes with it in a democratic idol-smashing society.

The idea of a meritocratic elite has gone by many names over the years. In his once trendy 1956 work, "The Power Elite," C. Wright Mills wrote of "prestigeful men and women" who "displace the society lady and the man of pedigreed wealth." In those days, the attack on Hollywood came from the left, attacking the TV industry for bland "Father Knows Best" images that were badly out of touch with the diversity of American life. The "counterculture" was just struggling to be born. Now many old hippies run the CE.

It used to be, of course, that "culture" meant serious literature and art. Prof. Alfred Appel of Northwestern University says that at first he thought Quayle's definition of "cultural elite" was a poor use of language: "Opportunistic, greedy, ill-educated, boorish TV and movie producers—is that *culture?*" But Appel concluded: "Movies and TV *are* the center of our culture, alas. The literary culture has become very minor. In the '50s, Time could put an intellectual like Jacques Barzun on the cover. Now you can't imagine a newsmagazine cover story that would feature a writer unless it was Stephen King."

For all of its connection to commerce, the new cultural elite is not the same as the economic elite—the people who control this country's wealth. Quayle would never have attacked that elite; it's mostly Republican. Much of the time, anti-elitism is democratically healthy. Unfortunately, it too often takes the form of attacks on intellectuals. When Yale man George Bush condemns Michael Dukakis for being part of "the Harvard Yard boutique" and Bill Clinton for going to Oxford, only a few "eggheads" (the 1950s term of derision) find it peculiar.

Wherever they matriculated, members of the CE are well schooled in hypocrisy. Conservatives who complain about lax family values don't seem to mind when Republican Arnold Schwarzenegger casually wipes out a few dozen men on screen. Concerned liberals almost never manage to speak out about rap music that advocates killing cops. (Imagine their reaction if a group called "KKK" sang about killing blacks.)

The conservative critique is unassailable on one point: the cultural elite is not made up of "average" middle-class Americans, though many were born that way. They are better educated, richer, more liberal, more mobile, less religious and less connected to conventional standards of morality than most of the public.

The citadels of the CE that Quayle identifies—Hollywood, the press, academia—include a disproportionate number of Jews. "We can drop the Republican code for cultural elite," director Mike Nichols deadpanned at the Clinton fund-raiser. "Good evening, fellow Jews." From McCarthyism to rumblings on the far right and far left about the "Jewish-dominated media," resentment against the cultural elite has often boiled down to simple anti-Semitism, though Quayle's Jewish speechwriters could hardly have meant it that way.

In truth, when Jewish studio bosses *really* ran Hollywood—in the old days—the movies were full of traditional values, as Neal Gabler points out in the book "An Empire of Their Own." Nowadays, there are large numbers of Jews—many of them nonreligious or intermarried—at all levels of the cultural elite. But at the top, power is fragmented and increasingly shared not just with Christians but with owners back in Japan. The pointlessness of the whole ar-

gument is conveyed by the fact that the only TV network owned by a Jew—
CBS—is also the network under the most fire (for a "60 Minutes" story) from
supporters of Israel.

A more useful way of understanding who comprises the cultural elite is to
look at it as a web of interconnected institutions. Each venue uses various
spawning grounds—e.g., the Harvard Lampoon, the Yale Daily News, the USC
School of Cinema—but also employs large numbers of people who worked
their way up without early connections. The values—or lack thereof—are
shared. "There are three elite groups in this country that professionally understand that they must function amorally: Hollywood, the media and politicians,"
says Howard Suber, cochairman of UCLA's film and TV producers program.
Each promotes and feeds off the other, as the "Murphy Brown" hype suggests.
It's no wonder that so many Americans think "they" are all in it together.

## What Do They Stand For?

Here are at least three ways to analyze the CE:

Under what could be called the Spiro Agnew analysis, "an effete corps
of impudent snobs" injects the culture with condescending liberalism. Clergy
and businessmen are generally portrayed as bad guys. Gays and minorities
are generally portrayed as good guys. Republicans are people to laugh at.
Obscenity is dressed up as "free expression" and sometimes paid for by the
government.

Then there's the Thomas Jefferson definition. He described "a natural
aristocracy among men. The grounds of this are virtue and talents." This is the
cultural elite that Clinton identified as a source of national pride—the social hierarchy in which people get ahead through education and moxie. Begrudging
then their status is to denigrate that which is good in American life.

And finally, the Andy Warhol analysis. "Art? I don't believe I've met the
man," Warhol said. This is the money first, art second theory. Or as Mike Me-
davoy, chairman of Tri-Star Pictures, puts it: "We have to make movies that
make money, not preach." People in Hollywood, says director John Milius,
"don't have a shred of honest ideology among them."

Could the "cultural elite" represent all three approaches? Could it include
both cynical purveyors of mindless junk, *and* artistic geniuses? The CE—like
any elite—reflects the best and worst of the culture. Both fresh cream and pond
scum rise to the top.

Quayle's central point is that the pond scum is the result of value-free liberalism. But when money's at stake, amorality knows no political bounds. The
occasional plugs for AIDS prevention notwithstanding, the media are generally
so politically *in*correct, that legions of p.c. professors make careers of decon-
structing the racism and sexism they see in it.

Similarly, most TV shows are situated in homey—not hostile—surroundings. Usually, the crook gets caught in the end. Most programs are still about
families, albeit extended or untraditional ones. "There's this perception that we

sit here and ask, 'How do we change the public's tastes?' " says John S. Pike, president of Paramount's TV division. "We don't do that. We are trying to produce mass-appeal programming." Indeed, several studios promise more "G" and "PG" moves, because box-office receipts show the boomers want them.

In the news media as well, the only meaningful ideology is capitalism. As the conservative William Bennett has argued, liberal reporters will chase anyone for a good story. How else to explain the media feeding frenzies that afflict Democrats at least as often as Republicans? Quayle has undoubtedly taken more media punches because he is conservative. But the cultural affinity between media elites and liberal political elites doesn't always work on behalf of the Democrat. Jimmy Carter received far worse press than Ronald Reagan, and Bill Clinton's press has veered between positive and negative extremes.

## How Influential Is It?

The conventional defense of Hollywood comes from Jack Valenti. "Movies reflect society. When people ask why Hollywood doesn't make movies like it used to, my answer is, 'Why isn't society like it used to be?' " Under this theory, all the Hollywood cultural elite does is hold a mirror to the world. "The last place any Hollywood producer wants to be is out in front of, or different than, the audience," says TV producer Gary David Goldberg. "This is a business that really runs on testing, polling, focus grouping." If they were honest, Goldberg's counterparts in publishing and politics would admit the same thing.

The mirror argument is convenient. But it dodges the question of ultimate responsibility, especially for what children so often see. *Of course* images affect behavior. If they didn't, there would be no such thing as advertising. Barry Diller, retired top executive at the Fox network, says studio executives should take on more responsibility for what they turn out. "There should be a process for companies to be sensitized to what the data tell us. The data says: films and TV have an effect." Apparently the process hasn't yet "sensitized" the coarseness at Fox: shows like "Married . . . With Children" and "Studs" are still very much on the air.

On the other hand, sometimes a laugh is just a laugh. If movies about sex directly affect behavior, why do most of the people who see them lead so much duller sex lives? If the liberal news media have so much clout, why have conservatives been running the country for 20 of the last 24 years? If that changes next month, it won't happen because the liberal cultural elite ordered America to dump George Bush and Dan Quayle.

It may be that the CE is less influential than we imagine—a conditioner of culture instead of its creator. At bottom, says critic Todd Gitlin, "The culture industry can lead, but it can't lead people anywhere it likes. It can take them down the road, but it doesn't build the road in the first place." Building a new moral road (or just voting with your ticket stubs and channel changers)—that's where the American public's ultimate power over the cultural elite comes in. If we build it, "They" will come, with a different set of wares to sell us.

# 69

# Culture in the Hands of Corporate Sponsors

## *by* Sarah Booth Conroy

*Editor's Note:* A long time ago President Calvin Coolidge told the American Society of Newspaper Editors, in a speech on January 17, 1925, "The business of America is business." That has not seemed to change. Indeed, we could say that "the business of American mass media is business."

We could also say that the culture of America is business, for not only does corporate America sponsor much of our mass media and popular culture. It even sponsors our elite culture, our arts and letters, and our historical heritage.

Sarah Booth Conroy is a *Washington Post* staff writer. This article was published in the *Washington Post* on November 12, 1989.

Philip Morris is bringing us the Bill of Rights, American Express has already delivered the Statue of Liberty (restored), and the National Archives has established the Corporate Circle to sponsor other sacred American documents.

Maison Taittinger, the champagne company of Reims, sponsored a toast to the armistice of World War I Thursday at Woodrow Wilson House.

Lafarge Corp., a construction materials company, made possible the Library of Congress's exhibit celebrating the Bicentennial of the French Revolution, "A Passion for Liberty: Alexis de Tocqueville on Democracy and Revolution."

The Baltimore Gas and Electric Co., C&P Telephone Co., and six banks, among others, joined with the Catholic Archdiocese of Baltimore in bringing masterworks from the Vatican to the Walters Art Gallery in Baltimore.

The Public Broadcasting Service, television and radio, comes to us through the support of business, as well as "you the listener."

And these are just a small number of the corporate sponsors of American life today. In Washington, where enormous and elegant dinners are fed nightly to black-tied and jeweled diners in the city's public palaces, hardly a loaf of bread is broken without being buttered by corporations. Few buy tickets to charity benefits; they come as guests of the corporate sponsors.

This week Public Citizen Health Research Group, a Ralph Nader organization, charged that the agreement between Philip Morris and the Archives "smears the Bill of Rights with the blood of all Americans killed as a result of smoking Marlboro and other Philip Morris cigarettes." Rep. John Conyers Jr. (D-Mich.), chairman of the committee on Government Operations, has asked the General Accounting Office to determine if the Archives is permitted to allow a private company to use its name, whether its building can be rented to a private group, and if the monies paid by Philip Morris must go to the Archives or the general treasury.

Philip Morris is conducting a two-year, $60 million celebration of the 200th anniversary of the Bill of Rights. On television and in newspapers, the firm quotes utterances about the "written guarantee of our personal freedoms" by everyone from Thomas Jefferson to Martin Luther King. The Archives and Philip Morris plan a countrywide traveling exhibit of Delaware's original copy of the Bill of Rights and an exhibit of political cartoons on American rights. Philip Morris has already sent out almost 300,000 free copies of the Bill of Rights.

Archives spokesperson Jill Brett explained that cultural institutions have a dilemma: "When we had the 200th anniversaries of the Declaration of Independence and the Constitution, we didn't have a corporate sponsor, so we didn't have any hoopla. The Archives can't afford to give every school kid a copy of the Bill of Rights. Or send one of the original Bill of Rights on tour. The money from Philip Morris will do all those things."

Big business, thanks to the tax laws, has largely replaced the philanthropists of yesteryear: James Smithson, who brought us the Smithsonian Institution; Charles Lang Freer (Gallery); Joseph Hirshhorn (Museum and Sculpture Garden); Duncan Phillips (Collection); W. W. Corcoran (Museum); Andrew Mellon, who declined to name the National Gallery of Art after himself, and his son, Paul, who followed the same restraint on the East Building of the National Gallery; and more recently, Arthur M. Sackler (Gallery).

In other countries, culture is supported by the crown and/or the government, with grants for everything from putting ballet companies on their toes to fixing the roofs on historic chateaus. And these countries' taxes reflect this largesse. In the United States, especially under the Ronald Reagan and George Bush presidencies, the bill has been passed to volunteers—individuals and corporations. Instead of paying the check for these amenities through tax money, Americans pay for them through the added cost on products or through tax writeoffs for business expenses.

Think of the additional possibilities. Gerber Food could bring us our babies (the stork having gone out of business because of the high cost of obstetricians and maternity wards). Beltone hearing aid could offer Elektra records. Macmillan Publishing could hold literary classes. Mitsubishi could sponsor displays of Ronald Reagan's speeches. BMW could send out the World War II peace treaty on tour. Dole Pineapple could sponsor displays of Imelda Marcos's shoes. The Chronicler could buy a cup of coffee for tattletales.

Kenneth Bowling, associate editor of the First Federal Congress Papers, put the matter into historic perspective the other day by saying, "I went to the party launching the Bill of Rights exhibit and campaign by Philip Morris, and it was the best Washington reception I ever went to—I've never eaten three kinds of oysters at one party before. But as I was leaving, I thought, it was rather a sacrilege to be eating oysters at the foot of the Bill of Rights. And then I considered, well, the founding fathers most likely went out after they wrote it and all ate oysters at the local tavern."

And had a smoke?

# 70

# The Fragmenting of America

## *by* Robert J. Samuelson

*Editor's Note:* Mass media of the past brought us together as a family and as a nation. There were fewer mass media, so most of us were audiences for the same messages. Critics pointed out the negative aspects of this process—it "homogenized" us all into one culture.

Now there are far more mass media available, as well as specialized media and personal media. The old critics would like these developments—they allow everyone to be an individual. The new critics decry the new media; they are fragmenting us, destroying our sense of unity, of nationhood, of culture.

One such critic is Robert J. Samuelson, an economist and widely syndicated newspaper columnist. This article appeared in the *Washington Post* and other papers on August 7, 1991.

Who would have thought that the three major television networks could be toppled from their pedestals? But they have been. Between 1975 and 1990, their share of the prime-time TV audience has fallen from 93 percent to 64 percent. It could go lower. Little wonder that network executives whine about how poor and beleaguered they've become. In an odd way, I mourn their plight.

Network dominance never consistently provided quality programming. But it did give us something that's now slipping away: shared experience and a sense of community. People in the 1950s watched "The Honeymooners." In the 1970s they watched "All in the Family." As the TV audience scatters to its many new choices—dozens of cable channels, VCR tapes, computer games—we're losing that. It wouldn't matter much, if the networks' eclipse were an isolated phenomenon. But it isn't. It's part of what I call the fragmenting of America.

If you examine recent economic and social trends, you will find that they emphasize (and sometimes exaggerate) our differences. By contrast, the great economic and social trends of the mid-1960s, emphasized and nurtured our similarities. The growing awareness of differences is a constant theme in today's politics. It underlies the raging debate over "multiculturalism." There is more to it, though, than race or immigration.

We have a deeper sense of accumulating differences. At some level, we don't like it. This explains a barely concealed public hunger for things that remind us of a common national heritage or destiny. Ronald Reagan was so

**429**

popular in part because he spoke above a splintered society to give voice to traditional (for some, merely nostalgic) values. This hunger also explains why the Persian Gulf War, once won, made most Americans feel good.

When I say that economic and social forces are fragmenting us, here's what I mean:

• *Technology:*   In the 1950s and 1960s, television gave us universal entertainment. The explosion in long-distance telephone service shrank distances. So did construction of interstate highways and the expansion of air travel. Now, technology transforms the "mass market" into endless "niche markets." Computers slice us by income, age, education and purchasing patterns into market "segments." Cable TV and direct mail cater to our micro tastes.

• *Economic Equality:*   There's less of it. We are more a society of haves and have-nots. Until the early 1970s family income rose rapidly and its distribution became more even. Between 1959 and 1973, the poverty rate dropped from 22.4 percent to 11.1 percent. In 1989 it was 12.8 percent. It's not just income but also the availability of health insurance and pension benefits that's becoming less equal. Coverage, once expanding, now isn't.

• *Regional Convergence:*   "Rolling recession" has become part of our vocabulary. In the 1980s, regions suffered severe slumps at different times. First the Rust Belt and the Farm Belt. Then the Oil Patch. And now the Northeast. Until 1980s regional per capita incomes were converging. Between 1950 and 1980, the South's income rose from 69 percent to 86 percent of the national average. In the 1980s the gap among regional incomes widened.

• *Lifestyles:*   Everyone knows that the "traditional" two-parent family with children is on the wane. Marrying later, divorcing more often and living longer, Americans have created new lifestyles, subcultures and market niches. In 1960 74 percent of households were married couples, and 44 percent were couples with children. By 1990 the same groups were 56 percent and 26 percent of the total.

• *Immigration:*   The huge influx of Hispanic and Asian immigrants (legal and illegal) beginning in the 1970s has literally changed the face of America. In the 1980s the Hispanic population of Los Angeles County—to take one example—increased by nearly 1.3 million, reports American Demographics magazine.

To the list, I'd also add the mere passage of time. In the 1950s and early 1960s, all adult Americans had lived through two great traumas: the Great Depression and World War II. They affected everyone powerfully. Today's Americans, spanning at least three generations, no longer have common, anchoring experiences of such intensity. Each has its own: For the baby boom, it was Vietnam. The generation gap has become the generations' gaps.

In some ways, the forces pulling America together in the early postwar period were unrepresentative of the economic and social tensions typical of U.S. history. In the 1920s immigration was a great source of conflict. Nor was the "traditional" family so traditional. It was less prevalent before World War II than in the 1950s. We have now reverted to a more normal state. Political calm was shattered in the 1960s by Vietnam and civil rights. Though less dramatic, the changes since then have quietly segregated us. A lot of little things have pulled us apart by creating many more separate worlds in which we all live.

The result is confusion. We celebrate diversity and individuality. We also crave a sense of nation and community. The two seem at odds. The unifying forces of the early postwar era involved a lot of social and political conformity ("bad" in our individualistic culture), but they also created a lot of consensus ("good" in a society that values compromise). Consensus is more elusive now. Too many groups move in different directions, preoccupied by different problems and navigating by different reference points. Politicians survive by offending no one, doing nothing and, in the process, disappointing almost everyone.

Our fragmented society exalts freedom and expands consumer choice. But it also sacrifices a larger sense of belonging. The less we have in common, the more we seek out people just like us. This isn't evil. It's human nature. But it isn't necessarily good, either. It builds isolation and makes more of everyday life strange and alien. There's no conspiracy here. It's history. The TV networks' decline is a small part of the story. Their eclipse is probably inevitable and maybe desirable. Or maybe not. Someday, we may yearn for a bit more of "The Honeymooners."

# ── XVI ──

# Technology
# and the Future

As we said in the beginning of this book, mass media are technology-based industries, and the technologies are in a constant state of change. We end by looking at the future and at some of our evolving technologies, which have the greatest possible implications for the changes that will affect mass media, the way we communicate, the ways we live, and our culture and our civilization. Given the changes in technology affecting mass media today, we can summarize in a few words the changes that will affect our society: diversity, multiculturalism, individualism, fragmentation.

In an earlier edition of this book, Professor Benjamin Barber of Rutgers University wrote that the "effects of the first age of television [from 1939 through the 1970s] on America's political culture were mixed." But in one clear sense, Barber noted, network television's homogenized programming benefited democracy: It provided a consensus indispensable to national unity.[1]

The new technologies are decentralizing not only television but also all the mass media.

All this programming diversity and special-interest narrowcasting replaces communication with group narcissism. The tube now becomes a mirror showing us only ourselves, relentlessly screening out any images that do not suit our own special prejudices and group norms. . . . Every parochial voice gets a hearing (though only before the already converted), and the public as a whole is left with no voice. No global village, but a Tower of Babel: a hundred chattering mouths bereft of any common language.[2]

Barber also points out that the very features of the new technology that make it versatile and exciting also make it frighteningly vulnerable to abuse.

433

He is thinking of the use of the new technologies to create sophisticated personal media for highly targeted advertising and marketing, using computer files to prepare profiles and dossiers that could make it possible for "big brother" corporations to know all about us, how to get to us, and how to sell to us.[3]

Of course, that is a dismal view, and there may be brighter ways of looking at the future. In this section we present a fairly optimistic view. You must make your own choice.

**Notes**

1. Benjamin Barber, "The Second American Revolution," reprinted in *Impact of Mass Media,* 2 ed. (New York: Longman, 1985), p. 501. Originally published in *Channels of Communication,* February/March 1982.
2. Ibid., p. 504.
3. Ibid., pp. 507–508.

# 71

# The Compleat Reporter

## by Gib Johnson

*Editor's Note:* What will the future be like for the journalist? Without doubt, given the new technologies, he or she will be wired to the world. Journalists will have far more information at their fingertips, and they will be able to analyze it in ways never before available. The problem will be to keep the machines from overwhelming the process of making judgments and writing effectively.

Gib Johnson, a freelance writer in Pasadena, teaches journalism at California State University, Los Angeles. This article appeared in the *Washington Journalism Review,* May 1990.

Late one night last September David Hawthorne boarded USAir's Flight 505 at LaGuardia Airport bound for North Carolina. The associate producer for CBS Newsnet was on his way to cover Hurricane Hugo. He didn't make it. The pilot decided to abort the takeoff, and the airliner crashed into the East River.

Hawthorne was knocked out on impact, and when he came to he helped several mothers get their children out on the wing of the plane. "Then it kind of came to me." says Hawthorne, "Wow, I've got a great story here, a plane crash!"

Although the flight crew was trying to keep people outside, Hawthorne managed to climb back into the shattered fuselage to retrieve his cellular phone from under seat 5C.

He immediately called Newsnet and then the CBS News national assignment desk. From the crash site he was put on the air with Dan Rather. Although another station may have had the first pictures or reported the crash earlier, "We were the first ones with any kind of actual live report from the scene," he says.

Now the cumbersome phone that he carries around means something more to Hawthorne. "The phone for me at the time was something to report the story, but it was also a bit of a security blanket," he says. "It gave me contact with the outside would and somebody calm to talk to."

Although Hawthorne's experience was unusual, even for a journalist, his use of high-tech gear isn't.

Journalists of every stripe now use a dazzling array of new gadgets to do their jobs more quickly and efficiently: laptop computers, cellular phones, transcontinental paging devices, camcorders, battery-operated printers, 9-band short-wave radios, microcassette recorders, mini color TV sets, and of course, the ubiquitous fax machine. But what were technological novelties yesterday are essential tools of the trade today.

That's not to mention services such as voice mail, electronic mail, databases, computer bulletin boards and computer access to airline guides and wire copy.

Besides giving journalists a competitive edge, as in Hawthorne's case, high-tech gear addresses a more basic need.

Speak to editors and reporters, and they'll tell you that one of the great advantages of this technology is that it allows them to communicate easily with their coworkers from virtually anywhere—from automobiles in West Germany, pay phones in Illinois, hotels in South Korea. It provides an electronic umbilical cord tethering journalists and their news organizations.

Political writer Mark Barabak of the *San Francisco Chronicle* says that using his laptop and modem on the road "ties me into the *Chronicle* computer as if I were sitting in the office." Barabak, who uses a Tandy 200, finds it especially helpful when his copy is being edited because he can see any changes before he updates the story. The laptop "gets you in sync" with the people in the office, he says.

For ABC News's Dan Noyes, the new technology means time saved.

During the 1988 presidential campaign, for example, Noyes carried the following in a canvas bag: laptop computer, miniature color TV, still camera, printer and tape recorder. Now a Midwest correspondent for ABC News in St. Louis, he says the only thing different is that his canvas bag is now leather, and he carries a more sophisticated tape recorder—a Sony Personal TCM-27, to be exact.

Introduced last year, it features a liquid-crystal display showing the date, time and a five-character slug for each interview. It also has a cue function that allows reporters to automatically fast forward specifically to sound bites they've already marked. It costs $160.

But again, for Noyes, it's time saved that's the big attraction of high-tech gear like his laptop. "I can actually be writing in the car as we're traveling someplace."

He recalls that he was once doing a story two hours out of ABC News's Chicago bureau and was running against deadline. "We stopped along the way at a pay phone, and I fed in my script using my modem. By the time I got to Chicago, the script had been looked over by people in New York and Washington and approved."

*Time* Deputy Chief of Correspondents Barrett Seaman says the new technology speeds paperwork too. When an overseas correspondent needs credentialing for a visa, they'll write the letter in New York and fax it to the embassy or *Time* bureau. And since the magazine is using more charts and graphs these days, they'll fax roughs to correspondents to "help us get it right."

Besides making them competitive, connecting them to their offices and saving time, the high-tech ware also keeps reporters up-to-date with the rest of the world. For Jonathan Kaufman, a foreign correspondent for *The Boston Globe,* "The big advantage (of the laptop) computer for me is you're able to get the wires." He carries the new Tandy 1100 FD, which weighs 6.4 pounds and costs $999.

His laptop allows him to put an eight-hour plane trip to use, making him "much more efficient."

Marc Cooper, a political-affairs freelancer and journalism professor at California State University took his Toshiba T1100 Plus laptop, telephone connecting cords, acoustic couplers and alligator clips behind guerrilla lines in El Salvador and to the U.S. invasion of Panama.

A contributor to *Mother Jones* and *The Village Voice,* Cooper gives his gadgetry heavy workouts at home too. The electronic mail fax function offered by CompuServe, an online information service, enables him to upload messages to electronic mail—but they are received as faxes. This lets him send copy to collaborators who don't have modem capability and ensures that editors get hard copy of important messages.

However, Cooper finds the word-processing functions of his desktop and laptop computers to be the most significant. It's made his job easier. "I found that when I switched from typewriters to word processing about six or seven years ago, I was moving from the dark ages into light, only because I'm such a terrible typist," he says. "The process of producing the manuscript physically was the greatest burden that I faced and greatly affected the amount and the quality of my work."

In the best of circumstances, new technology also allows overseas reporters to take superior technology with them and simply lay it down, like a magic electronic carpet. *Time*'s Seaman, for example, regularly gets called in New York by correspondents in Berlin and Bonn using their cellular phones. "Frankly, we find them more useful and dependable than hotel phones."

For correspondents in Africa, the laptop is the high-tech equivalent of the legendary Land Rover. It's essential. During their two months in Africa, husband-and-wife freelancers Richard O'Regan and Jeanmarie Condon took along his Toshiba T1100, a Kodak Diconix 150-Plus portable printer, three tape recorders and a pocket-sized shortwave radio. O'Regan was doing stories for National Public Radio, *Mother Jones* and *The Atlanta Journal* and *Constitution.* Condon was writing for *The Boston Globe.*

O'Regan calls Ethiopia and Sudan "the land of the laptops" because the computers can be found with every official from the United Nations and private charitable organizations. High-tech gear is the only way to get around unreliable electrical service and uncertain transportation between home and office. Even the Eritrean rebels in Ethiopia have a satellite dish and fax machine, says O'Regan.

Such technology is making reporters so self-sufficient that few trips back to a bureau or headquarters are necessary, he says. For example, before O'Regan left for Africa, he put historical and statistical information about every country he planned to visit on a computer disk and kept it in his shirt pocket throughout the trip. "For me, [research material is] the main thing that keeps you to a base at all," he says.

Ultimately, however, pushing the technology envelope helps reporters to get stories they couldn't get before—or at least would have great difficulty getting. Jay Fine, managing director of news production and technical services for NBC News, notes that his crews took along small consumer-quality camcorders to cover the rebellion at Tiananmen Square in China last year. He said the video cameras are inconspicuous and relatively inexpensive ($1,300 to $2,200 versus a $20,000 broadcast-quality camera) and allow them to get shots of otherwise anxious subjects. Even NBC News producers used them there on stories. "You look less like a professional photographer and more like a tourist," says Fine. NBC has also used them in Tibet and Albania.

Along with the enormous advantages of the new technology, glitches also arise.

Comedian Al Franken of "Saturday Night Live" captured the essence of the problem with his routine about a "one-man mobile uplink."

As a gung-ho reporter ready to cover breaking stories with the latest in electronic gadgetry, Franken carries a backpack crammed with high-tech gear, photographs himself by donning a Steadicam harness, and wears a motorcycle helmet topped with a small satellite dish.

In one skit Franken loses his uplink when his head moves, and immediately the viewer's TV screen turns to electronic snow. In another, he's hit by lightning. And in yet another skit, the satellite dish on his head is perforated by gunfire while the technojournalist is covering the arrival of smuggled cocaine.

Franken says his character is "fascinated with equipment and never gets the story." But, he adds, "He feels like he's a pioneer."

Being a SNL "pioneer" has its downside, however. Franken's character carries so much equipment that he has trouble with his knees and has become addicted to pain killers.

It's funny stuff—with a wisp of truth.

Brit Hume, chief White House correspondent for ABC News, coauthors a computer column for *The Washington Post* Writers Group. "Now, you know," says Hume, "if I carried everything they wanted me to, I would carry in my shoulder bag not only a computer but also a printer, and also a bunch of paper, and also a [two-way] radio and on top of that there'd be a cellular phone. I mean, I'd be a pack mule. So I try to avoid as much of it as I can. The downside of it is that there's so much of it now that there is a temptation or a tendency to carry all of it."

Sharon Spivak, a political writer for the *San Diego Tribune*, echoes Hume: "I'm five feet tall, and the lighter they make this equipment, the better." She travels with a Tandy 200 laptop and an Olympus microcassette recorder.

Traveling light doesn't mean traveling without problems. When *Newsweek* diplomatic correspondent Margaret Warner was in Hungary earlier this year, she couldn't get a phone line to work with her laptop, even with the help of a Hungarian electrician. "In the end," says Warner, "I had to dictate [over the phone]."

According to *The Boston Globe*'s Jonathan Kaufman, American journalists have put Yankee ingenuity to work to overcome similar frustrations, such as using alligator clips instead of complicated acoustic couplers to get good connections for their laptops in Eastern Europe.

But sometimes nothing works—especially in Africa, says O'Regan, where electronics don't fare well at all because of the jostling and dust. First his multi-band, pocket-sized shortwave radio broke. Then in Sudan one night, the electrical adapter he had plugged into a wall socket exploded. And he also found that odd-sized batteries are difficult to get. What's an odd size? "Anything not a D cell," deadpans O'Regan.

He suggests that any journalists planning to use electronic gadgets in Africa should carry a 12-volt adapter (to run off auto batteries), cover every seam of their equipment with gaffer's tape, and keep their gear in plastic bags as much as possible—even when it's being operated.

Time after time, however, journalists report that if one piece of equipment fails, there always seems to be something else to save the day.

When Los Angeles-based investigative reporter and syndicated columnist Peter Greenberg was staying in a Russian hotel last fall, he tried to get a phone line to send his story home from his Tandy 200 laptop. Unfortunately, the front desk told him that they were only booking calls for the next day. Unable to wait, Greenberg found some departing legislators from New Hampshire and gave them $40 to fax his three-page story to the U.S. when they got to Helsinki. That worked fine.

While the journalists interviewed for this article didn't express much concern over the possibility of competitors or hackers breaching their computer security, some worried about the danger from foreign governments. *Time*'s Barrett Seaman, for instance, says his magazine takes precautions in certain countries. Instead of sending electronic mail to the bureau's open computer system where it might be printed out on hard copy, *Time* uses personal electronic mail boxes accessible only with the correspondent's personal code.

And when it comes to security, sometimes it is the government that feels threatened. Says freelancer O'Regan, "The more repressive the country, the more likely they are to get freaked out by your computer. Computers are security threats. Journalists are suspicious. Therefore, if it's a journalist with a computer. . . ."

O'Regan says that when he arrived in Sudan, officials at the Khartoum airport almost didn't let him enter with his Toshiba laptop. He believes they viewed it as a security threat. O'Regan threatened to stay in the airport and write unless they relented. They did. However, the Sudanese officials made him write the laptop serial number in his passport and made sure he had the laptop when he left.

The sheer popularity and effectiveness of all this technology can also cause problems. After the crash of Avianca Flight 52 on Long Island last January 25, says Jay Fine of NBC News, there was so much cellular-phone traffic that circuits overloaded, causing delays.

Fine believes that as the popularity of "cell phones" grows, more circuits will be available, and the chance of overloading will lessen.

What's most amazing about the new technology is the forgiving attitude of the users when the gadgets don't work—not unlike misbehaving grandchildren who are never punished by their grandparents because they bring so much joy.

"Given the alternative, it's just been so much easier to use this equipment, so much more painless," says the *San Diego Tribune*'s Spivak.

Now, she says, major political announcements are made by fax, without even a phone call to alert the reporter. In addition, when politicians know she's working on a story, "They can get a message in the door even if we don't solicit it." That doesn't mean she uses it, however.

Electronic influence is keenly felt by reporters on the road. Spivak says that she can get a candidate's schedule faxed to her when she's doing a four-day sweep of California, cutting down on her lag time.

Time, indeed. Everything's up-tempo now with the high technology. "It has speeded up the process," says Susan Zirinsky, a senior producer at CBS News. "I always feel like we're on fast forward." The New York-based Zirinsky adds, "Where it wasn't possible, [it now] is possible. The reaction time is a nanosecond."

But has the new technology used by reporters changed the stories themselves? "I don't think so," says Zirinsky. "I think it's just changing the tools." During last year's rebellion in China, for example, she said there were some who felt that the story was altered by the media's presence. Zirinsky disagrees: "We're not participating in stories, we're just observers. It's just that we can observe—and report—a lot quicker than we ever did before."

Remember one thing, she cautions: "The story comes first"—because if you don't have the story, who cares how many cellular phones or fax machines you have?

# 72

# 2014: A Newspaper Odyssey

## *by* Joe Logan

**Editor's Note:** Newspapers in the 1990s are finding themselves in big trouble. Readership is down, and so is advertising. More people are turning to other mass media or to other activities, and newspapers are struggling to find a new audience. But this article says that there is a new role for today's newspapers and predicts that they will become tomorrow's information companies—if fear doesn't stifle the technology.

Joe Logan is a reporter for the *Philadelphia Inquirer*. This article was originally published in the *Washington Journalism Review* (now the *American Journalism Review*), May 1989.

*It's 4:35 on a clear, crisp October morning, and Bob Scribe, the night police reporter for the* Philadelphia Daily Inquirer, *is making his way across town to the scene of a reported shooting in north Philadelphia. The year is 2014. Scribe, 25, is too young to remember much about the* Philadelphia Daily News *or the* Philadelphia Inquirer. *All he's ever known is the* Philadelphia Daily Inquirer: An Information Company.

*"Whaddaya got, Lieutenant?" asks Scribe, stepping from his car.*

*"Dead man," says Lieutenant James Williams. "Louis Michael Reeve. Ventilation to the head. Forty-five caliber. My guess is drug wars."*

*Within minutes, Scribe is back in his car, dialing the main computer at the office. "Byline Scribe, 22136," he says, "filing for the city desk."*

*"Begin dictation," says the computer.*

*As Scribe dictates his story, the computer translates his spoken words into written text—no need to specify grammar: The computer makes those decisions from voice intonation.*

*"After the sixth graph, drop in five graphs of boilerplate background on these north Philly drug wars," Scribe instructs the computer. "And the whole story's got to come in at 10 inches exactly."*

*Thirty seconds later, Scribe's 10-inch story, with six graphs on this morning's homicide and five graphs of background, pops up on the night editor's screen, ready for editing.*

*Across town, Herbert Bilkington, the well-known criminal defense lawyer, is emerging from the shower, preparing to catch an early flight to Los Angeles. As he towels dry, Bilkington reaches over and switches on the small computer next to the washstand, a Dialog Audio Communications Center, put there by the* Philadelphia Daily Inquirer: An Information Company.

*"What's up, DACC?" asks Bilkington.*

*In a cheerful voice, DACC begins its overnight news and information summary.*

*"Good morning," says DACC. "Your flight to Los Angeles is running 15 minutes late. The good news is it's going to be a beautiful day in Los Angeles. Sunny, 80 degrees.*

*"Also, overnight the dollar fell against the Japanese yen, Hurricane Charlie hit the Florida Coast, coups toppled dictators in two Central American countries and there was another drug-related killing in north Philadelphia."*

*"Thanks, DACC," says Bilkington. "That's all for now."*

*Bilkington hurries out the door and does what he has done for years: He grabs his copy of the* Philadelphia Daily Inquirer *from the driveway. Then he jumps in his car and heads for the airport.*

The world Scribe and Bilkington inhabit is not as far away as you might think. We're talking about 25 years from now—possibly part of your working career if you're under age 40. And this isn't some far-fetched nonsense; futurists and communications experts insist that this is what the news and information business will be like in 2014.

Their only questions are: How big will the market be? And will today's newspapers initiate more research so they can stake out this territory before high-tech entrepreneurs do?

"All this is easily possible within 25 years," says Andrew Lippman, associate director of MIT's Media Lab. "And let me remind you, we are not futurists at the Media Lab. We are working on those kinds of things now."

"Look, you newspaper guys are lucky to have survived this far," contends Arthur Harkins, professor of anticipatory anthropology and education at the University of Minnesota and author of six books on the future. "If somebody came out with a low-power flat TV screen with an advanced micro-antenna that could be tucked under your arm, you'd already be in serious trouble. . . .

"You ought to be putting money into the Media Lab right now to develop the newspaper of tomorrow, because if you don't, somebody else will. You won't keep up with the Mitsubishis and the Sonys who are at the Media Lab now. If they develop a distribution system, hell, anybody can then go out and buy any big newspaper."

What will newspapers be like 25 years from now, a time when futurists believe human knowledge will double every nine to 10 days? Assuming newspapers are still around, what will the scope of their readerships be, given the present rate of decline? Will they continue to play a major role in setting national and local agendas? Or will they have degenerated from mass medium to niche-oriented medium, similar to most present-day cable channels, magazines and radio stations?

How will newspapers be delivered? Electronically? As hard copy? Both? And which companies and services will advertise in them? What will life be like for the reporter, editor and photographer? And what is to become of the entire production end of the newspaper?

No one can be certain what the future holds for newspapers, but there is agreement among futurists and communications experts on several counts:

• If newspapers work together and commit to considerably more research and planning than is currently under way, there is no reason the industry cannot thrive into the next century and well beyond.

• Newspapers as we know them today—ink on paper, tossed on your driveway or bought from a vendor—will still be with us, although in a diminished role. But newspapers will look different, with much more color, graphics and charts, and they may contain news and information tailored specifically for individual readers.

• Many newspapers, especially the big-city dailies and chains, must let go of their traditional roles and begin to think of themselves as full-service information companies with a variety of news services and distribution channels.

• Despite the industry's failures in launching videotext services (electronically disseminated news and information) for general consumers several years ago, such systems are definitely a major part of the future. The capability already exists, and as the cost of delivery plummets and the next generation of computer-era children grows up, the demand for advanced forms of videotext will go up. The key question is how much.

• If newspapers' household penetration continues to drop, they will become a medium of the educated and affluent. That, in turn, will have two major results: The advertising base will move away from mass retailers toward companies and services seeking demographically pinpointed audiences. And the shrunken readership will affect newspapers' ability to play a role in setting national and local agendas.

• Career outlooks for newspaper employees may depend on their roles. For production employees, the long-term outlook is bleak. In 25 years there will be almost no one between the touch of an editor's finger and the printed paper. Some of the employees who now do those jobs will be retrained; others no doubt will be laid off.

The outlook is better for reporters, photographers and editors. Indeed, cost cutting in the back shop may mean more money for news gathering, an investment that will become even more essential in the increasingly competitive world of news and information. But journalists may well need retraining to fill their new roles as multipurpose "communicators."

Despite their agreement that the next 25 years in newspapers will be volatile, the experts do not agree on how far newspapers will evolve by then. They foresee several potential scenarios revolving around new high-tech equipment, depending on technological innovation and demand. The possibilities include:

• A newspaper, or information center, similar to the *Philadelphia Daily Inquirer*'s DACC system, with audio and video electronic dissemination. Homes could be equipped with artificially intelligent computers that would scan a host of news services and, based on the owner's demonstrated areas of interest, pluck stories and display them or read them aloud.

• Highly advanced home video computers. These would project an entire newspaper page's image on a wall screen with the resolution of a 35-millimeter camera. But in the upper right-hand corner of, say, the front of the sports section, instead of a still photo of an Olympic athlete sprinting, the reader would see the actual moving video of the runner.

• In-home, high-resolution VDTs. Readers could glance at an overview of a front page, then zero in on the stories they want to read. Harkins, the Minnesota futurist, insists this technology will culminate in a screen that can be folded and tucked under one's arm and carried onto a commuter train like a small tabloid newspaper.

Many others predict, however, that newspapers will remain largely paper-based sources of general information and will closely resemble what we know today. These relative conservatives are quick to note that zoned editions may well become a thing of the past because computer scientists will have developed ways to tailor newspapers to individual readers.

All of this, of course, is speculation. The problem with trying to predict what newspapers will be in 25 years is that technology is expanding so fast. It's impossible to guess what the possibilities will be by then.

"There is no single technology that will affect newspapers," says Benjamin Compaine, a communications expert with Samara Associates in Cambridge, Massachusetts, and the author of *Issues In New Information Technology*. "Most things are a combination of technologies, and predicting what they are is notoriously bad.

"But 25 years from now is still short enough to say that most of what will be available then, we sort of know about today. It's just that anything in the information business will be smaller, faster, cheaper and better. Of course, there are always those couple of things that can come out of left field."

Compaine does point to one new technology that seems to have the most potential impact: fiber optics.

"If you bring fiber optics into the home—and it would be at least 15 to 20 years before it makes much of a dent—it really could open the door to do a lot of things that today would be too slow or too expensive." Compaine argues that fiber optics would reduce the price of transmitting a big-city paper into your home from today's $15 to $20 range to about 30 cents.

That naturally would have profound implications for the practical use of videotext. In the late 1970s and early 1980s, after Knight-Ridder and Times

Mirror lost millions in videotext products, the newspaper industry essentially pronounced the idea dead and breathed a collective sigh of relief.

Futurists say that attitude is a grave mistake.

"That may have been the general finding, but it was not the correct finding," says John Carey, a communications expert with Greystone Communications in New York. A combination of factors led to the failure of videotext: The technology wasn't there, the terminal was too expensive and it was very hard to get good graphics.

"The basic idea of trying to get information electronically at home is not going away," says Carey. "It is going to happen. When, I don't know. But the newspaper industry's attitude that people don't want it is a mistake."

Another well-known believer in the electronically based future of newspapers is futurist John Diebold, chairman of the Diebold Group consulting firm and the man who, 25 years ago, stood before the annual meeting of the American Society of Newspaper Editors and boldly predicted that reporters and editors would one day work at computer terminals, that much of the back shop would be automated and that electronic morgue and information services would be sold over telephone lines.

In April 1988 Diebold was invited to address ASNE again. This time his speech was no less dramatic. Diebold predicted that in the coming years the high cost of transmitting information electronically will drop to 1 percent of what it is today, thanks to fiber optics. He also forecasts that computers will respond to spoken commands, reporters will dictate stories to computers that translate them to text and consumers will talk to "smart" computers that scan and select information.

Diebold may be right about what is possible, say some industry experts, but that doesn't mean people will want instant access to information or be willing to spend the time, money and energy necessary to get it.

Indeed, some observers—futurists among them—say that while technology may present plenty of options for receiving news and information, you cannot underestimate the durability and staying power of today's newspapers.

People pick up newspapers today for a variety of reasons: They are cheap, portable, comprehensive and convenient. And unlike television, which dispenses information at its own speed, newspapers allow you to scan page after page in seconds. When you find something you like, you can even rip it out and put it in your pocket. For all this discussion of technology, media experts say the industry faces problems on two other, somewhat related, fronts.

Since the advent of television, newspapers have seen their household penetration figures decline, with the norm for many big-city papers now around 60 percent. If that drops—as it could—to, say, 40 percent, newspapers would no longer be regarded as a mass medium but rather as a niche-oriented medium.

If there is good news to be salvaged from the decline, it is that the people who continue to read newspapers tend to be the educated and the affluent, the very people who often influence public opinion.

At the same time, newspapers are facing a decline in national and mass-appeal advertising. Rather than pay to reach mass audiences, many advertisers prefer to reach selected target audiences. Even such traditional mass advertisers as department stores now market themselves as collections of boutiques with separate patrons and advertising campaigns.

If the mass-advertising base dissipates, and if strides in desktop publishing continue at the current rate, some futurists foresee the weakening of the big dailies, spawning an outcropping of small, designer dailies.

Greystone's John Carey says the advertising angle cannot be underestimated. "A lot of people, when they look at the future of newspapers, see it in terms of technology. But advertising is critical. The question for newspapers is, can they maintain that confidence?"

Beyond these issues lies what could be the biggest problem of all for newspapers: the industry's apparent dread of the future and what it might hold.

Indicative of that fear (and the resulting lethargy) is the amount of money the industry spends for research and development. In an era when the auto industry spends 2.4 percent of its profits on research, and computer companies spend 8.3 percent of their profits on research, the newspaper industry spends an estimated .0005 percent of sales on R&D, according to George Wilson, president of the *Concord* (New Hampshire) *Monitor* and former chairman of the American Newspaper Publishers Association.

This lack of support for R&D prompted something of a tongue lashing from John Diebold when he addressed editors at last year's ASNE convention. He pointed specifically to the 1982 divestiture of AT&T, which was followed by a successful lobbying campaign by the newspaper industry to convince Federal Judge Harold Greene to keep the phone companies out of the on-line information business—for seven years, anyway.

"What have you done with the six of those seven years that have already passed?" asked Diebold. "Are you or your advertisers and readers any better off as a result of the 'protection' you have secured from this potential source of competition?

"I do not wish to be unduly harsh in my criticism, but I believe that you have behaved the way most industries do when they have successfully practiced protectionism. You have enjoyed the protection but have done little to provide new services using the technology you so fear in the hands of others."

One ominous cloud hovering over the industry is Judge Greene's apparent growing impatience with newspapers.

"He has been taking things step by step," says Carey. "The most recent thing he said was that telephone companies can operate an information service but they cannot provide the information. So they can set up something called a gateway, which is the backbone of the system, and let others provide the information. But most people speculate that he will also, in steps, start to let them provide information through that system."

Despite all the criticism and the lack of overall research funding, several companies and press groups are taking the initiative on forward-looking projects. Among the leaders: Dow Jones, the New York Times Co., Knight-Ridder, Times Mirror, Gannett, the ANPA Institute and the University of Missouri's New Directions for News think tank.

Nancy Woodhull, president of Gannett New Media, a division established to explore new avenues to market and sell news and information, defends the industry's efforts. "I think the newspaper industry is taking a bad rap from futurists," she says. "The ASNE, for a couple of years, has had a Future of Newspapers Committee, which has been very active. At most conventions there is some kind of panel. People are very, very aware."

But even if the rest of the industry ignores the lead of Gannett and others, communications experts believe that there will be a place for newspapers in 2014.

"I'd have to say, yeah, newspapers are going to be there," says Benjamin Compaine. "But the trends that I've seen for the last 25 years or more are not going to change. . . . The newspaper has been dying at least since 1960, if not before, by almost any measure of circulation, penetration, role in society and in numbers of newspapers.

"But the reason the newspaper industry is healthy is because the survivors have sort of rallied the wagons in a circle and they have been able to stake out a territory of smaller turf. It will become less and less the vehicle of choice for those trying to reach the masses and more for those trying to reach a select audience."

Ironically, regardless of whether the industry galvanizes and faces the future head on as a formidable monolith—an anxious alliance similar to the one in which the three television networks now find themselves—media experts expect there will always be jobs for reporters, editors and photographers.

"You are in an industry that is going to be affected sharply by technological changes in society for the rest of your working life, so in a sense there is going to be a lot of uncertainty," says Carey. "But newspapers are not alone in that. Ten years ago everybody thought there was nothing more stable than IBM and the phone company. The economy, for good or ill, is becoming an information economy, and you're in the information business. I believe strongly that the skills of a journalist are going to become more and more important. Of course, you may be working for the phone company."

*Meanwhile, back in Philadelphia in the year 2014, where we left Bob Scribe, reporter, it's 6:30 a.m. He is now off duty, sipping a cup of coffee in a diner with Lieutenant Williams.*

*"I don't know about my future in this business," says Scribe.*

*"What do you mean?" asks Williams.*

*"I heard the other day that they're working on a new computer that writes better than reporters. They say that one day I'll go out to cover a shooting and all I'll do is call in my notes, real stream-of-consciousness stuff. The computer will write it. I'll be a legman for a computer.*

*"What are they going to do, give us a joint byline: by Bob Scribe and Xytron 2000?*

*"Where's it all gonna lead, man? Where's it all gonna lead?"*

# 73

# The Worst Is Yet to Come

## *by* Ted Koppel

*Editor's Note:* The new technologies have not necessarily made TV journalism better. In fact, as we've seen elsewhere in this book, TV news has deteriorated over the past decade for a variety of reasons.

In this article a distinguished TV journalist predicts that the future will not get any brighter for TV news. If you think today's television news is bad, he says, just wait!

Ted Koppel is anchor and managing editor of ABC News's "Nightline." This article is adapted from a speech given at Harvard University in March 1994. This version was reprinted in the *Washington Post,* April 3, 1994.

In the mid- to late '60s, when I went out to Vietnam for ABC television, we worked hard; but for reasons of technology, if nothing else, we operated at a more leisurely pace than reporters do now. And we focused far more on journalism. My fellow television reporters and I would spend a day, or two, or three in the field; bring the film back to Saigon, perhaps shipping it out the next morning, and 18 hours later—if it was deemed urgent enough—it might be taken off the plane in Los Angeles, processed, edited and then fed by telephone line to New York for use on the evening news.

You write differently when you know that your piece won't make it to the air for another day or two. You function differently in the field when you know that you and your competitors are at the mercy of just one connecting flight out of Saigon in the late afternoon. You have some time to think. You have some time to report. You even have some time, while the film is en route to the United States, to correct errors.

These days American reporters covering foreign wars (or at least those deemed important enough) are accompanied by portable ground stations, satellite phones, and a retinue of producers and technicians who can get you on the air "live" from anywhere in the world at any time. The technological tail is wagging the editorial dog.

The network schedule of news programs, or at least news-related programs, is such that a reporter is constantly on call. On major, breaking news there is literally no time for the reporter to go out and report the story. He or she is bound to the transmission point, while producers and camera crews go out and gather material. Frequently, *only* the camera crews actually go out and gather material. And they, for obvious reasons, are more concerned with the visuals.

So despite the fact that more people than ever before are in the field disseminating news, there is less time and less focus than ever before on the actual gathering of editorial material.

The capacity to "go live" also creates its own terrible dynamic. Much, if not most, of the process of good journalism lies in the evaluation, the assessment, the *editing* of raw material. Putting someone on the air while an event is unfolding is clearly a technological tour de force—but it is an impediment, not an aid, to good journalism.

Good reporting is to an event what a good map is to a city: It reduces the original in size and accessibility while remaining faithful to the basic features of the original. To simply train a camera on a complicated event is not journalism, any more than taking someone out on a boat and showing them a stretch of coastline is cartography.

If you're living in a participatory republic, you need good journalism—but the emphasis is on *good*. Bad journalism is no more useful than a bad chart. Journalism designed for the express purpose of entertaining is no more useful than the exquisite cartouches that adorned many early charts and maps. They were beautiful, but they were strategically placed to cover those areas that the mapmakers had not yet explored. When the cartographers had real information to impart, they didn't muck it up with pretty pictures.

It may shock you—but it will probably not surprise you—to learn that during the most intense two weeks of Tonya Harding-Nancy Kerrigan coverage, television devoted more time to that story than it did to the most intense two weeks after the downing of Pan Am 103 . . . or the collapse of the Berlin Wall.

Let that one carom around the inner caverns of your skull for a moment or two. It is an inevitable consequence of the marketplace bringing its economic forces to bear on journalism.

But we may yet—indeed, I predict we will—look back on these as the golden, halcyon days of television news programming.

In the marketplace today, the three networks still command an enormous share of the audience. While Fox has a number of youth-oriented programs, ABC, NBC and CBS still draw 60 to 70 out of every hundred homes watching television. In "Nightline's" time slot, the arrival of "Late Show With David Letterman" has taken away some audience from the "Tonight Show" (which never recovered from the departure of Johnny Carson), but our audience has actually grown by 25 percent over the past two years.

Are we at "Nightline" in competition with Letterman and "Tonight"? In a de facto sense, clearly—even though theirs are purely entertainment programs and no one at ABC News has ever suggested that we tailor our programming to compete with theirs. But the rules are implicit: In order to be able to produce the kinds of programs that we want to do, including investigative pieces, we cannot afford to ignore the kinds of stories that have always kept us competitive, going back to the days of Jim and Tammy Bakker and all the way through the current travails of Tonya Harding.

We may be in the waning years of mass communication as we've known it over the past 30 or 40 years, but *mass* communication it remains. Our audiences are several times those of our colleagues on cable or public television. For the time being at least, the commercial networks remain what they have always been: the most popular organs of the mass media, dependent upon the size of their audience to determine the size of their income.

Inevitably, that has some impact on the kind of news programming that we produce. Have we reached the level of lowest common denominator? I would argue strenuously that we have not. But are we aware of the continuing need to appeal to a mass audience? Absolutely.

We are also, however, on the cusp of a massive change. It may take a few years—five to 10 at the outside would be my guess—but the advent of the 500-channel supercommunications highway, and the ability of the audience to interact with its television set, will change our industry forever.

Just as the magazine world witnessed the demise of Collier's, Life and the Saturday Evening Post as ubiquitous giants of the publishing world; just as Time and Newsweek now frequently feature cover stories that have nothing to do with the breaking news of the previous week; just as mass circulation magazines have now been largely displaced by literally hundreds of special interest magazines—so too, we in network television news will either adjust or wither away.

The huge salaries being paid to those of us who anchor television news programs are in themselves an adjustment of sorts. As in the worlds of sports and entertainment, the simplest way to draw a crowd is with a recognizable star. But that's just a stopgap, a desperate quick fix.

The first major change is already happening: Time shifting. Those of you who like watching "Nightline," for example, but can't stay up until after midnight, already have the option of taping the program and watching it at your convenience. The lamentable fact, though, is that most of us can't even remove that blinking "12:00" from our VCRs, let alone set the machine to tape a program.

But help is at hand.

Imagine a three-button remote control: An on-off switch, a button that lets you scroll through a menu, and an "enter" button. Turn the set on; scroll through the menu until you come to the word "news"; hit enter. Now scroll through the available options until you come to "Nightline." Hit the enter button. At your convenience.

You could also, if you wish, scroll through the available "Nightline" programs by date or by subject matter—more than 3,500 of them. And as we all become more "interactively" literate, there will be a whole new world of options available. How about the entire interview that you did with Ross Perot in

1971, Ted? Not just the fragment that you replayed 23 years later on "Nightline." Play it for me. And I want to see all of your outtakes on that series of programs you did with President Clinton in Europe.

As for you, Peter and Dan and Tom, save me from all that Whitewater nonsense; I'm not interested. I want international news. My cousin, out in South Dakota, wants nothing but farm news. My son is a sports nut, my aging mother is worried about health care. My wife wants nothing but Whitewater. Each of them can shape and craft their own news programs according to their own special interests, and watch them at their own convenience. Gradually, the paternalistic world of television news as presented by a small group of reporters, producers and editors can be replaced by a brave new world of news you can choose.

Will there still be a place for the traditional network news division with its traditional programming? Of course. But probably not three of them anymore. And as programming reaches each home in America through direct satellite transmission, will there still be a need for local stations? Oh, sure. But not more than one or two to a market; and even then, only if they provide wide-ranging local coverage.

Commercials, with their shotgun approach to tens of millions of potential customers, can be far more direct, especially for big-ticket items. Scroll down your shopping list: "Automobiles." Enter. Scroll again. Chevrolet, Dodge, Ferrari, Ford. Enter. Scroll again. Escort, Falcon, Mustang. Enter. And so on, until you find the car you want. Would you prefer a simple one-minute commercial, or a ten-minute introduction to the car? Do you know which options you'd like? Scroll. Enter. Are you ready to talk with a member of our sales staff? Enter. And so on—through the sale, if you're ready to buy, or onto the next car if you're not.

Why is all of that relevant to the kind of television news coverage you'll be getting? Because we may no longer be sponsored. We may be selling our product to you directly. ("Nightline": 25 cents a program; 10 cents for the outtakes; a nickel for each old program you dial up.) Gradually, the audience will become more and more fragmented, and the information requested more and more oriented to the specific interests of the viewer. And the economic dynamics that have driven television news for the masses—with all its strengths and weaknesses—will cease to exist.

What I'm offering you here, of course, is simply an opinion, not revealed truth; but it disturbs me that so little attention is being paid to the changes that are all around us. We have traveled, during my relatively brief professional lifetime, from an era during which television news was regarded by its practitioners as almost a calling—when there really was no "business" of television news—to the present, when it is a massive, billion-dollar industry. That has imposed its own drawbacks. But still, there are top-flight professionals gathering, producing and editing excellent, free news programs for tens of millions of viewers.

The era upon which we are embarking, however, will winnow out the well-to-do, well-educated viewers. They will be ordering their news a la carte. They will do their high-priced shopping the same way. What will be left for the less well-to-do and the less well-educated among us will truly be television of the lowest common denominator: a National Enquirer of the air, sponsored by those products for whom demographics are irrelevant.

Television, which for so many years has been the great homogenizer in this country, seems poised to go the way of radio stations and newspapers and magazines. And since you were nice enough to ask, I'll tell you: I think it's a lousy idea.

# 74

# The Threat and the Promise

## *By* Peter F. Eder

*Editor's Note:* Finally, what about the new technologies and advertising and marketing? This article predicts that although in the future they will pose an increasing threat to privacy, sophisticated marketing will also lead to more customized products and services.

Author Peter F. Eder is senior vice president of member services for the Association of National Advertisers, Inc., New York. The views expressed here are the author's and do not necessarily reflect those of his association. This article was published in *The Futurist*, May/June 1990.

Advertising and mass marketing are growing more intensive and more invasive, spreading to almost every aspect of our lives. Yet, consumers also have a greater array of media from which to choose and more-sophisticated tools to avoid unwanted commercial messages.

The soaring number of media outlets is spurring this marketing boom. Sixty percent of American homes are now wired for cable television, and the average household can view 27 channels. Some 40,000 journals are published in the United States every year, and more than 10,000 radio stations crowd the airwaves.

Directly tied to the explosion in the number of media is an exponential increase in the number of commercial messages. Since 1965, the number of network television commercials has tripled from approximately 1,800 to nearly 5,400 a year, and this number is increasing by 20% annually, with more 15-second ads and more nonprogramming time. Networks often run five or six commercials in a row, and commercials during prime time average 10½ minutes per hour.

To get an idea of the sheer amount of advertising that forces itself upon us, try this simple experiment: Don't throw away any of the unsolicited mail that arrives at your home—catalogs, special offers, inserts into bill statements, and other "junk mail"—and see how long it takes you to accumulate a foot of material. I suspect that for most readers this would take less than two months.

Commercial sponsorship is also becoming increasingly omnipresent. Can you think of a bus-stop shelter, an amusement park, a marathon, a high-school dance, or a neighborhood clean-up effort that isn't commercially sponsored? In all likelihood, the only events left unsponsored are presidential press conferences, Supreme Court hearings, and celebrity funerals.

With the proliferation of sponsorship as a marketing device and the explosion in the number of media messages, the measurements of audience size, profile, and reactions have also increased exponentially. Within the next decade, media operators, manufacturers, and retailers will undoubtedly be able to measure the impact of individual commercial messages. They could assess who saw which television spot and when, what he purchased, how he reacted to the purchased product, and how likely he is to repurchase or switch brands.

But as market research grows more sophisticated, there may be a consumer backlash against it. Researchers are reporting a substantial decrease in consumers' willingness to participate in surveys. The assault of telephone selling—direct marketing disguised as information gathering—has sensitized customers and turned them off. This could create major problems for the data gatherers.

## Death of the Mass Consumer?

The growing sophistication of mass marketing isn't necessarily bad news for the consumer: Marketers are learning more about what increasingly heterogeneous customers really want. Thus, products are becoming less mass produced and more customized and specialized. In 1988, 33 new consumer products were introduced each day, not including 3,000 line extensions (modifications of existing products) that year. According to Laurel Cutler, vice chairman and director of marketing planning, FCB/Katz Partners: "The mass consumer is *dead.* . . . The focus of the '90s will be 'intensity' . . . pleasing one person at a time."

Media are becoming increasingly interactive, and there are more media variations to choose from. Three-dimensional television commercials are just the beginning: Viewers can play games with the game-show contestants, select optional endings to dramas, and express opinions by call-in voting.

And despite the assault by an ever growing number of appeals, we as message consumers have powerful tools to use to our advantage. We can not only tune out, but program our VCRs to record programs and even edit out the commercials. To a great extent, we can evade and avoid, and this makes us less homogeneous and more specialized.

We can have someone do the shopping for us, or we can do it ourselves any time of day or night. We can bank without tellers or with private investment counselors. We can purchase cars with an almost infinite array of options and preview on videotape where we want to spend our vacations. With this host of options available to us, we can be "demassified" as we individualize the mass market and the mass media.

Unfortunately, the same options aren't available to everyone, and the gap between the media-recipient "haves" and "have-nots" is widening. Several factors can create dramatically different levels of access to or assimilation of information: the degree of computer access, income and educational levels, geographic location, and ethnic and language barriers. These variations can lead to serious distortions of information, knowledge, and power, and they can ultimately affect our degree of control over our own lives.

Also keep in mind that the same array of tools—and hype—is available to all who have the funds or ability to generate active constituencies. Pressure and special-interest groups are in a position to manipulate information and promotional/publicity channels to their advantage. For example, "Moral Majority"-type organizations have led boycotts against products advertised on television programs with controversial subject matter, language, or sexual situations.

Regulators and organized bodies "acting in the public interest" are increasingly threatening the First Amendment guarantee of free speech to advertisers of legal products and services. In recent months, there have been attempts to ban all advertising and promotion for alcohol at any institution of higher education that receives federal funds. State attorneys general have begun regulating car-rental and airline advertising on a state-by-state basis.

Another area of concern is the potential for invasion of privacy. Marketers today can target mailings not only to ZIP codes, but to streets in a city, to generally defined income or educational levels, and to purchasers of a specific brand at a particular retail outlet. It's entirely within the realm of possibility that Mr. and Mrs. Jones and their 12-year-old daughter could be the source of a database that includes information on every aspect of their lives, such as the videos they rented last week, the causes they contribute to, and their "personal" opinions on everything from reproductive issues to drug use.

Consumers are faced with a barrage of messages, measurements, and solicited and unsolicited appeals, all making extraordinary demands on their attention. For consumers, this becomes a drain on their time and energy that many resent. For communicators, this creates the dilemma of ensuring memorability without causing the audience to tune out.

## Predictions for Advertising and Mass Marketing

To conclude, here are a few predictions for the next decade:

- We will live in a world of micro everything and macro nothing, with the personalization of media, messages, products, and services.
- We will be assaulted, in every area of our lives, by communications more intensive and more invasive than ever. A substantial portion of our time and probably an increase in our discretionary income will be required to selectively tune in and tune out. A San Francisco firm recently introduced SmarTV, a home-entertainment system that combines a VCR, a personal computer, and artificial intelligence. The system gives the user complete control over the

medium in program planning, viewing time, and editing.

• We will run the risk of having special-interest groups intrude upon our privacy, curtail our opportunities, and reduce our ability to make our own choices. We may find our constitutional protections abridged or more narrowly defined.

• Our media, our messages, our products, and our services will be provided by larger and larger firms and by foreign individuals and firms that may not share our heritage, our culture, and our national interest. Bertelsmann of West Germany, the world's second-largest media conglomerate (U.S.-owned Time Warner is number one), owns five major U.S. publishers and two of the largest record companies. The third-largest media conglomerate, Rupert Murdoch's Australian News Corporation, owns *TV Guide, Seventeen,* and 10 other U.S. publications, as well as newspapers in major U.S. cities.

But the 1990s also hold great promise. We will be able to choose as we never have before—where and how we live, what we buy, where and how we consume, what and how we learn, whom we communicate with, what we see, hear, and read. Our array of choices will be limitless. We will be more in control of our lives—where and how we work, commuters and telecommuters alike, and how we spend our leisure time and shape our opinions.

# Index

**459**